C++ Game Animation Programming

Learn modern animation techniques from theory to implementation using C++, OpenGL, and Vulkan

Michael Dunsky

Gabor Szauer

<packt>

BIRMINGHAM—MUMBAI

C++ Game Animation Programming

Group Product Manager: Rohit Rajkumar
Publishing Product Manager: Kaustubh Manglurkar
Book Project Manager: Sonam Pandey
Senior Editor: Rashi Dubey
Technical Editor: Simran Ali
Copy Editor: Safis Editing
Proofreader: Safis Editing
Indexer: Hemangini Bari
Production Designer: Shankar Kalbhor
DevRel Marketing Coordinators: Nivedita Pandey and Namita Velgekar

First published: June 2020
Second edition: December 2023

Production reference: 2221223

Published by
Packt Publishing Ltd.
Grosvenor House
11 St Paul's Square
Birmingham
B3 1RB, UK.

ISBN: 978-1-80324-652-9

www.packtpub.com

To my mother, Christel, for her patience as a single mother while raising a nerd.

To my kids, Eric and Greta, for following my footsteps into the tech world.

– Michael Dunsky

Contributors

About the authors

Michael Dunsky is an educated electronics technician, game developer, and console porting programmer with more than 20 years of programming experience. He started at the age of 14 with BASIC, adding along the way Assembly language, C, C++, Java, Python, VHDL, OpenGL, GLSL, and Vulkan to his portfolio. During his career, he has also gained extensive knowledge of virtual machines, server operation, infrastructure automation, and other DevOps topics. Michael holds a master of science degree in computer science from FernUniversität in Hagen, focused on computer graphics, parallel programming, and software systems.

Thanks to Fred and Mikkel for supporting my crazy idea of writing a book as a spare-time project – while working as a full-time programmer at Slipgate and in parallel to the completion of my Master of Science degree.

Gabor Szauer has been making games since 2010. He graduated from Full Sail University in 2010 with a bachelor's degree in game development. Gabor maintains an active Twitter/X presence and has a programming-oriented game development blog. Gabor's previously published books are *Game Physics Programming Cookbook* and *Lua Quick Start Guide*, both published by Packt Publishing.

About the reviewers

Hardik Dubal has been working in game development for the past 14 years. He has worked with gaming studios such as Gameloft, Gameshastra, Megarama, and Offworld Industries. He also co-founded and operated his own game studio known as Timeloop Technologies. Throughout his career in the gaming industry, he has worked with several game development technologies, including but not limited to C++, Unreal Engine, the Cocos2d-x Engine, Unity, C#, Box2D, Flash, and ActionScript 3.

Eric-Per Dunsky works as a programmer at Slipgate Ironworks. Eric started programming with Java at the age of 11, and he is also fluent in C++ and C#. Eric has experience in Unreal Engine and Unity, and he also has low-level knowledge of how to create 3D graphics with OpenGL, the Vulkan API, and GLSL.

Illina Bokareva is a game programmer with a passion for crafting immersive experiences. She skillfully navigates Unity, Unreal Engine, C#/C++, OpenGL, SDL, and Vulkan, weaving her expertise into diverse game projects. Her unquenchable desire for knowledge and collaboration makes her an invaluable asset to the gaming industry, where she continually embraces new technologies and thrives in the company of fellow professionals.

Table of Contents

3

Building a Vulkan Renderer 75

4

Working with Shaders 105

5

Adding Dear ImGui to Show Valuable Information 127

Part 2: Mathematics Roundup

6

Understanding Vector and Matrix 153

7

A Primer on Quaternions and Splines 181

Part 3: Working with Models and Animations

8

Loading Models in the glTF Format 213

9

The Model Skeleton and Skin 245

10

About Poses, Frames, and Clips 275

11

Blending between Animations 303

Part 4: Advancing Your Code to the Next Level

12

Cleaning Up the User Interface 333

13

Implementing Inverse Kinematics 357

14

Creating Instanced Crowds 389

15

Measuring Performance and Optimizing the Code 419

Preface

Character animations have existed since the first games were created for computers. The spaceships in *SpaceWar!*, written by Steve Russell in 1962 for a PDP-1, and *Computer Space* by Nolan Bushnell, released in 1971 as an arcade cabinet, were animated, with the animation showing the direction in which the spaceships headed.

Over time, the evolution of character animation went from these raster graphics, drawn by the electron beam inside the cathode-ray tube of old TV sets, to simple 2D pictures (so-called "sprites"). These sprites were drawn by hand, picture by picture, and every one of these pictures showed a different animation phase. To create the illusion of real-time animations, the pictures were shown quickly one after another, like cartoons. The main characters in *Pac-Man* and *Super Mario Bros.* are just a bunch of two-dimensional pictures, brought to life by proper timing between the sprites and their motion over the screen.

Eventually, the character models became real 3D objects. First, they were made of simply dozens of triangles, and as the graphics hardware became more powerful, the numbers got larger and larger. Current 3D models can have more than 500,000 polygons, and even these characters are animated smoothly in real time.

This book covers the animation of 3D game characters, taking a closer look at the principles of character components and animation. After explaining the theoretical elements of animation, we will provide an example implementation that will guide you from the conceptual stage to the real-world usage in an application. With this knowledge, you will be able to implement a similar animation system, regardless of the programming language or rendering API.

Who this book is for

This book is for programmers who want to "look behind the curtain" of character animation in games. You should be familiar with C++, and it would be best to have a modern version such as C++17. Basic knowledge of a rendering pipeline will come in handy too, but it is not required, as it will be covered in the book. The remaining skills, including opening a window, preparing a rendering API to draw triangles, and loading models and animating them, will also be explained throughout the book.

What this book covers

Chapter 1, Creating the Game Window, covers the initial steps to open a window using GLFW, a lightweight cross-platform window management library. The window will be enhanced to detect OpenGL 4.6 and Vulkan 1.1; code for handling window events such as resizing and moving will be added, followed by an introduction on using the keyboard and mouse as input devices.

Chapter 2, Building an OpenGL 4 Renderer, explains how to create a basic OpenGL 4 renderer that can display a textured quad consisting of two triangles.

Chapter 3, Building a Vulkan Renderer, explores the creation of a renderer, similar to *Chapter 2*, but instead using the newer Vulkan API to display the textured quad.

Chapter 4, Working with Shaders, covers the different shaders of the graphics pipeline for OpenGL and Vulkan, the buffer types, and how to access the variables of shaders from renderer code. At the end of the chapter, the parts of a vertex and a fragment shader will be discussed.

Chapter 5, Adding Dear ImGui to Show Valuable Information, explains how to add a simple UI to both renderers to display information about the rendering process, such as the frames per second or timing of code sections. Also, checkboxes, buttons, and sliders will be added to the UI to control the rendering parameters.

Chapter 6, Understanding Vector and Matrix, is a quick recap of the data types of a vector and a matrix, their transformations, and their operations.

Chapter 7, A Primer on Quaternions and Splines, explains the advantage of quaternions over matrix operations and introduces some spline types that are used in game character animations.

Chapter 8, Loading Models in the glTF format, covers the internals of the glTF file format. glTF is an open file format, supported by many 3D content creation tools. Being able to load this format will let you view models and animations authored in many 3D creation tools in the application.

Chapter 9, The Model Skeleton and Skin, covers the internal skeleton of a model as a base for animation, plus vertex skinning to match different poses of the skeleton. Different methods to apply vertex skinning will be discussed in this chapter.

Chapter 10, About Poses, Frames, and Clips, explains the different data types required for character animation, allowing you to get from a simple model pose to a complete animation clip.

Chapter 11, Blending between Animations, shows different blending methods for animated mode. The chapter covers simple blending between a basic pose and an animation clip, cross-blending between different clips, and additive blending to mix different clips.

Chapter 12, Cleaning Up the User Interface, enhances the UI created in *Chapter 4* with more user-interactable elements, such as combo boxes and radio buttons. These controls enable the modification of animation parameters in real time. In addition, the timer values for the code sections will be visualized as graphical plots.

Chapter 13, *Implementing Inverse Kinematics*, explains how to use inverse kinematics to achieve an interaction between a character and its environment. The two inverse kinematics methods, **Cyclic Coordinate Descent** (**CCD**) and **Forward And Backward Reaching Inverse Kinematics** (**FABRIK**), will be explained and implemented.

Chapter 14, *Creating Instanced Crowds*, shows how to add more than one model to a scene, plus different ways to transfer model data to the graphics memory.

Chapter 15, *Measuring Performance and Optimizing the Code*, introduces methods to find bottlenecks by profiling code and using RenderDoc to analyze the graphics pipeline. It also offers ideas to move calculations from runtime to compile time and examines the importance of scaling to get meaningful results.

To get the most out of this book

To follow the code snippets and the example code, you should have some experience using C++. Any special or advanced features will be explained, and resources to learn more about these features are included in the chapters when they are first used. However, you should be able to debug simple C++ problems (e.g., by using logging statements).

The code in this book is written for OpenGL 4.6 and Vulkan 1.1. These versions are widely supported in modern GPUs; the oldest graphics cards known to work with these API versions are from the Intel HD Graphics 4000 series, created about 10 years ago.

Software used in the book	Operating system requirements
OpenGL 4.6 and Vulkan 1.1	Windows or Linux

The example code presented in this book can be compiled on any desktop computer or laptop running a recent version of Windows and Linux. The code has been tested with the following combinations:

- Windows 10 with Visual Studio 2022
- Windows 10 with Eclipse 2023-06, using GCC from MSYS2 and Ninja as the build system
- Ubuntu 22.04 with Eclipse 2023-06, using GCC or Clang
- Ubuntu 22.04 compiling on the command line, using GCC or Clang

If you are using the digital version of this book, we advise you to type the code yourself or access the code from the book's GitHub repository (a link is available in the next section). Doing so will help you avoid any potential errors related to the copying and pasting of code.

The full source code for the examples is available from the book's GitHub repository (a link is available in the next section). The chapters in the book contain only excerpts from the code, covering the important parts.

Download the example code files

You can download the example code files for this book from GitHub at `https://github.com/PacktPublishing/Cpp-Game-Animation-Programming-Second-Edition`. If there's an update to the code, it will be updated in the GitHub repository.

We also have other code bundles from our rich catalog of books and videos available at `https://github.com/PacktPublishing/`. Check them out!

Conventions used

There are a number of text conventions used throughout this book.

`Code in text`: Indicates code words in text, database table names, folder names, filenames, file extensions, pathnames, dummy URLs, user input, and Twitter handles. Here is an example: "Now, the `include` directives for Glad will work in our code."

A block of code is set as follows:

```
public:
  bool init(unsigned int width, unsigned int height);
  bool resize(unsigned int newWidth, unsigned int newHeight);
  void bind();
  void unbind();
  void drawToScreen();
```

When we wish to draw your attention to a particular part of a code block, the relevant lines or items are set in bold:

```
> Set-ExecutionPolicy RemoteSigned -Scope CurrentUser
> irm get.scoop.sh | iex
```

Any command-line input or output is written as follows:

```
pacman -S base-devel
```

Bold: Indicates a new term, an important word, or words that you see on screen. For instance, words in menus or dialog boxes appear in **bold**. Here is an example: "Right-click the `CMakeLists.txt` file and choose **Build**."

> Note
>
> Important notes appear like this text.

Get in touch

Feedback from our readers is always welcome.

General feedback: If you have questions about any aspect of this book, email us at `customercare@packtpub.com` and mention the book title in the subject of your message.

Errata: Although we have taken every care to ensure the accuracy of our content, mistakes do happen. If you have found a mistake in this book, we would be grateful if you would report this to us. Please visit `www.packtpub.com/support/errata` and fill in the form.

Piracy: If you come across any illegal copies of our works in any form on the internet, we would be grateful if you would provide us with the location address or website name. Please contact us at `copyright@packt.com` with a link to the material.

If you are interested in becoming an author: If there is a topic that you have expertise in and you are interested in either writing or contributing to a book, please visit `authors.packtpub.com`.

Share Your Thoughts

Once you've read, we'd love to hear your thoughts! Scan the QR code below to go straight to the Amazon review page for this book and share your feedback.

`https://packt.link/r/1803246529`

Your review is important to us and the tech community and will help us make sure we're delivering excellent quality content.

Download a free PDF copy of this book

Thanks for purchasing this book!

Do you like to read on the go but are unable to carry your print books everywhere?

Is your eBook purchase not compatible with the device of your choice?

Don't worry, now with every Packt book you get a DRM-free PDF version of that book at no cost.

Read anywhere, any place, on any device. Search, copy, and paste code from your favorite technical books directly into your application.

The perks don't stop there, you can get exclusive access to discounts, newsletters, and great free content in your inbox daily

Follow these simple steps to get the benefits:

1. Scan the QR code or visit the link below

`https://packt.link/free-ebook/9781803246529`

2. Submit your proof of purchase
3. That's it! We'll send your free PDF and other benefits to your email directly

Part 1: Building a Graphics Renderer

In this part, you will get an overview of the steps to open a simple application window and handle keyboard and mouse input. In addition, you will learn how to draw textured 3D objects on a screen with OpenGL 4 and the Vulkan API. We will briefly explain GPU shaders, small programs running on a graphics card, working hard to calculate the pictures of the 3D objects you see on the screen. Finally, you will be introduced to Dear ImGui and learn how to add basic control elements to an application.

In this part, we will cover the following chapters:

- *Chapter 1, Creating the Game Window*
- *Chapter 2, Building an OpenGL 4 Renderer*
- *Chapter 3, Building a Vulkan Renderer*
- *Chapter 4, Working with Shaders*
- *Chapter 5, Adding Dear ImGui to Show Valuable Information*

1

Creating the Game Window

This is the start of your journey into the world of game character animation programming. In this book, you will open a window into a virtual world, enabling the user to take control and move around in it. The window will utilize hardware-accelerated graphics rendering to show detailed characters that have been loaded from a simple file on your system. You will be introduced to character animation, starting with basic steps such as how to show a single, static pose, and you will move on to more advanced topics such as **Inverse Kinematics**. By the end, the application will have a large crowd of animated people, who are the inhabitants of your virtual world. In addition, the window will have fancy UI elements that you can use to control the animations of the characters, and you will learn how to debug the application if you encounter any trouble, both on the CPU and the GPU. I hope you enjoy the ride – it will take you to various wonderful locations, steep hills, long roads, and nice cities. Buckle up!

To begin, welcome to *Chapter 1*! The first step might be the most important as it sets the foundation for all the other chapters in this book. Without a window to your virtual world, you won't be able to see your creations. But it's not as hard as you might expect, and the right tools can solve this quickly and easily.

As we are using open source software and platform-independent libraries in this book, you should be able to compile and run the code "out of the box" on Windows and Linux. You will find a detailed list of the required software and libraries in the *Technical requirements* section.

To that end, in this chapter, we will cover the following topics:

- Creating your first window
- Adding support for OpenGL or Vulkan to the window
- Event handling in GLFW
- The mouse and keyboard input for the game window

Technical requirements

For this chapter, you will need the following:

- A PC with Windows or Linux and the tools listed later in this section
- A text editor (such as Notepad++ or Kate) or a full IDE (such as Visual Studio or Eclipse)

Now, let's get the source code for this book and start unpacking the code.

Getting the source code and the basic tools

The code for this book is hosted on GitHub, which you can find here:

`https://github.com/PacktPublishing/Cpp-Game-Animation-Programming-Second-Edition`

To unpack the code, you can use any of the following methods.

Getting the code as a ZIP file

If you download the code as a ZIP file, you will need to unpack it onto your system. My suggested way is to create a subfolder inside the home directory of the local user account on your computer as the destination, that is, inside the `Documents` folder, and unpack it there. But any other place is also fine; it depends on your personal preference.

Please make sure the path contains no spaces or special characters such as umlauts, as this might confuse some compilers and development environments.

Getting the code using Git

To get the code of the book, you can also use Git. Using Git offers you additional features, such as reverting changes if you have broken the code during the exploration of the source, or while working on the practical sessions at the end of each chapter. For Linux systems, use your package manager. For Ubuntu,the following line installs `git`:

```
sudo apt install git
```

On Windows, you can download it here: `https://git-scm.com/downloads`

You can get a local checkout of the code in a specific location on your system either through the git GUI, or by executing the following command in CMD:

```
git clone (GitHub-Link)
```

Also, please make sure that you use a path without spaces or special characters.

Downloading and installing GLFW

If you use Windows, you can download the binary distribution here: `https://www.glfw.org/download`

Unpack it and copy the contents of the `include` folder here, as CMake will only search within this location:

```
C:\Program Files (x86)\glfw\include
```

Then, copy the libraries from the `lib-vc2022` subfolder into this `lib` folder:

```
C:\Program Files (x86)\glfw\lib
```

As a Linux user, you can install the development package of `glfw3` using the package manager of your distribution. For Ubuntu, this line installs GLFW:

```
sudo apt install libglfw3-dev
```

Downloading and installing CMake

To build the code, we will use CMake. CMake is a collection of tools used to create native Makefiles for your compiler and **operating system** (**OS**).CMake also searches for the libraries, the headers to include, and more. It refers to all that "dirty" stuff you don't want to lay your hands on during compilation time.

> **Important note**
>
> You only need CMake if you are using Eclipse or the command-line-based approach to compile the source code. Visual Studio installs its own version of CMake.

Windows users can download it here: `https://cmake.org/download/`.

Linux users can use the package manager of their distribution to install Cmake. If you use Ubuntu, the following line will install CMake on your system:

```
sudp apt install cmake
```

Using the example code with Visual Studio 2022 on Windows

If you want to use Visual Studio for the example files and don't have it installed yet, download the Community Edition of Visual Studio at `https://visualstudio.microsoft.com/de/downloads/`.

Then, follow these steps:

1. Choose the **Desktop development with C++** option so that the C++ compiler and the other required tools are installed on your machine:

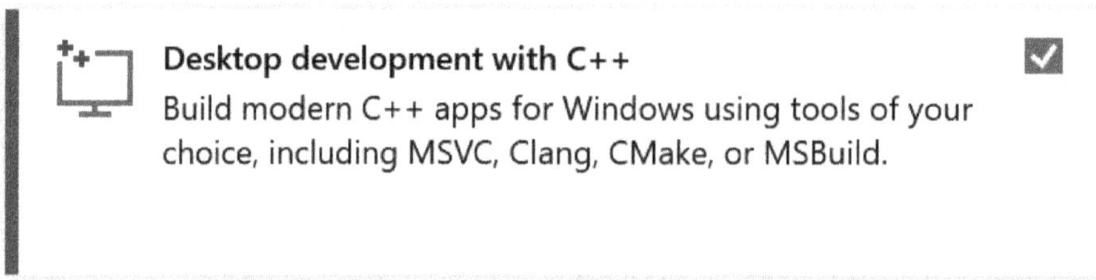

Figure 1.1: Installing the C++ Desktop development in VS 2022

2. Then, under **Individual components**, also check the **C++ CMake tools for Windows** option:

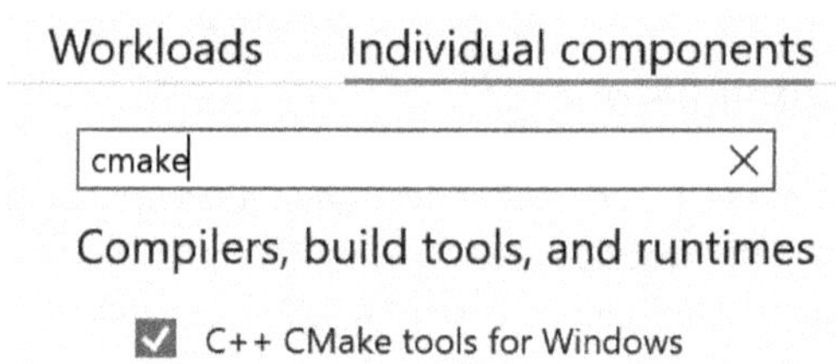

Figure 1.2: Installing the CMake tools in VS 2022

3. Finish the installation of Visual Studio, start it, and skip the initial project selection screen.

Compiling and starting the example code can be done using the following steps:

1. To open an example project, use the **CMake...** option, which appears after installing the CMake tools:

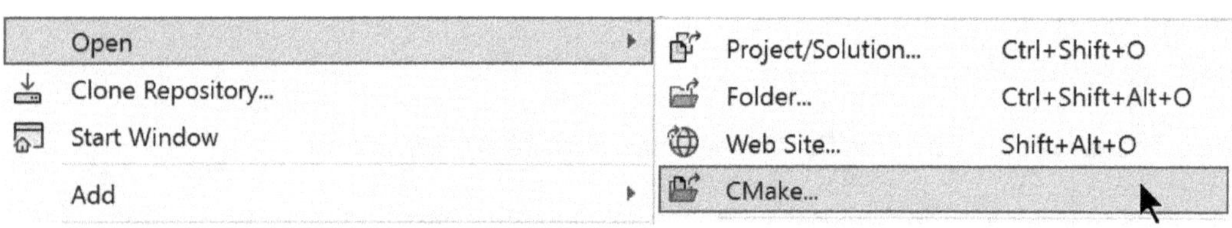

Figure 1.3: Open a CMake project in VS 2022

2. Navigate to the folder with the example file and select the `CMakeLists.txt` file. This is the main configuration file for CMake:

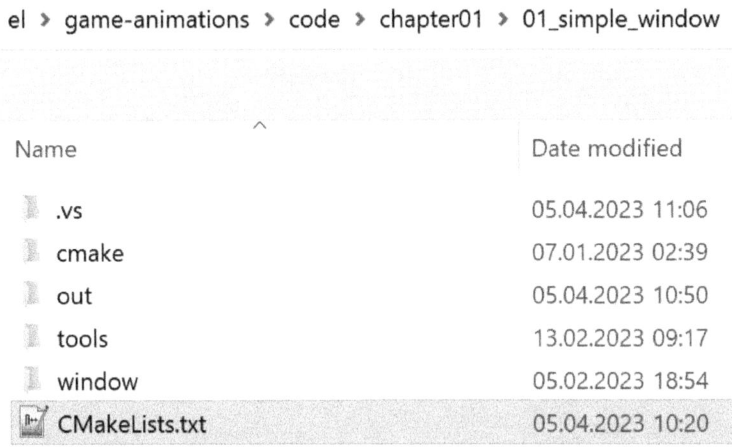

Figure 1.4: Selecting the CMakeLists.txt file in the project

Visual Studio will automatically configure CMake for you. The last line of the output window should be as follows:

```
1> CMake generation finished.
```

This confirms the successful run of the CMake file generation.

3. Now, set the startup item by right-clicking on the `CMakeLists.txt` file – this step is required to build and run the project:

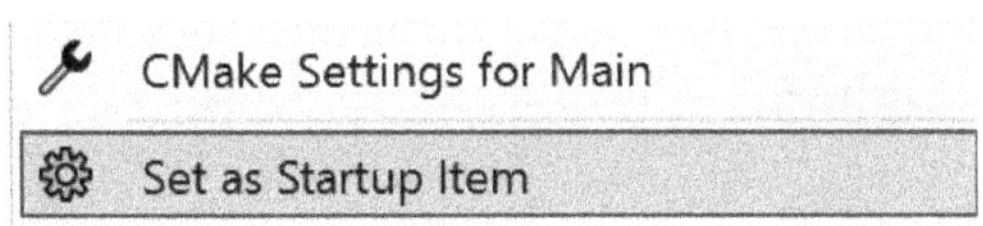

Figure 1.5: Configuring the startup item in VS 2022

4. After setting the startup item, we can build the current project. Right-click on the `CMakeLists.txt` file and choose **Build**:

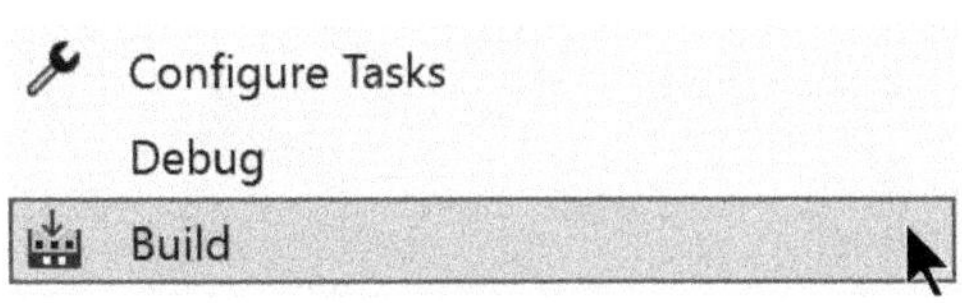

Figure 1.6: Building the VS 2022 CMake project

If the compilation succeeds, start the program using the green arrow:

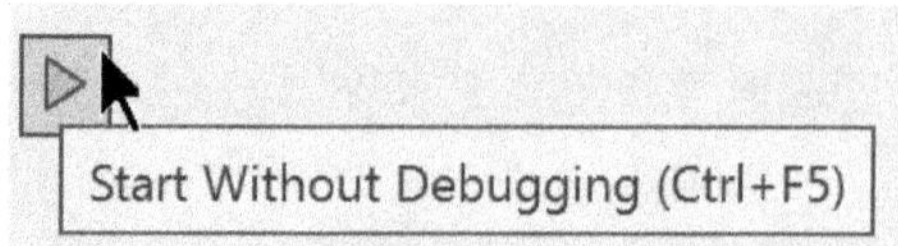

Figure 1.7: The program starting without debugging in VS 2022

Installing a C++ compiler on your Windows PC

If you don't use Visual Studio, you will need a C++ compiler first. You can use the MSYS2 tools and libs here: `https://www.msys2.org`.

Download the installation package, install `MSYS2` in the default location but do not start `MSYS2` at the end of the installation. Instead, start the `MSYS2 MINWG64` environment from the start menu and update the `MSYS2` system:

```
pacman -Syu
```

The `MSYS2` system will request to close the current console after the update. This is the normal behaviour.

Open the `MINGW64` environment again and install the `gcc` compiler suite, the `glwf3` library, and the basic development tools in the `MSYS2` console:

```
pacman -S mingw-x64-x86_64-gcc mingw-w64-x86_64-glfw base-devel
```

The preceding command installs the compilation tools you need for the book. We use the `glfw3` library included in `MSYS2` because it is compiled with the same compiler and version we will use in Eclipse.

You also need to include CMake and the installed compiler within the Windows `PATH` environment variable:

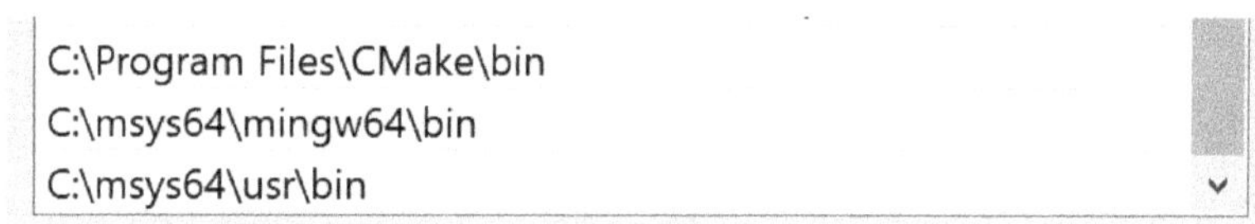

Figure 1.8: The Windows PATH settings when using MSYS2 on Windows

Eclipse for Windows uses Ninja to build CMake packages, so you need to install Ninja too. The easiest way to do this is by using the Windows package manager named **Scoop**, which you can access at `https://scoop.sh`.

Install Scoop in PowerShell Window:

```
> Set-ExecutionPolicy RemoteSigned -Scope CurrentUser
> irm get.scoop.sh | iex
```

The preceding code will download and install Scoop on your computer. Now use it to install Ninja:

```
scoop install ninja
```

Installing a C++ compiler in Linux

Linux users can install `g++` or `clang` with the package manager. For Ubuntu-based distributions, enter the following command in a Terminal window to install the compiler and the required libraries and tools for the book:

```
sudo apt install gcc build-essential ninja-build glslang-tools libglm-
dev
```

Using the example code with Eclipse on Windows or Linux

If you prefer Eclipse instead of Visual Studio, follow these steps:

1. Download and install **Eclipse IDE for C/C++ Developers** from `https://www.eclipse.org/downloads/packages/`.
2. After installing Eclipse, head to the marketplace under **Help**:

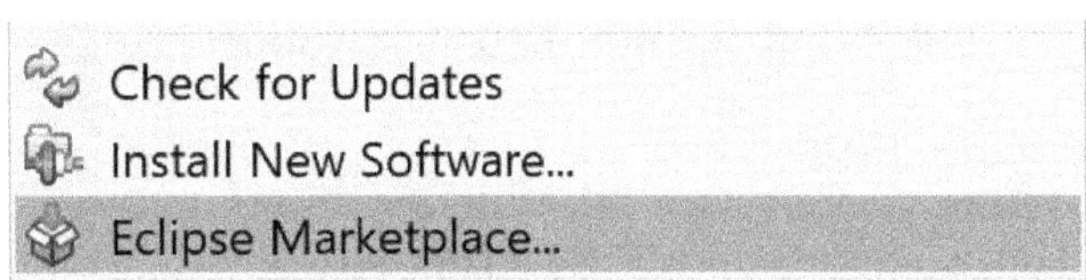

Figure 1.9: Accessing the Eclipse marketplace

3. Install the **cmake4eclipse** and **CMake Editor** packages. The first one enables CMake support in Eclipse, with all the features we need, and the second one adds syntax coloring to the CMake files. This makes it more convenient to edit the files:

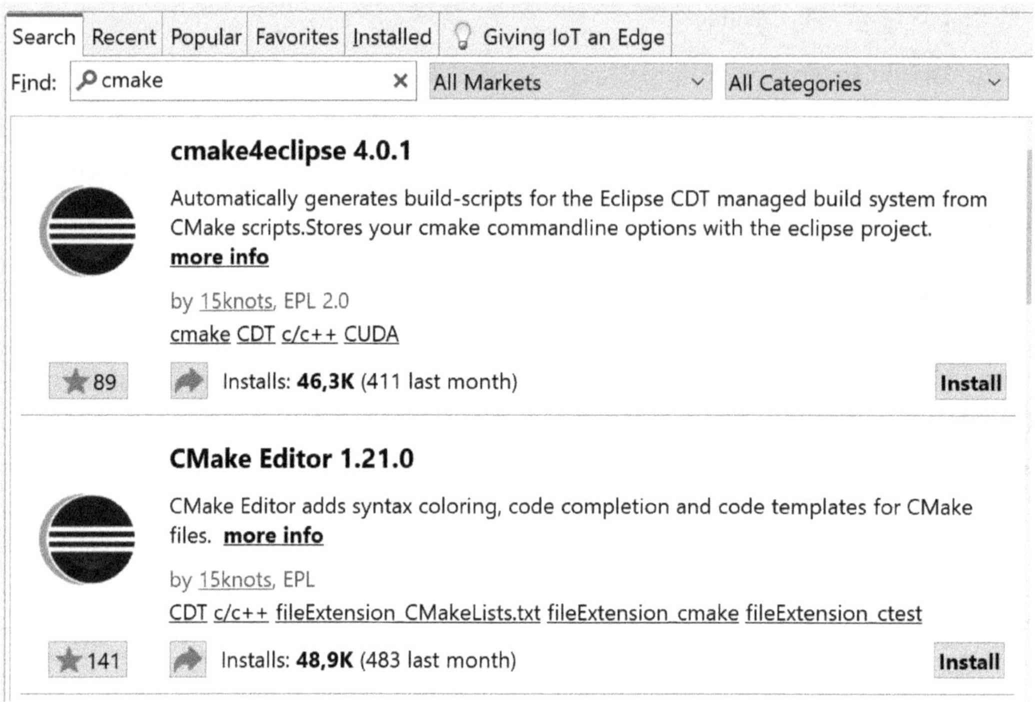

Figure 1.10: Installing the Eclipse CMake solutions

Compiling and starting the example code can be done in the following steps:

1. First, open a project from the filesystem:

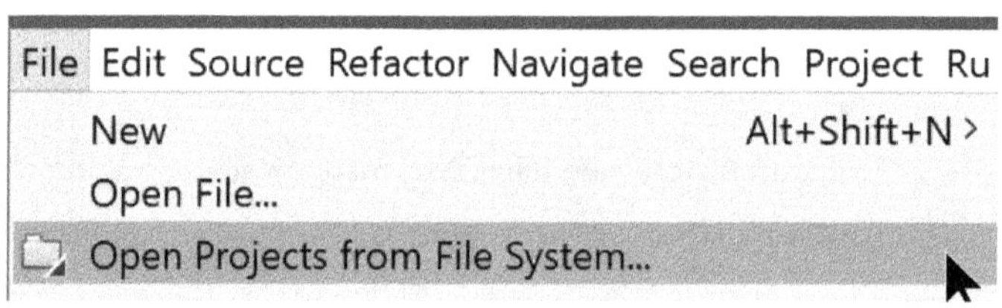

Figure 1.11: Opening a project in Eclipse

2. Choose **Directory...** and navigate to the folder with the source code:

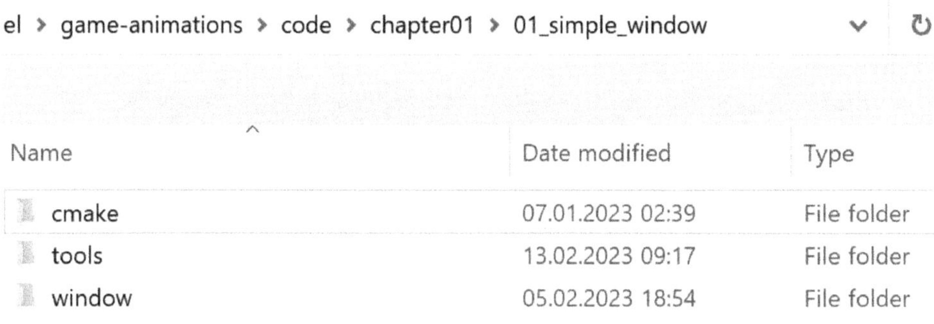

Figure 1.12: Navigating to the folder with the Eclipse project

3. Click on **Finish** to open the project. Next, choose **Build Project** from the context menu. You can do this by clicking on the right mouse button while hovering over the project folder:

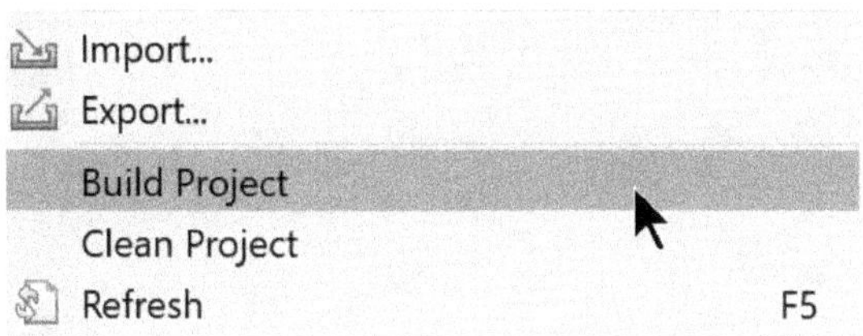

Figure 1.13: Building the project in Eclipse

4. Sometimes, Eclipse does not automatically refresh the content of the project. You must force this via the context menu. Select **Refresh** or press *F5*:

Figure 1.14: Refreshing the Eclipse project

5. Now the executable is visible and can be run. Choose **Run As**, and select the second option, **Local C/C++ Application**:

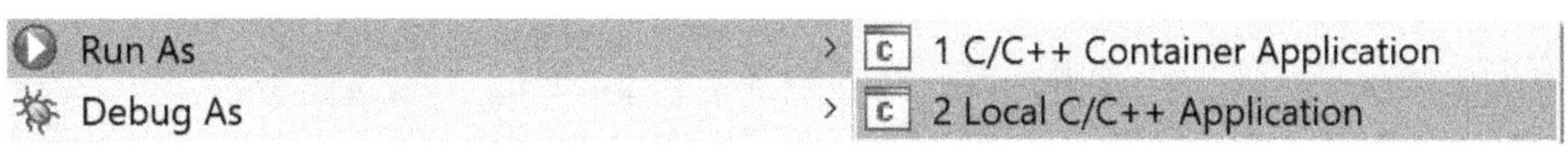

Figure 1.15: Starting the executable generated by Eclipse

6. In the following dialog, choose the `Main.exe` (Windows) or `Main` (Linux) binary file from the list:

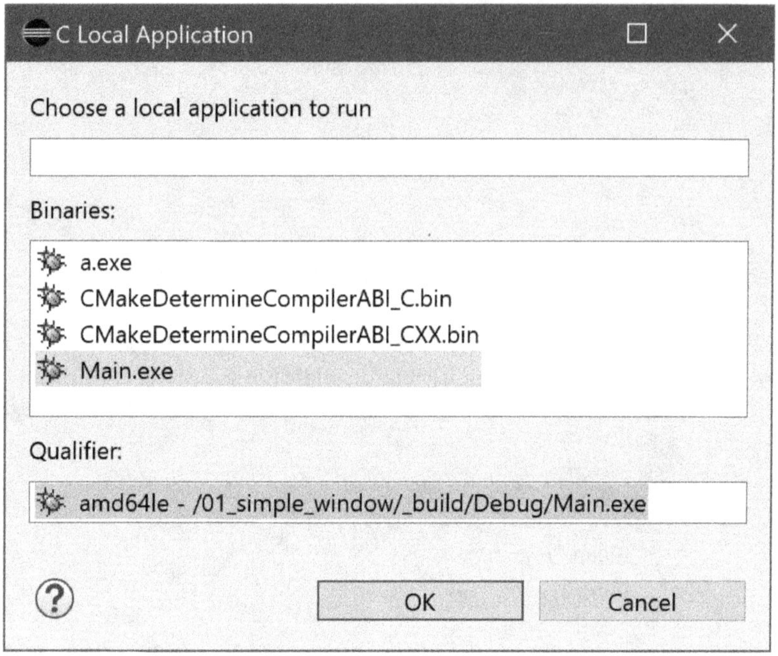

Figure 1.16: Selecting the generated executable in Eclipse

The Vulkan SDK

For Vulkan support, you also need to have the Vulkan SDK installed. Get it here: `https://vulkan.lunarg.com/sdk/home`. Then, do a default installation, and make sure to add **GLM** and **Vulkan Memory Allocator**, as we will need both of them later in the book:

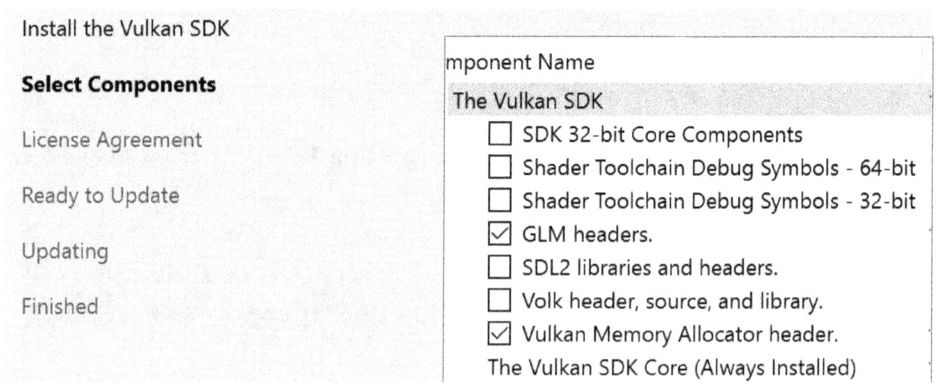

Figure 1.17: Adding GLM and VMA during the Vulkan SDK installation

Code organization in this book

The code for every chapter is stored in the GitHub repository, in a separate folder with the relevant chapter number. The number uses two digits to get the ordering right. Inside each folder, one or more subfolders can be found. These subfolders contain the code of the chapter, depending on the progress of that specific chapter:

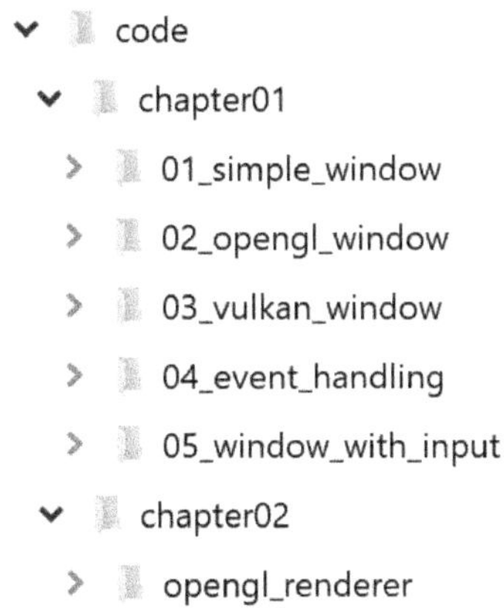

Figure 1.18: Folder organization with the chapters in the example code

For all chapters, we put the `Main.cpp` class and the CMake configuration file, `CMakeLists.txt`, into the project root folder. Inside the `cmake` folder, helper files for CMake are stored. These files are required to find additional header and library files. All C++ classes are located inside folders, collecting the classes of the objects we create. The `Window` class will be stored in the `window` subfolder to hold all files related to the class itself, and the same applies to the logger:

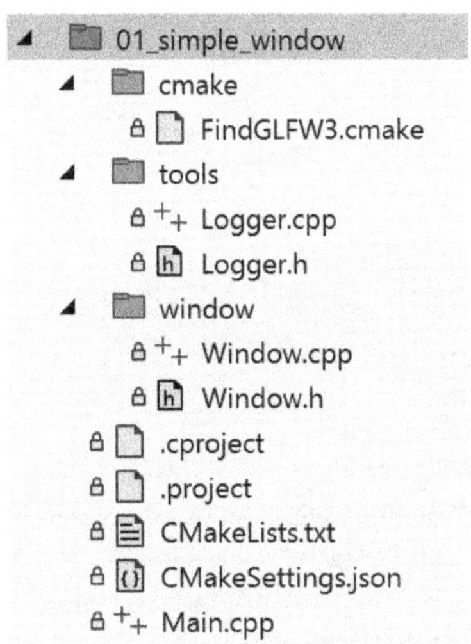

Figure 1.19: Folders and files in one example code project

In the other chapters, more folders will be created.

The basic code for our application

Our future character rendering application needs some additional code to work.

A program can't be started without an initial function called by the operating system. On Windows and Linux, this initial function in the code must be named `main()`. Inside this function, the application window will be created, and the control is moved over to the window.

As long as a graphical output is unavailable, we must have the capability to print text within the application to update the user on its status. Instead of the `std::cout` call, we will use a simple logging function in a separate class. This extra output will be kept for debugging purposes even after we have completed the rendering, as this makes a programmer's life much easier.

The main entry point

The `main()` function is embedded in a C++ class file, but as it has no class definition, it just contains the code to open and close the application window and call the main loop of our `Window` class.

This is the content of the `Main.cpp` file, located in the project root:

```
#include <memory>
#include "Window.h"
#include "Logger.h"

int main(int argc, char *argv[]) {
  std::unique_ptr<Window> w = std::make_unique<Window>();

  if (!w->init(640, 480, "Test Window")) {
    Logger::log(1, "%s error: Window init error\n",
      __FUNCTION__);
    return -1;
  }
  w->mainLoop();
  w->cleanup();

  return 0;
}
```

The preceding class includes the memory header, as we will use a unique smart pointer here. Additionally, it includes the headers for the `Window` and `Logger` classes. Inside the `main()` function, we create the smart pointer with the w object of the `Window` class. Next, we try to initialize the window using the width, height, and title text. If this initialization fails, we print out a log message and exit the program with a value of `-1` to tell the OS we ran into an error. The `log()` call has the same verbosity level as the first parameter, followed by a C-style `printf` string. The `__FUNCTION__` macro is recommended to print out the function where the logging call was issued.

If the `init()` call was successful, we enter the `mainLoop()` function of the `Windows` class. This handles all the window events, drawings, and more. Closing the window ends the main loop. After this, we clean up the window and return the value of `0` to signal a successful termination.

The Logger class

Additionally, I added a small and simple `Logger` class to simplify the debugging process. This allows you to add logging messages with different logging levels, enabling you to control the number of logs being shown. If you encounter problems with the code, you can use the `Logger` class to print out the content of the variables and success/error messages. In the case of a crash, you will see which part of the code has been reached before the termination of the program.

The following is the content of the `Logger.h` file:

```
#pragma once
#include <cstdio>

class Logger {
  public:
    /* log if input log level is equal or smaller to log level set */
    template <typename... Args>
    static void log(unsigned int logLevel, Args ... args) {
      if (logLevel <= mLogLevel) {
        std::printf(args ...);
        /* force output, i.e. for Eclipse */
        std::fflush(stdout);
      }
    }
    static void setLogLevel(unsigned int inLogLevel) {
      inLogLevel <= 9 ? mLogLevel = inLogLevel :
          mLogLevel = 9;
    }
  private:
    static unsigned int mLogLevel;
};
```

The preceding file starts with the `#pragma once` directive, which is called a *header guard*. The header guard line is used to prevent multiple inclusions of the same header file during the compilation. Then, we include the `cstdio` C++ headers so that the `std::printf()` and `std::fflush()` functions are available. Here, I use the old C-style of printing as it is both easy to implement and use. The `log()` function is implemented as a C++ template to enable us to use a varying number of arguments to print to the screen. Inside the function, the current log level of the call is compared with the stored log level, suppressing all messages with higher log levels. If the log level fits, we use `printf` to output the arguments to the terminal. Forced flushing with `std::fflush()` is required for Eclipse; without the line, the output will be displayed after the termination of the program. The `setLogLevel()` function enables you to change the desired verbosity at runtime. That means you could also add UI elements to set the logging level using mGui controls, which are explained in *Chapter 5*. The only data member is the global log level.

The `Logger.cpp` file is only two lines long:

```
#include "Logger.h"
unsigned int Logger::mLogLevel = 1;
```

The first line includes the class header, while the second line is responsible for initializing the member variable holding the current log level. This initialization has to be done in the `.cpp` file, or else we will get a linker error during compilation.

We will come back to debugging in *Chapter 4*, which discusses different ways in which to show what's going on in your code.

NULL versus nullptr

As GLFW is a C library, you will see a lot of `NULL` values in the examples and function calls. Modern C++ has redefined `NULL` to `nullptr`, which is still compatible with the pointer type in C code. From the technical perspective, the values of `NULL` for a pointer and `0` as a number are the same in C, and `nullptr` helps to avoid ambiguous cases where a pointer was intended but a number was used (and vice versa). I will only use `nullptr` as there is no reason to stick with ancient definitions in 2023.

Now that you've worked through the source code, let's move on and create our first window!

Creating your first window

After all the necessary software products have been installed, we are ready for our first smoke test. We will create a small, non-resizable window, and its only purpose is to check your system for the correct path and configuration. You will be able to move it around, minimize and restore it, and close it… that's mostly all at this stage.

But believe me, seeing your first test window on the screen will make you smile. For basic window operations, we are going to use GLFW to open and close a window.

GLFW is an open source toolkit that is used to handle the tasks around the application window, and it is available for different OSs and hardware platforms.

GLFW will do the following tasks with a few lines of code, independent of your OS:

- Create and destroy the application window
- Handle the window events (such as minimize, resize, or close)
- Add an OpenGL context or Vulkan support to enable 3D rendering
- Get the input from the mouse, keyboard, and gamepads/joysticks

If you want to check the source for this example, head to the `chapter01` folder in the Git checkout or the extracted source for this book, and then go to the `01_simple_window` folder. You can follow the explanation of the code snippets, or in case you have no questions about the intention of the code lines, you can compile the code in advance and check the code snippets only for clarification.

For the window code, start with the `Window.h` header file:

```
#pragma once
#include <string>
#include <GLFW/glfw3.h>

class Window {
  public:
    bool init(unsigned int width, unsigned int height,
      std::string title);
    void mainLoop();
    void cleanup();

  private:
    GLFWwindow *mWindow = nullptr;
};
```

After the `include` guard, we need to include the `std::string` header, which we will use to pass the window title to the instance, and the GLFW header for the GLFW functions.

The `Window` class contains a handle for the GLFW window that we will create as a `private` member, along with three other `public` methods.The `init()` method is used to initialize the new window; the `mainLoop()` method runs the code of the main loop of the window where we do all the work; and the `cleanup()` method cleans up the window to shut down the application properly.

The implementation of the three functions is done in the `Window.cpp` file:

```
#include "Window.h"
#include "Logger.h"
```

We include our previously created header file for the `Window` class, plus the header file for the `Logger` class to ensure the console logging is available:

```
bool Window::init(unsigned int width, unsigned int height, std::string
title) {
  if (!glfwInit()) {
    Logger::log(1, "%s: glfwInit() error\n",
      __FUNCTION__);
    return false;
  }
  /* set a "hint" for the NEXT window created*/
  glfwWindowHint(GLFW_RESIZABLE, GLFW_FALSE);

  mWindow = glfwCreateWindow(width, height,
    title.c_str(), nullptr, nullptr);
  if (!mWindow) {
    Logger::log(1, "%s: Could not create window\n",
      __FUNCTION__);
    glfwTerminate();
    return false;
  }
  Logger::log(1, "%s: Window successfully initialized\n",
     __FUNCTION__);
  return true;
}
```

The `init()` function checks whether GLFW could be initialized at all. If something unexpected happens, it will return `false` in the `main()` function and stop the program.

The **window hint** set with the `glfwWindowHint()` call is a special property in GLFW, which changes the settings for the creation of the next window. For example, we can disable the ability to resize our window. After this, the creation of the window itself is done, and the result is saved inside our member variable. If the window cannot be created, the process of creating a window will also be aborted and GLFW will be terminated. In a successful window creation, we output a log line to the console and return to the `main()` function, stating that everything went fine.

The `mainLoop()` function does nothing special for the first window; it simply checks whether the user generated an event to close the window, that is, by selecting the close button. If this is not the case, it instructs GLFW to poll any events. This call is required to react to anything happening to the window itself – keyboard presses, mouse events, and window operations such as minimizing or even closing:

```
void Window::mainLoop() {
  while (!glfwWindowShouldClose(mWindow)) {
    /* poll events in a loop */
```

```
        glfwPollEvents();
    }
}
```

Finally, the `cleanup()` function destroys the window and terminates GLFW, removing our window from the screen and ending the usage of GLFW. At this point, the destroy window operation is slightly redundant, as `glfwTerminate()` also kills all windows that are still onscreen. But using the explicit `destroy` function on the application window should remain here, in case of later additions to the termination process of the application:

```
void Window::cleanup() {
  Logger::log(1, "%s: Terminating Window\n",
      __FUNCTION__);
  glfwDestroyWindow(mWindow);
  glfwTerminate();
}
```

To compile the preceding code, we also need a file named `CMakeLists.txt` in our project folder. This file instructs the CMake build system about the configuration of the project; it states which files to compile and how to add the required additional dependencies.

In the following code snippet, at the top of the file, we set the *minimum version* of CMake to `3.19`. This is the first version that provides support to find the shader compiler for Vulkan. We will need this in *Chapter 3* for the Vulkan renderer:

```
cmake_minimum_required(VERSION 3.19)
```

Setting C++17 as the minimum version might seem a bit overkill for the projects in this book, but as I stated earlier, I will try to get rid of the legacy features of C++ and use the newer ones instead:

```
set(CMAKE_CXX_STANDARD 17)
set(CMAKE_CXX_STANDARD_REQUIRED ON)
```

The next lines add the `cmake` folder inside the project folder to the list of locations CMake uses to store helper scripts for the `find_package` command:

```
# use custom file to find libraries
if(WIN32)
  list(APPEND CMAKE_MODULE_PATH "${CMAKE_CUR
  RENT_LIST_DIR}/cmake")
endif()
```

As the current version of CMake does not search for GLFW, I have added a script to search for it. This extra script requires GLFW to be stored in a fixed location on the system, and by using the location we have chosen at installation time, we are able to use the single GLFW installation for all projects in the book, instead of having a copy per project.The GLFW search script is only needed on Windows, as Linux already includes a helper script in the GLFW package. So,we instruct CMake to only add this on Windows by using a check to `WIN32`. This variable is only defined on Windows.

Next, we name our project `Main`. You could use any arbitrary name here, and this could be used in other commands by referencing a variable. Then, we add the C++ (`*.cpp`) and header (`.h`) files in the local folder via a `GLOB` search and add them to the list of files to compile to our main executable, which will also be named `Main`. Under Windows, this will automatically get an extension, resulting in `Main.exe`:

```
project(Main)
file(GLOB SOURCES
      .h
      .cpp)
add_executable(Main ${SOURCES})
```

Now, the CMake command called `find_package` is used to locate the GLFW headers in version 3.3 or higher, marking GLFW also as required for the code compilation. The corresponding CMake helper script will set a couple of variables if GLFW has been found – here, the two important ones are `GWLF3_LIBRARY` and `GLFW3_INCLUDE_DIR`. Due to the different searches on Windows and Linux, we will reuse the `GLFW3_LIBRARY` variable to avoid any further splits in the control structures:

```
find_package(glfw3 3.3 REQUIRED)

#variable is set by FindGLFW3.cmake, reuse for Linux
if(UNIX)
  set(GLFW3_LIBRARY glfw)
endif()
```

Finally, the last two lines of the following code add the GLFW3 headers to the list of `include` paths for the compiler and the library to link to the final executable:

```
include_directories(${GLFW3_INCLUDE_DIR})
target_link_libraries(Main ${GLFW3_LIBRARY})
```

Now you can build the project, and it should compile the code without any errors or warnings. If the compilation fails, please check the *Technical requirements* section for all the required tools and libraries.

Start the executable file, `Main.exe` (Windows) or `Main` (Linux), and you will see a small window appear on the screen, as shown in the following screenshot:

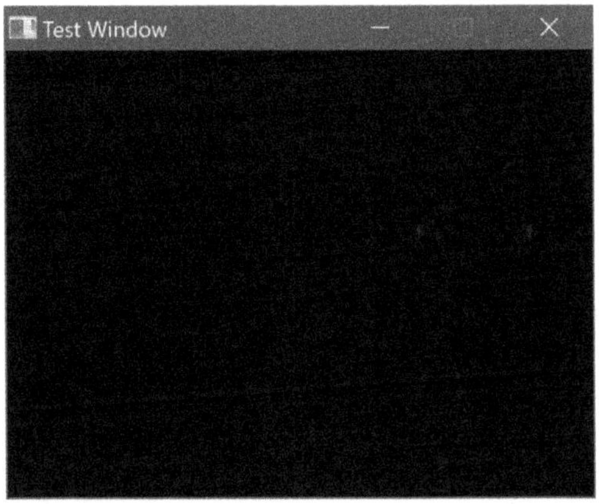

Figure 1.20: Your first window

Depending on your OS, the window might be filled in black, white, or even contain some parts of the screen where it was opened. The system does a "cheap" copy when creating the window, and we don't clear the window content. So, don't be alarmed if you don't get exactly the same picture as *Figure 1.1*. As long as your window has the proper caption and the OS-specific buttons to close and minimize, everything has worked fine.

Now, let's check out the available 3D-rendering APIs on the system.

Adding support for OpenGL or Vulkan to the window

Having a simple window is cool, but we need to go a bit further to draw our models using OpenGL or Vulkan. These changes will add the bare minimum of code to initialize the window for 3D rendering. It is a "smoke test" to see whether you have all the libraries and headers for *Chapters 2* and *3*, where we will create two triangle renderers, one for OpenGL and one for Vulkan.

GLFW and OpenGL

GLFW includes basic support for OpenGL; you only need a bunch of calls and a link to the OpenGL library. You can find the code in the `02_opengl_window` folder.

Add the following lines to the `Window.cpp` file:

```
bool Window::init(unsigned int width, unsigned int height, std::string
title) {
  if (!glfwInit()) {
  ...
  glfwMakeContextCurrent(mWindow);

  Logger::log(1, "%s: Window successfully initialized\n",
```

```
      __FUNCTION__);
    return true;
  }
```

The first call is `glfwMakeContextCurrent()` – it gets the OpenGL context, which contains the global state of the rendering, and makes it the context of the current thread. This needs to be added to the end of the `init()` call.

Having the context in place, we can use some simple OpenGL calls inside the main loop of the window. Without an extension loader, this is fairly basic (Windows may be down for OpenGL version 1.x), but for pure initialization, the following is sufficient:

```
void Window::mainLoop() {

  glfwSwapInterval(1);
  float color = 0.0f;
```

Before going into the loop, we will activate the wait for the vertical sync with a call to the GLFW function, `glfwSwapInterval()`. Without waiting for it, the window might flicker, or tearing might occur, as the update and buffer switch will be done as fast as possible. Also, we add a `color` float variable, which holds our background color.

Inside the `while` loop, which is, again, waiting for the window to close, the `color` variable is incremented in small amounts and reset to zero if it reaches a value of one. The value is set using a call to the `glClearColor()` function as the new color to be used when clearing the draw buffer – setting the red, green, and blue results in a gray color. The call to the `glClear()` function, with the value set to clear only the color buffer, gives the window a simple gray background:

```
  while (!glfwWindowShouldClose(mWindow)) {
    color >= 1.0f ? color = 0.0f : color += 0.01f;
    glClearColor(color, color, color, 1.0f);
    glClear(GL_COLOR_BUFFER_BIT);
```

By default, GLFW activates **double buffering** for the OpenGL window. This means we have two separate graphics buffers of the same size, a **front buffer** and a **back buffer**. All the changes to the final picture occur in the back buffer while showing the front buffer, which contains the image created by the previous rendering calls. This hides the creation process from the user. After the drawing of the back buffer has finished, `glfwSwapBuffers()` swaps the two buffers and displays the content of the back buffer, making the previous front buffer the new back buffer for the hidden drawing:

```
    /* swap buffers */
    glfwSwapBuffers(mWindow);
```

The event polling stays at the end of the loop, enabling it to move and close the window:

```
        /* poll events in a loop */
        glfwPollEvents();
    }
}
```

Note that `CMakeLists.txt` also needs to be extended for proper usage of OpenGL:

```
set(OpenGL_GL_PREFERENCE GLVND)
find_package(OpenGL REQUIRED)

target_link_libraries(Main ${GLFW3_LIBRARY} OpenGL::GL)
```

We have to set a variable to define the type of OpenGL; here, we are using the "vendor neutral dispatch" implementation (hence the name GLVND), and we use the `find_package` command to locate the OpenGL library. In addition, we have to add the OpenGL library to the command to link the final executable to it.

After compiling and starting the program, you should see a slowly flashing window. This means that your system has all the required libraries for the OpenGL renderer, which will be discussed in *Chapter 2*:

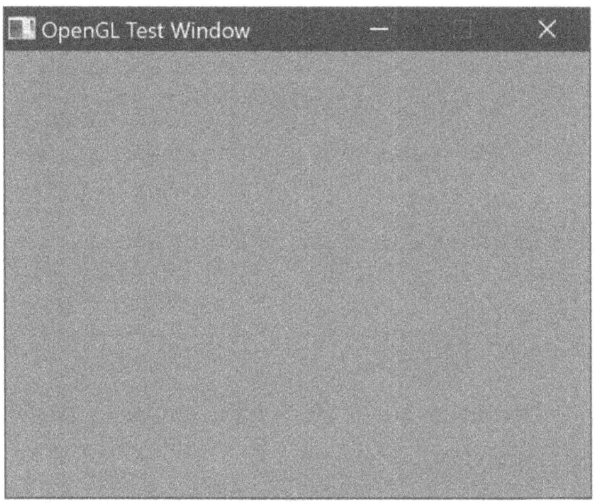

Figure 1.21: The filled OpenGL window

After checking the OS for OpenGL support to draw our characters, next, we will test whether the Vulkan-rendering API is also available.

GLFW and Vulkan

GLFW also supports the newer Vulkan API, and compared to OpenGL, this is much closer to the GPU. You can get a lot more power out of your graphics card, but with great power comes great responsibility. As you will learn, the first basic steps to initialize the Vulkan system already require a lot of work. And even with this amount of code, we are far, far away from drawing a triangle or just clearing the screen like in the OpenGL code.

The code for this example can be found in the `03_vulkan_window` folder.

First, the `Window.h` file needs to be extended:

```
#include <string>
/* include Vulkan header BEFORE GLFW */
#include <vulkan/vulkan.h>
#include <GLFW/glfw3.h>
```

We need to include the Vulkan header, `<vulkan/vulkan.h>`. This has to be done *before* the GLFW, as the GLFW switches on specific features if it detects Vulkan.

To encapsulate all of the new Vulkan-specific code, create an `initVulkan()` function:

```
public:
  bool initVulkan();
```

Two new member variables must be added in the `private` section of the class. We need a handle for the Vulkan instance and another handle for the Vulkan surface:

```
private:
  GLFWwindow *mWindow = nullptr;
  std::string mApplicationName;
  VkInstance mInstance{};
  VkSurfaceKHR mSurface{};
```

Here, `VkInstance` stores information about the Vulkan settings in the current application, and `VkSurfaceKHR` is a drawable "surface" in Vulkan. This will be enhanced in *Chapter 3* when we create a Vulkan renderer.

The application name has been stored as `std::string` since we need it in two positions.

The `init()` function in the `Window.cpp` file will be extended by two additional calls:

```
if (!glfwVulkanSupported()) {
  glfwTerminate();
  Logger::log(1, "%s: Vulkan is not supported\n",
    __FUNCTION__);
  return false;
}
```

The first call, `glfwVulkanSupported()`, checks whether Vulkan is available at all. If this fails, the machine might be missing the software or hardware capabilities in which to use Vulkan.

The second call is the new `initVulkan()` function; the program run will also fail if something goes wrong during the initialization process:

```
if (!initVulkan()) {
  Logger::log(1, "%s: Could not init Vulkan\n",
    __FUNCTION__);
  glfwTerminate();
  return false;
}
```

The new `initVulkan()` function starts with a data structure called `VkApplicationInfo`:

```
VkApplicationInfo mAppInfo{};
mAppInfo.sType = VK_STRUCTURE_TYPE_APPLICATION_INFO;
mAppInfo.pNext = nullptr;
....
mAppInfo.apiVersion = VK_MAKE_API_VERSION(0, 1, 1, 0);
```

This contains basic information about the application, such as the name and the version. Most of the fields are optional, but we need at least three of them:

- You will see `.sType` in many of the Vulkan data structures. This is required for Vulkan to know what kind of struct you pass to it. The naming is always `VK_STRUCTURE_TYPE_*`.
- Here, `.pNext` will always be `nullptr`. It could be used to link different Vulkan structures.
- `.apiVersion` must be set to the minimum Vulkan API version that we want to use. Here, we generate version 1.1.0.

With a call to `glfwGetRequiredInstanceExtensions()`, we check whether we have the required extensions to run a Vulkan application:

```
uint32_t extensionCount = 0;
const char** extensions =
    glfwGetRequiredInstanceExtensions(&extensionCount);

if (extensionCount == 0) {
  Logger::log(1, "%s error: no Vulkan extensions
    found\n", __FUNCTION__);
  return false;
}
```

The preceding code block returns the number of extensions and the extension names as a C-style array. We need extension names for the Vulkan initialization, but if we get no extensions at all, then again, there is no proper support for Vulkan, and we terminate the program by returning `false` from the Vulkan `init` function.

The next structure is `VkInstanceCreateInfo`:

```
VkInstanceCreateInfo mCreateInfo{};
mCreateInfo.sType =
  VK_STRUCTURE_TYPE_INSTANCE_CREATE_INFO;
mCreateInfo.pNext = nullptr;
mCreateInfo.pApplicationInfo = &mAppInfo;
mCreateInfo.enabledExtensionCount = extensionCount;
mCreateInfo.ppEnabledExtensionNames = extensions;
mCreateInfo.enabledLayerCount = 0;

result = vkCreateInstance(&mCreateInfo, nullptr,
  &mInstance);
if (result != VK_SUCCESS) {
  Logger::log(1, "%s: Could not create Instance
    (%i)\n", __FUNCTION__, result);
  return false;
}
```

The `VkInstanceCreateInfo` struct also contains the `.sType` and `.pNext` fields, along with a link to the application info structure and the extensions we found. Having this information collected, we can call `vkCreateInstance()` to create a Vulkan instance. The instance includes the storage for the Vulkan state on the application level, and there is no longer a system global state ("context") like in OpenGL.

Now, let's see how many graphics cards we can find in the system:

```
uint32_t physicalDeviceCount = 0;
vkEnumeratePhysicalDevices(mInstance,
  &physicalDeviceCount, nullptr);

if (physicalDeviceCount == 0) {
  Logger::log(1, "%s: No Vulkan capable GPU found\n",
    __FUNCTION__);
  return false;
}

std::vector<VkPhysicalDevice> devices;
vkEnumeratePhysicalDevices(mInstance,
  &physicalDeviceCount, devices.data());
```

The call to `vkEnumeratePhysicalDevices()` has to be done twice. The first time, we will only get the number of GPUs, and if we find one or more GPUs, the second call will be used to fill the corresponding array with data about the GPUs.

For the last step, we will create the Vulkan surface using `glfwCreateWindowSurface()`:

```
  result = glfwCreateWindowSurface(mInstance, mWindow,
    nullptr, &mSurface);
  if (result != VK_SUCCESS) {
    Logger::log(1, "%s: Could not create Vulkan
      surface\n", __FUNCTION__);
    return false;
  }
```

If this call is successful, full support for Vulkan will become available on your machine.

The Vulkan surface and the instance need to be deleted in the `cleanup()` function, along with the GLFW window:

```
void Window::cleanup() {
  Logger::log(1, "%s: Terminating Window\n",
    __FUNCTION__);
  vkDestroySurfaceKHR(mInstance, mSurface, nullptr);
  vkDestroyInstance(mInstance, nullptr);
  glfwDestroyWindow(mWindow);
  glfwTerminate();
}
```

Additionally, the configuration of CMake needs to be changed, and we have to find Vulkan. Add the respective change specified in the following lines to the `CmakeLists.txt` file:

```
find_package(Vulkan REQUIRED)
target_link_libraries(Main ${GLFW3_LIBRARY} Vulkan::Vulkan)
```

Note that `find_package` is used to locate the Vulkan SDK, which contains the header and libraries. Also, we have to link the final executable to the Vulkan library to be able to use the Vulkan calls.

The output window that is created when you run the code is similar to *Figure 1.1*. Again, you will get a simple window, but this time, it will be filled with a static color or with fragments of your current screen. The code from this example does not clear the screen, but in this chapter, we want to check only for the general availability of the Vulkan API. So, we need to rely on the log output. If you see a line saying **Found physical device(s)** and that the window was successfully initialized after running the code, you are ready to go for the Vulkan renderer in *Chapter 3*:

```
initVulkan: Found 2 Vulkan extensions
initVulkan: VK_KHR_surface
```

```
initVulkan: VK_KHR_xcb_surface
initVulkan: Found 1 physical device(s)
init: Window successfully initialized
```

At the very least, you need the `VK_KHR_surface` extension that is listed in the output. Other extensions might appear too, depending on your OS and the graphics drivers.

After we have checked the OS for support of one or both rendering APIs, we will add some code to the `Window` class. This code will ensure our application behaves like every other application window on the system.

Event handling in GLFW

Many modern OSs are event-based – the programs don't just sit there and ask the OS over and over if any mouse or keyboard input has occurred or if the window has been moved, minimized, or resized. All these events are stored in an **event queue** and must be handled by the application code. If you never request the events of that queue, your application window won't even close in a proper manner, that is, it can only be killed using Task Manager.

You can find the example code for these additions in the `04_event_handling` folder.

Let's have a look at how GLFW handles the events from the OS.

The GLFW event queue handling

You have already seen a bit of the event handling in the code for the `Window` class – we used these two GLFW calls to close our window and end the application:

```
int glfwWindowShouldClose(GLFWwindow *win);
void glfwPollEvents();
```

The first call, `glfwWindowShouldClose()`, checks whether an application window should be closed. This event is generated after the user clicks on the top-right close icon of the window. We are using this as a condition to step out of our `while()` loop, end the `mainLoop()` method of the `Window` class, and start the cleanup process.

> **Important note**
>
> The call to `glfwPollEvents()` is required in order to empty the event queue. It will also run any configured callbacks. If you forget this call, your window will do nothing, not even close down.

You should call `glfwPollEvents()` at the end of the main loop to process the newly arrived events.

There is another call to clear the event queue and fire the callbacks:

```
void glfwWaitEvents();
```

This one puts the thread to sleep and waits until at least one event has been generated for the window. Usually, this is used in non-interactive applications that are waiting for any input from the user.

Mixing the C++ classes and the C callbacks

A simple starting point is to react to the window close request and just output a message to the user. To get this to work, we need two parts – the function called by GLFW and a call that sets the function as a **callback**.

This sounds easy to do, but only at first glance. As GLFW is pure C code, it has no knowledge about C++ classes, member functions, the `this` pointer, and all the other moving parts. However, there are some solutions to this.

The first way is that we could use a **static** function of our `Window` class as it is technically similar to a C function. At the moment, we won't use more than one application window, but if we add support for a pop-out window later, we might be in trouble with the static class function. It is the same for all objects of that class, and as it can only access static members, you have to take extra steps to avoid even more trouble when starting with multithreaded code.

So, let's consider the second way and use a "free" function, outside the class, to dispatch the call to the C++ class. However, instead of having to define two separate functions for every callback, we will use a **Lambda**.

Lambda functions

A lambda is a small piece of code, running as an **anonymous** function. It has no visible name, takes the number and types of arguments from its definition, and runs the code. Internally, the lambda function is converted into a small class by your compiler; there is no magic applied here. It's only a convenient way to help reduce the code you write. If you want to know more about lambda functions, you can find a link to a tutorial in the *Additional resources* section.

The authors of GLFW are aware of this problem and have added a small helper to every window that might be created – a pointer that can be set and read by the user:

```
void glfwSetWindowUserPointer(GLFWwindow *win, void *ptr);
```

You can store any arbitrary data in the user pointer – it doesn't have to be the `this` pointer of the class object, but it is only a pointer and must be accessible by your code. We will use it to store the pointer in our C++ `Window` object, and inside the lambda, this pointer will be read and used just like in any other C++ call.

The callback function itself looks a bit weird if you have never used C-style callbacks:

```
GLFWwindowclosefun glfwSetWindowCloseCallback (GLFWwindow *window,
GLFWwindowclosefun callback);
```

It requires a pointer to a function and returns either `NULL`, if this is the first call, or the pointer to a previously set callback function. You could change this callback during runtime, which means moving to a different dialog to display any unsaved changes.

The last part of the puzzle is the window close function, which is called by the callback:

```
typedef void(* GLFWwindowclosefun) (GLFWwindow *window)
```

The `GLFWwindowclosefun` function is created using `typedef`, just like the other functions used for callbacks. This is done to avoid writing the expression in the second braces every time we use the function. As this is still C code, sadly, no modern C++ enhancements are available to change it.

And this is how you should put all the parts together – by adding the following lines to the `init()` function of the `Window.cpp` file:

```
  glfwSetWindowUserPointer(mWindow, this);
  glfwSetWindowCloseCallback(mWindow, [](GLFWwindow *win) {
    auto thisWindow = static_cast<Window*>(
      glfwGetWindowUserPointer(win));
    thisWindow->handleWindowCloseEvents();
  });
```

Here, the lambda is introduced by the square brackets, `[]`, followed by the parameters the function takes. You could even *capture* some data from the outside of the function using the brackets, making it available, like in normal functions. We can't use this capturing method for C-style callbacks, as such captures are not compatible with a function pointer.

Inside the lambda function, we can retrieve the user pointer set by `glfwSetWindowUserPointer()`, cast it back to a pointer to an instance of our `Window` class (this is our application window), and call the member function to handle the event. The function does not need to get the `GLFWwindow` parameter, as we already saved it as a private member in the `Window` class. The result of `glfwSetWindowCloseCallback()` can be safely ignored. It returns the address of the callback function that was set in a previous call. This is the first call in the code, so it will simply return `NULL`.

The class member function needs to be added to `Window.cpp`:

```
void Window::handleWindowCloseEvents() {
  Logger::log(1, "%s: Window got close event... bye!\n",
    __FUNCTION__);
}
```

Currently, the `handleWindowCloseEvents()` function just prints out a log line and does nothing else. But this is the perfect place to check whether the user really wants to quit or if unsaved changes have been made.

This function has to be declared in the `Window.h` header file, too:

```
private:
  void handleWindowCloseEvents();
```

If you start the compiled code and close the window, you should get an output like this:

```
init: Window successfully initialized
handleWindowCloseEvents: Window got close event... bye!
cleanup: Terminating Window
```

You can check the other events in the GLFW documentation and add other callback functions plus the respective lambdas. Additionally, you can check the example code for more calls – it has simple support for window movement, minimizing and maximizing, and printing out some log messages when the events are processed.

> **Important note**
>
> Some OSs stall the window content update if your application window has been moved or resized. So, don't be alarmed if this happens – it is not a bug in your code. Workarounds are available to keep the window content updated on these window events, and you can check the GLFW documentation to find a way to solve this.

Now that our application window behaves in the way we would expect, we should add methods for a user to control what happens in our program.

The mouse and keyboard input for the game window

Adding support for the keys pressed on the keyboard, the buttons on the mouse, or moving the mouse around is a simple copy-and-paste task from the window events – create a member function to be called and add the lambda-encapsulated call to GLFW. The next time you press a key or move the mouse after a successful recompilation, the new callbacks will run.

You can find the enhanced example code in the `05_window_with_input` folder.

Let's start by retrieving the key presses before we add the keyboard callbacks and functions. After this, we will continue to get mouse events and also add the respective functions for them to the code.

Key code, scan code, and modifiers

To get the events for the keys the user presses or releases on their keyboard, GLFW offers another callback. The following callback for a plain key input receives four values:

```
glfwSetKeyCallback(window, key_callback);
void key_callback(GLFWwindow* window, int key, int scancode, int
action, int mods)
```

These values are listed as follows:

- The ASCII key code of the key
- The (platform-specific) scan code of that key
- The action you carried out (press the key, release it, or hold it until the key repeat starts)
- The status of the modifier key, such as *Shift*, *Ctrl*, or *Alt*

The key can be compared with internal GLFW values such as `GLFW_KEY_A`, as they emit the 7-bit ASCII code of the letter you pressed. The function keys, the separate keypad, and the modifier keys return values >256.

The scan code is specific to your system. While it stays the same on your system, the code may differ on another platform. So, hardcoding it into your code is a bad idea.

The action is one of the three values `GLFW_PRESS`, `GLFW_RELEASE`, or `GLFW_REPEAT`, if the key is pressed for longer, but note that the `GLFW_REPEAT` action is not issued for all keys.

The modifier status is a bitmap to see whether the users pressed keys such as *Shift*, *Ctrl*, or *Alt*. You can also enable the reporting of *Caps Lock* and *Num Lock* – this is not enabled in the normal input mode.

For example, we could add a simple keyboard logging to the code. First, add a new function to the `Window.h` header file:

```
public:
  void handleKeyEvents(int key, int scancode, int action,
    int mods);
```

As you can see in the preceding code, we don't need `GLFWwindow` in our functions, as we already saved it as a private data member of the class.

Next, add the callback to the GLFW function using a lambda:

```
  glfwSetKeyCallback(mWindow, [](GLFWwindow *win, int key,
    int scancode, int action, int mods) {
    auto thisWindow = static_cast<Window*>(
      glfwGetWindowUserPointer(win));
```

```
    thisWindow->handleKeyEvents(key, scancode, action,
      mods);
    }
  );
```

This is the same as it was for the window event – get the `this` pointer of the current instance of the `Window` class from the user pointer set by `glfwSetWindowUserPointer()` and call the new member functions of the class.

For now, the member function for the keys can be simple:

```
void Window::handleKeyEvents(int key, int scancode, int action, int
mods) {
  std::string actionName;
  switch (action) {
    case GLFW_PRESS:
      actionName = "pressed";
      break;
    case GLFW_RELEASE:
      actionName = "released";
      break;
    case GLFW_REPEAT:
      actionName = "repeated";
      break;
    default:
      actionName = "invalid";
      break;
  }
  const char *keyName = glfwGetKeyName(key, 0);
  Logger::log(1, "%s: key %s (key %i, scancode %i) %s\n",
    __FUNCTION__, keyName, key, scancode,
    actionName.c_str());
}
```

Here, we use a `switch()` statement to set a string depending on the action that has occurred and also call `glfwGetKeyName()` to get a human-readable name of the key. If no name has been set, it prints out `(null)`. You will also see the key code, which is the ASCII code for letters and numbers, as mentioned earlier in this section, and the platform-specific scan code of the key. As a last field, it will print out if the key was pressed, released, or held until the key repeat from the OS started. The `default` option is used for completeness here; it should never be called in the current GLFW version as it would indicate a bug.

Different styles of mouse movement

GLFW knows two types of mouse movement: the movement adjusted by the OS and a **raw** movement.

The first one returns the value with all the optional settings you might have defined, such as mouse acceleration, which speeds up the cursor if you need to move the cursor across the screen.

The following is a callback function, which gets informed if the mouse position changes:

```
glfwSetCursorPosCallback(window, cursor_position_callback);
void cursor_position_callback(GLFWwindow* window,
  double xpos, double ypos)
```

Alternatively, you can poll the current mouse position in your code manually:

```
double xpos, ypos;
glfwGetCursorPos(window, &xpos, &ypos);
```

The raw mode excludes these settings and provides you with the precise level of movement on your desk or mouse mat. To enable raw mode, first, you have to disable the mouse cursor in the window (not only hide it), and then you can try to activate it:

```
glfwSetInputMode(window, GLFW_CURSOR,
  GLFW_CURSOR_DISABLED);
if (glfwRawMouseMotionSupported()) {
    glfwSetInputMode(window, GLFW_RAW_MOUSE_MOTION,
      GLFW_TRUE);
}
```

To exit raw mode, go back to the normal mouse mode:

```
glfwSetInputMode(window, GLFW_CURSOR, GLFW_CURSOR_NORMAL);
```

Keeping both movement styles apart will be interesting for the kind of application we are creating. If we want to adjust the settings using an onscreen menu, having the mouse pointer react like it would in other applications on your computer is perfect. But once we need to rotate or move the model, or change the view in the virtual world, any acceleration could lead to unexpected results. For this kind of mouse movement, we should use the raw mode instead.

To add a mouse button callback, add the function call to `Window.h`:

```
private:
  void handleMouseButtonEvents(int button, int action,
    int mods);
```

And in `Window.cpp`, add the callback handling and the function itself:

```
glfwSetMouseButtonCallback(mWindow, [](GLFWwindow *win,
  int button, int action, int mods) {
  auto thisWindow = static_cast<Window*>(
    glfwGetWindowUserPointer(win));
  thisWindow->handleMouseButtonEvents(button, action,
    mods);
  }
);
```

This is similar to the keyboard callback discussed earlier in this chapter; we get back the pressed button, the action (`GLFW_PRESS` or `GLFW_RELEASE`), and also any pressed modifiers such as the *Shift* or *Alt* keys.

The handler itself is pretty basic in the first version. The first `switch()` block is similar to the keyboard function, as it checks whether the button has been pressed or released:

```
void Window::handleMouseButtonEvents(int button,
  int action, int mods) {
  std::string actionName;
  switch (action) {
    case GLFW_PRESS:
      actionName = "pressed";
      break;
    case GLFW_RELEASE:
      actionName = "released";
      break;
    default:
      actionName = "invalid";
      break;
  }
```

The second `switch()` block checks which mouse button was pressed, and it prints out the names of the left, right, or middle buttons. GLFW supports up to eight buttons on the mouse, and more than the basic three are printed out as `"other"`:

```
  std::string mouseButtonName;
  switch(button) {
    case GLFW_MOUSE_BUTTON_LEFT:
      mouseButtonName = "left";
      break;
    case GLFW_MOUSE_BUTTON_MIDDLE:
      mouseButtonName = "middle";
      break;
```

```
    case GLFW_MOUSE_BUTTON_RIGHT:
      mouseButtonName = "right";
      break;
    default:
      mouseButtonName = "other";
      break;
  }

  Logger::log(1, "%s: %s mouse button (%i) %s\n",
    __FUNCTION__, mouseButtonName.c_str(), button,
    actionName.c_str());
}
```

When running the code, you should see messages like this:

```
init: Window successfully initialized
handleWindowMoveEvents: Window has been moved to 0/248
handleMouseButtonEvents: left mouse button (0) pressed
handleMouseButtonEvents: left mouse button (0) released
handleMouseButtonEvents: middle mouse button (2) pressed
handleMouseButtonEvents: middle mouse button (2) released
handleWindowCloseEvents: Window got close event... bye!
cleanup: Terminating Window
```

You could add more handlers. The example code also uses the callbacks for mouse movement, which gives you the current mouse position inside the window, and the callback for entering and leaving the window.

Summary

In this chapter, we made the first steps toward a much bigger project. We started with a simple window, whose only task was to be closed again. This showed us the general usage of GLFW. In the next section, we added OpenGL support, and we also tried to detect support for the Vulkan API. If one of them fails (most probably Vulkan), you could continue with OpenGL and skip *Chapter 3*. The remaining code in this book will be built independently of the renderer and run with OpenGL and Vulkan as the rendering APIs. After the 3D rendering capabilities, we added the handling of the basic window events. Finally, we added the handling of the keyboard for mouse events, allowing us to build view controls and movement in our virtual 3D world.

With these building blocks, you can now create application windows using only a few lines of code. Additionally, you can retrieve input from the mouse and keyboard and prepare the window to display hardware-accelerated graphics. What is shown inside this window is up to your imagination.

In *Chapter 2*, we will create a basic OpenGL renderer.

Practical sessions

You will see this section at the end of every chapter in the book. Here, I will add a bunch of suggestions and exercises that you can try out with the code on GitHub.

Usually, there's no danger in doing something wrong while experimenting. Changing lines, deleting, or adding new code may end in your program no longer compiling or even crashing, but your computer will not explode if you make mistakes. In the few cases where hazardous behavior can occur (such as overwriting some of your files), I will attach a big red warning sticker.

So, here's something for you to try. After you have created the window, you might notice that you still can't resize it (the setting was done intentionally). You might also want to change the title of the window to make it more like your very own application. And the handling of the mouse and keyboard could also use a little bit of polish.

You could try to do the following:

- Play around with the window title. You can change it at any time after its creation, and it can store a lot of information in an easily accessible place. You could use it for the name of the model you loaded, the animation replay speed, and more.
- Set a callback for the handling of window resizing. This will be handy once we have enabled 3D rendering, and you will need to adjust the sizes of the other buffers too.
- Store information about some keys, such as *W*, *A*, *S*, and *D* or the cursor keys. Set the status when pressed and clear it on release. We will need the stored status of the keys in *Chapter 5* to move around inside the virtual world.
- Add support for mouse movement on a mouse button press only. Imagine you would like to rotate the view around your animated model while the left button is being pressed or zoom in and out while the right button is being pressed.

Additional resources

For further reading, please take a look at the following resources:

- An introduction to lambdas: `https://www.programiz.com/cpp-programming/lambda-expression`
- The official GLFW documentation: `https://www.glfw.org/documentation.html`

2

Building an OpenGL 4 Renderer

Welcome to *Chapter 2*! In the previous chapter, you learned how to open an application window, including the OpenGL context, and how to perform a very basic operation: clearing the screen in different colors. More actions were not possible due to the limited OpenGL support included in GLFW.

In this chapter, you will learn how to get access to the OpenGL function calls and extensions using a "loader" helper, which is a small piece of code that maps the OpenGL functions to the entry points of the installed system library. We could also do this mapping in our own code, but this would require a lot of extra work. The OpenGL renderer will be enhanced during the book – as the first step, we will only display a textured quad on the screen, consisting of two triangles.

In this chapter, we will cover the following topics:

- The rendering pipeline of OpenGL 4
- Basic elements of our OpenGL 4 renderer
- Buffer types for the OpenGL renderer
- Loading and compiling shaders

Technical requirements

For this chapter, you will need the following:

- `Main.cpp` and the OpenGL window code from *Chapter 1*
- Glad, the OpenGL loader generator
- `stb_image`, a single-header loader for image files
- The **OpenGL Mathematics** (**GLM**) library (installed with the Vulkan SDK)

The rendering pipeline of OpenGL 4

OpenGL is one of the most used graphics libraries to render objects in 3D, and also 2D, to the screen. It is not just the world, buildings, trees, or characters that are drawn using OpenGL; other elements (such as the user interface or a 2D map) are brought to the screen with the help of OpenGL draw calls.

The library has faced several evolutionary steps since its initial release in 1992, with each version giving the developer more and more control of the underlying graphics hardware. While the rendering pipeline in OpenGL had only limited features and fixed operations, the latest version (4.6) offers high flexibility for all components. All green components are programmable in the later versions:

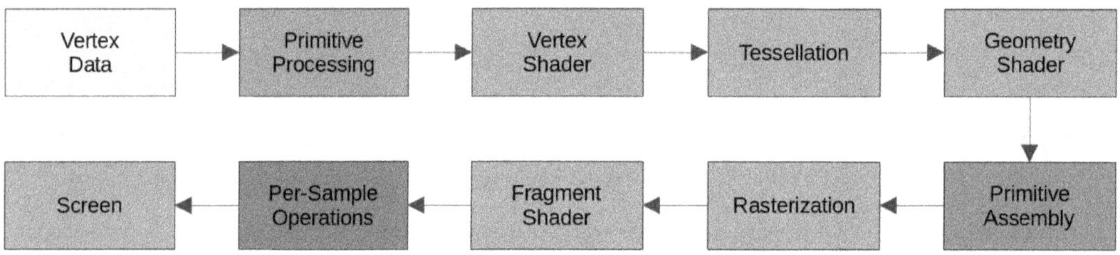

Figure 2.1: The OpenGL graphics pipeline

Figure 2.1 can be understood as follows:

1. The characters we will draw are made of triangles, and the **Vertex Data** of these triangles is sent from our application to the graphics card.
2. This input data is processed per **Primitive** – that is, for every triangle we send (OpenGL sends the primitive type with the draw call).
3. The **Vertex Shader** transforms the per-vertex data into the so-called clip space, a normalized space with a range between -1.0 and 1.0. This makes the processing of further transformation easier; any coordinate outside the range will not be visible.
4. The **Tessellation** stage runs only for a special OpenGL primitive, the **patch**. The tessellation operation will subdivide the patch into smaller primitives such as triangles. This stage can be controlled by shader programs too.
5. For triangles, the **Geometry Shader** comes next. This shader can generate new primitives in addition to the currently processed ones, and you can use it to easily add debug information to your scene.
6. During the **Primitive Assembly** stage, all primitives are converted into triangles, transformed into viewport space (our screen dimensions), and clipped to the visible part in the viewport.
7. The **Rasterization** stage converts the incoming primitives into so-called fragments, which will eventually become screen pixels. It also interpolates the vertex values, such as color or texture, across the face of the primitive.

8. The **Fragment Shader** determines the final color of the fragment. It can be used to blend textures or add fog.
9. **Per-Sample Operations** include scissor or stencil tests (to "cut out" parts of the screen) or the depth test, which decides whether the fragment will be used for the final screen or discarded.
10. At the end of the stage, we have created the final picture. During the **Screen** stage, this picture will eventually be displayed on the computer screen.

We will use only a subset of all features in this renderer, just the required components to draw textured triangles to the screen – the vertex and the fragment shader.

Basic elements of the OpenGL 4 renderer

To be able to use OpenGL in our code, we need access to its functions and extensions. Unfortunately, the graphics card vendors do not create these functions in an easy-to-use way. They are stored as function pointers, which will be hard to use.

To translate the function pointers back to more human-readable function names, several helper libraries exist. We will use the **Glad** tool for this translation.

The OpenGL loader generator Glad

Glad is a free and open source **loader generator**; all parts to make OpenGL fully available for us are included. Glad supports all OpenGL versions, even back to the first version (1.0), plus the mobile variant OpenGL for **Embedded Systems** (**ES**) and the platform-specific APIs for Microsoft Windows and the X Window System of Unix.

You can access the web service at `https://glad.dav1d.de`, which should open this screen:

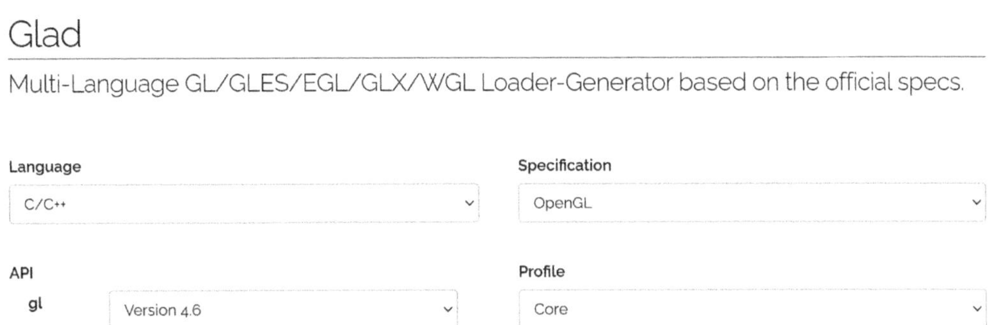

Figure 2.2: The Glad web service, version selection

Select **OpenGL** for **Specification**, **Version 4.6** for **API**, and **Core** for **Profile**. The other option you could choose for **Profile** is the **Compatibility** profile, which may contain older extensions; we don't need that here.

For **Extensions**, choose **ADD ALL**. We may not need them all, or even have support for all these extensions, but manually sorting out the good from the bad would be a huge task. As it does not break anything, we can simply include all of them.

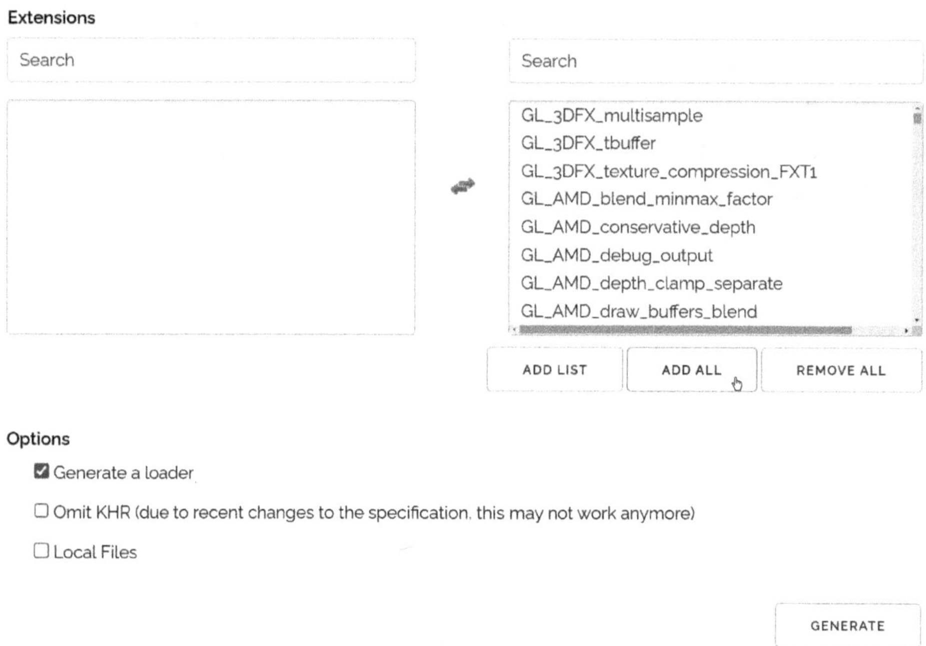

Figure 2.3: The Glad web service, extension selection

Keep **Generate a loader** checked and the other two options unchecked, and press the **GENERATE** button.

You are redirected to a new website, containing the header files as separate files and as a ZIP file. The website is generated "on the fly" for your settings:

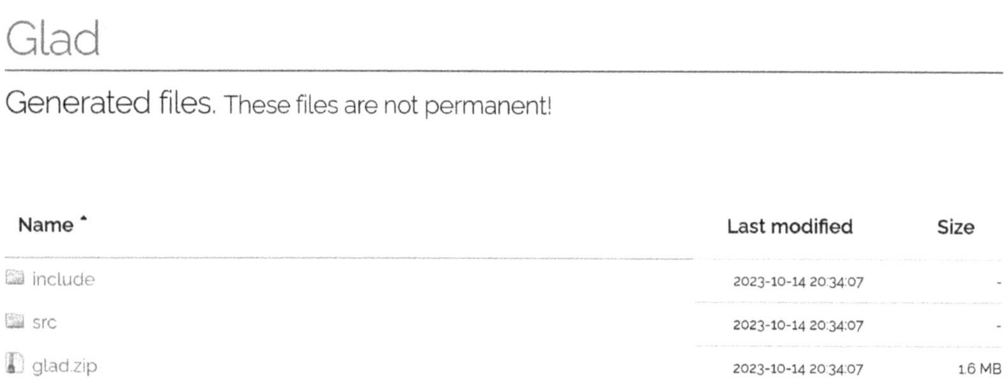

Figure 2.4: The Glad web service, header download

Please download the ZIP file and unpack it to the project root, including the folders. You should have the two folders (`src` and `include`) now, containing the `glad.c` file for the loader and `glad.h` for the OpenGL functions, plus `khrplatform.h`, an extra file with some definitions from the Khronos Group, which maintains OpenGL.

To use these files, we have to adjust the `CMakeLists` file again:

```
file(GLOB SOURCES
  src/glad.c
  ...
)
```

The `glad.c` loader file needs to be included in our sources, as functions from it will be used during OpenGL initialization, and the `include` directories have to be extended too:

```
target_include_directories(Main PUBLIC include src window tools opengl
model)
```

Now, the `include` directives for Glad will work in our code.

Anatomy of the OpenGL renderer

Our renderer will be split into five classes to collect all operations and data required for different OpenGL objects:

- The main renderer class, which is called from `mainLoop()` in the `Window` class
- A `Framebuffer` class, which is responsible for the creation of the buffers we need
- A vertex array class, which stores the vertex data that will be drawn to the screen
- A shader class, which loads and compiles the shader programs
- A texture class, which loads PNG image files from the system and creates an OpenGL texture out of them

In addition to these classes, we will create a "mock" `Model` class, holding some static vertex data for now. In this chapter, this `Model` class will contain only the data for the two triangles to draw to the screen, but a separate class allows us to implement a full loop in the `Window` class main loop: get the current vertex data from our model(s), store it in the renderer class, and draw the triangles of the 3D objects to the screen.

The main OpenGL class

We will start implementing the main OpenGL renderer class, and, step by step, the remaining parts of the renderer in this chapter. So, compiling the code will work only at the end of this chapter, after all classes have been created.

Creating the header for the OpenGL renderer class

Inside the `opengl` folder, create the `OGLRenderer.h` file and add these lines:

```
#pragma once

#include <vector>
#include <string>
#include <glm/glm.hpp>
#include <glad/glad.h>
#include <GLFW/glfw3.h>

#include "Framebuffer.h"
#include "VertexBuffer.h"
#include "Texture.h"
#include "Shader.h"

#include "OGLRenderData.h"
```

We start – as always in header files – with the `#pragma once` header guard, which guards against problems due to including the header multiple times during compiling. Next, we include the `string` system header, for the `std::string` type. Additionally, we include the header for the OpenGL Mathematics library, `glm` (which will be explained in *Chapter 4* in depth), our previously downloaded `glad.h` with the OpenGL functions, and the `glfw3.h` GLFW header for the window operations.

Make sure `glad.h` is included *before* `glfw3.h` as GLFW changes its behavior and will not include the basic system headers if OpenGL functionality is already found. This is important, especially for Windows, as the original system headers are still using OpenGL version 1.2, which is far too old for our code.

The next four headers are from the classes we will create in the next parts of this chapter: **framebuffer objects**, **vertex buffers**, **textures**, and **shaders**. The `OGLRenderData.h` header defines the structures we use to upload the model data.

Implementing the OpenGL renderer methods

Continue in the `OGLRenderer.cpp` file and create the class itself:

```
class OGLRenderer {
  public:
    bool init(unsigned int width, unsigned int height);
    void setSize(unsigned int width, unsigned int height);
    void cleanup();
    void uploadData(OGLMesh vertexData);
    void draw();
```

The `init()` method is used for the first initialization; it creates the OpenGL objects we need to draw anything at all. These objects will be removed by the `cleanup()` method, called from the `Window` class after we close the application window.

The `setSize()` method is used during window resizes; it will be called from the `Window` class. In the `uploadData()` method, we store triangle and texture data from the model in the renderer class, and the triangles will be drawn to the framebuffer using the `draw()` call.

Continue in `OGLRenderer.cpp` with the `private` members:

```
  private:

    Shader mBasicShader{};
    Framebuffer mFramebuffer{};
    VertexBuffer mVertexBuffer{};
    Texture mTex{};
    int mTriangleCount = 0;
};
```

As `private` members, we add local objects of our four classes in the list to create, and a counter of the triangles we upload to the renderer. The counter is needed for the `draw()` call to display the correct amount of triangles from the vertex array.

Now, create the `OGLRenderer.cpp` file and start it with the `include` directive:

```
#include "OGLRenderer.h"
```

We will include our class header – it also includes the other headers we use.

The `init()` method starts with the OpenGL initialization:

```
bool OGLRenderer::init(unsigned int width,
unsigned int height) {
  if (!gladLoadGLLoader((GLADloadproc)glfwGetProcAddress)){
    return false;
  }

  if (!GLAD_GL_VERSION_4_6) {
    return false;
  }
```

The call to `gladLoadGLLoader()` initializes OpenGL via Glad. If this fails, we return `false` to signal a failure to the creating `Window` class. The check for the value of the `GLAD_GL_VERSION_4_6` integer is only satisfied if the graphics card and driver support OpenGL 4.6; if this is not supported, we also return an error.

Now let's use the `init()` methods of the classes:

```
    if (!mFramebuffer.init(width, height)) {
      return false;
    }

    if (!mTex.loadTexture( "textures/crate.png")) {
      return false;
    }
    MVertexBuffer.init();

    if (!mShader.loadShaders( "shader/basic.vert",
      "shader/basic.frag")) {
      return false;
    }
    return true;
  }
```

Here, we check whether the creation of the `Framebuffer` class with the given width and height works and whether the texture is loaded from the `textures` folder. The vertex array initialization needs no separate check as this operation can only fail in a fatal way (such as out-of-memory errors), and the `Shader` class will be advised to load two files – a vertex shader and a fragment shader – from the `shaders` folder on disk.

If none of the steps fails, we return `true` to signal that the OpenGL initialization succeeded.

The `setSize()` method has only two lines:

```
void OGLRenderer::setSize(unsigned int width,
unsigned int height) {
  mFramebuffer.resize(width, height);
  glViewport(0, 0, width, height);
}
```

It resizes the framebuffer object and also the OpenGL viewport – the viewport information is important for the driver to know how to map the framebuffer to the output window.

The `uploadData()` method is also short:

```
void OGLRenderer::uploadData( OGLMesh vertexData) {
  mTriangleCount = vertexData.vertices.size();
  mVertexBuffer.uploadData(vertexData);
}
```

For correct usage of the uploaded vertex and triangle data, the `uploadData()` method needs to store the size of `std::vector` with the triangle data. It hands over the input data to the vertex array object.

Finalizing the OpenGL renderer

The last method in the class is `draw()`, which is responsible for displaying the triangles from the vertex array object to the framebuffers, and then to the screen (our window):

```
void OGLRenderer::draw() {
  mFramebuffer.bind();
  glClearColor(0.1f, 0.1f, 0.1f, 1.0f);
  glClear(GL_COLOR_BUFFER_BIT | GL_DEPTH_BUFFER_BIT);
  glEnable(GL_CULL_FACE);
```

We start by binding the framebuffer object, which will let the framebuffer receive our vertex data. After this, we clear the screen with a very low gray color. We also clear the depth buffer – a detailed description of the framebuffer follows in the *Buffer types for the OpenGL renderer* section.

The last setting enables the so-called **back-face culling**. Every triangle in the virtual world has two sides, front and back. The front side of the triangle usually faces the outside of the virtual objects we draw, while the back side faces the inside. As the back of the objects will never be seen, they are occluded by the front faces, so the triangles facing "away" from us don't need to be drawn. This also gives speedups, as the triangles are discarded early in the graphics pipeline before much work has been done with them. OpenGL gladly takes over the task of removing these never-seen triangles with this back-face culling.

Now, we can draw the triangles stored in the vertex buffer:

```
  mShader.use();
  mTex.bind();
  mVertexBuffer.bind();
  mVertexBuffer.draw(GL_TRIANGLES, 0, mTriangleCount);
  mVertexBuffer.unbind();
  mTex.unbind();
  mFramebuffer.unbind();
```

We load our shader program, which enables the processing of the vertex data. Next, we bind the texture to be able to draw textured triangles. We also bind the vertex array, so we have our triangle data available.

The `draw()` call of `mVertexBuffer` is where "all the magic happens." As we will see in the implementation of the `VertexBuffer` class, this is the point where the vertex data is sent to the GPU to be processed by the shaders.

As a last instruction, we will draw the content of the framebuffer to our screen:

```
  mFramebuffer.drawToScreen();
}
```

When the renderer object gets destroyed, it must also free the OpenGL resources it had used. This is done in the `cleanup()` method:

```
void OGLRenderer::cleanup() {
  mShader.cleanup();
  mTex.cleanup();
  mVertexBuffer.cleanup();
  mFramebuffer.cleanup();
}
```

The `cleanup()` method in the renderer simply calls the `cleanup()` method of all other objects we created.

To simplify the management of the vertex data, two structs will be used. The first struct holds the data for a single vertex, consisting of a three-element GLM vector for its position and a two-element vector for the texture coordinates. The second struct is a C++-style vector with elements of the first struct, creating a collection of all the vertices of a model.

Due to the usage of GLM, this data is organized in the same way in the system memory as it would be on the GPU memory, allowing a simple copy to transfer the vertex data to the graphics card.

The first part of the `OGLRenderData.h` file inside the `opengl` folder is again the header definition of the headers:

```
#pragma once
#include <glm/glm.hpp>
#include <vector>
```

After the header guard, we include the headers for GLM and `std::vector`. Next, we define the two new structs:

```
struct OGLVertex {
  glm::vec3 position;
  glm::vec2 uv;
};
struct OGLMesh {
  std::vector<OGLVertex> vertices;
};
```

The `OGLVertex` struct is used for a single vertex, and the `OGLMesh` struct collects all vertices of a single character model.

This ends the implementation of the main renderer class. We will fill the other four OpenGL classes in the next sections.

> **Note**
>
> Feel free to add custom logging to the calls. It is always helpful to see which part of the call fails during the initialization. Don't forget to include the header for the logger class: `#include "Logger.h"`.

Buffer types for the OpenGL renderer

The memory of the graphics cards is managed by the driver; usually, all memory is seen as a single, large block. This block will be divided into smaller parts – that is, for triangle data, textures, frame buffers, and more. Each of the smaller blocks can be seen as a buffer in OpenGL terms, accessible from your code via the driver, just like the RAM in the machine.

Your program will get a "handle" to the buffer, which is usually an integer value, and the driver maps this value internally to the correct buffer to identify it and modify the contents. The details are hidden from you – you just create such a buffer by an OpenGL call, upload data to it by another call, and destroy it when you no longer need it.

Let's take a look at the types of buffers we will use in the code of this chapter. The first type is framebuffer.

Framebuffers

A framebuffer is the most "visible" buffer type for a user: the final picture shown on the screen is created in a framebuffer, and the intermediate results of rendering steps are stored in framebuffers too.

We will add our framebuffer management class now, which is already referenced and used in the renderer class. Create the `Framebuffer.h` file in the `opengl` folder, starting with the headers:

```
#pragma once
#include <glad/glad.h>
#include <GLFW/glfw3.h>
```

After the header guard, we again include Glad and GLFW in the correct order – Glad first and GLFW second. This is required for the OpenGL calls in the class to work.

The class starts with the `public` methods:

```
class Framebuffer {
  public:
    bool init(unsigned int width, unsigned int height);
    bool resize(unsigned int newWidth,
      unsigned int newHeight);
    void bind();
    void unbind();
    void drawToScreen();
    void cleanup();
```

The `init()` method takes `size` and `width` as parameters and initializes the framebuffers. The next method, `resize()`, has the same parameters and recreates the framebuffers to the given, new size. The latter is called from the renderer on window size changes to have matching framebuffer sizes.

The `bind()` method enables the drawing to the framebuffers, while `unbind()` disables this drawing again. This makes it possible to use multiple `Framebuffer` objects in a single function – "deferred rendering" uses this technique and combines the buffers in a final method to the output picture. Even if we use only one framebuffer here, it is a good style to remove the binding to avoid surprises with OpenGL draw or clean calls. The last method, `drawToScreen()`, copies the data to our GLFW window. We draw internally to a separate buffer and not directly to the screen, which is intended to show you the flexibility of the rendering.

Add these `private` data members to the `Framebuffer.h` file:

```
  private:
    unsigned int mBufferWidth = 640;
    unsigned int mBufferHeight = 480;
    GLuint mBuffer = 0;
    GLuint mColorTex = 0;
    GLuint mDepthBuffer = 0;
    bool checkComplete();
};
```

The `mBufferWidth` and `mBufferHeight` members are used to store the current dimensions of the buffer; they are required in the method for the final drawing to the output window. The next three `GLuint` typed values are integers for internal buffers: the overall framebuffer we draw to, the color texture we use as data storage for the framebuffer, and the depth buffer. The depth buffer stores the distance from the viewer for every pixel and ensures that only the color value nearest to the viewer will be drawn.

The `checkComplete()` method is used to check whether the framebuffer contains all components required to draw. You should always do this check when creating a framebuffer. If the created framebuffer is missing parts of the configuration, accessing them would result in errors.

The class is implemented in the `Framebuffer.cpp` file, residing also in the `opengl` folder. We start, as always, with the header we just created:

```
#include "Framebuffer.h"
```

Next, we will add the `init()` method:

```
bool Framebuffer::init(unsigned int width, unsigned int height) {
  mBufferWidth = width;
  mBufferHeight = height;
```

We store the `width` and `height` values for later calls to draw the content to the screen.

The `glGenFramebuffers()` call creates an OpenGL framebuffer object for us:

```
glGenFramebuffers(1, &mBuffer);
glBindFramebuffer(GL_FRAMEBUFFER, mBuffer);
```

> **Important**
>
> When the ampersand (&) is in front of the member variable, the call will write the result to that variable. This write access is used for all `glGen*()` and `glDelete*()` calls, while the rest of the calls will only read the value.

After the framebuffer, we create a texture with the same size as the window, but without data. It can be left uninitialized as we will clear it before we ever display it to the user, so any possible content in the graphics card memory will be deleted. Then, we bind the created texture as a 2D texture type to alter it in the following code lines:

```
glGenTextures(1, &mColorTex);
glBindTexture(GL_TEXTURE_2D, mColorTex);
glTexImage2D(GL_TEXTURE_2D, 0, GL_RGBA, width,
  height, 0, GL_RGBA, GL_UNSIGNED_BYTE, NULL);
```

The texture will now be created with four 8-bit wide components: red, green, blue, and an alpha component for transparency. This value will always be set to the maximum of `1.0` as we don't use transparency here. Drawing transparent objects in OpenGL is a quite big topic, which we won't cover in this book.

We need some additional properties as some drivers refuse to display the texture if they are not set:

```
glTexParameteri(GL_TEXTURE_2D, GL_TEXTURE_MIN_FILTER,
  GL_NEAREST);
glTexParameteri(GL_TEXTURE_2D, GL_TEXTURE_MAG_FILTER,
  GL_NEAREST);
glTexParameteri(GL_TEXTURE_2D, GL_TEXTURE_WRAP_S,
  GL_CLAMP_TO_EDGE);
glTexParameteri(GL_TEXTURE_2D, GL_TEXTURE_WRAP_T,
  GL_CLAMP_TO_EDGE);
```

The `GL_TEXTURE_MIN_FILTER` and `GL_TEXTURE_MAG_FILTER` properties are responsible for the handling of downscaling (minification) the texture if it is drawn far away, or upscaling (magnification) when it is close to the viewer. We set both to the `GL_NEAREST` value, which is the fastest as it does no filtering at all.

The texture wrap decides what happens on the positive and negative edges of the texture when we draw outside the defined area of the texture. The edge-clamping sets the value of the texture data of the *x* or *y* position to `0.0` if the requested position is <0, and the texture data of the position to `1.0` if we are requesting a position of >1.

Now we unbind the texture by binding the (invalid) texture ID of 0:

```
glBindTexture(GL_TEXTURE_2D, 0);
```

This avoids further modifications. This style is required due to the way OpenGL works internally and is one of the reasons for using Vulkan.

The next step is binding the texture as so-called texture attachment zero:

```
glFramebufferTexture(GL_FRAMEBUFFER,
  GL_COLOR_ATTACHMENT0, mColorTex, 0);
```

We can bind multiple texture attachments to a single frame buffer and draw to all or some of them within our shaders. This is also an advanced rendering topic that we will not cover in this book as we don't need it. Please check the *Additional resources* section at the end of the chapter for sources to learn about those.

Renderbuffers

In the case that we don't need to show or reuse the result of a drawing operation, we may use a renderbuffer instead of a texture. A renderbuffer can be written to like the texture in the framebuffer before, but it cannot be read out easily. This is most useful for intermediate buffers that are valid for a single frame, where the content is not needed for more than this single draw processing. Here we use a renderbuffer to create the depth buffer:

```
glGenRenderbuffers(1, &mDepthBuffer);
glBindRenderbuffer(GL_RENDERBUFFER, mDepthBuffer);
glRenderbufferStorage(GL_RENDERBUFFER,
  GL_DEPTH_COMPONENT24, width, height);
```

While a pixel in the color attachment is about to be written, the depth buffer will be checked to see whether the pixel is closer to the viewer compared to a pixel already in that position (if any). If the new pixel is from a triangle closer to the viewer position, the depth buffer will be updated with the new, nearer value and the color attachment will be drawn. If it is further away, both writes are discarded.

We bind the created renderbuffer as a depth attachment:

```
glFramebufferRenderbuffer(GL_FRAMEBUFFER,
  GL_DEPTH_ATTACHMENT, GL_RENDERBUFFER, mDepthBuffer);
```

This is a special type, so OpenGL knows it is a depth buffer instead of a color buffer.

We unbind the renderbuffer plus the framebuffer, as the setup should be finished:

```
glBindRenderbuffer(GL_RENDERBUFFER, 0);
glBindFramebuffer(GL_FRAMEBUFFER, 0);
```

This disabled modification to both buffers with later calls.

Finally, we return the value of the `checkComplete()` method:

```
  return checkComplete();
}
```

This method is responsible for the "completeness" check of the created framebuffer:

```
bool Framebuffer::checkComplete() {
  glBindFramebuffer(GL_FRAMEBUFFER, mBuffer);
  GLenum result = glCheckFramebufferStatus(GL_FRAMEBUFFER);
  if (result != GL_FRAMEBUFFER_COMPLETE) {
    return false;
  }
  glBindFramebuffer(GL_FRAMEBUFFER, 0);
  return true;
}
```

We bind our framebuffer just as if we want to modify it, but instead of modifications, we call `glCheckFramebufferStatus()`. This OpenGL function verifies that the framebuffer has all the data it needs to work and that all buffer types are complete and correct. If anything is wrong, it returns without the `GL_FRAMEBUFFER_COMPLETE` result, which we signal back to the calling function. This extra check helps to avoid using broken framebuffers.

The `resize()` method is called to change the size of the framebuffer:

```
bool Framebuffer::resize(unsigned int newWidth,
unsigned int newHeight) {
  mBufferWidth = newWidth;
  mBufferHeight = newHeight;

  glBindFramebuffer(GL_DRAW_FRAMEBUFFER, 0);
  glDeleteTextures(1, &mColorTex);
  glDeleteRenderbuffers(1, &mDepthBuffer);
  glDeleteFramebuffers(1, &mBuffer);

  return init(newWidth, newHeight);
}
```

To achieve this, we store the new width and height, unbind the framebuffer, and remove the created OpenGL objects for the framebuffer. At the end, the method simply calls `init()` with the new values to create new objects. If this call or the completeness check fails during resize, this is signaled back to the caller.

The `bind()` and `unbind()` methods are really simple:

```
void Framebuffer::bind() {
  glBindFramebuffer(GL_DRAW_FRAMEBUFFER, mBuffer);
}
void Framebuffer::unbind() {
  glBindFramebuffer(GL_DRAW_FRAMEBUFFER, 0);
}
```

The `bind()` call activates the framebuffer of the object, while `unbind()` deactivates it.

At the end of the program, the created texture, renderbuffer, and framebuffer need to be removed from the OpenGL context. This is done in the `cleanup()` method:

```
void Framebuffer::cleanup() {
  unbind();
  glDeleteTextures(1, &mColorTex);
  glDeleteRenderbuffers(1, &mDepthBuffer);
  glDeleteFramebuffers(1, &mBuffer);
}
```

To be sure that the framebuffer is no longer used, we unbind it first, and we delete the objects we created in the `init()` method.

Finally, we need to copy the color attachment to the screen:

```
void Framebuffer::drawToScreen() {
  glBindFramebuffer(GL_READ_FRAMEBUFFER, mBuffer);
  glBindFramebuffer(GL_DRAW_FRAMEBUFFER, 0);
  glBlitFramebuffer(0, 0, mBufferWidth, mBufferHeight, 0,
    0, mBufferWidth, mBufferHeight, GL_COLOR_BUFFER_BIT,
    GL_NEAREST);
  glBindFramebuffer(GL_READ_FRAMEBUFFER, 0);
}
```

The `drawToScreen()` method binds the framebuffer we draw to as the framebuffer to read from, and the window as the output (draw) framebuffer. Then, we "blit" the contents of the internal framebuffer to the window. Blitting is a memory copy; this is a fast method to copy the contents of one framebuffer to another. In the end, we unbind our internal framebuffer to stop reading from it.

Our `Framebuffer` class is finished, but we need triangles to draw to the buffer. One method to store triangle data is vertex buffers, plus vertex arrays as an additional organizational element in OpenGL.

Vertex buffers and vertex arrays

One of the simple ways to store all the data about the vertices we want to draw is using vertex buffers. These are OpenGL data structures that hold all the required information for the rendering, such as the ordering of the data, and how many elements are used per vertex (such as three for vertex coordinates, four for color, and two for the texture coordinates). To combine multiple vertex buffers, a vertex array can be used. It is a collection of the same or even different kinds of vertex buffers, bound together to be enabled or disabled by a single call as the source to draw from. This method makes it easy to use different data formats during the rendering.

The vertex buffers inside a vertex array are bound tight to the shaders we use, as the buffers will be used to "feed" the vertex data to the GPU. The format and positions in the vertex array have to match the shader input definition; if there are any differences, the data will be misinterpreted, resulting in garbage on the screen.

Create a new file called `VertexBuffer.h` in the `opengl` folder:

```
#pragma once
#include <vector>
#include <glm/glm.hpp>
#include <glad/glad.h>
#include <GLFW/glfw3.h>
#include "OGLRenderData.h"
```

We start again with the headers we need in the declaration – we will use `std::vector`, `glm`, `glad`, and `GLFW` in this class. We need the `OGLMesh` struct for the storage of the vertices of the model, so the `OGLRenderData.h` header is required too:

```
class VertexBuffer {
  public:
    void init();
    void uploadData(OGLMesh vertexData);
    void bind();
    void unbind();
    void draw(GLuint mode, unsigned int start,
      unsigned int num);
    void cleanup()
```

This class also contains an `init()` method to set up the buffers, and the `uploadData()` method, which copies the data to the vertex buffers. We are using our own data type here to have all the per-vertex data as a single element. The `bind()` and `unbind()` methods are similar to the `Framebuffer` class, and the `draw()` method is the one that moves the data to the GPU. The `cleanup()` method frees the OpenGL resources, as in the other classes.

Next, we add some data members to the `VertexBuffer` class:

```
    private:
      GLuint mVAO = 0;
      GLuint mVertexVBO = 0;
};
```

These OpenGL handles store the vertex array, plus the vertex buffer, for the vertex data.

Let's implement the class now: create the `VertexBuffer.cpp` file in the `opengl` folder. We start with the `VertexBuffer` header:

```
#include "VertexBuffer.h"
```

The `init()` method is responsible for the creation and configuration of the OpenGL objects:

```
void VertexBuffer::init() {
   glGenVertexArrays(1, &mVAO);
   glGenBuffers(1, &mVertexVBO);
```

The `glGenVertexArray()` function creates a new vertex array object, and the `glGenBuffers()` function creates a vertex buffer object. The buffer objects will contain the vertex and texture data, while the vertex array object contains the vertex buffer.

We bind the vertex array object and the first buffer for the vertex data:

```
   glBindVertexArray(mVAO);
   glBindBuffer(GL_ARRAY_BUFFER, mVertexVBO);
```

The `glVertexAttribPointer()` method configures the buffer object – it has input location `0` in shaders, and it has three elements of the `float` type. The elements are not normalized as they are floating-point values; they are packed tight with a stride of the size of the vertex struct we created, consisting of the position and the texture coordinate. The last parameter is the offset inside the `OGLVertex` struct; we use the C++ `offsetof` macro to get the offsets of the position and the texture coordinates elements. We need to cast the offset values to `void *` to match the signature of the call. A similar initialization is made for the texture data, but it uses location `1` with only two floats:

```
   glVertexAttribPointer(0, 3, GL_FLOAT, GL_FALSE,
     sizeof(OGLVertex), (void*) offsetof(OGLVertex,
     position));
   glVertexAttribPointer(1, 2, GL_FLOAT, GL_FALSE,
     sizeof(OGLVertex), (void*) offsetof(OGLVertex, uv));
```

The two `glEnableVertexAttribArray()` calls enable the vertex buffers of `0` and `1`, which we just configured. The enabled status of the arrays will be stored in the vertex array object too:

```
    glEnableVertexAttribArray(0);
    glEnableVertexAttribArray(1);
```

At the end, we unbind the array buffer and the vertex array:

```
    glBindBuffer(GL_ARRAY_BUFFER, 0);
    glBindVertexArray(0);
  }
```

The `cleanup()` method is used for the cleanup again:

```
  void VertexBuffer::cleanup() {
    glDeleteBuffers(1, &mVertexVBO);
    glDeleteVertexArrays(1, &mVAO);
  }
```

It deletes the vertex buffer and the vertex array on the destruction of the object. To upload data to the vertex buffers, the `uploadData()` method has our custom vertex data as `std::vector` parameters:

```
  void VAO::uploadData(OGLMesh vertexData) {
    glBindVertexArray(mVAO);
    glBindBuffer(GL_ARRAY_BUFFER, mVertexVBO);
    glBufferData(GL_ARRAY_BUFFER, vertexData.vertices.size()
      * sizeof(OGLVertex), &vertexData.vertices.at(0),
      GL_DYNAMIC_DRAW);

    glBindVertexArray(0);
  }
```

The method starts with the binding of the vertex array and the vertex buffer. The call to `glBufferData()` uploads the vertex data to the OpenGL buffer; it calculates the size by multiplying the number of elements in the vector by the size of our custom vertex data type. And it needs the starting address for the memory copy, given by the address of the first vertex element. `GL_DYNAMIC_DRAW` is a hint for the driver that the data will be written and used multiple times, but it is just a hint – the driver will decide where to store the data internally. The same upload follows for the texture data, and at the end of the method, we unbind the buffers.

The `bind()` and `unbind()` methods are similar to the FBO class:

```
  void VertexBuffer::bind() {
    glBindVertexArray(mVAO);
  }
  void VertexBuffer::unbind() {
```

```
  glBindVertexArray(0);
}
```

We can use them to bind the vertex array object or to unbind any previously bound vertex array object by using the special value `0`.

The `draw()` method has only a single OpenGL call:

```
void VertexBuffer::draw(GLuint mode, unsigned int start,
unsigned int num) {
  glDrawArrays(mode, start, num);
}
```

The `glDrawArrays()` method instructs OpenGL to draw the vertex array from the currently bound vertex array object, starting at the `start` index and rendering `num` elements. They are drawn in a rendering mode. To draw our triangles, we will use the `GL_TRIANGLES` value, defined as an integer. Other values are possible to draw in a different mode, such as lines or different triangle styles. We will use the normal triangle mode here as it is easier to understand.

This ends the implementation of the `VertexBuffer` class. Let's go to the next buffer type: textures.

Textures

Textures are used to make objects in the virtual world appear more realistic. They can be generated procedurally, or generated from pictures taken from the real world, and may be altered by graphics tools. In *Chapter 14*, we will see another usage for textures: they can also be used to transport vertex data to the GPU in a very efficient way.

We will use a small class to load an image using the STB image header. STB is a free header to load any type of images from the system, such as PNG or JPEG, and make them available as a byte buffer for further usage.

To use the header, download the `stb_image.h` file from the official repository (`https://github.com/nothings/stb`) and store it in the `include` folder. Linux users should be able to install the header using the package manager of their distribution.

Create the `Texture.cpp` file in the `opengl` folder, starting again with the headers:

```
#pragma once
#include <string>
#include <glad/glad.h>
#include <GLFW/glfw3.h>
```

After the header guard, we include the `std::string` header, `glad`, and `GLFW` (again, `glad` before `GLFW`) to use OpenGL methods.

The class is rather short:

```
class Texture {
  public:
    bool loadTexture(std::string textureFilename);
    void bind();
    void unbind();
    void cleanup();
```

The `loadTexture()` method will load the file given as a parameter from the system and generate an OpenGL texture. The `bind()` and `unbind()` methods are used to be able to use the texture and stop using it, as in the FBO and VAO classes.

The data elements follow in the `private` sections of the class:

```
  private:
    GLuint mTexture = 0;
};
```

The `mTexture` variable will store the generated OpenGL texture handle. We don't need to save other data here for the basic functionality.

The implementation is done in the `Texture.cpp` file in the `opengl` folder:

```
#define STB_IMAGE_IMPLEMENTATION
#include <stb_image.h>
#include "Texture.h"
```

The definition of `STB_IMAGE_IMPLEMENTATION` before the header is required only in a C++ file, to advise the header to activate the functions, and we include our declaration header, `Texture.h`.

The `loadTexture()` method loads the file using the STB functions and creates the OpenGL texture itself:

```
bool Texture::loadTexture(std::string textureFilename) {
  int mTexWidth, mTexHeight, mNumberOfChannels;
```

The three integer values are required for the STB loading function, which will return the dimension of the loaded image and the number of channels (usually `3` for a color picture without transparency and `4` with an extra transparency channel).

The call to `stbi_set_flip_vertically_on_load()` is used to flip the image on the vertical axis, as the coordinate systems of the texture and the picture differ on the axis: the picture has its `(0,0)` coordinate in the top-left corner, and the texture in the bottom left:

```
  stbi_set_flip_vertically_on_load(true);
  unsigned char *textureData =
```

```
    stbi_load(textureFilename.c_str(), &mTexWidth,
    &mTexHeight, &mNumberOfChannels, 0);
```

Then, `stbi_load()` creates a memory area, reads the file from the system, flips the image as instructed before, and fills the width, height, and channels with the values found in the image.

If the image can't be loaded for some reason, such as the file was not found, we free the memory allocated by STB and return `false` to signal a loading error:

```
  if (!textureData) {
    stbi_image_free(textureData);
    return false;
  }
```

It is our responsibility to free the memory; if we forget it, we will create a memory leak.

Next, we generate a `Texture` object with a `glGenTextures()` call and bind the new texture as the current 2D texture:

```
  glGenTextures(1, &mTexture);
  glBindTexture(GL_TEXTURE_2D, mTexture);
```

We start by generating and binding a new 2D texture.

The texture parameters are different from the `Framebuffer` class as we will apply texture filtering here:

```
  glTexParameteri(GL_TEXTURE_2D, GL_TEXTURE_MIN_FILTER,
    GL_LINEAR_MIPMAP_LINEAR);
  glTexParameteri(GL_TEXTURE_2D, GL_TEXTURE_MAG_FILTER,
    GL_LINEAR);
  glTexParameteri(GL_TEXTURE_2D, GL_TEXTURE_WRAP_S,
    GL_REPEAT);
  glTexParameteri(GL_TEXTURE_2D, GL_TEXTURE_WRAP_T,
    GL_REPEAT);
```

For the minification, we use trilinear sampling; for the magnification, there is only linear filtering available. The wrapping parameter is also different; we repeat the texture outside the range of `0` to `1`. Think of it as using only the fractional part of the texture coordinate, ignoring the integer part.

The real loading of the data to the graphics part is done with the `glTexImage2D()` call. It uses the loaded byte data from `stbi_load()` and the width plus height to push the data from system memory to the GPU:

```
  glTexImage2D(GL_TEXTURE_2D, 0, GL_RGBA, mTexWidth,
    mTexHeight, 0, GL_RGBA, GL_UNSIGNED_BYTE, textureData);
```

We are using a four-component image here (`GL_RGBA` – red, green, blue, and alpha) as we will use PNG images for now, but an extension of the loader class to switch between three and four components can be easily implemented later.

Next, we generate the so-called **mipmaps**. These are scaled-down versions of the original image, halving the width and height in every step:

```
    glGenerateMipmap(GL_TEXTURE_2D);
```

The reduced images will be 1/4, 1/16, 1/256, and so on of the original size, until a configurable limit is reached, or the size is 1x1 pixel. The mipmaps are used to increase rendering speed, as less data is read if the texture is far away, and it also reduces artifacts.

To disable accidental changes to the texture, we unbind it after configuration and data upload are finished:

```
    glBindTexture(GL_TEXTURE_2D, 0);
```

In the end, we free the memory allocated by the STB load call and return `true` to signal that everything went fine:

```
    stbi_image_free(textureData);
    return true;
  }
```

The `Texture` class also contains simple `bind()` and `unbind()` methods:

```
  void Texture::bind() {
    glBindTexture(GL_TEXTURE_2D, mTexture);
  }

  void Texture::unbind() {
    glBindTexture(GL_TEXTURE_2D, 0);
  }
```

Similar to the other classes, the `Texture` class binds the object to be used in the next OpenGL calls and unbinds the 2D texture to stop using it.

After we have created classes for the framebuffers, vertex storage, and textures, one last puzzle piece is left to complete our renderer – the shader.

Loading and compiling shaders

A shader is a small program running on the graphics card, which has special computing units for them. Modern GPUs have thousands of shader units to be able to run the shaders in a massively parallel fashion, which is one of the reasons for the high-speed drawing of pictures of 3D worlds.

The OpenGL rendering pipeline uses several shader types, as seen in *Figure 2.1*, but we will use only two of the types here: vertex shaders and fragment shaders, the first and last steps in the pipeline. There are more shader types, such as geometry or tessellation shaders, and also shaders outside the normal pipeline such as compute shaders, which are used for simple but fast computation in the shader units.

Let's take a closer look at the two shader types we will use in the OpenGL renderer to draw the objects to the screen: the vertex and fragment shaders.

Vertex and fragment shaders

A vertex shader uses the uploaded vertex data as input and transforms the incoming primitive types, such as triangles, from 3D to 2D screen space. It passes the generated data into the remaining parts of the pipeline, with the fragment shader at the end. The fragment shader computes the color value for every "fragment" of the final picture. A fragment is an internal unit – usually, it maps 1:1 to a pixel. A fragment shader type can also be used to make post-processing changes to an image, such as blurring parts of the picture.

We are using very simple shaders here, but we will advance them in later chapters.

The vertex shader will be called `basic.vert` and resides in the `shaders` folder. The `.vert` extension is used here to clarify that we have a vertex shader. The fragment shader will have a `.frag` extension.

We are using **GLSL** (which stands for **OpenGL Shading Language**) version 4.6 in the `core` profile here, matching the OpenGL version:

```
#version 460 core
```

Every OpenGL shader *must* start with a version string; this is required for the driver to see which data types and functions are available.

The two `layout` lines are for the input of the vertex shader: the vertex buffers in our vertex array object. The two `location` definitions in the shader must match the vertex buffer definition in the *Vertex buffers and vertex arrays* section to produce correct results:

```
layout (location = 0) in vec3 aPos;
layout (location = 1) in vec2 aTexCoord;
```

In our shader, we create a variable called `aPos` ("a position") of the `vec3` type for the incoming data on input `location 0` – a vector with three elements for the *x*, *y*, and *z* coordinates. For the incoming data on input `location 1`, we create the `aTexCoord` variable ("a texture coordinate"). The texture coordinate variable will contain a two-element `vec2` type, again matching the vertex buffer defintion.

The `out` prefix defines an output parameter; we have only a single `vec2` type variable that is passed to the next shader stage. The variable has the name `texCoord` for *texture coordinate*:

```
out vec2 texCoord;
```

The `main()` function itself is similar to C code; you can call functions and assign variables:

```
void main() {
  gl_Position = vec4(aPos, 1.0);
  texCoord = aTexCoord;
}
```

One of the variables – `glPosition` – is very important as this four-element vector is always passed to the next shader stage. We use the incoming `aPos` for it, adding another element called `w`, and setting it to `1.0`. We pass the incoming `aTexCoord` to the next shader stage without altering it.

The `basic.frag` fragment shader in the `shaders` folders is also short. We start again with the mandatory version string, using the OpenGL 4.6 `core` profile:

```
#version 460 core
```

The next line defines the internal name for the incoming `vec2` data element:

```
in vec2 texCoord;
```

Important note

The internal name for the incoming data element *must* match the name given to the output element of the previous shader stage. Here, the output name (`texCoord`) from the vertex shader must match the input name in the fragment shader. If the names do not match, the shader compiling will fail!

Our output from the fragment shader is called `FragColor`, and it has to be written in the `main()` function, just like the vertex shader:

```
out vec4 FragColor;
```

The final fragment color is a four-element vector, containing values for red, green, blue, plus alpha for transparency.

A `uniform` data type marks the parameter as non-changing for all parallel invocations of the shader during a draw call. Here, we have a `sampler2D` data type, which is a 2D texture:

```
uniform sampler2D Tex;
```

Finally, the `main()` function assigns the `FragColor` output parameter the result of the call to the `texture()` GLSL function:

```
void main() {
  FragColor = texture(Tex, texCoord);
}
```

The `texture()` function of the fragment shader does a color lookup in the texture given as the first parameter. It uses the *x* and *y* coordinates given as the second parameter to find the color on that position and returns this value. This lookup process maps the texture to our drawn primitive objects, such as a triangle, creating a natural-looking appearance of the object.

We could alter the final color here in different ways, such as adding another vertex array with a color value for every vertex, which will be interpolated along the primitive edge between two adjacent vertices and also between the edges.

Creating our shader loader

Now that we have the two shaders, we can start with our shader loading class.

Adding the header file for the shader loader

Create a new file named `Shader.h` in the `opengl` folder:

```
#pragma once
#include <string>
#include <glad/glad.h>
#include <GLFW/glfw3.h>
```

These are the usual `include` directives; nothing special is used in this class.

The `Shader` class itself has three `public` methods:

```
class Shader {
  public:
    bool loadShaders(std::string vertexShaderFileName,
      std::string fragmentShaderFileName);
    void use();
    void cleanup();
```

The `loadShaders()` method will load two files from the system and generate an OpenGL shader, and the `cleanup()` method will free the created OpenGL shader object at the end of our program.

A call to `use()` will instruct the graphics card to use this shader for the next draw operation. There is no "unuse" method in the class as we will always need a shader bound to generate an output to our window.

The `private` section of the `Shader` class contains a member plus two internal methods:

```
  private:
    GLuint mShaderProgram = 0;
    GLuint readShader(std::string shaderFileName,
      GLuint shaderType);
};
```

The mShaderProgram variable contains the OpenGL handle to our shader program, and readShader() is a helper to avoid code duplication, as the operations to load a vertex or a fragment shader differ only in a single parameter to one of the calls.

Implementing the shader loader logic

The class itself will be implemented in the Shader.cpp file in the opengl folder. We start again with the required headers:

```
#include <fstream>
#include "Shader.h"
```

The fstream header is required for C++ functions used inside the loading method to read the file contents into std::string. The C array representation of the string is later used as input to the OpenGL function compiling the shader code.

The main shader-loading function uses the private method to load the shader code:

```
bool Shader::loadShaders(std::string vertexShaderFileName, std::string
fragmentShaderFileName) {
  GLuint vertexShader = readShader(vertexShaderFileName,
    GL_VERTEX_SHADER);
  if (!vertexShader) {
    return false;
  }
  GLuint fragmentShader =
    readShader(fragmentShaderFileName, GL_FRAGMENT_SHADER);
  if (!fragmentShader) {
    return false;
  }
```

We are loading the vertex shader first, and the fragment shader second. If the loading fails, the return value of loadShader() is set to 0, and our check returns false to signal that something went wrong.

After this, we call a couple of OpenGL functions to create the shader objects:

```
  mShaderProgram = glCreateProgram();
  glAttachShader(mShaderProgram, vertexShader);
  glAttachShader(mShaderProgram, fragmentShader);
  glLinkProgram(mShaderProgram);
```

The glCreateProgram() function creates an empty shader program, and we attach both shaders we loaded. As the next step, we link the shaders together to create our final shader program in the graphics card memory.

To make sure the linking was successful, we should check the status of the shader program link result:

```
  GLint isProgramLinked;
  glGetProgramiv(mShaderProgram, GL_LINK_STATUS,
    &isProgramLinked);
  if (!isProgramLinked) {
    return false;
  }
```

This part reads the link status of our shader program, and if the linking fails, we abort the shader loading. It is possible to get the detailed error message with `glGetProgramInfoLog()`, which could be useful for real shader development.

Now we clean a bit and return from the `loadShaders()` method:

```
  glDeleteShader(vertexShader);
  glDeleteShader(fragmentShader);
  return true;
}
```

It is safe to delete the two loaded shader programs at this point, as this will just mark them to be removed. But all intermediate data inside the graphics cards will be cleaned, freeing up some space.

The `cleanup()` method is again short and simple:

```
void Shader::cleanup() {
  glDeleteProgram(mShaderProgram);
}
```

It deletes the created shader program, which also removes the two shaders.

The last method to implement is `readShader()`:

```
GLuint Shader::readShader(std::string shaderFileName,
GLuint shaderType) {
  Gluint shader;
  std::string shaderAsText;
  std::ifstream inFile(shaderFileName);
```

We create a variable to temporarily store the shader file content in a string, and we open the file given as a parameter as `std::ifstream`. This allows easier file handling.

We get the length of the shader file by seeking the end and reserving the number of bytes in our destination string:

```
if (inFile.is_open()) {
  inFile.seekg(0, std::ios::end);
  shaderAsText.reserve(inFile.tellg());
  inFile.seekg(0, std::ios::beg);
  shaderAsText.assign((std::istreambuf_iterator<char>(
    inFile)), std::istreambuf_iterator<char>());
  inFile.close();
```

The call to `shaderAsText.assign()` reads the content of `ifstream` into our string, and we can close the file.

If `std::ifstream` cannot be opened for reading, we return `0` to signal the error:

```
} else {
  return 0;
}
```

And if the read failed, or if `ifstream` is in a bad state for some reason, we close the file and also return `0` to signal that the loading has failed:

```
if (inFile.bad() || inFile.fail()) {
inFile.close();
return 0;
}

inFile.close();
```

As we have the shader code from the file in our string, we can compile the shader:

```
const char* shaderSource = shaderAsText.c_str();
```

We need a `char` array for `glShaderSource()`, so we get the C-style array from our string first.

Next, we create an empty shader with the type given as a parameter. This is the reason for using the separate function as this is the only difference between loading and compiling a vertex shader and a fragment shader:

```
GLuint shader = glCreateShader(shaderType);
```

Then, we load the shader code into the yet-empty shader and the OpenGL library compiles it:

```
glShaderSource(shader, 1, (const GLchar**) &shaderSource, 0);
glCompileShader(shader);
```

A check follows if the compiling was successful:

```
  GLint isShaderCompiled;
  glGetShaderiv(shader, GL_COMPILE_STATUS,
    &isShaderCompiled);
  if (!isShaderCompiled) {
    return 0;
  }
```

This is the same way we checked the link status of the final program. If everything went fine up to this point, we can return our created `shader` handle:

```
  return shader;
}
```

Finally, add the `use()` method:

```
void Shader::use() {
  glUseProgram(mShaderProgram);
}
```

It uses the `glUseProgram()` OpenGL function to activate the shader program. There is no "unuse" like in the binding and unbinding of the texture and the vertex buffer, as there needs to be an active shader every time to avoid undefined results.

This completes our `Shader` class. With this code, we can load the two text files (`basic.vert` and `basic.frag`) from the system, compile them, and link them to a final shader program.

Updating the Window class

The `Window` class needs more adjustments. First, we add some headers to it:

```
#include <memory>
...
#include "OGLRenderer.h"
#include "Model.h"
```

The `memory` header is for the smart pointer we will use, and the other two are for the main renderer and the `Model` class.

The smart pointers for the renderer and the model file are added to the `private` section:

```
    std::unique_ptr<OGLRenderer> mRenderer;
    std::unique_ptr<Model> mModel;
```

We use smart pointers here to avoid trouble with the memory allocation; `unique_ptr` will call the destructor automatically once the objects managed by the smart pointers fall out of the scope of a method or code block.

While the `cleanup()` method is the same as in *Chapter 1*, `init()` needs some modifications. After the `glfwInit()` check, add some window hints for the OpenGL version and remove the non-resizable hint:

```
glfwWindowHint(GLFW_CONTEXT_VERSION_MAJOR, 4);
glfwWindowHint(GLFW_CONTEXT_VERSION_MINOR, 6);
glfwWindowHint(GLFW_OPENGL_PROFILE,
  GLFW_OPENGL_CORE_PROFILE);
```

This instructs GLFW to create an OpenGL 4.6 window with the `core` profile set. Now, we create the renderer object with the folder of the executable file:

```
mRenderer = std::make_unique<OGLRenderer>();
if (!mRenderer->init(width, height)) {
  glfwTerminate();
  return false;
}
```

If the initialization fails, we stop the window here. To have a working window resize, we need a lambda-style callback:

```
glfwSetWindowUserPointer(mWindow, mRenderer.get());
glfwSetWindowSizeCallback(mWindow, [](GLFWwindow *win,
  int width, int height) {
  auto renderer = static_cast<OGLRenderer*>(
    glfwGetWindowUserPointer(win));
  renderer->setSize(width, height);
  }
);
```

In this callback, we call `setSize()` of the renderer instead of the window; this will resize the OpenGL viewport and framebuffer, matching the size of the window. Finally, we create and initialize the model object:

```
mModel = std::make_unique<Model>();
mModel->init();
```

What's left now is the updated `mainLoop()` of the window. We can remove the old code for clearing the screen, as this is now done in the rendering process:

```
void Window::mainLoop() {
  glfwSwapInterval(1);
```

In the main loop, we still activate the vertical sync to avoid tearing on window resizes.

We grab the vertex and texture data from the model and feed the renderer with it:

```
  mRenderer->uploadData(mModel->getVertexData());
```

Inside the `while()` loop, the only operation (next to buffer swapping and event polling) is the `draw()` call to the renderer:

```
  while (!glfwWindowShouldClose(mWindow)) {
    mRendere->draw();
    glfwSwapBuffers(mWindow);
    glfwPollEvents();
  }
}
```

The `draw()` call draws the vertex data of the model to the back buffer, and the `glfwSwapBuffers()` call swaps the front buffer and the back buffer to make the model visible on the screen. Finally, the GLFW events will be polled.

Creating the simple Model class

To have some vertex data available, we will create a simple `Model` class. Create a new file named `Model.h` in the `model` folder:

```
#pragma once
#include <vector>
#include <glm/glm.hpp>
#include "OGLRenderData.h"
```

This time, we include the header to use `std::vector` and the header for the OpenGL Mathematics library, `glm`. We also add the header for our custom data structures.

The `Model` class has only a few methods and elements:

```
class Model {
  public:
    void init();
    OGLMesh getVertexData();


  private:
    OGLMesh mVertexData{};

};
```

The `init()` method is used to fill in the vectors with data, and we add a function to read out the vertex. As a data element, we have just our custom `OGLMesh` structure, which contains a `std::vector` type vector of the vertices.

The implementation in the `Model.cpp` file in the `model` folder starts with the header:

```
#include "Model.h"
```

Now we fill the vectors in the `init()` method:

```
void Model::init() {

  mVertexData.vertices[0].position =  glm::vec3(-0.5f,
    -0.5f,  0.5f);
  mVertexData.vertices[1].position = glm::vec3(
    0.5f,  0.5f,  0.5f);
  mVertexData.vertices[2].position = glm::vec3(-
    0.5f,  0.5f,  0.5f);
  mVertexData.vertices[3].position = glm::vec3(-0.5f,
    -0.5f,  0.5f);
  mVertexData.vertices[4].position = glm::vec3( 0.5f,
    -0.5f,  0.5f);
  mVertexData.vertices[5].position = glm::vec3(
    0.5f,  0.5f,  0.5f);
  mVertexData.vertices[0].uv = glm::vec2(0.0, 0.0);
  mVertexData.vertices[1].uv = glm::vec2(1.0, 1.0);
  mVertexData.vertices[2].uv = glm::vec2(0.0, 1.0);
  mVertexData.vertices[3].uv = glm::vec2(0.0, 0.0);
  mVertexData.vertices[4].uv = glm::vec2(1.0, 0.0);
  mVertexData.vertices[5].uv = glm::vec2(1.0, 1.0);
}
```

Here we create six three-element vectors for two triangles to draw, plus the texture data.

After this, we add the getter methods for the data:

```
OGLMesh Model::getVertexData() {
  return mVertexData;
}
```

We simply return the vertex data to the caller here.

Getting an image for the texture

As a final step, you need to get a PNG file as a texture for the quad we will draw. You may search the internet or use a local file, add it to a folder named `textures`, and adjust the texture name in the corresponding line in `OGLRenderer.cpp`:

```
    if (!mTex.loadTexture(mtextures/crate.png")) {
```

If you compile and run the executable, you should see a textured rectangle on the screen, which will be resized along with the window:

Figure 2.5: Textured box created by the OpenGL renderer

The shaders are complete now, along with the first version of our `Model` class that will later store the vertex data of the character. This completes the OpenGL renderer – you have learned all the steps you need to draw textured triangles to the screen. This result is still a quite flat object, but the real "third dimension" will be added in *Chapter 4*.

Summary

In this chapter, we created a quite simple OpenGL renderer, consisting of the renderer itself, plus helper classes for a framebuffer, vertex array objects, textures, and shaders. This renderer enables us to draw triangles on the screen, and the data is taken from a `Model` class. The current minimalistic model will be extended in later chapters when we will take care of model loading and animations.

In the next chapter, we will take a look at the Vulkan API and create a renderer to show the same textured two triangles with it. You will learn about the similarities and differences between OpenGL and Vulkan, and we will use helper libraries to lower the amount of code.

Practical sessions

There are some additions you could make to the code:

- Add log lines with the `Logger` class to all the methods we implemented. This will help a lot if you need to debug problems, as you can also output values used in the methods.
- Read the failure logs during shader compilation and linking. This is a bit tricky because you need to get the length of the log first, allocate a dynamic buffer (that is, by using `std::vector`), and get the log contents into this buffer. You will get a detailed error log and see the faulty line and operation or data type.
- Add support for different file formats in the `Texture` class. Right now, there's only support for PNGs in the RGBA component order. Try to also add other formats, such as JPG, or even more exotic variants such as ARGB or the reversed BGRA.

Additional resources

For further reading, please check these links:

- A series of tutorials for OpenGL: `https://learnopengl.com`
- Another great tutorial series to learn about OpenGL: `https://open.gl`
- The official OpenGL docs from the Khronos Group: `https://www.khronos.org/opengl/`
- A curated list of OpenGL resources: `https://github.com/eug/awesome-opengl`

3

Building a Vulkan Renderer

Welcome to *Chapter 3*! In the previous chapter, we took a deeper look into OpenGL as a method to get some polygons onto your screen. In this chapter, we will move on to its successor, Vulkan, which aims to give you much more control of your graphics hardware, thus resulting in improved performance.

Vulkan is a quite complex and also verbose API. You will have to create a lot of objects to get even a single colored triangle onto your screen, resulting in the creation of hundreds of C++ lines before you see anything. But you also get advanced error handling and debugging with an extra validation layer, allowing you to easily see where you have missed something or where an operation failed.

Due to the extensive amount of code needed for the basics, this chapter gives only a broad overview of the internals of Vulkan, plus some code snippets to explain how to initialize some of the objects. The complete rendering code for this chapter can be found in the `chapter 02` | `vulkan_renderer` folder in the GitHub repo of this book.

In this chapter, we will cover the following topics:

- Basic anatomy of a Vulkan application
- Differences and similarities between OpenGL 4 and Vulkan
- Using helper libraries for Vulkan
- Fitting Vulkan's nuts and bolts together

Let's start with an overview of the Vulkan API.

Technical requirements

For this chapter, you will need the Vulkan SDK, installed according to the *Getting the source code and the basic tools* section of *Chapter 1*.

Basic anatomy of a Vulkan application

Vulkan was released in 2016 as a successor to OpenGL. The goal was to develop a modern, scalable, low-overhead, cross-platform, 3D graphics API capable of matching the growing number of processors in computers and polygons in games and graphics applications. At the same time, the development of new features for OpenGL had slowed down. The latest version, 4.6, was released in 2017, and it will be still maintained for many more years, but we should look at the changes Vulkan brings to the 3D rendering process.

This is a picture of the – more or less – most important required objects to draw colorful triangles on the screen. Additionally, approximately 30 Vulkan C-style struct definitions must be constructed to create these objects:

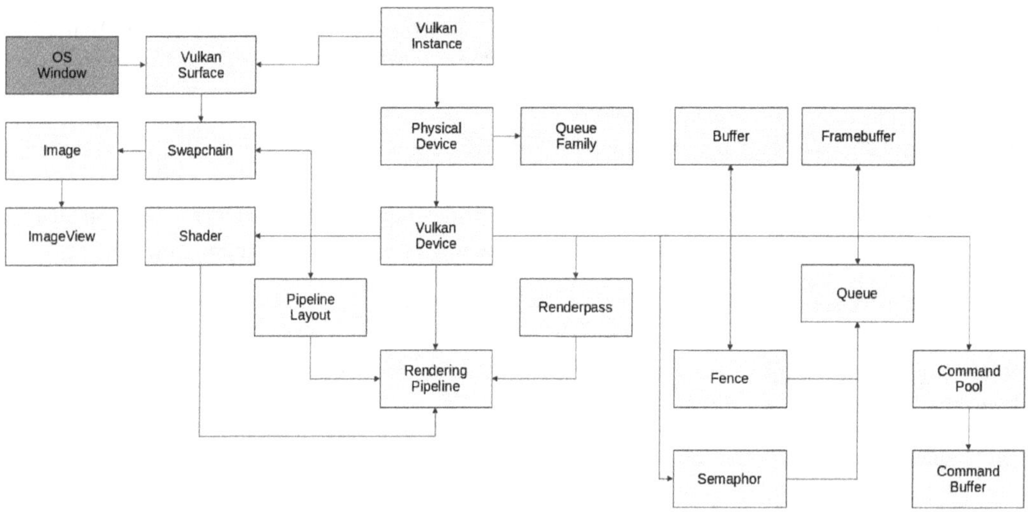

Figure 3.1: Main Vulkan objects and their dependencies

We will take a closer look at these objects and their functions in the rendering process:

- OS Window: This is the window created by **Graphics Library Framework** (**GLFW**), or by any other method (i.e., via native calls to the OS). The window is maintained by the OS.
- Vulkan Instance: The Vulkan instance is the connection between the application and the Vulkan library. It maintains some basic data about the application and the required Vulkan version.
- Vulkan Surface: As Vulkan is OS independent, it needs some help from the underlying system to display the rendered graphics on the screen. This is done by a memory region of the OS, managed together with the window. It is exposed as a so-called surface.
- Physical Device: The physical devices are the GPUs inside your computer. This could be one or multiple graphics cards, depending on your setup. Dedicated GPUs may be preferred over integrated GPUs, as they deliver more power.

- Queue Families: All Vulkan operations, such as drawing or uploading data, are submitted to queues; there are no direct operations. A graphics card may offer multiple queue families for drawing or computing commands, for example. They may be handled in different ways in the GPU.
- Vulkan Device: The logical device provides an abstraction of the physical device with Vulkan capabilities. The logical device is the connection between the physical device (the GPU) and the Vulkan library. It contains function pointers to various Vulkan functions, which are configured at creation time.

  A physical device can have more than one logical device.
- Swapchain: Vulkan knows no default framebuffer, unlike OpenGL. It maintains a queue of images instead. The application will acquire one image, render the triangles to the image, and put the image back into the queue. The Vulkan library will present this image on the surface, showing it to the user.
- Image: A Vulkan image is a memory area containing the pixels to display on screen. It depends on the window system and may be completely different on Windows and Linux. Vulkan stores the data in an optimized way in the images.
- ImageView: The image view describes the image type, that is, whether it is a normal 2D texture, a 2D depth texture, or a 3D texture. It also manages how the image will be rendered and whether mipmap levels are available. Every image needs an image view to be use in the render pipeline.
- Buffer: In addition to images, Vulkan can manage the GPU memory in buffers. Buffers need no additional structure; they can be used directly in the rendering pipeline. You can store arbitrary data in a buffer, such as color or vertex data to render, or use it for read-only data for access in the shaders (so-called uniform buffers).
- Framebuffer: A framebuffer in Vulkan is like the framebuffer in OpenGL – it contains one or more attachments to be used in a rendering pass. For our Vulkan renderer, we will attach a color attachment and a depth attachment to the framebuffer. We need to create a framebuffer object for every image of the swapchain; while a single depth attachment may be reused in rendering passes, it can be bound to all framebuffers.
- Command Pool and Command Buffer: Operations in Vulkan need to be recorded in command buffer objects, and after the recording, the commands will be submitted together to the Vulkan library. The command recording is also possible from multiple threads.
- Queue: All commands sent to the Vulkan library are committed into queues and not sent directly to the GPU. The queues are created from the queue families of the physical devices when creating the logical device.
- Shader: We are using the same graphics hardware as with OpenGL, and the shader and shader stages are identical in both APIs. Vulkan uses a slightly different way to upload the shader code to the GPU; they are precompiled into an intermediate format instead of being uploaded and compiled inside the GPU. More details follow in the*Fitting the Vulkan nuts and bolts together* section.

- Render Pass: The render pass object contains information about the attachments used in a rendering process. A render pass can also contain subpasses, with dependencies between subsequent subpasses, for instance, for post-processing stages. You need no additional memory barriers or synchronization mechanisms.
- Pipeline Layout: A pipeline layout is used to track the shader inputs, separate from the vertex data sent from the vertex buffer. These inputs could be so-called descriptor sets to map textures to the shader, or small amounts of data available in multiple shader stages.
- Rendering Pipeline: The rendering pipeline is the biggest part of the Vulkan API. It needs a lot of information about the configuration in its structures. Examples are the kind of objects to draw from the incoming vertices, such as points, lines or triangles, color blending values for transparency, the removal of the backsides of the triangles, a depth buffer (if configured), and the shaders to use to draw the configured object type to an image or buffer.
- Fences and Semaphores: Vulkan is full of asynchronous operations – we record commands to a buffer, submit the buffer to a queue, and continue in the application. To find out when the GPU has finished an operation, we need additional operations. A semaphore is used to synchronize operations inside the GPU, while fences are used to let the CPU know the GPU has reached a specific command in the queue.

After a short description of the significant objects we will see in a Vulkan renderer, we will look at the similarities and differences between OpenGL and Vulkan.

Differences and similarities between OpenGL 4 and Vulkan

It shouldn't be a surprise that Vulkan is unable to create any kind of rendering miracles when used instead of OpenGL, as the underlying hardware remains the same. However, there are a number of improvements in the management of the GPU.

Let's take a look at some of the most visible points.

Technical similarities

These are a few technical similarities – things you may find familiar when switching from OpenGL to Vulkan:

- The framebuffer works quite similarly in Vulkan and OpenGL. You create a special object and attach one or more textures (images in Vulkan) to it, and the GPU renders the picture to it.
- If you use deferred rendering, a technique where different intermediate steps write their passes into buffers, this is similar to a Vulkan render pass and its subpasses.
- The shader stages of the GPU are the same. We are using only vertex and fragment shaders, but the remaining stages are similar to OpenGL.

- The **OpenGL Shading Language** (**GLSL**), the programming language for the shaders, can be used with small adjustments as the source language for Vulkan shaders. This means you don't have to learn a new language for the shaders; the current shader can be adjusted.

Differences

The remaining parts of Vulkan are different. Some of these may look a bit similar, but others need a completely new approach in your mind to use them:

- While OpenGL maintains a global state (the so-called context), which can be changed from anywhere in the thread that created it, Vulkan maintains its state in the `Instance` object you use. There are cases where you use multiple instances (such as graphics and computing).
- Vulkan is safe to use in multiple threads. The information about the instance can be shared and the Vulkan library controls the access to it. OpenGL has only a limited ability to share the global context between threads, causing more problems than benefits. Plus, drivers tend to be single-threaded, creating a bottleneck during the rendering process.
- OpenGL uses an implicit way of programming. Many parts are hidden in the driver, and you have only limited control of details. Vulkan has a quite verbose and explicit API. It moves the resource management to the programmer's shoulders. And with great power comes great responsibility… you don't get a choice to control all the knobs and levers; you are forced to do so.
- The rendering pipeline in OpenGL is filled synchronously with data. You send the commands and data, and they will be saved in the driver. Once the buffer swapping occurs, or if an explicit pipeline flush is initiated, the API call blocks, and OpenGL begins its operation. Doing the same steps in Vulkan is not possible; you send the commands asynchronously to a queue and continue with your program. If you need to wait for the GPU to finish its drawing steps, you need to use sync objects such as the fence.
- Vulkan moves a lot of logic to compile time, while OpenGL processes most tasks at runtime. As an example, Vulkan needs precompiled shaders; the compilation with the syntax checks occurs before program startup. OpenGL compiles the shaders at runtime; any errors may lead to incomplete renderings or even crash the application.
- Vulkan uses a new format as it generates the shader files called **SPIR-V** (**SPIR** stands for **Standard Portable Intermediate Representation**, and the **V** is for **Vulkan**). SPIR-V is an intermediate binary format, and there are several ways and many source languages to generate a SPIR-V shader. One of the source languages is GLSL, and another is HLSL from Microsoft, which is used in DirectX.
- Locating errors in an OpenGL application is a time-consuming task. You need to get the error status after each command you suspect of some sort of misbehavior. Vulkan, on the other hand, has a validation layer, which can be enabled at development time and disabled in the final product. This validation layer checks many aspects of the rendering, down to the correct order of constructing and destroying objects.

- Most parts of the rendering pipeline and many objects in Vulkan are immutable. This means you can't change parts of it, such as attaching other shaders; you have to recreate it or use a second object, a third, and so on, all with different configurations. This enables a lot of optimizations as the configuration can be seen as fixed from the Vulkan side. In OpenGL, you can change the objects at runtime. This could lead to an invalid configuration, resulting in drawing errors or crashing applications.

The Vulkan API can be seen as an evolutionary step, using lessons learned during the development of the OpenGL API. It fulfills the needs of the current generation of games, applications, and graphics hardware to achieve the best performance when rendering 3D images and interactive virtual worlds.

Due to the verbosity of the API, several helper libraries have been created. We will use two of them in our renderer code, so let's check them out.

Using helper libraries for Vulkan

Having full control of your graphics hardware sounds cool, but the extensive amount of code for the basic initialization might scare people who are new to Vulkan. Writing about 1,000 lines of code just to get a colored triangle onto the screen may sound frightening.

To reduce the code a bit, two helper libraries are integrated:

- vk-bootstrap, the Vulkan Bootstrap, which is for the first steps of creating the instance, device, and swapchain
- The **Vulkan Memory Allocator** (**VMA**), taking some of the complexity out of the memory management out of the code

We start with the simplification of the creation of the most important objects.

Initializing Vulkan via vk-bootstrap

If you visit the GitHub page for vk-bootstrap at `https://github.com/charles-lunarg/vk-bootstrap`, the benefits are listed right at the top of the `README` file. It will help you with all the steps needed for the following:

- Instance creation, enabling the validation layers, if desired
- Selection of the physical device (also with additional criteria)
- Device and swapchain creation, plus queue retrieving

Next, we will see how to use vk-bootstrap.

You need to download and include three files in your project:

- `VkBootstrap.h`
- `VkBootstrapDispatch.h`
- `VkBootstrap.cpp`

Only the first header file has to be in the files with functions and objects of vk-bootstrap:

```
#include <VkBootstrap.h>
```

After this line, you are ready to go. The example code in the **Basic Usage** section of the vk-bootstrap GitHub page shows the steps to create a Vulkan instance:

```
vkb::InstanceBuilder builder;
auto inst_ret =
  builder.set_app_name ("Example Vulkan Application")
    .request_validation_layers ()
    .use_default_debug_messenger ()
    .build ();
```

Here `vkb::InstanceBuilder` simplifies the creation of the Vulkan instance object. The application name is set first, here just to an example string. The graphics driver could use the name to apply optimizations or bug fixes. The instance will have the validation layers enabled, helping to find incorrect resource usage. The default debug messenger is used by the validation layers, printing out any errors to the command window or the console of the program. With the `build()` call in the last step, the instance is finally created.

If the Vulkan instance creation fails, we signal this failure to the calling function. And if the creation succeeds, we read the instance value from the builder:

```
if (!inst_ret) {
  std::cerr << "Failed to create Vulkan instance" << "\n";
  std::cerr << "Error: " << inst_ret.error().message() <<
    "\n";
  return false;
}

vkb::Instance vkb_inst = inst_ret.value();
```

The vk-bootstrap objects reside in the C++ namespace called `vkb`. Also, a lot of functions are attached to these objects; this makes the function calls for all important initialization steps available directly on the vk-bootstrap objects.

You may check the code in the Vulkan tutorial (see the *Additional resources* section) and compare the amount of code required to create a Vulkan instance with the validation layers enabled at `https://github.com/Overv/VulkanTutorial/blob/main/code/02_validation_layers.cpp`.

The preceding vk-bootstrap code takes less than 15 lines of code; the full-featured Vulkan code of the tutorial is about 200 lines long. And that's just the instance creation; you also need to select the physical device, the logical device, and the queues.

As we need to acquire and free the memory for every Vulkan image and buffer, we use the **Vulkan Memory Allocator** (**VMA**). VMA was created by **Advanced Micro Devices** (**AMD**), and the source code is freely available as Open Source library. Working with VMA makes our lives a bit easier compared to using only the built-in Vulkan functions.

Memory management with VMA

The memory management of Vulkan images and buffers lies entirely in the hands of the programmers.

OpenGL hides the process of the creation and deletion of textures behind a single line. You just have to point it to the source image loaded into the memory of your computer. But Vulkan forces you to allocate and free the memory, in addition to the definition of all resources for the image. This includes finding the right memory type for the image you want to create, calculating the correct size, and binding the acquired memory to the buffer. Even with some helper code to detect the memory types, you will be far away from the simplicity of VMA.

To use VMA, download the `vk_mem_alloc.h` file from the GitHub project page (see the *Additional resources* section), put it into the `include` path of your project, and include it:

```
#include <vk_mem_alloc.h>
```

After initializing the allocator, you only need a structure and a single call:

```
VmaAllocationCreateInfo vmaAllocInfo{};
vmaAllocInfo.usage = VMA_MEMORY_USAGE_CPU_TO_GPU;
vmaCreateBuffer(allocator, &bufferInfoStruct,
  &vmaAllocInfo, &mVertexBuffer, &mVertexBufferAlloc,
  nullptr);
```

All remaining calculations of the size, memory type, and binding are hidden behind this one call.

After all the theoretical parts of the Vulkan API, let's take a closer look at some implementation details, including more about vk-bootstrap and VMA.

Fitting the Vulkan nuts and bolts together

Going from zero to hero in Vulkan is not hard. It takes a couple of hours if you copy and paste the example code from one of the tutorials, and even longer if you type it. Once you understand the roles and dependencies of the objects, your adventure begins.

The example code for the Vulkan renderer can be found in the `chapter03 | vulkan_renderer` folder of this book's GitHub repo.

We start with the basic classes of the Vulkan renderer.

General considerations about classes

Similar to the OpenGL renderer, the creation and management of some Vulkan objects has been moved to separate classes. This helps to avoid creating a so-called "god class," which is huge and a maintenance nightmare for developers, and it enables us to quickly add more objects of a specific type. In *Chapter 4*, we will create new shaders and switch between them, and having a separate `Pipeline` class to hand makes this possible with a few changes.

> **Remember**
>
> The Vulkan Pipeline object is immutable. We can't switch the shader in an existing object. Instead, we have to create two pipelines, one for each shader.

Changes in the Window class

The most notable point about the `Window` class: there are only minimal differences between the OpenGL and the Vulkan versions. This was the goal of the animation application design: you should be able to use either of the rendering APIs, or even both, without having to bother about the details.

We have to adjust some of the `include` statements, swapping the OpenGL headers with their Vulkan counterparts in the `Window.h` file:

```
...
#include <vulkan/vulkan.h>
#include <GLFW/glfw3.h>

#include "VkRenderer.h"
#include "Model.h"
...
```

The Vulkan header must be included again before the GLFW header because GLFW adjusts some internals when it finds Vulkan variables. We use `VkRenderer.h` instead of `OGLRenderer.h`.

The type of the `mRenderer` variable has to be changed too:

```
std::unique_ptr<VkRenderer> mRenderer;
```

In the `Window.cpp` file, we make the type of the renderer when the smart pointer is created match the one in the header file:

```
mRenderer = std::make_unique<VkRenderer>(mWindow);
```

Finally, we add a check for a possible failure of the `draw()` call of the renderer:

```
while (!glfwWindowShouldClose(mWindow)) {
  if (!mRenderer->draw()) {
    break;
  }
...
```

We may return `false` if we encounter major problems during the `draw()` call of the Vulkan renderer. In this case, we will end the application in a slightly forceful way without waiting for the closing event. But this may be better than a crash during the next draw.

Passing around the VkRenderData structure

Due to the splitting of the Vulkan render into separate classes, a method for passing other Vulkan objects around is required. While OpenGL maintains many settings in the global context, we need at least a logical device for many Vulkan calls, and Vulkan returns other objects that are needed in different classes.

If we do this in the usual way, by passing the logical device as parameters plus the changed objects as references, we would end up with long and complicated functions.

> **Note**
>
> As a general rule for C++ functions, if the function has more than four or five parameters, or many of the same type, create a struct or class out of them and pass that instead. This frees you from remembering tens of parameters, plus their exact positions in the list.

Here's another observation I made while I was writing the renderer code: some Vulkan objects are a little bit picky about being given as a value or reference to another function. The Vulkan validation layer tracks the creation, usage, and destruction of all the objects and may complain about an incomplete deletion when passing an object by value. Using the struct containing all object data fixed this behavior.

The struct itself is plain and simple; it's just a collection of all the Vulkan objects we need in various stages of the rendering process:

```
struct VkRenderData {
  VmaAllocator rdAllocator;
  vkb::Instance rdVkbInstance{};
  vkb::Device rdVkbDevice{};
  vkb::Swapchain rdVkbSwapchain{};

  std::vector<VkImage> rdSwapchainImages;
  std::vector<VkImageView> rdSwapchainImageViews;
  std::vector<VkFramebuffer> rdFramebuffers;
  ...
}
```

For the `VkImage`, `VkImageView`, and `VkFramebuffer` objects, we use C++ vectors because they are multiple instances of unknown size. The number of buffers depends on your local configuration. We are safe if we can use dynamic storage for them.

Vulkan object initialization structs

During the initialization of all the Vulkan objects you need, you will encounter a lot of struct definitions for Vulkan objects. Most of these objects are handled similarly, so let's explain this with an example. We define a struct, in this case `VkPipelineVertexInputStateCreateInfo`, which is one of the helper objects we need during the rendering pipeline creation:

```
VkPipelineVertexInputStateCreateInfo vertexInputInfo{};
vertexInputInfo.sType =
  VK_STRUCTURE_TYPE_PIPELINE_VERTEX_INPUT_STATE_CREATE
  _INFO;
```

As mentioned in the *GLFW and Vulkan* section in *Chapter 1*, many of the Vulkan structs have a member called `.sType`. It sometimes takes quite a long type description as a parameter, identifying it for usage within Vulkan.

Then, we add two required struct types, vertex bindings and vertex attributes:

```
vertexInputInfo.vertexBindingDescriptionCount = 1;
vertexInputInfo.pVertexBindingDescriptions =
  &mainBinding;
vertexInputInfo.vertexAttributeDescriptionCount = 2;
vertexInputInfo.pVertexAttributeDescriptions =
  attributes;
```

Both these struct types are connected to the vertex buffer. This buffer is like the OpenGL vertex array object, and it contains the vertices of the objects we would like to draw, which reside on the GPU.

Any members ending with the word `Count` expect you to specify the number of objects or struct definitions you will add. Usually, there is a second member with the same name prefixed by the letter `p` with `Count` removed. Here, you must specify a pointer to that number of objects or structs (hence the letter `p`: pointer).

If you have only one object to add, specify that object by its address (add `&`). If you have more than one object, use a C-style array of this type, or use a C++ `std::vector` and access the contents via `.data()`.

To visualize this, here are three short example snippets:

- The first one is for a single struct:

```
VkVertexInputAttributeDescription
positionAttribute{};
...
vertexInputInfo.vertexAttributeDescriptionCount = 1;
vertexInputInfo.pVertexAttributeDescriptions =
  &positionAttribute;
```

- The second snippet is with a C-style array:

```
VkVertexInputAttributeDescription
positionAttribute{};
...
VkVertexInputAttributeDescription uvAttribute{};
...
VkVertexInputAttributeDescription attributes[] =
  { positionAttribute, uvAttribute };
...
vertexInputInfo.vertexAttributeDescriptionCount = 2;
vertexInputInfo.pVertexAttributeDescriptions =
  attributes;
```

- The last example is in the C++ style using `std::vector`. The C++ vector is handy if you need to have some control structures and create the other objects dynamically:

```
VkVertexInputAttributeDescription
positionAttribute{};
...
VkVertexInputAttributeDescription uvAttribute{};
...
std::vector<VkVertexInputAttributeDescription>
```

```
    attributes;
  attributes.push_back(positionAttribute);
  attributes.push_back(uvAttribute);
  ...
  vertexInputInfo.vertexAttributeDescriptionCount =
      static_cast<uint32_t>attributes.size();
  vertexInputInfo.pVertexAttributeDescriptions =
    attributes.data();
```

> **Note**
>
> In the last example, `static_cast` is connected to the alignment inside Vulkan. This alignment needs to be 32 bits. You may encounter this type of casting in some objects. Skipping this cast may lead to unexpected behavior.

Other member initializations are in the usual C style. A value may be specified either as `int` or `float`, a bitmask consisting of integer values (combined with a logical `OR`), a Boolean for true and false, or values from `enum` data types defined by Vulkan.

Required changes to the shaders

As we mentioned in the *Differences and similarities between OpenGL 4 and Vulkan* section, Vulkan uploads shaders to the GPU in a different way to OpenGL. While OpenGL shaders are pure text, Vulkan needs these shaders to be compiled into the intermediate SPIR-V format. Luckily, shaders written in GLSL can be used as input with some minor modifications. This means you do not need to start from scratch when OpenGL shaders are available, such as the ones created in *Chapter 2*.

The differences between an OpenGL shader and a Vulkan-compatible shader primarily lie in the input and output parts, along with the sampler definitions. While OpenGL matches the variables between the shader stages and the textures by their literal names in the file, Vulkan requires you to explicitly specify the order for variables and a so-called binding for the texture.

This is the start of the vertex shader from the OpenGL renderer:

```
#version 460 core
layout (location = 0) in vec3 aPos;
layout (location = 1) in vec2 aTexCoord;
out vec2 texCoord;
```

We need the locations set in the shaders, but only if we have more than one input to the shader or send more than one output variable to the next stage.

Vulkan forces the usage of the location definition, so we must specify the location even if there is a single input or output:

```
#version 460 core
layout (location = 0) in vec3 aPos;
layout (location = 1) in vec2 aTexCoord;

layout (location = 0) out vec2 texCoord;
```

In the fragment shader, the requirement for the location can be seen clearly. This is the start of the OpenGL version, without a location:

```
#version 460 core
in vec2 texCoord;
out vec4 FragColor;
uniform sampler2D Tex;
```

And here are the first lines from the Vulkan fragment shader. We need the location for input and output:

```
#version 460 core
layout (location = 0) in vec2 texCoord;
layout (location = 0) out vec4 FragColor;
layout (binding = 0) uniform sampler2D Tex;
```

The remaining code is identical in both shaders, so the number of changes is small.

After all the theoretical explanations, let's go to one of the functions of the code.

Drawing the triangles on the screen

Drawing the polygons of your model to the framebuffer and displaying the final picture via one of the swapchain images on the screen is a complex synchronized operation in Vulkan. OpenGL lets you send all drawing commands in the desired order to the library, and the buffer-swapping API call blocks the application while OpenGL works on the drawing operations. Vulkan does not block the application after all data is sent to the GPU; we need to do some extra work to avoid pulling away buffers in the middle of the drawing process.

We will walk through the `draw()` method next; this should give you detailed insights into the process that brings the triangles of your models from the buffers to the screen.

The starting point is the definition of the function:

```
bool VkRenderer::draw() {
```

We need no extra parameters here, as `mRenderData` is a local variable in the `VkRenderer` class, which is filled by the calls in this class and the other ones.

We start with waiting for a Vulkan fence.

Waiting for the previous Vulkan commands to complete

We defined a Vulkan fence as a `rdRenderFence` variable in the `VkRenderData` struct and initialized this fence during the `SyncObjects` class initialization. The fence signals the end of the processing of the previous commands sent to the command buffer; it is a GPU-to-CPU synchronization mechanism:

```
if (vkWaitForFences(mRenderData.rdVkbDevice.device, 1,
    &mRenderData.rdRenderFence, VK_TRUE, UINT64_MAX) !=
      VK_SUCCESS) {
  Logger::log(1, "%s error: waiting for fence failed",
    __FUNCTION__);
  return false;
}
```

The first parameter is the logical Vulkan device, which is required by many Vulkan calls. The device is followed by the count of fences it waits on. The function can wait for multiple fences, but we will wait for only one in the call. The address of the fence object is given next because a pointer is required here. Multiple fences may be added using a C-style array or `std::vector`, where `.data()` returns a pointer. `VK_TRUE` tells `vkWaitForFences()` to wait for all the fences given; if we use `VK_FALSE`, the `vkWaitForFences()` call returns if at least one of the fences in the array signals that it has been triggered. The last parameter is the timeout, or how long the function waits for the fence. Using `UINT64_MAX` is a way to tell the `vkWaitForFences()` call to wait for a very long time because this is a really large number, even if the parameter is in nanoseconds.

The return value is checked for `VK_SUCCESS`. If the fence was signaled within the timeout, we continue with the drawing. In every other case, we return from the `draw()` call with a value of `false`.

Every other result from `vkWaitForFences()` means our GPU is in serious trouble. We may even have lost the Vulkan device. In this case, the best thing to do is to abort completely.

The fence object must be reset to the unsignaled state, which is done next:

```
if (vkResetFences(mRenderData.rdVkbDevice.device, 1,
  &mRenderData.rdRenderFence) != VK_SUCCESS) {
  Logger::log(1, "%s error:  fence reset failed",
    __FUNCTION__);
  return false;
}
```

The call to `vkResetFences()` is similar to the waiting call. It needs the logical device as the first parameter, followed by the number of fences found at the pointer as the last parameter. As we have only one fence to reset, the values are the same as before.

The call could also fail, so we had better check for VK_SUCCESS again and return from the drawing if we cannot reset the fences.

Acquiring an image from the swapchain

The next code block tries to get the next free image from the swapchain. The swapchain manages multiple images so that at least one is available for drawing while one is shown via the VkSurface object to the user:

```
uint32_t imageIndex = 0;
VkResult result =
  vkAcquireNextImageKHR(mRenderData.rdVkbDevice.device,
    mRenderData.rdVkbSwapchain.swapchain, UINT64_MAX,
    mRenderData.rdPresentSemaphore, VK_NULL_HANDLE,
    &imageIndex);
```

We define a local variable named imageIndex. This variable will be filled with the number of the next free image of the swapchain.

The call to vkAcquireNextImageKHR() again has the logical device as the first parameter. The next parameter is our swapchain object. This object has been created using vk-bootstrap, and we could use this different object type directly as a parameter but we will refer to the original VkSwapchainKHR inside the vk-bootstrap object here. After the swapchain, there is a timeout again; this time, it states how long to wait in nanoseconds for the next available image from the swapchain. It is again set to a very long time span.

The rdPresentSemaphore object is a Vulkan semaphore object. Semaphore objects are used for GPU-internal synchronization tasks. The semaphore is signaled as soon as at least one free swapchain image is available. We will see this semaphore again later in this section in the code of the draw() method. VK_NULL_HANDLE is given as the penultimate parameter, through which we can set a Vulkan fence instead to let the call wait for an instruction in the command buffer. The last parameter is the pointer to our imageIndex variable, which will be filled with the index of the next available image in the swapchain once the vkAcquireNextImageKHR() function returns.

The check for the return value is a bit more complex, as it includes some magic:

```
if (result == VK_ERROR_OUT_OF_DATE_KHR) {
  return recreateSwapchain();
} else {
    if (result != VK_SUCCESS && result !=
    VK_SUBOPTIMAL_KHR) {
      Logger::log(1, "%s error: failed to acquire
        swapchain image. Error is '%i'\n", __FUNCTION__,
        result);
```

```
        return false;
      }
  }
```

If `vkAcquireNextImageKHR()` gives us an out-of-date error, this means the swapchain is no longer usable because the images differ too much from the Vulkan surface properties. This happens on changes such as a window resize, which also changes the Vulkan surface parameters. The call to `recreateSwapchain()` destroys the swapchain with all dependent objects and recreates them with the parameters from the surface.

Reacting this way handles any window resizes internally, and we do not need to set a callback for that event. Neat, huh?

The other possible result, next to `VK_SUCCESS`, is `VK_SUBOPTIMAL_KHR`. This means that the surface has changed but the swapchain can still be used to display the images. We may recreate the swapchain on this result to have it in an optimal configuration for the next `draw()`.

Preparing the Vulkan objects for the command buffer

Once a swapchain image is available, we can start the command buffer preparation:

```
  if (vkResetCommandBuffer(mRenderData.rdCommandBuffer, 0)
  != VK_SUCCESS) {
    Logger::log(1, "%s error: failed to reset command
      buffer\n", __FUNCTION__);
    return false;
  }
```

We have created only a single command buffer, which is enough for this demonstration. After the command buffer has been sent to the queue and the commands have been processed, it must be reset to its initial state. This is done by calling `vkResetCommandBuffer()` with the command buffer object. We do not need the logical device as the first parameter because the object was initialized using the logical device. The second parameter is used for additional flags; we can leave this at zero.

The result needs to be checked again because we are unable to continue if we cannot reset the command buffer.

Now it is time to start recording commands:

```
  VkCommandBufferBeginInfo cmdBeginInfo{};
  cmdBeginInfo.sType =
    VK_STRUCTURE_TYPE_COMMAND_BUFFER_BEGIN_INFO;
  cmdBeginInfo.flags =
    VK_COMMAND_BUFFER_USAGE_ONE_TIME_SUBMIT_BIT;
```

The call to `vkBeginCommandBuffer()` starts the process of recording commands. It needs a `VkCommandBufferBeginInfo` struct as the first parameter and the command buffer object as the second.

`VkCommandBufferBeginInfo` has only two values set. The type of the struct is explicitly set in `.sType`, and `.flags` tells Vulkan that these commands will be sent only once, and the buffer will be reset after the usage. It's also possible to create a reusable command buffer object, which could be submitted multiple times to the queue:

```
if(vkBeginCommandBuffer(mRenderData.rdCommandBuffer,
&cmdBeginInfo) != VK_SUCCESS) {
  Logger::log(1, "%s error: failed to begin command
    buffer\n", __FUNCTION__);
  return false;
}
```

And, as we've seen before in this section, we check for a successful result or abort the `draw()` call.

Prior to sending commands, we need to create another Vulkan structure, and we will initialize a couple of helper variables:

```
VkClearValue colorClearValue;
colorClearValue.color = { { 0.1f, 0.1f, 0.1f, 1.0f } };
```

`VkClearValue` is a C-style union containing either a Vulkan type to store a color using up to four parameters (red, green, blue, and transparency), or a combined depth and stencil type. The depth value is in the range from `0.0f` to `1.0f`, where `1.0f` is the maximum depth. The range is normalized within the pipeline, scaling the *z* values of the polygons drawn to this range:

```
VkClearValue depthValue;
depthValue.depthStencil.depth = 1.0f;
```

A small depth value for a pixel usually lets the new color value pass, while a large depth discards the pixel color because it will be hidden behind some other pixel. Many aspects of this testing behavior can be changed in the pipeline configuration.

The stencil buffer can be seen as some sort of silhouette. During a rendering pass, the stencil buffer can be updated, that is, by setting a value if the color attachment is written. In a later rendering pass or subpass, this stencil buffer may be used to mask parts of the framebuffer, ignoring writes if the stencil buffer in that position has a special value:

```
VkClearValue clearValues[] = { colorClearValue,
  depthValue };
```

The value of the `colorClearValue` variable will be set to a dark gray, and the depth of the `depthValue` variable will be set to `1.0`, the maximum depth of the depth buffer. These variables are combined to the C-style `clearValues` array, as the following `VkRenderPassBeginInfo` struct uses a single pointer member for those values.

To begin the rendering process, we have to collect some more data:

```
VkRenderPassBeginInfo rpInfo{};
rpInfo.sType = VK_STRUCTURE_TYPE_RENDER_PASS_BEGIN_INFO;
rpInfo.renderPass = mRenderData.rdRenderpass;
```

The `VkRenderPassBeginInfo` struct has the usual `.sType` to identify the type. It needs our created render pass object, but only as a value to read the data from it.

Next, we define a rendering area:

```
rpInfo.renderArea.offset.x = 0;
rpInfo.renderArea.offset.y = 0;
rpInfo.renderArea.extent =
  mRenderData.rdVkbSwapchain.extent;
rpInfo.framebuffer =
  mRenderData.rdFramebuffers[imageIndex];
```

This may limit the rendering to a rectangular sub-part of the framebuffer. Our rendering should be done on the entire size of the framebuffer, so we specify the origin of the image as `offset`, and the size of the images in the swapchain as `size`. We also need to set the correct index in the `framebuffer` vector, selecting the swapchain image with `imageIndex` retrieved from the `vkAcquireNextImageKHR` call.

As the last two members, we set the clearing values:

```
rpInfo.clearValueCount = 2;
rpInfo.pClearValues = clearValues;
```

The count member is set to `2`, which is the number of elements in the `clearValues` array defined before. We set the clear value pointer member to the `clearValues` array; this works because the address to a C-style array is a pointer.

There are two more Vulkan objects required to support the dynamic window size change: the viewport and a `scissor` object. The viewport defines the mapping of the internal Vulkan coordinates to the window coordinates. This has to be adjusted when the window size changes. The `scissor` object is used to define a rectangular part of the drawing, ignoring draws to all pixels around it. If you don't adjust it as the window changes, you will get blank areas around the previous size.

We start with the viewport:

```
VkViewport viewport{};
viewport.x = 0.0f;
viewport.y = 0.0f;
```

The viewport will start at the position (0,0) of our window, which is the top-left corner in Vulkan. This is different from OpenGL; it had the position (0,0) in the bottom-left corner.

The height and width of the viewport are identical to the window dimensions. Both values are taken from the swapchain and the new values for height and width are updated in the swapchain after the recreation during the `vkAcquireNextImageKHR()` call:

```
viewport.width = static_cast<float>(
  mRenderData.rdVkbSwapchain.extent.width);
viewport.height = static_cast<float>(
  mRenderData.rdVkbSwapchain.extent.height);
```

There is some attention needed; the `Viewport` object expects the height and width values to be floats instead of integers, so we do `static_cast` to convert them in place:

```
viewport.minDepth = 0.0f;
viewport.maxDepth = 1.0f
```

Finally, we include the full depth range in the viewport.

The `scissor` object is simple:

```
VkRect2D scissor{};
scissor.offset = { 0, 0 };
scissor.extent = mRenderData.rdVkbSwapchain.extent;
```

We only need the offset, which is zero in both coordinates, and the (potentially new) size of the window, taken again from the swapchain.

Starting a new render pass

Now we are ready to begin a new rendering pass. A rendering pass collects all buffers, pipelines, and descriptor sets that will be used to render the image:

```
vkCmdBeginRenderPass(mRenderData.rdCommandBuffer,
  &rpInfo,VK_SUBPASS_CONTENTS_INLINE);
```

The call to `vkCmdBeginRenderPass()` has a command buffer object as the first parameter. All following commands are recorded into this buffer. The `VkRenderPassBeginInfo` struct is the next parameter. It specifies which render pass and framebuffer to use for the drawing calls. The last parameter defines the usage of subpasses inside the render pass, telling the render pass to use only a so-called primary command buffer. There are also secondary command buffers that could be used to record reusable sequences, which could be included in primary command buffers.

The `vkCmdBeginRenderPass()` function has no return parameter, so we don't need additional checks here.

Next, we need to bind our rendering pipeline:

```
vkCmdBindPipeline(mRenderData.rdCommandBuffer,
  VK_PIPELINE_BIND_POINT_GRAPHICS,mRenderData.rdPipeline);
```

The first parameter is again our command buffer object, as we want to bind the pipeline to it. The next parameter specifies the pipeline usage to draw graphics, and other values are for compute or raytracing pipelines. The rendering pipeline object is set as the last parameter. It contains the settings Vulkan needs to know to start the rendering process. Pipeline creation is one of the biggest tasks. You can check out the implementation of the `Pipeline` class in the `Pipeline.cpp` file.

To use the vertices from a vertex array on the GPU, we need to bind the buffer containing the vertex data:

```
VkDeviceSize offset = 0;
vkCmdBindVertexBuffers(mRenderData.rdCommandBuffer, 0, 1,
  &mVertexBuffer,&offset);
```

The `offset` variable is used as offset into the vertex buffer; we could use this to draw only parts of the vertices in such a buffer. In our case, it is set to zero, to start at the very beginning of the buffer. Then, we use `vkCmdBindVertexBuffers()` to also record this into our command buffer object, as the selection of the vertex buffer is also a Vulkan command.

The next two values are for Vulkan bindings; these are additional pipeline properties to select different "slots" in the shaders. Bindings are not immutable, unlike most parts of the pipeline, allowing a bit more flexibility. The first value specifies the first binding number, which is `0` in our case, and the second value defines the total number of bindings to use. As we have only one binding, the value is `1`.

Now we set the Vulkan buffer object containing the vertex data, plus the offset, which was set to zero in the previous statement. At this point, the pipeline knows where to find the vertex data for the triangles we want to draw.

Drawing textured triangles requires another binding call:

```
vkCmdBindDescriptorSets(mRenderData.rdCommandBuffer,
  VK_PIPELINE_BIND_POINT_GRAPHICS,
  mRenderData.rdPipelineLayout, 0, 1,
  &mRenderData.rdDescriptorSet, 0, nullptr);
```

The `vkCmdBindDescriptorSets()` call binds a Vulkan `DescriptorSet` to our command buffer object. This descriptor set contains the required information about the Vulkan image that we want to use. You could see the creation steps in the `Texture` class, inside the `Texture.cpp` file.

The first parameter is the command buffer. We will also record the binding of `DescriptorSet` as a command. Then, we choose again to draw graphics in the pipeline, and we set a pipeline layout. The pipeline layout is a helper object collecting information related to the pipeline, created along with the graphics pipeline.

The next two numbers are like the vertex buffer values. Instead of the first binding number and the count of bindings, we have the first descriptor number and the count of descriptors here. The pointer to the single descriptor set follows this definition.

The last two parameters are for dynamic buffers. This feature enables us to bind a large buffer with different model matrix data and choose the offset into the buffer at draw time. The alternative would be a lot of smaller buffers with one matrix each; which option you choose depends on the architecture and performance needs. Doing this is out of the scope of our basic renderer – we only want to draw two triangles for now.

As the viewport and the scissor object are used in a dynamic fashion, we must add them to the command buffer object too:

```
vkCmdSetViewport(mRenderData.rdCommandBuffer, 0, 1,
  &viewport);
vkCmdSetScissor(mRenderData.rdCommandBuffer, 0, 1,
  &scissor);
```

After all the preparation steps, the real drawing command will be sent:

```
vkCmdDraw(mRenderData.rdCommandBuffer, mTriangleCount *
  3, 1, 0, 0);
```

The call to `vkCmdDraw` tells the GPU to draw the triangles from the vertex buffer into the framebuffer defined in the rendering pass struct, using the pipeline with the shaders and the descriptor set with the Vulkan image as the texture. This is the most important command for us; this is where the magic happens.

The first parameter is the command buffer object that gets the drawing call recorded. The second parameter is the number of vertices to draw in this call. The value of the `mTriangleCount` variable is calculated from the model data sent. We need to multiply it by 3 because every triangle here is drawn separately, but other drawing modes are supported that reuse vertices sent to the graphics pipeline.

The next parameter is the number of instances to draw. Instanced rendering will be added in *Chapter 14*. Here, we want to draw only one instance, so we set the value to one. The last two parameters are the first vertex and the first instance number to draw. With the four parameters that control the start and the skip of vertices and indexes, we are able to draw only parts of the model data or some of the model instances during a `vkCmdDraw()` call.

The last four parameters allow us to draw the same set of vertices multiple times but with some parameters changed inside the shader, such as the position or rotation. This method enables highly efficient drawings of the same objects without having to specify every object by itself. There's no need to define every single blade of grass in a meadow. You could essentially draw the entire meadow with a single object, which is moved around by the GPU.

After the draw command, we will end the rendering pass:

```
vkCmdEndRenderPass(mRenderData.rdCommandBuffer);
```

This call records the command to end the render pass to the command buffer object.

In bigger graphics renderers, multiple render passes could follow, but we use only this one and don't want to send more commands. So, let's end the recording:

```
if (vkEndCommandBuffer(mRenderData.rdCommandBuffer) !=
VK_SUCCESS) {
  Logger::log(1, "%s error: failed to end command
    buffer\n", __FUNCTION__);
  return false;
}
```

The call to `vkEndCommandBuffer()` tells Vulkan that we have finished adding commands to the command buffer object. The buffer will be internally marked as executable.

Submitting the command buffer to the Vulkan queue

The rendering will still not start at this point. The Vulkan command buffers must be submitted to the queues of the logical Vulkan device: in our case, to the graphics queue of the GPU. To do this, another struct is needed:

```
VkSubmitInfo submitInfo{};
submitInfo.sType = VK_STRUCTURE_TYPE_SUBMIT_INFO;
```

`VkSubmitInfo` collects all the information needed to submit the recorded commands inside the command buffer to the Vulkan queue. We set `.sType` according to the structure type.

Next, we define a wait stage and set the struct member to it:

```
VkPipelineStageFlags waitStage =
  VK_PIPELINE_STAGE_COLOR_ATTACHMENT_OUTPUT_BIT;
submitInfo.pWaitDstStageMask = &waitStage;
```

We need two semaphores to coordinate the drawing process in the GPU:

```
submitInfo.waitSemaphoreCount = 1;
submitInfo.pWaitSemaphores =
  &mRenderData.rdPresentSemaphore;
```

The first semaphore, `waitSemaphore`, will block the Vulkan rendering before the given wait stage: in our case, before reaching the stage where the color attachments of the framebuffer are written. The semaphore is used in the `vkAcquireNextImageKHR()` call at the start of the `draw()` call and informs the rendering process that the previously used image of the swapchain is now free, and the rendering to the framebuffer can start:

```
submitInfo.signalSemaphoreCount = 1;
submitInfo.pSignalSemaphores =
  &mRenderData.rdRenderSemaphore;
```

The second semaphore, `signalSemaphore`, does the synchronization in the other direction. It signals the end of the command buffer execution, and another Vulkan function can be blocked with this semaphore until all the commands have been worked on. In our case, the second semaphore will be used by `vkQueuePresentKHR()` at the end of the `draw()` call. This queues the presentation of the next swapchain image to the Vulkan surface.

The final step is adding the command buffer to the struct:

```
submitInfo.commandBufferCount = 1;
submitInfo.pCommandBuffers =
  &mRenderData.rdCommandBuffer;
```

The command buffer object completes the information required for the queue submission. Now we are ready to submit to the queue:

```
if (vkQueueSubmit(mGraphicsQueue, 1, &submitInfo,
  mRenderData.rdRenderFence) != VK_SUCCESS) {
  Logger::log(1, "%s error: failed to submit draw command
    buffer\n",__FUNCTION__);
  return false;
}
```

The `vkQueueSubmit()` call needs the queue as the first parameter; we use the graphics queue here, which is read during the initialization phase. Next is the number of submit info structs we send, and a pointer to the submit info struct(s). As we have only a single struct, the number is `1`, and we use the address of that struct.

The last parameter is our rendering fence. This is the one we waited for with the very first command of the `draw()` call: `vkWaitForFences()`. This fence signals the execution of all of the commands recorded in the given command buffer object – it simply informs about the completed drawing process.

This information allows fully asynchronous drawing. We can immediately grab the next swapchain image and start recording the new command buffer. The `vkWaitForFences()` command will be blocked by the semaphore until we have a free image. Ideally, we should always keep at least one finished image of our 3D scene in the swapchain.

Queuing the presentation of the swapchain image

As the very last step of the `draw()` call, we must inform Vulkan to copy the drawn swapchain image to the surface, finally displaying the image on the screen and presenting it to the viewer – to you. This is done by starting with another struct definition, `VkPresentInfoKHR`:

```
VkPresentInfoKHR presentInfo{};
presentInfo.sType = VK_STRUCTURE_TYPE_PRESENT_INFO_KHR;
```

Here `.sType` is again set to the type of the struct. Next, we will use the rendering semaphore set in the submit info struct earlier in this section:

```
presentInfo.waitSemaphoreCount = 1;
presentInfo.pWaitSemaphores =
  &mRenderData.rdRenderSemaphore;
```

This semaphore will be signaled once all commands in the command buffer object have been executed. This is similar to the fence but is a pure GPU internal signaling mechanism.

The presentation of the swapchain image waits with this semaphore until all the draw commands are finished and the final image in the framebuffer is completed. To let the presentation call know which of the images to present, we must also set this information in the struct:

```
presentInfo.swapchainCount = 1;
presentInfo.pSwapchains =
  &mRenderData.rdVkbSwapchain.swapchain;
presentInfo.pImageIndices = &imageIndex;
```

We have only one swapchain in this example, and we set the swapchain and the index of the last image drawn. The image presentation to the surface is also queued in the graphics queue and not executed immediately:

```
  result = vkQueuePresentKHR(mRenderData.rdPresentQueue,
&presentInfo);
  if (result == VK_ERROR_OUT_OF_DATE_KHR || result ==
    VK_SUBOPTIMAL_KHR) {
    return recreateSwapchain();
  } else {
      if (result != VK_SUCCESS) {
        Logger::log(1, "%s error: failed to present
          swapchain image\n",
            __FUNCTION__);
        return false;
      }
  }
```

We also check the result if the Vulkan surface no longer matches the swapchain image properties and make sure to recreate the swapchain if the surface has been changed. This enables Vulkan to work with optimal performance because we disable expensive copy transitions due to different settings or sizes in the surface and the swapchain. By using fences and semaphores, the asynchronous Vulkan rendering will be smooth and coordinated.

If you compile and run the renderer code, you should get a picture of a textures box, like the picture of the OpenGL renderer in *Chapter 2*:

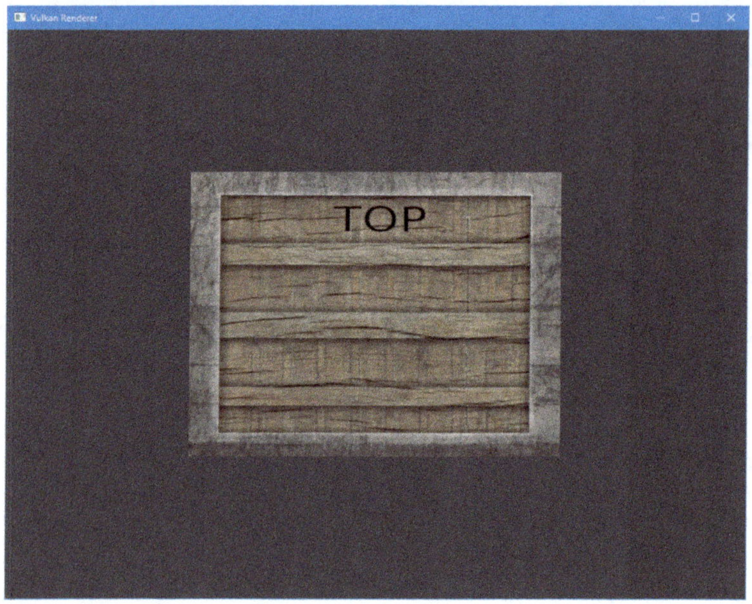

Figure 3.2: Textured box created by the Vulkan renderer

The Vulkan picture you see on your screen may be brighter than the OpenGL output of the same example code, similar brightness as the OpenGL output, or darker. The brightness depends on a configuration of your operating system that we do not take into account here: the internal gamma correction. This gamma correction was required for older CRT screens to display the colors at different brightness values correctly and is still in use in modern displays, although in an adjusted manner, but the configuration of the gamma correction lies outside of the scope of this book.

Differences and similarities between OpenGL and Vulkan, reprised

Now, let's compare the `draw()` call (from the previous section) from Vulkan with the same drawing steps as OpenGL. I have cheated a bit here and added the commands. They are distributed across different classes in the OpenGL renderer we created in *Chapter 2*.

First, we bind a framebuffer. It has color and depth attachments, like in Vulkan:

```
glBindFramebuffer(GL_DRAW_FRAMEBUFFER, mBuffer);
```

Then, we clear the color and depth attachments of the framebuffer:

```
glClearColor(0.1f, 0.1f, 0.1f, 1.0f);
glClearDepth();
glClear(GL_COLOR_BUFFER_BIT | GL_DEPTH_BUFFER_BIT);
```

Next, we bind our shader program, the vertex buffer, and the texture:

```
glUseProgram(mShaderProgram);
glBindVertexArray(mVAO);
glBindTexture(GL_TEXTURE_2D, mTexture);
```

This must be done every time we need to set or change one of them.

A context change follows. We want to draw only the triangles facing us, hiding all the triangles we would never see:

```
glEnable(GL_CULL_FACE);
```

The call to `glDrawArrays()` is the "real" drawing command, instructing OpenGL to draw the triangles given in the vertex buffer using the active texture:

```
glDrawArrays(GL_TRIANGLES, 0, mTriangleCount);
```

After the drawing, we need to explicitly disable the vertex buffer and texture, preventing further uses of it:

```
glBindVertexArray(0);
glBindTexture(GL_TEXTURE_2D, 0);
```

The next four commands copy the content of the framebuffer to the window:

```
glBindFramebuffer(GL_DRAW_FRAMEBUFFER, 0);
glBindFramebuffer(GL_READ_FRAMEBUFFER, mBuffer);
glBlitFramebuffer(0, 0, mBufferWidth, mBufferHeight,
  0, 0, mBufferWidth, mBufferHeight, GL_COLOR_BUFFER_BIT,
  GL_NEAREST);
glBindFramebuffer(GL_READ_FRAMEBUFFER, 0);
```

Finally, we instruct GLFW to swap the front and back buffers:

```
glfwSwapBuffers(mWindow);
```

You get the same result on the screen using these 14 OpenGL calls, plus the GLFW call to swap the buffers. Yes, it looks much easier, but on the downside, you do not have much control over the steps. There is no explicit synchronization; most of the synchronization is hidden from you and will be done by the OpenGL library and the underlying driver. You must enable and disable all the OpenGL objects you want to use, such as shaders, vertex buffers, and textures.

You have to take care of the settings in the global context. Other OpenGL calls, even far away from these lines in your code, could possibly change the context, altering the behavior of the OpenGL functions used in the `draw()` call. You may need a lot of time to debug such issues.

Summary

In this chapter, you learned how a Vulkan renderer can be created. After an overview of some of the objects and the relations between them, two helper libraries were introduced. Using vk-bootstrap and the VMA helps to reduce the number of lines of code needed for a renderer, and there are more abstraction layers that can be used to make it even more compact.

In the last section of the chapter, we inspected the implementation details of some of the Vulkan objects. You will find the pattern with one or more `VK_STRUCTURE` objects carrying the desired properties of all Vulkan objects, making it easy to read the code once you get into it. Even if you will not extend the code or experiment with it, knowing details about the structures and objects of Vulkan should help you to build a mental model of the components needed for the rendering process in our game character animations.

In the next chapter, we will dive deeper into vertex and fragment shaders. You will learn how they work together to display the final picture, and what kind of data is passed between the shader stages. You will be introduced to methods of sending small amounts of data to the shaders on the GPU, allowing you to control parts of the rendering pipeline from within your application.

Practical sessions

As in the previous chapters, here are some ideas to try out with the example Vulkan rendering code. If you break anything, just roll back to the downloaded version:

- Add some more triangles to the model class. You can achieve this by adding more vertex and texture lines to `std::vector`. See what happens if you change the last value of the `glm::vec3` position of the vertices. This is the *z*-value (or depth) of the vertex. The renderer has a depth buffer as an attachment on the framebuffer. The current ordering of the triangles from front to back should be independent of their position in the vertex's vectors of `VkMesh`.

- Use another image type as a texture, such as a JPG file from your system. You will break the display for sure because the number of channels is hardcoded for a PNG file (four channels: red, green, blue, and transparency), and a JPG file has no transparency. The `stbi_load()` function returns the number of channels of the loaded image, adding a switch between three and four channels should be fairly easy to implement.
- Experiment with the validation layer. Re-order the statements in the `cleanup()` method of the main renderer class, or comment one out, and watch what the validation layer prints to the screen. Or, as another example, remove one of the incoming vertex data lines of the vertex shader, recompile it, and start the application. You will get detailed messages about the problems.

Additional resources

For more information, take a look at the following:

- The official website of the Vulkan API: `https://www.vulkan.org`
- The Vulkan Guide: `https://vkguide.dev`
- The Vulkan Tutorial: `https://vulkan-tutorial.com`
- vk-bootstrap: `https://github.com/charles-lunarg/vk-bootstrap`
- VMA: `https://github.com/GPUOpen-LibrariesAndSDKs/VulkanMemoryAllocator`
- 3D Graphics Rendering Cookbook: `https://www.amazon.com/-/dp/1838986197`
- A curated list of Vulkan links: `https://github.com/vinjn/awesome-vulkan`

4
Working with Shaders

Welcome to *Chapter 4*! In the previous two chapters, we created renderers for OpenGL and Vulkan, but we addressed only the application part of the drawing: how to store the data in a simplified model and how to copy the data over to the GPU via a vertex buffer.

The GPU needs to know what to do with the data too. We must tell the graphics card in which format, sizes, and order the data for the vertices arrives, whether and how we would like to transform it, and how to apply colors or textures to the objects we sent.These steps are done in so-called **shaders**, which are small programs running on the compute units of your graphics card.

In this chapter, we will take a deeper look into the basic functionality of shaders. You will learn more about the way data is sent to the GPU – the vertex data itself, and additional data, such as transformation matrices.

We will also discuss the **OpenGL Mathematics** (**GLM**) library, allowing you to use the same data types and transformations in your code as in the shaders. We will also explore the code of a simple vertex and a simple fragment shader.

In this chapter, we will cover the following topics:

- Shader basics
- GLM, the OpenGL Mathematics library
- Vertex data transfer to the GPU
- Switching shaders at runtime
- Sending additional data to the GPU

Technical requirements

For this chapter, you will need the OpenGL code from *Chapter 2* and the Vulkan code from *Chapter 3*.

We will start with an overview of the shaders themselves: what they are and how they are used.

Shader basics

Today's GPUs are powerful computing units. While the main job of older graphics cards was just to display the graphics memory (consisting of 2D images of the windows and their contents), the evolution to 3D has shifted some tasks from the CPU to the GPU.

The main "workhorses" in a GPU are the shader units. These are small and simple processing units with a limited instruction set, compared to the system processor. However, they utilize large registers and can operate on more than one data value at once, calculating multiple results in a single step. This is called **Single Instruction, Multiple Data** (**SIMD**). You may also have heard terms such as SSE as being included in your CPU (older readers may also remember the predecessors, MMX and 3DNow!). With SIMD, each one of the registers can load more than one value, usually two or four of them. Mathematical operations, such as multiplication or addition, are done on each pair of values in two registers, leading to four results instead of only one per operation.

And there are lots of shader units in a GPU. An NVIDIA RTX 3090 has approximately 10,000 shader units, and an AMD Radeon 6900XT has around 5,000, running at clock rates of 1.5–1.8 GHz. Even if the raw unit numbers of both models cannot be compared directly due to different implementations, you should be able to imagine the raw power that can be unleashed with this number of small processors, all running in parallel, plus computing multiple values at once with SIMD.

This amount of computational power is much more than your CPU would be able to achieve. Current desktop processors have between four and sixteen cores, and with a "trick" called **simultaneous multithreading** (**SMT**), they are able to work on twice the number of processes at the same time. The actual desktop processors also have higher clock rates than the GPU shader units – the top models can reach speeds of up to 5 GHz. However, even if we multiply the values for the cores and the clock rates for CPUs and GPUs and interpret the results in a CPU-friendly manner, desktop processors are still far from matching the power of the enormous amount of shader units. And shader units can do their work in parallel, calculating multiple vertex positions or colors on the same picture at once, without explicit synchronization by the programmer. This massive computational power can be used not only for the pure rendering of the virtual world but also for additional work, such as calculating occlusions between objects, which can be offloaded in the so-called compute shaders stage of the GPU.

There are mostly two languages used to program shaders, **OpenGL Shading Language** (**GLSL**) and **High-Level Shading Language** (**HLSL**), used in DirectX. Vulkan uses a different format, called SPIR-V, but the Vulkan shaders can be generated from one of the preceding two languages, as well as others (even C++).

In the example code for this chapter, GLSL in version 4.60 is used, the latest version to date. The OpenGL renderer uses it directly, and the Vulkan shaders will be compiled to SPIR-V.

Before we dive deeper into shaders, let us take a detour to another helper library we will use in this book: GLM.

GLM, the OpenGL Mathematics library

One important limit when working with OpenGL and Vulkan is that all data must be available in GPU memory so the graphics card can access it directly. We must copy the information about every vertex to the memory of the graphics card, including the vertex position, color, texture coordinates, and more. All or part of this data may be copied in every frame to the graphics card, so the fastest way to copy the data to the GPU memory is a simple memory copy command. In C and C++, this command is called `memcpy`. The compiler may utilize the best fitting internal method to achieve the data duplication, such as by using the large SIMD registers on a modern CPU.

But a question arises from this transfer: how do we ensure we make a simple copy, without having to touch and adjust every data element?

This may happen if the data is stored in the system memory in a different format compared to the GPU memory. It may differ in element sizes or the alignment of small data elements, complex structures may be packed differently, or they might even be in a different endianness (order of the single bytes of larger data types).

To ensure we can use a simple high-bandwidth memory-to-memory copy command, the data in the system memory must be the same as in the GPU. This is the main purpose of GLM.

GLM data types and basic operations

The main goal of GLM is to have the same data types in your C++ code available as in the GPU shaders. This prevents CPU-intense conversions during the transfer to the GPU. The main difference in C++ is the namespace prefix, at least if we avoid the *using namespace* directive. Even if the GLM namespace prefix takes five more characters to type for every variable and command, it makes the intention clearer and avoids clashes with other libraries, or some self-written 2D or 3D vector or matrix types.

The most used data types are as follows:

- `glm::vec2` – A vector with two elements (i.e., a texture coordinate)
- `glm::vec3` – A vector with three elements (i.e., a position in 3D space)
- `glm::vec4` – A vector with four elements (i.e., a color with transparency or a position with an additional element for the perspective)
- `glm::mat3` – A 3 x 3 matrix, mostly used for scaling, rotations, or translations
- `glm::mat4` – A 4 x 4 matrix, mostly used for transformations combined with perspective changes

The vector types can have different prefixes for the internal data type:

- `glm::vec3` – A three-element vector of `float`-type elements
- `glm::bvec3` – A three-element vector of `bool`-type elements

- `glm::dvec3` – A three-element vector of `double`-type elements
- `glm::ivec3` – A three-element vector of "signed integers"
- `glm::uvec3` – A three-element vector of "unsigned integers"

The matrix types only know a single prefix:

- `glm::mat3` – A 3 x 3 matrix of `float`-type elements
- `glm::dmat3` – A 3 x 3 matrix of `double`-type elements

The GLM data types have many operations tied to the classes, so you could use them like normal variables, without having to call specialized functions. Let's take a look at some examples of vector mathematics with GLM.

To add two vectors together, just do it as you would for basic types:

```
glm::vec3 a = glm::vec3(1.0, 2.0, 4.0);
glm::vec3 b = glm::vec3(0.5, 1.0, 2.0);
glm::vec3 c = a + b; // glm::vec3(1.5, 3.0, 6.0)
```

And this is how to multiply every element of the vector with a scalar number:

```
glm::vec3 d = glm::vec3(1.0f, 2.0f, 3.0f);
glm::vec3 e = d * 3.0f; // glm::vec3(3.0f, 6.0f, 9.0f)
```

The scalar division works similarly, as follows:

```
glm::vec3 f = glm::vec3(12.0f, 16.0f, 40.0f);
glm::vec3 g = f / 4.0f; // glm::vec3(3.0f, 4.0f, 10.0f)
```

Using GLM instead of some self-made classes may save you a lot of time and headaches, especially when it comes to matrix-matrix and vector-matrix operations. Implementing those operations is a nice exercise to learn or recap the math rules, and if small errors remain undetected, you will have a lot of fun debugging your code.

GLM transformations

In addition to the class-based operations, the GLM data types also have useful functions for transformations. We will use some of these functions in this chapter and the remaining parts of the book.

One example is to **normalize** a vector, scaling it to the length of `1`:

```
glm::vec3 h = glm::vec3(1.0f, 2.0f, 4.0f);
glm::vec3 i = glm::normalize(h); // glm::vec3(0.218218, 0.436436,
  0.872872)
float j = glm::length(h) // 4.582576
float k = glm::length(i) // 1.000000
```

This normalization is important, as we only need the direction of a vector in several transformation operations. And the vector length of `1` will not change the scaling of the other operators.

> **Note**
>
> You should also be aware of pitfalls when working with GLM, as some of them are easy to get wrong. One of the most common errors is trying to calculate the magnitude of a vector by using the `length()` function, which gets the number of elements: `int m = h.length() // number of floats in the glm::vec3`.

We will take a more detailed look at GLM transformations in *Chapter 6*, which will cover a roundup of vectors, matrices, and their operations.

Now, let us see how the vertex data in the first step finds its way into the GPU, and what is done between the pipeline stages.

Vertex data transfer to the GPU

The basic data flow in the graphics pipeline is shown in *Figure 2.1* of *Chapter 2*. The input of the first shader stage is defined by you, the programmer. There are some rules and limits, but mostly it is between "nothing at all" in simple `Hello World` tutorial code, and extraordinarily complex, structured, and interleaved vertex data from games and 3D applications. As already stated at the start of the *GLM, the OpenGL Mathematics library* section, all data must reside in the GPU memory to be drawn.

We will copy the vertex data of the 3D models to the GPU by using vertex buffers. These are, like all other buffers, just parts of the GPU memory – in this case, dedicated to storing vertex data in it. Other methods exist, and we will talk about one of them in *Chapter 14*, where we will use textures as data storage instead of vertex buffers.

The OpenGL renderer from *Chapter 2* and the Vulkan renderer from *Chapter 3* already contain vertex buffers to upload the vertex data. In both versions of the application, we store two different properties for every vertex:

```
struct OGLVertex {
  glm::vec3 position;
  glm::vec2 uv;
};
```

We store the position in 3D space as a three-element vector, and the position inside the texture as a two-element vector. In the Vulkan renderer, we do the same, only the name of the struct is different. For the sake of simplicity, we continue with the OpenGL renderer – the full Vulkan code can be found in the GitHub repository of this book.

The goal of this section is to add a third property for every vertex: a color. By the end, you will know how to extend the vertex data of the model even further.

The data for every vertex is stored interleaved – this means, position and texture data are mixed in the buffer. The three position values from each vertex come first, followed by the two texture values, starting again with the position for the next vertex:

```
v1.position.x v1.position.y v1.position.z v1.uv.u v1.uv.v
v2.position.x v2.position.y v2.position.z v2.uv.u v2.uv.v
v3.position.x v3.position.y v3.position.z v3.uv.u v3.uv.v
```

An alternative way would be to use a separate buffer for every property. Both methods have pros and cons, and only profiling your application with interleaved and non-interleaved buffers can tell you the better one. As we are not aiming for the most efficient renderer code but for easy understanding, the interleaved buffers are fine.

For the OpenGL renderer, the vertex buffer is configured in the `VertexBuffer.cpp` file, inside the `opengl` folder:

```
glBindVertexArray(mVAO);
glBindBuffer(GL_ARRAY_BUFFER, mVertexVBO);
glVertexAttribPointer(0, 3, GL_FLOAT, GL_FALSE,
  sizeof(OGLVertex),
  (void*) offsetof(OGLVertex, position));
glVertexAttribPointer(1, 2, GL_FLOAT, GL_FALSE,
  sizeof(OGLVertex),
  (void*) offsetof(OGLVertex, uv));
glEnableVertexAttribArray(0);
glEnableVertexAttribArray(1);
```

The parameters to `glVertexAttribPointer()` define the layout of the vertex buffer. The first parameter is the index to be set. This is an ascending index; every call needs a unique one. The second and third parameters are the size and type of the elements in the vertex buffer. At index `0`, we have `3` float elements (the position), and at index `1`, we have `2` float elements (the texture location), just as in the `OGLVertex` struct. The next parameter will allow us to normalize the data into the range between `-1` and `1` for signed values, or between `0` and `1` for unsigned values. Setting this to `GL_FALSE` disables the normalization, and the values that are transferred remain unchanged. The second last parameter is the so-called **stride**, the offset between two consecutive data elements. This value is set to the size of our struct – 5 * the size of a `float` value.

The last parameter is the offset into one of those data elements. We use a little C++ macro called `offsetof` here, which gives us more flexibility in the definition as it also counts in the data type.

The position is stored at an offset of `0`, right at the start, and the `uv` parameter is stored at the offset of `3` floats. These values enable the OpenGL library to access the elements correctly. We must use C-style casting to cast them to a pointer to void; OpenGL sometimes requires this kind of casting to allow several types.

Failing to get the stride and offset values right will result in distorted drawings, as the values for the texture may be misinterpreted as positions. So, if your final drawing has a lot of odd-colored triangles in the center, you should check for mistakes here.

As we see in the `basic.vert` file, this also matches the definition in the vertex shader:

```
layout (location = 0) in vec3 aPos;
layout (location = 1) in vec2 aTexCoord;
```

Now, it is time to add the `color` value. As a first step, add it to the `OGLVertex` struct in the `OGLRenderData.h` header file, inside the `opengl` folder:

```
struct OGLVertex {
  glm::vec3 position;
  glm::vec3 color;
  glm::vec2 uv;
};
```

We will move it to the second spot, between the position and texture coordinates, as it "feels" better when going for the vertex color first and applying the texture after this. You may use a different order, but that order must match in all three places: the `OGLVertex` struct, the `glVertexAttribPointer()` calls, and the incoming variable definitions of the vertex shader code.

Thanks to using a struct, the only part to adjust outside the renderer code is the mockup model. Add these lines to the `Model.cpp` file in the `model` folder:

```
mVertexData.vertices[0].color=glm::vec3(0.0f,0.0f,1.0f);
mVertexData.vertices[1].color=glm::vec3(0.0f,1.0f,1.0f);
mVertexData.vertices[2].color=glm::vec3(1.0f,1.0f,0.0f);
mVertexData.vertices[3].color=glm::vec3(1.0f,0.0f,1.0f);
mVertexData.vertices[4].color=glm::vec3(0.0f,1.0f,0.0f);
mVertexData.vertices[5].color=glm::vec3(1.0f,1.0f,1.0f);
```

The values are stored as red, green, and blue. You may use different color values in the range of `0.0` (for "no color") to `1.0` (for "full color") – these are just examples.

Now, head back to the renderer and change the layout in the `VAO.cpp` file:

```
glVertexAttribPointer(0, 3, GL_FLOAT, GL_FALSE,
  sizeof(OGLVertex),
  (void*) offsetof(OGLVertex, position));
glVertexAttribPointer(1, 3, GL_FLOAT, GL_FALSE,
  sizeof(OGLVertex),
  (void*) offsetof(OGLVertex, color));
glVertexAttribPointer(2, 2, GL_FLOAT, GL_FALSE,
  sizeof(OGLVertex),
  (void*) offsetof(OGLVertex, uv));
```

The position remains in index `0`, the 3 floats for the color are added as index `1`, and the texture coordinates move to index `2`.

Do not forget to enable the index numbers `0`, `1`, and `2`:

```
glEnableVertexAttribArray(0);
glEnableVertexAttribArray(1);
glEnableVertexAttribArray(2);
```

As a last step, we need to take care of both shaders. The vertex shader in the `basic.vert` file needs to know the changes in the input, as we have added the color and moved the texture coordinates:

```
layout (location = 0) in vec3 aPos;
layout (location = 1) in vec3 aColor;
layout (location = 2) in vec2 aTexCoord;
```

The color is not used in the vertex shader; it needs to be passed to the fragment shader:

```
layout (location = 0) out vec4 texColor;
layout (location = 1) out vec2 texCoord;
```

You may wonder why we do not pass the incoming `color` variable directly as an output variable to the fragment shader. Sadly, this is not possible in GLSL; we must create a "dummy" assignment in the `main()` function.

We add a fourth element here:

```
texColor = vec4(aColor, 1.0);
texCoord = aTexCoord;
```

This last element is for transparency, and the value of `1.0` means we have no transparency here. The fragment shader in the `basic.frag` file must be made aware of the new, incoming `color` variable too:

```
layout (location = 0) in vec4 texColor;
layout (location = 1) in vec2 texCoord;
```

Remember to use the same variable names as in the outgoing parameters of the vertex shader, as a mismatch between the names will fail the shader compilation.

Finally, in the `main()` function of the fragment shader, we multiply the color taken from the texture location with the vertex color:

```
FragColor = texture(Tex, texCoord) * texColor;
```

This operation does an element-wise multiplication of the `color` value from the texture and the vertex color, mixing both to give a final value. The fragment shader interpolates the colors between the vertices, so you will get a nice and smooth colored crate:

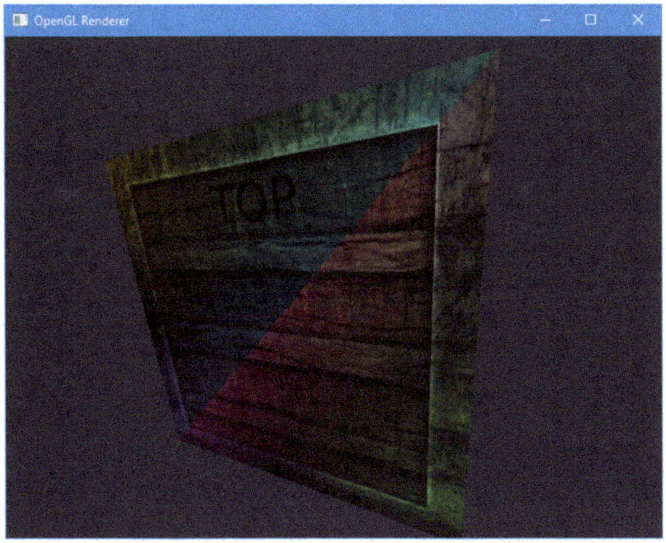

Figure 4.1: The textured box with colored vertices

Changing the behavior of the shader is still completely static. To adjust the color settings or the box position, we must change the code in the shader files and restart the application. If we want to switch faster, we need to add more shaders and switch between them while the application is still running.

Switching shaders at runtime

In a real 3D renderer, you will need a lot of shader switches. The final picture is often created in many consecutive rendering steps, and the drawing operations need to reflect the tasks to be done in that single step. The vertex data sent to the GPU may be the same among many of the shaders, as changes in the data structures would require expensive transformations or lead to duplicate data storage with another set of attributes. But in many cases, the rest of the shader code itself will be completely different, depending on the input to that shader and the expected output.

Adding new shaders is done in only a couple of steps for the OpenGL renderer, so we will walk through the changes here. The Vulkan renderer needs different adjustments, and we will only check the broad steps.

The full example code can be found in the `chapter04` | `01_opengl_shader_switch` folder.

Creating a new set of shaders

The first step is to have multiple shaders available. In our case, we simply copy both files: `basic.vert` to `changed.vert`, and `basic.frag` to `changed.frag`.

Now, change the shader code to get a different result on the screen. First, adjust the code inside the `main()` function in the `changed.vert` file:

```
vec3 offset = vec3(0.1, 0.1, 0.0);
gl_Position = vec4(aPos + offset, 1.0);
```

We define a small offset in the *x* and *y* direction; our textures box will be moved a bit upward and to the right when drawn using the new shader.

In the `main()` function of the `changed.frag` file, change this:

```
FragColor = texture(Tex, texCoord) *
    (vec4(1.0) - texColor);
```

This subtraction inverts the colors of the vertices; you will also see a difference in the colors if you switch between shaders.

These new shaders and the old shaders must be loaded into the renderer, so head for the `OGLRenderer.h` file in the `opengl` folder and adjust the `Shader` classes:

```
private:
  Shader mBasicShader{};
  Shader mChangedShader{};
```

The `mShader` instance becomes `mBasicShader`, and the new `mChangedShader` instance will be added.

In the `OGLRenderer.cpp` file, we need to load both shaders in the `init()` function:

```
if (!mBasicShader.loadShaders("shader/basic.vert",
  "shader/basic.frag")) {
    return false;
}
if (!mChangedShader.loadShaders("shader/changed.vert",
  "shader/changed.frag")) {
    return false;
}
```

This `mShader` instance is renamed here to `mBasicShader` too; the `mChangedShader` instance is new.

In the `cleanup()` function, we also remove the old and the new shader:

```
mBasicShader.cleanup();
mChangedShader.cleanup();
```

Again, the `mShader` instance is renamed, and the `mChangedShader` instance is added.

If we compile this code… nothing changes. The reason is simple: the basic shader is still in use when we draw the textured box. We could change the shader in the code and recompile it, but a better solution is to add some functionality to make the switch between the old and new shader at runtime.

Binding the shader switching to a key

A common way to achieve switching between various kinds of behavior in our application is currently by using a key on our keyboard and a variable in the class responsible for the switching. We will add UI controls in *Chapter 5*; using a button or a list will allow us to easily choose between two or more options. But for now, we will go for the keyboard version.

As a first step, we need to activate the keyboard callback again, but this time, we bind it to the renderer instead of the window. Add the key event handler to the `Window.cpp` file in the `window` folder, pointing to a function in the renderer:

```
glfwSetKeyCallback(mWindow, [](GLFWwindow* win, int key, int scancode,
  int action, int mods) {
    auto renderer = static_cast<OGLRenderer*>
    (glfwGetWindowUserPointer(win));
    renderer->handleKeyEvents(key, scancode, action, mods);
  }
);
```

Now, the key presses will be sent to the `handleKeyEvents()` function in the `OGLRenderer` class. We must implement this function too. Add the declaration of the new `public` method in the `OGLRenderer.h` file:

```
void handleKeyEvents(int key, int scancode, int action, int mods);
```

Also add a new `private` variable to the `OGLRenderer.h` file, called `mUseChangedShader`:

```
bool mUseChangedShader = false;
```

This variable is used to decide whether we want to use the original shader (now named `mBasicShader`) or the new one (`mChangedShader`).

Add the definition of the `handleKeyEvents()` function to the `OLGRenderer.cpp` file:

```
void OGLRenderer::handleKeyEvents(int key, int scancode, int action,
  int mods) {
  if (glfwGetKey(mWindow, GLFW_KEY_SPACE) == GLFW_PRESS){
    mUseChangedShader = !mUseChangedShader;
  }
}
```

This function simply flips the Boolean value between `true` and `false` when we press the spacebar. This enables the switch back and forth between both shaders.

The shader switch in the draw call

The decision between both shaders is made in the `draw()` function. Replace `mShader.use()` with this block:

```
if (mUseChangedShader) {
  mChangedShader.use();
} else {
  mBasicShader.use();
}
```

Depending on the value of the `mUseChangedShader` variable, the new or the original shader will be used. So, if you press the spacebar, the active shader for the next frame will be toggled. The box is drawn with different colors and moved to the top right. Pressing the spacebar again toggles the shader back to the first one:

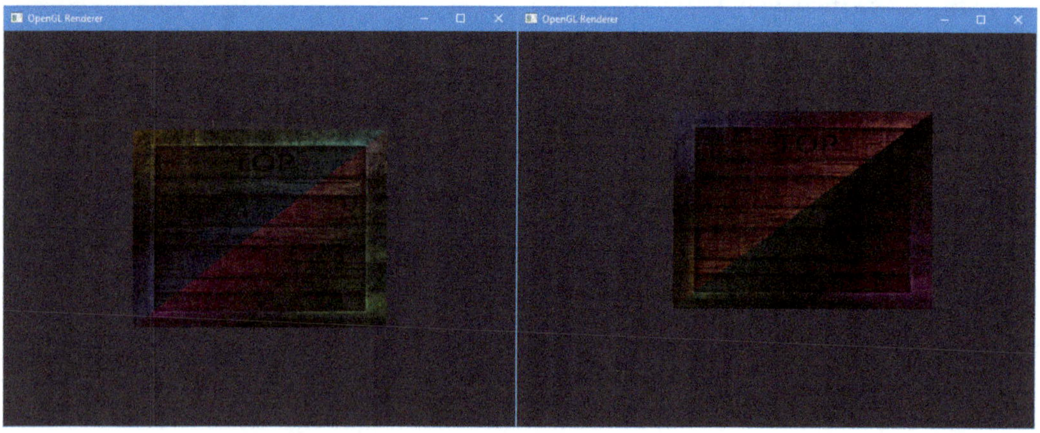

Figure 4.2: Alternating images during the shader switching

> **Note**
>
> In a larger rendering application, the switching and usage of the variable should be guarded by some kind of lock (i.e., a mutex) as the key press is an asynchronous event. If the request to change the shader arrives in the middle of the drawing, this may cause undefined behavior during the current frame.

Shader switching in Vulkan

Using different shaders in Vulkan is done with a different approach, and due to the size of the code, only the basic outline is explained. The full code for the Vulkan renderer with the required changes is available in the `chapter 04` | `03_vulkan_shader_switch` folder.

As the Vulkan rendering pipeline object is immutable, we cannot just swap the shader before drawing the next frame. In Vulkan, we must make two pipeline objects to switch between the shaders, one for each shader set.

The remaining part of the first step is similar. We can also copy the shader files and adjust the `changed.vert` and `changed.frag` lines. But, instead of loading the shaders directly, we create two separate rendering pipelines.

The key binding step is identical, only the class in the callback differs: we need to use the `VKRenderer` class instead of the `OGLRenderer` class.

In the Vulkan renderer `draw()` call, the corresponding change must be done for the `vkCmdBindPipeline()` call. The function gets the rendering pipeline as the last parameter, as it binds the pipeline to the command buffer. The call needs to be included in the switch using the `mUseChangedShader` variable.

If you compile the Vulkan example code and compare the results, you will see a notable difference: the box moves to the right and down on shader switches, as opposed to moving right and up, as seen in the OpenGL renderer.

This is related to the different coordinate systems. Vulkan uses a more natural approach, and the *Y* coordinate starts with a value of `0` at the top of the window, while in OpenGL, for historical reasons, the `0` value for *Y* is at the bottom of the window.

Switching the shaders at runtime is already nice, but the textured box is still completely static. As a naive solution, we could loop over all the vertices in the models to translate or rotate them, before sending them to the GPU. But for more vertices per character or to draw in the final application, this would create a bottleneck on the CPU side. Transforming every single vertex of every character that would have to be transformed for every frame is expensive for the processor – but one of the easiest tasks a shader on the graphics card can do. So, let us explore a method to upload other data to the GPU, and use it to modify the vertices in the graphics pipeline.

Sending additional data to the GPU

The data sent from the vertex buffer has one important drawback: it changes for every vertex. If we need some sort of values to remain constant during a frame, such as a transformation matrix, we must take a different approach. Using the CPU for this has already been ruled out as it would be too expensive and time-consuming, so we will utilize the GPU for this task.

Both OpenGL and Vulkan have a special type of buffer for this use case: the uniform buffer.

Using uniform buffers to upload constant data

Uniform buffers have two important properties:

- They are shared among all shaders on the graphics card
- They are read-only inside the shaders

Any data, such as the aforementioned transformation matrices, needs to be uploaded only once per frame before the drawing starts. In the shader code, the data can be referenced like local variables, but in contrast to vertex positions, colors, and so on, it is the same for every vertex.

Because of this sharing, uniform buffers are set to read-only for the shader code. The execution order of the parallel shader invocations in the GPU cannot be determined, so some shaders would use the old values and some the new ones. To avoid this kind of trouble, any kind of writing to the values uploaded to the uniform buffers is forbidden from within the shaders – uniform buffers are always read-only.

As in the previous section, we will inspect only the OpenGL code. The full source code for this section can be found in the `chapter04` | `02_opengl_ubo` folder. The Vulkan implementation contains more code, which can be found in the `chapter04` |`04_vulkan_ubo` folder.

Creating a uniform buffer

To encapsulate the handling of uniform buffers, a new class will be created. The header file is named `UniformBuffer.h`, and it resides in the `opengl` folder:

```
#pragma once
#include <glm/glm.hpp>
#include <glad/glad.h>
```

We start with the header guard to avoid double inclusions, and include the GLM and the GLAD header, as we need data types from both.

Now, we define the class itself, starting with the `public` methods:

```
class UniformBuffer {
  public:
    void init();
    void uploadUboData(glm::mat4 viewMatrix, glm::mat4
      projectionMatrix);
    void cleanup();
```

The `init()` and `cleanup()` functions are like the other OpenGL classes: they create and destroy the OpenGL objects. The `uploadUboData()` method copies the data of two 4 x 4 matrices to the uniform buffer, making it available on the GPU.

The class contains only one `private` data member, the buffer handle:

```
private:
  GLuint mUboBuffer = 0;
};
```

The implementation in the `UniformBuffer.cpp` file is also straightforward. First, we have two headers to include:

```
#include <glm/gtc/type_ptr.hpp>
#include "UniformBuffer.h"
```

The `glm/gtc/type_ptr.hpp` header is required to create a pointer from a GLM matrix, and we need this during the upload.

Next in the file is the `init()` method:

```
void UniformBuffer::init() {
  glGenBuffers(1, &mUboBuffer);
  glBindBuffer(GL_UNIFORM_BUFFER, mUboBuffer);
  glBufferData(GL_UNIFORM_BUFFER, 2 * sizeof(glm::mat4), NULL,
    GL_STATIC_DRAW);
  glBindBuffer(GL_UNIFORM_BUFFER, 0);
}
```

The call to `glGenBuffers()` creates a new OpenGL buffer, and `glBindBuffer()` binds this buffer for further commands. Using `glBufferData()`, we allocate the memory for the two 4 x 4 matrices; `GL_STATIC_DRAW` is here as just a usage hint for the driver, and after the reservation, we unbind the buffer again.

To clean up the buffer when we exit the program, the usual `cleanup()` is created:

```
void UniformBuffer::cleanup() {
  glDeleteBuffers(1, &mUboBuffer);
}
```

Here, we simply delete the OpenGL buffer object.

The largest method in this class is `uploadUbodata()`:

```
void UniformBuffer::uploadUboData(glm::mat4 viewMatrix, glm::mat4
projectionMatrix) {
  glBindBuffer(GL_UNIFORM_BUFFER, mUboBuffer);
  glBufferSubData(GL_UNIFORM_BUFFER, 0,
      sizeof(glm::mat4),
      glm::value_ptr(viewMatrix));
  glBufferSubData(GL_UNIFORM_BUFFER, sizeof(glm::mat4),
      sizeof(glm::mat4),
      glm::value_ptr(projectionMatrix));
  glBindBufferRange(GL_UNIFORM_BUFFER, 0, mUboBuffer, 0,
    2 * sizeof(glm::mat4));
    glBindBuffer(GL_UNIFORM_BUFFER, 0);
}
```

We bind the created uniform buffer object again and upload the data to the buffer using two `glBufferSubData()` calls. The first parameter is the buffer type, and the second is the offset into the buffer, which must be the size of a 4 x 4 matrix in the second call. The third parameter is the size of the data we upload, and the last is a pointer to the data itself. Here, we need the special GLM header to create a pointer from the matrix data. The last step is unbinding the buffer again.

Shader changes to use the data in the buffer

The `basic.vert` and `changed.vert` vertex shaders must be extended to use the uniform buffer. We call the buffer `Matrices` to show the purpose:

```
layout (std140, binding = 0) uniform Matrices {
  mat4 view;
  mat4 projection;
};
```

The `std140` keyword defines the memory layout inside the shader, while the `binding` keyword is used with an index number, in case multiple uniform buffers are used.

The buffer has two 4 x 4 matrices, one called `view` and one called `projection`. They can be used in the `main()` method of the shaders like other variables. Adjust `basic.vert` like this:

```
gl_Position = projection * view * vec4(aPos, 1.0);
```

And adjust `changed.vert` like this:

```
gl_Position = projection * view * vec4(aPos + offset, 1.0);
```

We use the matrices to multiply the vertex data with it: first the view matrix, then the projection matrix. The matrices will be filled with data in the renderer itself.

> **Note**
> Matrix multiplication is applied from right to left!

The shader class also needs a small addition. We must get the location of the `Matrices` block and bind it to the `binding` value we use in the shader. This is done by adding these two lines right before the deletion of the shader objects:

```
GLint uboIndex = glGetUniformBlockIndex(mShaderProgram, "Matrices");
glUniformBlockBinding(mShaderProgram, uboIndex, 0);
```

The `glGetUniformBlockIndex()` call extracts the location of the block with the literal name `Matrices` from the compiled shader program. This location is then bound in the second call, `glUniformBlockBinding()`, to index 0 for the uniform buffer in the shader code. As we have only one uniform buffer, this may seem redundant, but without this call, the OpenGL library will not find the data in the shader.

Preparing and uploading data

The uniform buffer has been created and the shader modified, so now it is time to tell the OpenGL renderer to upload data. As the first step, we need to add the two 4 x 4 matrices to the `OpenGL.h` file as `private` members:

```
glm::mat4 mViewMatrix = glm::mat4(1.0f);
glm::mat4 mProjectionMatrix = glm::mat4(1.0f);
```

We initialize the matrices with the identity matrix, which allows us to leave one or both of them untouched during the next steps, but we still get a valid result in the renderer.

To activate the upload of the data, simply add it to our shader selection:

```
if (!mUseChangedShader) {
  mBasicShader.use();
} else {
  mChangedShader.use();
}
mUniformBuffer.uploadUboData(mViewMatrix, mProjectionMatrix;
```

If you compile this code, you will see no changes. The multiplication with the unit matrices does not change the value of the vertices; everything is still the same.

To see a difference, add this line to one of the shader selection blocks, either for the basic or the changed shader, but after `mBasicShader.use()` or `mChangedShader.use()`:

```
mViewMatrix = glm::rotate(glm::mat4(1.0f), 0.2f,
    glm::vec3(0.0f, 0.0f, 1.0f));
```

The preceding line creates a rotation matrix with a rotation around the *z* axis by an amount of `0.2` radians, which is about 14.5 °. The *z* axis is the axis of the 3-dimensional OpenGL coordinate system that points to the depth of the virtual scene. So, the vertices of our box would be rotated counter-clockwise by 14.5° around the centre of the screen.

We could also set the rotation angle value directly from a degree value between 0° and 360° by converting the angle with the GLM function `glm::radians()`:

```
mViewMatrix = glm::rotate(glm::mat4(1.0f),
   glm::radians(30.0f),
   glm::vec3(0.0f, 0.0f, 1.0f));
```

This line would rotate the box by 30° counter-clockwise around the center of the screen.

As the data is shared between the shaders, both versions of the quad are affected. Depending on the location, you will see two different behaviors:

- Adding the `mViewMatrix` update to the first block, with the original shader, results in an immediately rotated box
- Adding the `mViewMatrix` update to the second block, with the changed shader, results in a normal box, which will be rotated after pressing the spacebar

The rotation stays active, no matter what we do, just because we upload static data again. Let us bring some movement to the scene. Add this line right before the `if` shader selection:

```
float t = glfwGetTime();
```

The `glfwGetTime()` call returns the system time in seconds, and as this is in the drawing loop, the number will increase constantly.

Now, use this number as input to the rotation call instead of a fixed angle:

```
mViewMatrix = glm::rotate(glm::mat4(1.0f), t,
  glm::vec3(0.0f, 0.0f, 1.0f));
```

This results in a rotating box for one shader and a static box for the other shader. The rotation for the static box is the last rotation sent to the shader, as the missing `mViewMatrix` update in the opposite branch of `if` never changes it. Add the line to the other shader selection too, but now with `-t`:

```
mViewMatrix = glm::rotate(glm::mat4(1.0f), -t,
  glm::vec3(0.0f, 0.0f, 1.0f));
```

After this change, you have two boxes, with different colors and rotating in opposite directions if you switch the shaders.

To bring even more fun into the code, let us add another small feature. Put these lines right before the `glfwGetTime()` call:

```
glm::vec3 cameraPosition = glm::vec3(0.4f, 0.3f, 1.0f);
glm::vec3 cameraLookAtPosition = glm::vec3(0.0f, 0.0f, 0.0f);
glm::vec3 cameraUpVector = glm::vec3(0.0f, 1.0f, 0.0f);

mProjectionMatrix = glm::perspective(glm::radians(90.0f),
  static_cast<float>(mWidth) / static_cast<float>(mHeight),
  0.1f, 100.f);
```

The first three define a camera position, slightly to the top and right, plus it is moved a bit to the viewer. We also have a destination to look at (the center) and a so-called up-vector, set to the *Y* axis. This is the natural upward vector in OpenGL.

The `glm::perspective()` call creates a matrix suitable for a perspective view – the view we have of the world, with parallel lines appearing to get closer to each other in the distance. The first parameter is the so-called **field of view**, a measurement factor for visible distortion. The second parameter is the aspect ratio – the ratio between the width and the height of the screen. We take the saved values from the `init()` and `resize()` calls here, casting them to `float` to get a float as a result. The last two parameters are the near and far *Z* distance. The depth buffer has a range from `0.0f` (near) to `1.0f` (far), and all the vertex *Z* values are scaled from the two values to the depth buffer.

Now add a new 4 x 4 matrix, right above the `if` block used for the shader selection:

```
glm::mat4 view = glm::mat4(1.0);
```

This matrix will contain the rotation matrix we create.

Add this line to the top of the basic shader block, replacing the old `mViewMatrix` line:

```
view = glm::rotate(glm::mat4(1.0f), t, glm::vec3(0.0f, 0.0f, 1.0f));
```

This new line comes to the bottom block, with the changed shader:

```
view = glm::rotate(glm::mat4(1.0f), -t, glm::vec3(0.0f, 0.0f, 1.0f));
```

Finally, add this line right above the `mUniformBuffer.uploadUboData()` call:

```
mViewMatrix = glm::lookAt(cameraPosition, cameraLookAtPosition,
  cameraUpVector) * view;
```

To make the desired perspective effect clearly visible, we use a different offset in the second shader. Adjust the variable in `changed.vert`:

```
vec3 offset = vec3(0.0, 0.0, -1.0);
```

Having an offset in the *Z* direction will move the box away from the viewpoint, while the previous offset in the *X* and *Y* directions will only shift the center of rotation a bit.

Now, compile the code, start the executable... and smile. You will be able to switch between two boxes with different colors and opposite rotation directions, as shown here:

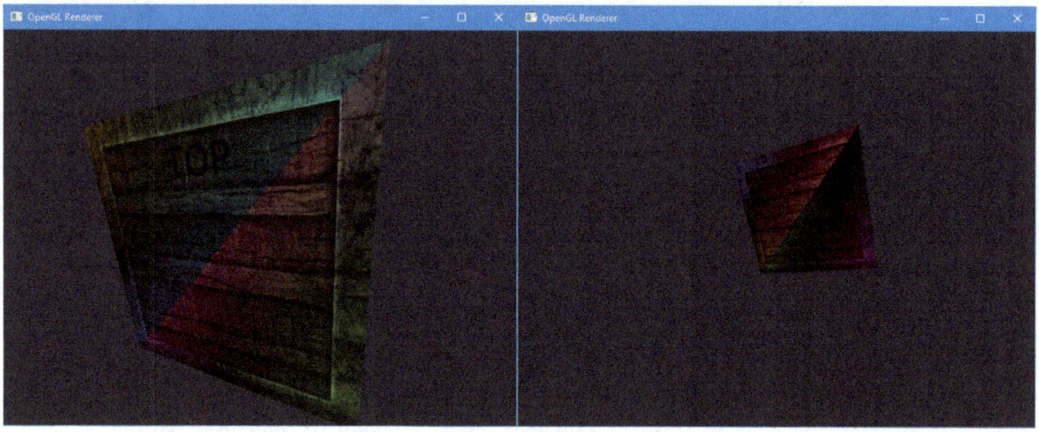

Figure 4.3: Perspective distortion and different distances when switching shaders

Both the boxes appear to be at a different distance too, plus we have some perspective distortion.

Using uniform buffers in Vulkan

The Vulkan way is like OpenGL but, again, with more initialization code.

The uniform buffer must be created as a separate buffer, like the vertex buffer, and allocated via the Vulkan Memory Allocator. In addition, a new descriptor set is required to make the buffer usable in the pipeline and the shaders.

The view and perspective matrices need to be allocated in different ways. Vulkan uses a memory copy to get the data into the GPU, so we add both matrices to a struct. Prior to the drawing process, the matrices inside the struct are updated with the new values. After the new values are set, the whole struct is copied to the uniform buffer on the graphics card, using only a single `memcpy` command.

Then, we bind the texture descriptor set and the new uniform buffer descriptor set before we issue the `vkCmdDraw()` command.

Vulkan knows another method to upload tiny amounts of data to the GPU: push constants. We will take only a quick look at them; the full implementation is available in the folder for `chapter 04`, `05_vulkan_push_constants` subfolder.

Using push constants in Vulkan

Vulkan push constants have two interesting limits, which make their usage somehow special:

- The minimal guaranteed size is 128 bytes
- Only one push constant block per shader is allowed

You have read the size limit correctly. That is not 128 KB or larger – only 128 bytes are guaranteed by the Vulkan standard. Some implementations may give you more space, but please do not rely on that and check the limit during runtime. The maximum size for the Vulkan push constants can be retrieved via the `vk-bootstrap` helper, introduced in *Initializing Vulkan via vk-bootstrap* section in *Chapter 3*; the value is stored in the properties of the physical device: `VkPhysicalDeviceLimits::maxPushConstantsSize`.

The push constants have another unique feature: they are not stored in some sort of buffer on the GPU, and no separate upload is required. The push constants can be set directly at any time in the drawing process, and the definitions of the stage(s) and the size are done when the Vulkan pipeline is created.

Summary

In this chapter, you learned about some of the methods to move data from your application to the graphics card so that shaders can use it and draw the triangles on the screen. While the data inside the vertex buffers changes for every vertex, uniform buffers and push constants enable you to upload tiny amounts of constant data to the shaders. This enables you to offload the transformation work (such as scaling, translating, or perspective changes) to the shader units on your graphics card. By using GLM for the vertex data, you avoid expensive transformations during the process of copying the vertex data to the GPU.

In *Chapter 5*, we will add some fancy UI elements to the rendering window. This will allow us to have critical data at hand, such as the frame rate or various timings inside the application. By using buttons, we are also able to switch options on and off using the mouse. For many operations, using a mouse is more convenient compared to remembering all the keys on the keyboard we may have mapped.

Practical sessions

As in the previous chapters, here are some additional suggestions on what to do after you finish reading this chapter:

- Add more vertices to the mockup model object, and create a fully textured, six-faced cube. Check for the face orientation of the single triangles, as they may be in the wrong direction and create holes in the cube. Also, watch out for the proper orientation of the texture (i.e., add some text to the texture and try to have it readable on all six faces). This will add a lot of duplicated code, though, but in *Part 3* of the book, we will load real models from files.

- Duplicate the model after creating a cube and try to transform and concatenate the vertex data to draw all models at once. You could create three or four cubes, translate them to some place in 3D space, and rotate them around their center. Check out the differences between local rotation and translation, and global rotation and translation, and observe the results if you change the order of operations.

Additional resources

For further reading, please check the following links:

- A tutorial on shaders: `https://learnopengl.com/Getting-started/Shaders`
- A curated list of shader-related resources: `https://github.com/vanrez-nez/awesome-glsl`

5

Adding Dear ImGui to Show Valuable Information

Welcome to *Chapter 5*! In the previous chapter, we took a close look at shaders, small programs running on the GPU that do the main work in the process of creating stunning 3D worlds on your screen. In this chapter, we will go from the internals of the drawing process to the visual side and create a user interface for both renderers.

Displaying 3D objects without any additional information is nice for a purely graphical demonstration, but an application should also give the user some kind of data about the objects visible on the screen. In addition, the application could display details about its internal state, such as the amount of resources used. On the other hand, the manipulation of object properties should also be possible without having to remember dozens of key combinations. UI elements such as buttons, sliders, or color selectors simplify the process of changing model data, enabling easy-to-use workflows, even for inexperienced users.

In this chapter, we will cover the following topics:

- What is Dear ImGui?
- Adding ImGui to the OpenGL and Vulkan renderers
- How to create an FPS counter
- Timing sections of your code and showing the results
- Adding UI elements to control the application

Creating a user interface for an application can be a challenging task. Drawing the characters in the correct place, adding UI elements, and also the possibility of adjusting values are only a small part of the work required to get a user interface done. Luckily, some ready-to-use variants are available. And one of them is Dear ImGui.

Technical requirements

For this chapter, you will need the OpenGL and/or Vulkan renderer code from *Chapter 4*.

What is Dear ImGui?

Dear ImGui, or **ImGui** for short, is a graphical user interface library for C++, using the pipelines of modern 3D APIs to render texts and elements in framebuffers. In addition, ImGui is self-contained, which means we do not need additional dependencies besides GLFW, OpenGL, and Vulkan. It is also platform-independent, so the application code still runs on both Windows and Linux.

To get a first impression, here is a screenshot of some of the elements of ImGui:

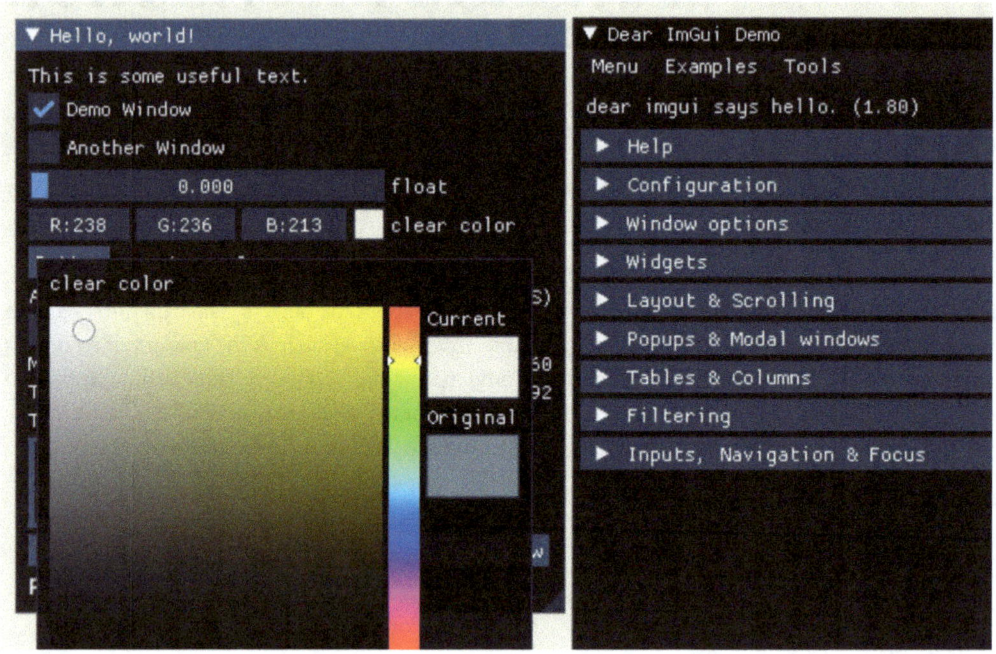

Figure 5.1: Some widgets of the Dear ImGui demo code

The ImGui code consists of three parts:

- The widget rendering
- The input backend
- The output backend

ImGui aims to create an identical look and feel across all supported operating systems, helper libraries, and rendering backends. To draw the widgets independently of the underlying system, the widget rendering functions are separated from the backends.

The function calls we use are only at the widget level. ImGui translates them to OS-level calls using the corresponding backends. So, both the input and the output backend must match the libraries we use in the application code. For our renderers, we need the GLFW input backend and the respective OpenGL or Vulkan output backends.

The separation of input and output backends is done for technical reasons. Libraries such as GLFW or the **Simple DirectMedia Layer** (**SDL**) are used for inputs such as a mouse or keyboard, to have the position of the mouse pointer available to click the UI elements or input text. Libraries such as OpenGL, Vulkan, or DirectX are only used to draw the UI elements on the screen. This split between input and output allows a great amount of flexibility in using ImGui, as it does not limit the libraries you choose or create additional dependencies between them.

Let's take a look at how we can integrate ImGui into our application.

Adding ImGui to the OpenGL and Vulkan renderers

To use ImGui in our code, we need a couple of files from the ImGui GitHub repository at `https://github.com/ocornut/imgui`

Download the following files to a folder named `imgui`:

- `imconfig.h`
- `imgui.cpp`
- `imgui.h`
- `imgui_draw.cpp`
- `imgui_internal.h`
- `imgui_tables.cpp`
- `imgui_widgets.cpp`
- `imstb_rectpack.h`
- `imstb_textedit.h`
- `imstb_truetype.h`

These downloaded files are the backend-independent code, containing the implementations of the widgets. We have to include them in our project for ImGui to work in general.

For the GLFW input backend, two additional files are required. Download these two files and put them into the `imgui` folder:

- `imgui_impl_glfw.cpp`
- `imgui_impl_glfw.h`

To include the GLFW backend, this line will be needed:

```
#include <imgui_impl_glfw.h>
```

You can find the code for this section in the `chapter05` folder's `01_opengl_ui` subfolder for OpenGL and `05_vulkan_ui` subfolder for Vulkan.

Let's take the first step to create a user interface for the application, by downloading and adding the header files to the code.

Adding the headers to the OpenGL renderer

To use ImGui in the OpenGL renderer, we need the OpenGL-specific output backend files. Download these files for the OpenGL renderer and add them to the `imgui` folder:

- `imgui_impl_opengl3.cpp`
- `imgui_impl_opengl3.h`
- `imgui_impl_opengl3_loader.h`

The `imgui_impl_opengl3_loader.h` file is like the **glad** loader we used in *Chapter 2* for the OpenGL renderer. Do not worry about the files being named after OpenGL 3 as OpenGL 4 is backward compatible with version 3. The following `#include` line with the OpenGL implementation header is required to work with ImGui:

```
#include <imgui_impl_opengl3.h>
```

Adding the headers to the Vulkan renderer

The Vulkan renderer also needs specific files to draw ImGui widgets. For Vulkan, download these two files to the `imgui` folder:

- `imgui_impl_vulkan.cpp`
- `imgui_impl_vulkan.h`

Vulkan uses no loader, like OpenGL, so these two files are all we need. The header files are the ones included in the C++ code using ImGui widgets:

```
#include <imgui_impl_vulkan.h>
```

CMake adjustments needed for ImGui

To allow the compiler to find the files, the `imgui` folder must be added to the `CMakeLists.txt` file in two places:

```
file(GLOB SOURCES
  ...
  model/*.cpp
  imgui/*.cpp
)
...
target_include_directories(Main … opengl model imgui)
```

The first change ensures that all the ImGui C++ files are compiled along with all the other code, so the final link to the executable finds all the function calls. The second change adds the header files to the search path, enabling us to use the header to be included without extra paths in our code.

Moving the shared data to the OGLRenderData header

To make the GLFW window, its width and height, and the number of drawn triangles available for the `UserInterface` class, we use the `OGLRenderData` struct.

Append these lines to the `OGLRenderData.h` file in the `opengl` folder:

```
struct OGLRenderData {
  GLFWwindow *rdWindow = nullptr;
  unsigned int rdWidth = 0;
  unsigned int rdHeight = 0;
  unsigned int rdTriangleCount = 0;
};
```

We also need the GLFW header in the `OGLRenderData.h` file as we'll use the `GLFWwindow` type here. Add it to the top, where the other include is as follows:

```
#include <GLFW/glfw3.h>
```

Next, add an instance of the `OGLRenderData` struct as a `private` member variable in the `OGLRenderer` class, in the `OGLRenderer.h` file:

```
    OGLRenderData mRenderData{};
```

The next part is a bit tricky: you need to catch all variable usage to compile the code. *Remove* the four private member variables from the `OGLRenderer` class:

```
    GLFWwindow* mWindow;
    unsigned int mWidth;
```

```
    unsigned int mHeight;
    int mTriangleCount = 0;
```

These four variables will be used from the new `mRenderData` variable, and no longer from the `OGLRenderer` class. Now *replace all* usages of the previous local variables with the new ones. As an example, all occurrences of the `mWindow` variable become `mRenderData.rdWindow`, everywhere in the `OGLRender.cpp` file.

Do the same search and replace for `mWidth`, `mHeight`, and `mTriangleCount`. These variables will become `mRenderData.rdWidth`, `mRenderData.rdHeight`, and `mRenderData.rdTriangleCount`.

Replacing the local variable usages with the `OLGRenderData` variables makes sure we can share them with other classes, such as the `UserInterface` class.

As the last step to show the UI, we have to add an instance of the `UserInterface` class to the OpenGL renderer and call the functions of that `UserInterface` instance.

Creating the UserInterface class

Instead of putting the UI code directly into the renderer calls, a new class will be added. It encapsulates the drawing; this keeps the main renderer code more readable. The values and data to be shown in the UI will be transferred via the `OGLRenderData` / `VkRenderData` struct to the class. This frees us from adding each new data element as a parameter to the calls.

For this walk-through, the OpenGL renderer code is used. The drawing calls for the Vulkan renderer are the same, but the initialization is quite complex. You can check it out in the example code in the `05_vulkan_ui` folder.

To start the new `UserInterface` class, add the `UserInterface.h` file in the `opengl` folder:

```
#pragma once
#include "OGLRenderData.h"
```

The first line is the header guard, as in every header we create. The second line includes our `OGLRenderData` struct, our generic transport method between the classes.

Now add the four `public` method declarations to the `UserInterface.h` file:

```
class UserInterface {
  public:
    void init(OGLRenderData &renderData);
    void createFrame(OGLRenderData &renderData);
    void render();
    void cleanup();
};
```

The `init()` function of the `UserInterface` class calls the ImGui functions to initialize the GLFW and OpenGL backends and `cleanup()` is called at the end of the program, to free all resources ImGui reserved. Calling `createFrame()` draws the ImGui widgets into an internal ImGui buffer. The `render()` function finally draws the internal buffer to our framebuffer and the widgets are visible on the screen.

> **Important note**
>
> ImGui draws all widgets on *every* frame, so the calls to `createFrame()` and `render()` must be included in the `draw()` call to display the UI. The `render()` call draws to the framebuffer at that specific state. So, it may happen that some objects overlay the ImGui widgets if `render()` is called too early.

Adding the implementation of the UserInterface class

Now let us complete the `UserInterface` class and add the `UserInterface.cpp` file in the `opengl` folder, starting with the headers:

```
#include <string>
#include <imgui_impl_glfw.h>
#include <imgui_impl_opengl3.h>
#include "UserInterface.h"
```

The `string` header is required as we will convert some numbers to C++ strings using the `std::to_string()` function. And, as ImGui is written in C, we will use the `c_str()` function of the C++ strings to retrieve the raw C strings. Next, the two ImGui backend headers are included, one for GLFW and one for OpenGL. The last header is from the `UserInterface` class itself.

Continue the `UserInterface` class with the code for the `init()` method. We use a reference of the `OGLRenderData` struct as a parameter to have the shared data available:

```
void UserInterface::init(OGLRenderData &renderData) {
  IMGUI_CHECKVERSION();
  ImGui::CreateContext();
  ImGui_ImplGlfw_InitForOpenGL(renderData.rdWindow, true);
  const char *glslVersion = "#version 460 core";
  ImGui_ImplOpenGL3_Init(glslVersion);
}
```

The calls to `IMGUI_CHECKVERSION()` and `ImGui::CreateContext()` are required from the ImGui side for proper initialization. The context created by the `ImGui::CreateContext()` function searches for a file named `imgui.ini`, containing the settings of the ImGui widgets that need to be available across application restarts. The `imgui.ini` file will be created by ImGui if it does not exist yet.

As an example, this information is stored in the `imgui.ini` file for the ImGui window named `Control`:

```
[Window] [Control]
Pos=60,60
Size=374,341
Collapsed=0
```

Next, the GLFW backend is initialized using `ImGui_ImplGlfw_InitForOpenGL()`. The first parameter is the GLFW window created in the `Window` class, taken from the `OGLRenderData` struct. The second parameter instructs ImGui to install its own keyboard/mouse callbacks. These callbacks will be chained, so any callbacks we install will still be called from ImGui.

The `glslVersion` C-string is used internally for the ImGui shaders. This string will be used as the first line in the shaders. We set it to the same value as the other shaders we use and use GLSL version 4.60 here. The last line initializes the OpenGL backend of ImGui.

To release the resources acquired by ImGui, the `cleanup()` method calls the shutdown functions of ImGui in the inverse order:

```
void UserInterface::cleanup() {
  ImGui_ImplOpenGL3_Shutdown();
  ImGui_ImplGlfw_Shutdown();
  ImGui::DestroyContext();
}
```

The first call ends the OpenGL backend, the second call the GLFW backend, and the last call finally frees the internal ImGui data.

Next, we add the `createFrame()` method to create the widgets and fill them with the data we hand over, using the `OGLRendeData` reference:

```
void UserInterface::createFrame(OGLRenderData &renderData) {
  ImGui_ImplOpenGL3_NewFrame();
  ImGui_ImplGlfw_NewFrame();
  ImGui::NewFrame();
```

These three calls create new frames in the two backends and the ImGui itself. They are needed every time we start a new ImGui draw call.

We continue with the creation of the overlay window from ImGui:

```
  ImGuiWindowFlags imguiWindowFlags = 0;
  ImGui::SetNextWindowBgAlpha(0.8f);
  ImGui::Begin("Control", nullptr, imguiWindowFlags);
```

The `imguiWindowFlags` variable is set to allow changing some of the properties of the ImGui window, such as disabling it to be moved or resized. The definition of the flags is left in the code for further experiments, see the *Practical sessions* section at the end of the chapter.

In the next call, the background transparency of the ImGui window is set. It is nice to see what happens behind the window, without having to move it first.

Calling `ImGui::Begin()` starts a new ImGui window. The name shown in the title bar of the ImGui window is given as the first parameter. We simply use `Control` here. A pointer to a bool could be used as the second parameter. ImGui updates the bool to `true` if the closing **X** is pressed. We do not want this signaling functionality here, so we set `nullptr` here. The window flags are given as the last parameter.

At this point, ImGui has created an internal window named `Control`, and all widgets created will be now drawn into this window. So, let us create the first widget:

```
ImGui::Text("Triangles:");
ImGui::SameLine();
ImGui::Text(
  std::to_string(renderData.rdTriangleCount).c_str());
```

The `ImGui::Text()` function creates a line with text on the next line. Normally, every text widget in ImGui is drawn on its own line. ImGui takes care of proper spacing. But there is an exception: in the second line, `ImGui::SameLine()` instructs ImGui to stay on the current line. Then, we take the triangle count, transferred via the `OGLRenderData` struct, convert it to `std::string`, and extract the C-style string from it, as ImGui does not understand the C++ string type.

Next, we add three more text widgets to show:

```
std::string windowDims =
  std::to_string(renderData.rdWidth) + "x" +
  std::to_string(renderData.rdHeight);
ImGui::Text("Window Dimensions:");
ImGui::SameLine();
ImGui::Text(windowDims.c_str());
```

In this widget, we read the width and height of the GLFW window from the `OGLRenderData` struct and create a single `std::string` from the two text lines.

Our last added widget is an example of how to get internal data from ImGui itself:

```
std::string imgWindowPos =
  std::to_string(static_cast<int>(
    ImGui::GetWindowPos().x)) + "/" +
std::to_string(static_cast<int>(
  ImGui::GetWindowPos().y));
```

```
    ImGui::Text("ImGui Window Position:");
    ImGui::SameLine();
    ImGui::Text(imgWindowPos.c_str());
```

Here, we read the position of the ImGui window itself and add it as output to the same window. This way, the position will be updated whenever we move the ImGui window.

Now we end drawing the current ImGui window:

```
    ImGui::End();
  }
```

The call to `ImGui::End()` tells ImGui to stop drawing widgets in the window. We could start another window using `ImGui::Begin()` from the start of the `createFrame()` method. The two windows would be usable independently in the application window.

To see all the windows and widgets ImGui created, we must call two of the ImGui functions in the `render()` method of the `UserInterface` class:

```
  void UserInterface::render() {
    ImGui::Render();
    ImGui_ImplOpenGL3_RenderDrawData(ImGui::GetDrawData());
  }
```

Up to this call, we have created only data structures containing windows and text widgets. The call to `ImGui::Render()` draws the windows and widgets internally into an ImGui buffer. The call to `ImGui_ImplOpenGL3_RenderDrawData()` copies the data of the internal framebuffer to our currently active framebuffer in the application. After these two calls, the UI will be drawn to our application window.

After the `UserInterface` class has been created, we also must make some changes to the rest of the code to call the methods of the class. First, we need to move the shared elements to the `OGLRenderData` header.

Adding the UserInterface class to the OpenGL renderer

To make the `UserInterface` class available for the renderer, add the `UserInterface.h` header file to the top of the `OGLRenderer.h` file:

```
  #include "UserInterface.h"
```

Create an instance of the `UserInterface` class as a `private` data member:

```
      UserInterface mUserInterface{};
```

Now we are just four calls away from the fresh and all-new ImGui window.

The first call is for the ImGui initialization. Add the call to the `init()` method of the `UserInterface` instance at the end of the `init()` method in the `OGLRenderer.cpp` file, right before the last line of the method, containing the return from the method with the Boolean value `true`:

```
  ...
  mUserInterface.init(mRenderData);
  return true;
}
```

The second and third calls are for the rendering of the ImGui widgets. Add the calls to `createFrame()` and `render()` at the end of the `draw()` method of the `OGLRenderer.cpp` file:

```
  ...
  mFramebuffer.drawToScreen();
  mUserInterface.createFrame(mRenderData);
  mUserInterface.render();
}
```

The last call to add is the `cleanup()` call of the `UserInterface` instance. Add it as the first call in the `cleanup()` method of the `OGLRenderer` class, to destroy the objects again in the reverse order of their creation:

```
  mUserInterface.cleanup();
```

If you compile the code now and run the application, you will see a small ImGui window inside the application window, in front of the rotating textured box:

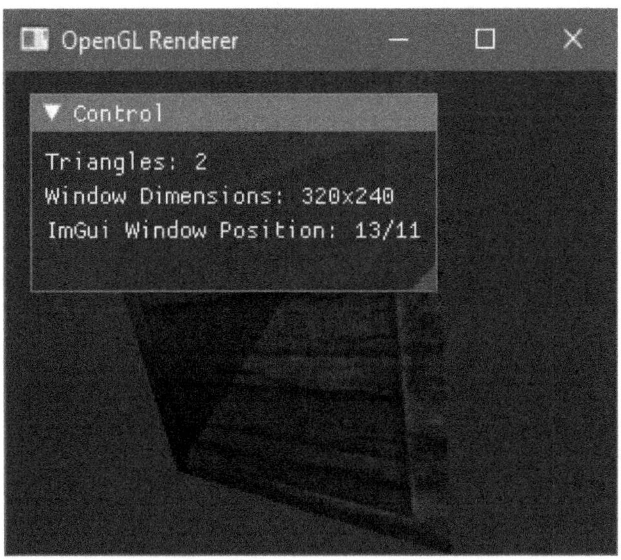

Figure 5.2: The ImGui window and the created widgets

You can collapse the window (the small down arrow on the left of **Control**), move it around by holding the left mouse button when clicking on the ImGui window, or resize it by grabbing the triangle at the bottom right of the window. The small window is controlled entirely by ImGui and is updated every frame with any new data. Try to move the ImGui window around, resize, or maximize the application window. This will change the data inside the ImGui window.

Having some internal data such as the window size is nice, but other data would be more of the user's interest. One of those data points is the **frames per second** (**FPS**). This number gives the number of frames the application can draw within a second, and the higher the number is, the smoother any movement inside the application window. So let us add an FPS counter to the application, showing us how many frames we draw every second.

Creating an FPS counter

To measure the time it takes to draw a frame, we need a stable time source. Luckily, GLFW has a function we could use for our virtual stopwatch: `glfwGetTime()`. This function returns the number of seconds since GLFW was initialized as a double type. The resolution of the returned value is system-dependent, but GLFW should use the time with the highest resolution. We should get the time down to micro- or nanoseconds.

We start by using GLFW as a simple timer.

Using GLFW as a simple timer

To measure the time the renderer needs to draw the objects to the screen, we save the time given by `glfwGetTime()` at the start of the `draw()` method. To be able to calculate the full frame time, including the code in the `Window` class, we also store the starting time of the previous draw in a static variable. Then, we use a new variable in the `OGLRenderData` struct to transfer the difference of both time values to the `UserInterface` class. This difference is simply converted to FPS with the inverse function.

The example code for the FPS timer is in the `02_opengl_ui_fps` and `06_vulkan_ui_fps` folders.

As the first step to measure the frame time in the `Renderer` class, add the new variable to the `OGLRenderData` struct in the `OGLRenderData.h` file, below the other variables of that struct:

```
float rdFrameTime = 0.0f;
```

Using a `float` variable instead of a `double` variable here to store the difference and the values is okay. We do not need the FPS value with super-high precision.

Next, add the two time-taking calls to the `draw()` method of the `OGLRenderer` class, in `OGLRenderer.cpp`. The time is taken at the start of the drawing:

```
void OGLRenderer::draw() {
  static float prevFrameStartTime = 0.0;
  float frameStartTime = glfwGetTime();
```

We save the current time in a static variable to store these intermediate values across multiple frames.

At the end of the `draw()` method, the difference is calculated:

```
  mRenderData.rdFrameTime =
    frameStartTime - prevFrameStartTime;
  prevFrameStartTime = frameStartTime;
}
```

The result is stored in the `mRenderData.rdFrameTime` variable and the current value is saved in the `prevFrameStartTime` variable for the next loop.

Adding the values to the user interface

To show the new values in the ImGui window, we must add some lines to the `UserInterface` class. First, add two new private data members in the `UserInterface.h` file in the `opengl` folder:

```
  private:
    float framesPerSecond = 0.0f;
    float averagingAlpha = 0.96f;
```

The `framesPerSecond` variable will contain the FPS value calculated out of the frame time. To get a more stable number, a so-called moving average will be used.

The moving average adds only a fraction of the new values to the current FPS counter; the major part will be taken from the current value of the FPS counter variable. This method "flattens" out spikes with much more or much less frame time a bit, resulting in a more stable number in the ImGui field with the FPS counter. The `averagingAlpha` variable controls how much of the current `framesPerSecond` value will be used. Here, 96%, while new values will be added with only 4%.

Next, add these lines to the `UserInterface.cpp` file in the `opengl` folder, after the `ImGui::Begin()` function call for the new window:

```
  static float newFps = 0.0f;
  if (renderData.rdFrameTime > 0.0) {
    newFps = 1.0f / renderData.rdFrameTime;
  }
```

We store the value for the FPS counter to be added in a static variable, to have it regardless of the next `if` block. A check for a zero frame time is needed because a value close to zero would lead to a high number in the division, or even a division by zero could happen, terminating the program. But if the frame time from the renderer is greater than zero, we calculate the inverse and save it in the `newFps` variable.

Now we add the moving average calculation:

```
framesPerSecond = (averagingAlpha * framesPerSecond) +
  (1.0f - averagingAlpha) * newFps;
```

Here, we multiply the current `framesPerSecond` value with the averaging value, while the newly calculated FPS value is multiplied by the result of 1 minus the averaging value, and both results are added. This calculation ensures that higher or lower values for the new frames per second will affect value in the the `framesPerSecond` variable only by a small amount.

The FPS value is added to the window with a new text line:

```
ImGui::Text("FPS:");
ImGui::SameLine();
ImGui::Text(std::to_string(framesPerSecond).c_str());
ImGui::Separator();
```

The ImGui text for the FPS value is created like the previous ImGui text lines: we start a new `ImGui::Text()` function with the `FPS:` string and append the converted value of the `framesPerSecond` variable. The `ImGui::Separator()` function at the end adds a horizontal line below the FPS text, separating it from the already drawn number of triangles, window dimension, and ImGui window position.

After compiling and starting the code, you should see a window like this:

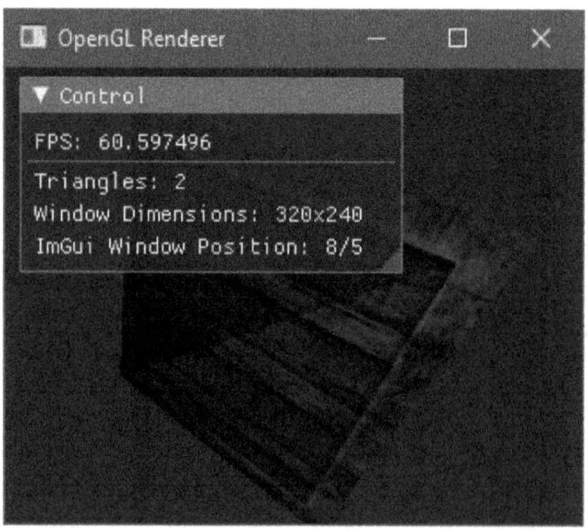

Figure 5.3: The OpenGL renderer with the FPS counter

The FPS value may be as low as 60 on a normal system. You may also get a bit more, such as 144 on some high-end systems. The reason for this frame rate limit is the active vertical sync (VSync) in the `Window` class, synchronizing the `draw()` calls to the refresh rate of your monitor. Some drivers may ignore the VSync setting in the code, and you'll get thousands of frames per second for the two triangles we draw to the screen. So do not be alarmed if your value differs.

To see more than just the FPS in the UI, such as how much time single functions or longer slices of the code take, we need to take the time between the start and the end of that code too. For easier handling, we will add a separate `Timer` class.

Timing sections of your code and showing the results

Our new `Timer` class uses the C++ `chrono` library, a specialized part of C++ dealing with clocks, durations, and points in time.

You can find the example code of this section in the `03_opengl_ui_timer` and `07_vulkan_ui_timer` folders.

Adding the Timer class

Create the new `Timer` class by adding the `Timer.h` file in the `tools` folder:

```
#pragma once
#include <chrono>
```

After the header guard, we include the `chrono` header. The elements from the `chrono` header can be found in the `std::chrono` namespace.

Next, add the `Timer` class itself in the `Timer.h` file:

```
class Timer {
  public:
    void start();
    float stop();
  private:
    bool mRunning = false;
    std::chrono::time_point<std::chrono::steady_clock>
      mStartTime{};
};
```

The `Timer` class has two `public` methods: the `start()` method will start the timer, and the `stop()` method will stop the timer, returning the time elapsed since the call to `start()` as a float.

The implementation of the `Timer` class is in the `Timer.cpp` file in the `tools` folder:

```
#include "Timer.h"
void Timer::start() {
  if (mRunning) {
    return;
  }
  mRunning = true;
  mStartTime = std::chrono::steady_clock::now();
}
```

After including the class header, we define the `start()` method. To avoid errors due to multiple `start()` calls in the code, we first check for an already running timer. If the timer did not run, we set the `mRunning` flag and take the current time from the system.

The second method of the `Timer` class follows:

```
float Timer::stop() {
  if (!mRunning) {
    return 0;
  }
  mRunning = false;
  auto stopTime = std::chrono::steady_clock::now();
  float timerMilliSeconds =
    std::chrono::duration_cast<std::chrono::microseconds>
    (stopTime - mStartTime).count() / 1000.0f;
  return timerMilliSeconds;
}
```

In the `stop()` method, we check again for a running timer to avoid trouble taking the time from a timer stopped before. After this check, we clear the `mRunning` flag and take the time from the system again. Then, we calculate the difference between the time our timer was stopped and the time it was started. To have a higher resolution of time difference, we take the duration in microseconds, but we divide it by 1,000 to get the millisecond value from the result.

Measuring time with the `Timer` class needs a couple of adjustments to the `OGLRenderer` and `UserInterface` classes, along with new variables in the `OGLRenderData` struct.

Integrating the new Timer class into the renderer

For the `OGLRenderer` class, add the `Timer` header to the `OGLRenderer.h` file:

```
#include "Timer.h"
```

Then, define a new `private` data member of the `Timer` type, that is, for taking the time of the ImGui window and widget generation:

```
    Timer mUIGenerateTimer{};
```

Surround the piece of code to time with the `start()` and `stop()` calls to the new timer:

```
  mUIGenerateTimer.start();
  mUserInterface.createFrame(mRenderData);
  mRenderData.rdUIGenerateTime = mUIGenerateTimer.stop();
```

We save the result to the `OGLRenderData` struct in the `OGLRenderData.h` file:

```
  float rdUIGenerateTime = 0.0f;
```

To show the value in the ImGui window, we have to add a new text line to the `createFrame()` call of the `UserInterface` class:

```
  ImGui::Text("UI Generation Time:");
  ImGui::SameLine();
  ImGui::Text(std::to_string
    (renderData.rdUIGenerateTime).c_str());
  ImGui::SameLine();
  ImGui::Text("ms");
```

We start a new text line in the first `ImGui::Text()` function, append the C-style string from the transformed time taken from the timer, and append the `"ms"` string to state the time is taken in milliseconds.

You may add more timers and separate the section containing the timer values from the other ImGui widgets using `ImGui::Separator()` calls. The GitHub example uses four more timers, and it looks like this:

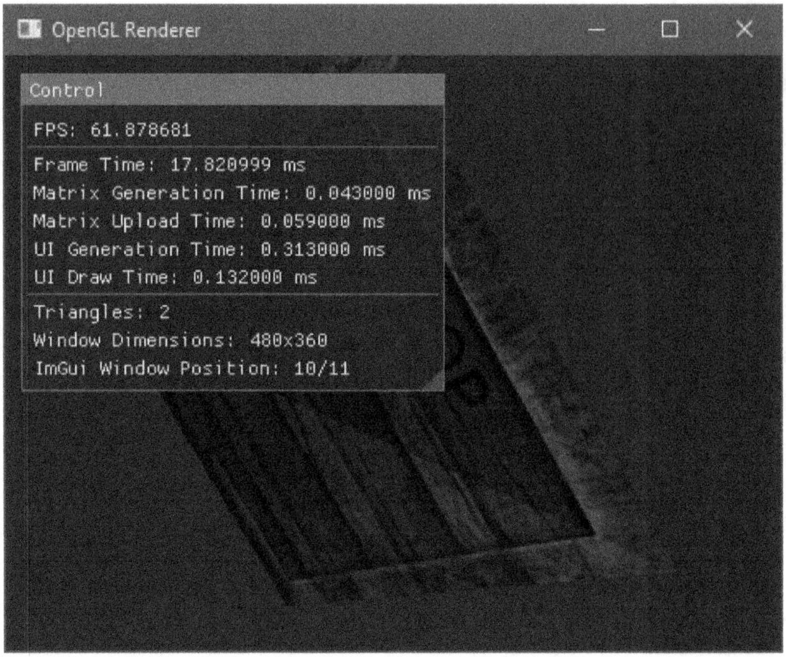

Figure 5.4: OpenGL renderer with FPS counter and five different timings

In the example code of the GitHub repository, some timings were added. The code measures the time of the creation and update of the matrices in the `draw()` call, plus the time it takes to upload the matrices to the uniform buffers in the GPU. In addition to the ImGui window and widget generation time, the example also measures the time it takes to draw the ImGui data to the framebuffer.

In the last section, we will add elements to control parts of the application's behavior.

Adding UI elements to control the application

Having values such as the FPS counter of the timers shown in the ImGui window is nice, but ImGui is also capable of sending input to the application. This sending of input enables us to add control elements to the ImGui window and change the values of our running program, without the need to recompile or remember key mappings.

The example code for this last section is in the `04_opengl_ui_control` and `08_vulkan_ui_control` folders.

To see the generic principle of input controls in ImGui, let's create a simple example: a checkbox that toggles a Boolean value.

Adding a checkbox

Create the checkbox widget in the `UserInterface` class by adding these lines to the `createFrame()` method of the `UserInterface.cpp` file between the ImGui window position text output widget and the `ImGui::End()` call:

```
static bool checkBoxChecked = false;
ImGui::Checkbox("Check Me", &checkBoxChecked);

if (checkBoxChecked) {
  ImGui::SameLine();
  ImGui::PushStyleColor(ImGuiCol_Text,
    IM_COL32(0,255,0,255));
  ImGui::Text("Yes");
  ImGui::PopStyleColor();
}
```

In the first line, we define a `static` Boolean variable called `checkBoxChecked`. Due to declaring it `static`, the variable will remember its value across different invocations of the `createFrame()` method. The `ImGui::Checkbox()` call creates a new checkbox widget named `"Check Me"`, requiring a pointer to a `bool` variable as the second parameter. We use the address of the static `checkBoxChecked` variable here.

ImGui updates the `checkBoxChecked` variable with the status of the check mark inside the checkbox, setting the variable to true if we set the check mark, and setting the variable to `false` after the check mark has been cleared.

Next, we check the value of the `checkBoxChecked` variable, and if the value is `true`, we add another text widget on the same line as the checkbox: the green **Yes**. To change the color of the text, set the color using `ImGui::PushStyleColor()` and reset it with an `ImGui::PopStyleColor()` call. Between these two calls, all text widgets created with `ImGui::Text()` will be drawn in green.

The resulting checkbox will look like this:

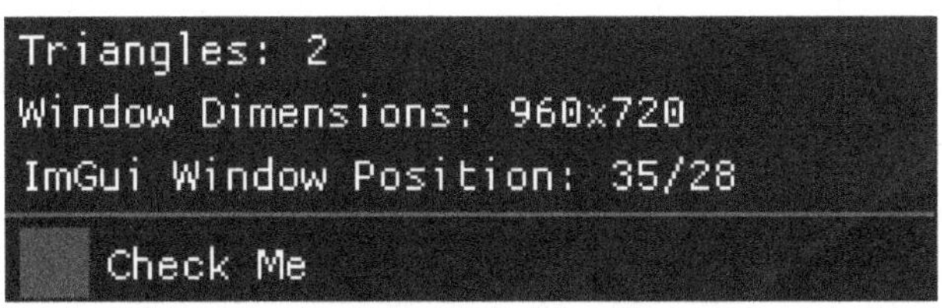

Figure 5.5: Unchecked checkbox

And the toggled text will look like this:

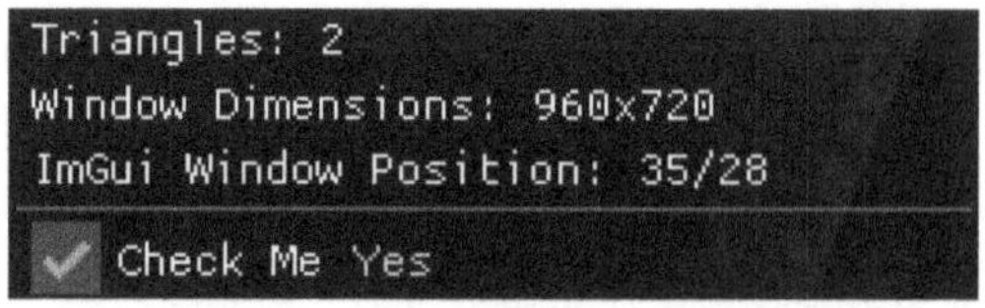

Figure 5.6: Checked checkbox

Adding only a changeable text field is a good start. Now, let us add two more control elements: a button and a slider. The button reacts to a left mouse button click, and the slider gives us a choice to choose a value out of a self-defined range.

Adding a button to switch between the shaders

To switch between the basic and the changed shader, we use the spacebar as a toggle key. Using an ImGui button widget, we can also switch the shaders with a mouse click, in addition to the spacebar.

Changing the behavior of the shader switching needs the same adjustments we needed in the *Moving the shared data to the OGLRenderData.h* section. We have to move the private `mUseChangedShader` member variable from the `OGLRenderer.h` file to the `rdUseChangedShader` shared variable in the `OGLRenderData.h` file.

So, add this line to the `OGLRenderData` struct in the `OGLRenderData.h` file:

```
bool rdUseChangedShader = false;
```

And *remove* this line from the `private` members in the `OGLRenderer.h` file:

```
bool mUseChangedShader = false;
```

Plus, all usages of `mUseChangedShader` in the `OGLRenderer` class have to be changed to the new `mRenderData.rdUseChangedShader` value. The `mUseChangedShader` variable is used only in the `toggleShader()` and `draw()` methods of the `OGLRenderer` class. This is a quick task.

Having the variable change in place, we can add another ImGui widget to the `UserInterface` class. Add these lines right below the checkbox widget in the `createFrame()` method:

```
if (ImGui::Button("Toggle Shader")){
  renderData.rdUseChangedShader =
    !renderData.rdUseChangedShader;
}
ImGui::SameLine();
if (!renderData.rdUseChangedShader) {
  ImGui::Text("Basic Shader");
} else {
```

```
    ImGui::Text("Changed Shader");
  }
```

The call to `ImGui::Button()` returns the Boolean value `true` whenever it is clicked, and `false` if it is not clicked. This behavior enables us to toggle the `renderData.rdUseChangedShader` shader variable directly when checking the button for being clicked. After the check for a mouse click, we stay on the same line and output the text **Basic Shader** or **Changed Shader**, depending on the shader variable, giving us direct feedback on which of the two shaders is used to render the textured box.

Adding a slider to control the field of view

As the third control element, we will add a slider. Using a slider, you can choose a value from a range between a minimum and a maximum value – perfect for the field of view of our application now.

The **Field of View**, abbreviated to **FOV**, is the part of the scene you see on the screen. Usual FOV values in games are around 90°, which is about ¼ of the entire scene around you. Widening the field of view gives you a larger overview of what happens to the left and right of you, but narrows the upward and downward view. In addition, a large field of view produces visible distortions on the left and right sides of the screen, caused by the perspective correction in the rendering process. Narrowing the field of view lets you "zoom in" to a small part of the screen, just like you are looking through a telescope.

To use the slider, add a new variable to the `OGLRenderData` struct in the `OGLRenderData.h` file:

```
int rdFieldOfView = 90;
```

We initialize the FOV variable with a reasonable value – in this case, `90` for 90°.

Next, we need to remove the hardcoded value from the `glm::perspective()` call in the `draw()` method of the `OGLRenderer` class:

```
mProjectionMatrix = glm::perspective(glm::radians
  (static_cast<float>(mRenderData.rdFieldOfView)),
  static_cast<float>(mRenderData.rdWidth) /
  static_cast<float>(mRenderData.rdHeight), 0.1f, 10.0f);
```

Earlier, the first parameter of `glm::perspective()` was set to `90`. Now, we are moving that value to a variable, `mRenderData.rdFieldOfView`, which is accessible from the `OGLRenderer` and `UserInterface` classes. Now add the slider widget to `UserInterface.cpp`, that is, below the shader switch button:

```
ImGui::Text("Field of View");
ImGui::SameLine();
ImGui::SliderInt("##FOV", &renderData.rdFieldOfView,
  40, 150);
```

We start again with a text widget and append the slider on the same line. The double hash in front of the first parameter, the name of the slider, disables the display of the first parameter as trailing text, appended to the widget. The second parameter is a pointer to the value that will be changed if the slider is moved, and the third and the last parameters are the minimum value at the left end of the slider and the maximum value at the right end of the slider.

Running the application now should result in something like this screen:

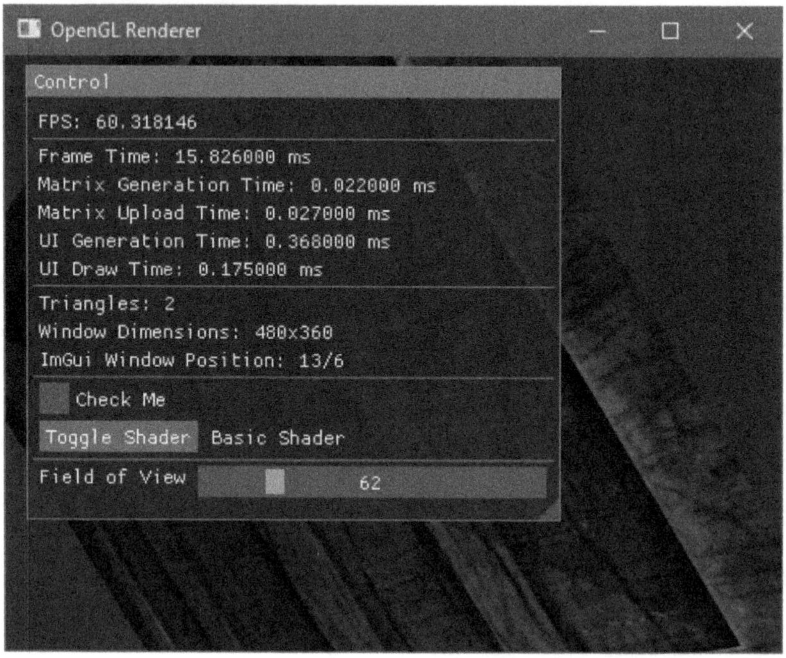

Figure 5.7: OpenGL renderer with a shader toggle button and FOV slider

Clicking the button will switch between the two shaders, in addition to the spacebar handling added before. And moving around the FOV slider will "zoom" the textured box in and out, resulting in a large, square box toward the minimal field of view value and a small, distorted box toward the maximal value.

That is all for the basic steps with ImGui. The other widgets follow the same principles as the checkbox, the button, and the slider: you set a name to identify them and a pointer to the value(s) to be changed on user interaction. You may check out the widget demo file in the GitHub repository – see the *Additional resources* section.

Summary

In this chapter, you learned how to add ImGui to the application to create a simple, widget-based UI, enabling you to output valuable data from your application, such as the FPS counter and various timings of code passages and functions. You also learned how to use ImGui widgets as input elements to control your application using a mouse.

A large variety of ImGui widgets is available already in the official GitHub repository, and many more have been created and contributed by users around the world. So, if you need a widget for some kind of UI task, there's a chance such a widget is already available and waiting to be used.

In the next chapter, we take a closer look at vector and matrix data types and the operations between them using GLM. Having the operations at hand, without the need to define them for all data types, makes our lives much easier. We will peek into the mathematical background of some operations to understand what happens in the code and in the shaders if these operations are used.

Practical sessions

Here are some additional suggestions to implement after you have finished reading:

- Adjust the ImGui window properties by using the window flags to disable properties such as the collapsing of the window, or the movement of it, and watch the result. You can find all supported flags in the `imgui.h` file.
- Change the checkbox to enable or disable vertical sync. This may be a bit tricky, as the `UserInterface` class may have no direct access to all the data you need. One idea to achieve this VSync change is toggling a Boolean variable in the `OGLRenderData` struct as a flag when the checkbox has been clicked and handling the change of this flag in the `draw()` method of the renderer.
- Add additional output to the ImGui window, such as the contents of the perspective and view matrix. You have to move them to the `OGLRenderData` / `VkRenderData` struct to access them from the `UserInterface` class. GLM has a `glm::to_string()` function, which works like `std::to_string()`. Watch the changes during the rotation of the textured box and during the FOV change.

Additional resources

- The Dear ImGui home page: `https://www.dearimgui.org`
- The Dear ImGui GitHub repository: `https://github.com/ocornut/imgui`
- A Dear ImGui widget demo: `https://jnmaloney.github.io/WebGui/imgui.html`

Part 2: Mathematics Roundup

In this part, we will cover the basic mathematical elements of vectors and matrices. Both element types are important to draw and manipulate objects in the virtual world. In addition, you will be introduced to quaternions and splines, two complex mathematical element types that will be used for advanced object manipulation.

In this part, we will cover the following chapters:

- *Chapter 6, Understanding Vector and Matrix*
- *Chapter 7, A Primer on Quaternions and Splines*

6
Understanding Vector and Matrix

Welcome to *Chapter 6*! In the previous chapter, we added a simple UI with elements to show the status of the program and timings for some of the functions, plus some simple controls to change the behavior of the program.

In this chapter, we will explore both the mathematical elements and the computer data types vector and matrix. We start with a review of the basic properties of each type and the operations between the same data types, as well as operations between vectors and matrices. The focus here is on the execution of these operations using the **OpenGL Mathematics** (**GLM**) library, as the library does all the operations we need with simple function calls.

At the end of the chapter, a practical exercise on matrix and vector operations follows: we will add a freely rotating and freely moving camera to the virtual world, both in the OpenGL and Vulkan renderer, allowing us to view objects from every angle.

In this chapter, we will cover the following topics:

- A review of the vector and its operations
- A review of the matrix and its operations
- Adding a camera to the renderer
- Adding camera movement

Technical requirements

For this chapter, you will need the following:

- The OpenGL and Vulkan renderer code from *Chapter 5*
- Basic mathematical understanding of vectors and matrices

A review of the vector and its operations

A **vector** is the most important element of any 3D renderer. Vectors are used to store the position, color, and texture coordinates for all vertices of all triangles we draw. In addition, we use vectors to define static camera parameters.

A vector can be seen as a mathematical object with two independent properties:

- A direction, from the start point to the end point
- A length, or magnitude

Let us recap some basics about vectors.

Representations of vectors

The usual representation is a simple arrow, starting somewhere in the coordinate system. All the vectors in *Figure 6.1* represent the same vector, as they all have the same directions and lengths, even if they do not share the same start and end points:

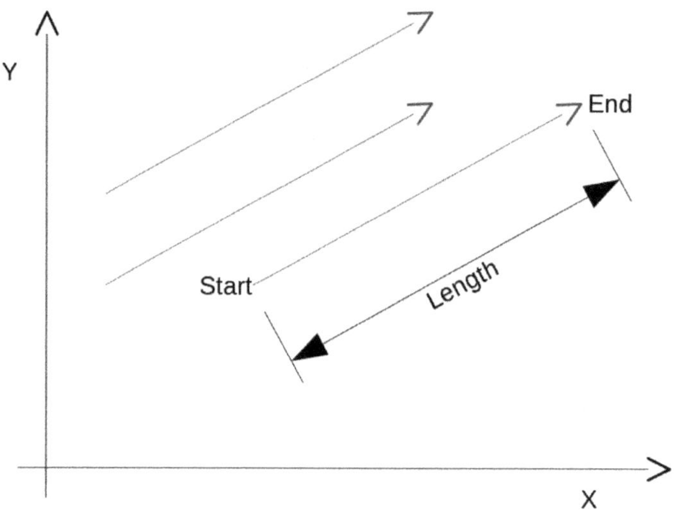

Figure 6.1: Graphical representations of a 2D vector

For a better visualization, think of every vector starting at the origin of the coordinate system. The origin is the point in the coordinate system where all the coordinates are `0`, so for a 2D coordinate system, this is the point at (`0, 0`), and for a 3D coordinate system, this is the point at (`0, 0, 0`). This maps all vector representations into one, and the end point for all these vectors is the same point in the coordinate system.

Figure 6.2 shows a few different vectors. All vectors with the same values are represented by the same arrow, while different vector values result in different arrows:

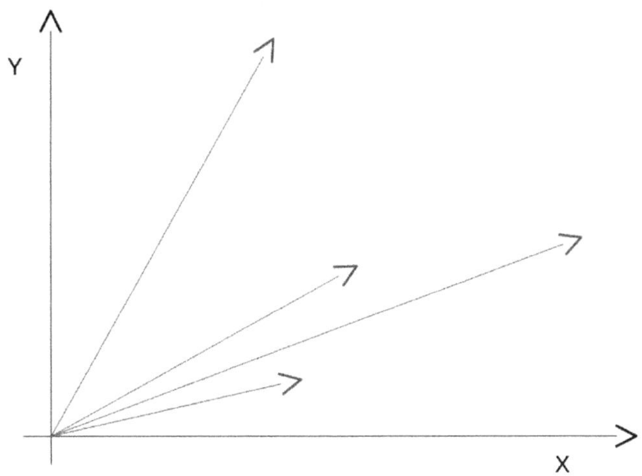

Figure 6.2: All 2D vectors start at the origin of the coordinate system

The mathematical representation is a lowercase letter with an arrow above it, and round brackets containing its components. In the following example, the vector v_1 represents a 2D vector, while the vector v_2 represents a 3D vector:

$$\vec{v}_1 = (9.5, 3.2)$$
$$\vec{v}_2 = (-1, 11,7)$$

The technical representation of the vector data type stores the differences between the end and the start point in every coordinate. This allows us to reconstruct the mathematical representation from the values saved in the data type. In GLM, these data vectors may have the following representation:

```
glm::vec2 v1 = glm::vec2(9.5f, 3.2f);
glm::ivec3 v2 = glm::ivec3(-1, 11, 7);
```

The `v1` vector uses the float version of a 2D vector, `glm::vec2`, while the `v2` vector uses the integer version of a 3D vector, `glm::ivec3`.

Adding and subtracting vectors

A vector addition is just an addition of the components in the same position, while vector subtraction is a component-wise subtraction. Because we need to add or subtract the components of the same index position in the vector, only vectors with the same number of components can be used for addition and subtraction. Here, you can see the addition and the subtraction of the 3D vectors, *a* and *b*:

$$\vec{a} + \vec{b} = \begin{pmatrix} a_x \\ a_y \\ a_z \end{pmatrix} + \begin{pmatrix} b_x \\ b_y \\ b_z \end{pmatrix} = \begin{pmatrix} a_x + b_x \\ a_y + b_y \\ a_z + b_z \end{pmatrix}$$

$$\vec{a} - \vec{b} = \begin{pmatrix} a_x \\ a_y \\ a_z \end{pmatrix} - \begin{pmatrix} b_x \\ b_y \\ b_z \end{pmatrix} = \begin{pmatrix} a_x - b_x \\ a_y - b_y \\ a_z - b_z \end{pmatrix}$$

GLM has overloaded the + and - operators for the vector data types, resulting in a simple way to add two vectors or subtract one from another:

```
glm::vec3 a = glm::vec3(1.0f, 4.0f, 3.0f);
glm::vec3 b = glm::vec3(2.0f, 1.0f, 2.0f);
glm::vec3 added = a + b; // (3.0f, 5.0f, 5.0f)
glm::vec3 subst = a - b; // (-1.0f, 3.0, 1.0f)
```

We can work with vectors in the same way as we work with the basic data types and add or subtract two vectors as we would add integers or floats.

Calculating the length of a vector

From a vector's representation, we can read the differences between the start and end points but not the length. If we work in a Cartesian coordinate system, where the coordinates are perpendicular to each other, we could make use of the Pythagorean theorem to obtain the length, by getting the square root of the squares of the components added up. Here is an example of the length calculation for the 2D vector, *c*, and the 3D vector, *d*:

$$|\vec{c}| = \sqrt{c_x^2 + c_y^2}$$

$$|\vec{d}| = \sqrt{d_x^2 + d_y^2 + d_z^2}$$

In order to refer to the length of a vector, we use the notation of adding vertical bars around the name of the vector – for example, $|v_1|$

GLM has a separate function to calculate the length:

```
float l1 = glm::length(v1);
float l2 = glm::length(v2);
```

> **Important note**
>
> Using `v1.length()` is *not* the correct way to get the mathematical length of a vector. This is a common error. The `length()` function returns only the number of components in the vector.

Zero and unit vectors

The zero vector and the unit vector are important vector variants we should understand, as they play an important role in virtual 3D worlds.

The **zero vector** has a length of zero, thus no length at all. Without a length, there is also no direction – the direction of a zero vector is not defined. In 2D, a zero vector is written as `(0, 0)`, and in 3D, it is written as `(0, 0, 0)`. It is important to distinguish between the center of a Cartesian coordinate system and the zero vector. Here, we mean to say the following:

- The center of a Cartesian coordinate system is a point at the coordinates `(0,0)`
- A zero vector `(0,0)` is a vector with a length of zero

The second type, the **unit vector**, has a length of exactly one. It is used in many operations where we are required to specify only the direction of a vector and don't need the length.

An **axis vector** is a special variant of a unit vector, where only one of the two or three components of the vector is `1` while all other components are `0`. This kind of unit vector represents one unit on the respective axis in the coordinate system, depending on the component set to `1`.

These are examples of the zero vector, a generic unit vector with a length of `1`, and a unit vector along an axis, respectively:

$$\vec{v}_{zero} = \left(0.0, 0.0, 0.0\right)$$

$$\vec{v}_{unit} = \left(0.218218, 0.436436, 0.872872\right)$$

$$\vec{v}_{axis} = \left(1.0, 0.0, 0.0\right)$$

Using GLM, the three variants would look like this:

```
glm::vec3 zero = glm::vec3(0.0f, 0.0f, 0.0f);
glm::vec3 unit = glm::vec3(0.218218f, 0.436436f, 0.872872f);
glm::vec3 axis = glm::vec3(1.0f, 0.0f, 0.0f);
```

In the preceding code, the vector named `zero` is a zero vector; the vector named `unit` has an approximate length of `1` (depending upon rounding errors); and the vector named `axis` is a unit vector pointing only in the direction of the *x* axis.

Vector normalization

The unit vector in the previous code example may look interesting, and the question will arise about how we get those numbers and the length of exactly `1`. This is done by normalizing the vector, thus resizing the vector to the length of `1`, and making a unit vector out of it. Mathematically normalizing a vector is a two-step process:

- First, we get the length of the vector
- Then, we divide each of the vector elements by the length

This is an example of the normalization of the vector *e*:

$$l_e = \sqrt{e_x^{\,2} + e_y^{\,2} + e_z^{\,2}}$$

$$e_x = \frac{e_x}{l_e}\ ;\ e_y = \frac{e_y}{l_e}\ ;\ e_z = \frac{e_z}{l_e}$$

Having GLM at hand, this can be done as a single operation:

```
glm::vec3 v3 = glm::vec3(1.0f, 2.0f, 4.0f);
glm::vec3 unit = glm::normalize(v3);
```

The call to `glm::normalize()` does both mathematical operations for us and will scale the `v3` input vector to a unit vector.

Vector multiplication

As the last operation, we will look at multiplication. For the vector data type, a whole family of multiplications is defined.

Scaling and element-wise multiplication

To scale a vector, each component is multiplied by the same scalar value. Scaling changes the length of a vector, but not its direction. As an example, we multiply the vector *g* with the scalar value *s*:

$$s * \vec{g} = s * \begin{pmatrix} g_x \\ g_y \\ g_z \end{pmatrix} = \begin{pmatrix} s * g_x \\ s * g_y \\ s * g_z \end{pmatrix}$$

Multiplying each component of a vector with different values results in scaling the vector non-uniformly. Such a multiplication will not only change the length of the vector but it will also change the direction of the vector. Here, you can see the vector multiplication of the vectors *f* and *g*:

$$\vec{f} * \vec{g} = \begin{pmatrix} f_x \\ f_y \\ f_z \end{pmatrix} * \begin{pmatrix} g_x \\ g_y \\ g_z \end{pmatrix} = \begin{pmatrix} f_x * g_x \\ f_y * g_y \\ f_z * g_z \end{pmatrix}$$

The inner product or dot product

The **inner product** (the so-called **dot product**) outputs a single number instead of a vector. For the dot product, all elements are multiplied pairwise, and the results are added up.

The following example shows the calculation of the dot product of the vectors *h* and *l*:

$$\vec{h} \cdot \vec{l} = \begin{pmatrix} h_x \\ h_y \\ h_z \end{pmatrix} \cdot \begin{pmatrix} l_x \\ l_y \\ l_z \end{pmatrix} = h_x l_x + h_y l_y + h_z l_z$$

The result is also the cosine of the angle between the vectors, but the cosine needs normalized vectors for the correct result, or the result must be divided by the length of both vectors.

The cosine of the angle between vectors *h* and *l* is calculated like this:

$$\vec{h} \cdot \vec{l} = |\vec{h}||\vec{l}| cos(\phi)$$

$$cos(\phi) = \frac{\vec{h} \cdot \vec{l}}{|\vec{h}||\vec{l}|}$$

The outer product or cross product

The last multiplication, the **outer product** or **cross product**, is defined only for 3D vectors. The result of the cross product is another vector, standing perpendicular to both input vectors, which means it has an angle of 90 degrees to both of the other vectors. For 2D vectors, the cross product can be obtained, but the result will be a 3D vector that is perpendicular to the plane in which the 2D vectors exist. The cross product m of the vectors *k* and *l* is defined in this formula:

$$\vec{m} = \vec{k} \times \vec{l} = \begin{pmatrix} k_y l_z - k_z l_y \\ k_z l_x - k_x l_z \\ k_x l_y - k_y l_x \end{pmatrix}$$

To calculate the cross product of two 3D vectors, *k* and *l*, use the rules shown here:

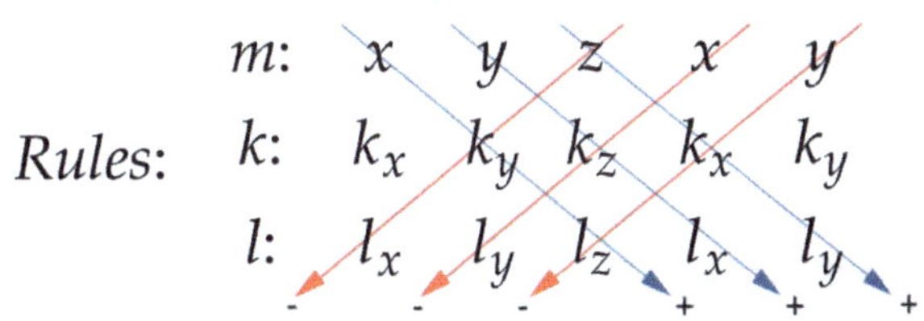

For the component of the result vector in the row labeled *m*, follow the diagonal blue line for the minuend, and the opposite red diagonal line for the subtrahend. The result and source vector components are continued at the end, as this simplifies the understanding of which of the vector components to use for the cross product.

Vector multiplication in GLM

In GLM, the multiplications are single operations. First, we define some vectors:

```
glm::vec3 v6 = glm::vec3(1.0f, 2.0f, 3.0f);
glm::vec3 v7 = glm::vec3(2.0f, 3.0f, -1.0f);
glm::vec3 s1 = glm::vec3(2.0f);
glm::vec3 s2 = glm::vec3(1.0f, 0.5, 3.0f);
```

Scaling is done by multiplication with another vector:

```
glm::vec3 uniform = v6 * s1; // (2.0f, 4.0f, 6.0f)
glm::vec3 nonuni = v6 * s2; // (1.0f, 1.0f, 9.0f)
```

The dot product can be computed with the `glm::dot()` function, and the result of the dot product is a single number, such as a float:

```
float dot = glm::dot(glm::normalize(v6),
    glm::normalize(v7)); // 0.357143f, cosine of ~69°
```

The cross product is calculated with the `glm::cross()` function, and the result of the cross product is another vector:

```
glm::vec3 cross = glm::cross(v6, v7);
    // (-11.0f, 7.0f, -1.0f)
```

Calculating the dot product between two perpendicular vectors will result in `0`. This is because the cosine of 90 degrees is 0. In the preceding code, the new vector, `cross`, is perpendicular to both the vectors, `v6` and `v7`. Hence, if we obtain the cross product of `cross` with either `v6` or `v7`, it will give a result of `0.0`.

The second data type to recapitulate is the matrix, which we will discuss next.

A review of the matrix and its operations

A matrix is used for operations that require storing more than three or four values, as in a vector, such as a rotation of a vector or a perspective change for all objects in a scene.

The matrix data type consists of rows and columns, creating a 2D collection of elements. All elements of the matrix must have the same data type.

Let's start with the mathematical representation to get an understanding of what a matrix is.

Matrix representation

A matrix is written as a grid of elements, and the elements are identified by the indices for the row (first index) and the column (second index) of their position. The dimensions of a matrix are given as *rows x columns*, so a 2 x 3 matrix has 2 rows and 3 columns.

These two matrices, *A* and *B*, have the dimensions 2 x 2 and 3 x 3:

$$A = \begin{bmatrix} a_{11} & a_{12} \\ a_{21} & a_{22} \end{bmatrix} \quad B = \begin{bmatrix} b_{11} & b_{12} & b_{13} \\ b_{21} & b_{22} & b_{23} \\ b_{31} & b_{32} & b_{33} \end{bmatrix}$$

Null matrix and identity matrix

As with vectors, matrices also have two types with special meanings:

- The **identity matrix** is one of the most important matrices. The main diagonal of the identity matrix is set to `1`, while all other elements are `0`. The identity matrix is the neutral element regarding multiplication, making it the perfect starting point for the multiplication of more matrices, as every matrix stays identical when multiplied by the identity matrix, or vice versa.
- The **null matrix**, or **zero matrix**, has all elements set to `0`. It is the neutral element for addition, so it could be a good starting point if we need to add different matrices. For multiplication, the null matrix has no use, as all elements of the result would also be set to `0`.

Here you can see the identity matrix, *I*, with the values `1` along the main diagonal, and the zero matrix, *N*:

$$I = \begin{bmatrix} 1 & 0 & 0 \\ 0 & 1 & 0 \\ 0 & 0 & 1 \end{bmatrix} \quad N = \begin{bmatrix} 0 & 0 & 0 \\ 0 & 0 & 0 \\ 0 & 0 & 0 \end{bmatrix}$$

In GLM, we can create both types with single commands:

```
glm::mat3 m3  = glm::mat3(0.0f);
glm::mat3 m4  = glm::mat3(1.0f);
```

The 3 x 3 `m3` matrix is constructed as a null or zero matrix. GLM uses the special constructor for the zero matrix if the only parameter is the value `0.0`. The 3 x 3 `m4` matrix is generated as an identity matrix.

Matrix addition and subtraction

To add two matrices together, every element of the first matrix is added up with the element in the same position in the second matrix. These calculations are done for all rows and columns. Matrix addition and subtraction only work for matrices with the same number of rows and columns.

The following example shows the addition of two 2 x 2 matrices, *C* and *D*:

$$C + D = \begin{bmatrix} c_{11} & c_{12} \\ c_{21} & c_{22} \end{bmatrix} + \begin{bmatrix} d_{11} & d_{12} \\ d_{21} & d_{22} \end{bmatrix} = \begin{bmatrix} c_{11} + d_{11} & c_{12} + d_{12} \\ c_{21} + d_{21} & c_{22} + d_{22} \end{bmatrix}$$

The subtraction works in the same way, by subtracting every element of the second matrix from the element at the same position in the first matrix.

In GLM, the normal addition and subtraction operators are overloaded again:

```
glm::mat3 matA = glm::mat3(1.0f);
glm::mat3 matB = glm::mat3(1.0f);
glm::mat3 zeroMat = matA - matB;
```

First, we define the 3 x 3 matrices, `matA` and `matB`, as identity matrices. GLM uses the constructor for the identity matrix if given the value of `1.0` as the only parameter.

Then, we subtract `matB` from `matA`, and the result, `zeroMat`, will be the zero matrix.

> **Note**
> You can only add or subtract matrices with the same number of rows and columns.

Matrix multiplication

One of the most used operations in graphics programming is the multiplication of two matrices. For every element of the resulting matrix, the elements in the same *rows* of the multiplier matrix and the same *column* of the multiplicand matrix are multiplied, element by element, and the products are added up. This is like the calculation of the dot product of the vectors.

The 2 x 2 matrices, *E* and *F*, are multiplied into the resulting 2 x 2 matrix *G*. The first operation is done with the highlighted row of *E* and the highlighted column of *F*, and the remaining elements of *G* are calculated according to the same schema:

$$E = \begin{bmatrix} e_{11} & e_{12} \\ e_{21} & e_{22} \end{bmatrix}; F = \begin{bmatrix} f_{11} & f_{12} \\ f_{21} & f_{22} \end{bmatrix}$$

$$G = E * F = \begin{bmatrix} e_{11} & e_{12} \\ e_{21} & e_{22} \end{bmatrix} * \begin{bmatrix} f_{11} & f_{12} \\ f_{21} & f_{22} \end{bmatrix} = \begin{bmatrix} e_{11}f_{11} + e_{12}f_{21} & e_{11}f_{12} + e_{12}f_{22} \\ e_{21}f_{11} + e_{22}f_{21} & e_{22}f_{12} + e_{22}f_{22} \end{bmatrix}$$

Matrix multiplication is *not* commutative. The order of the multiplications and additions shows that the positions of the two matrices cannot be changed without altering the resulting matrix. If we swap the matrices E and F in the preceding formula, we would multiply the elements of the first row of F with the first column of E, leading to a completely different result in matrix G.

In GLM, the `*` multiplication operator is overloaded for matrices:

```
glm::mat3 matE = glm::mat3(...);
glm::mat3 matF = glm::mat3(...);
glm::mat3 matG = matE * matF;
```

The 3 x 3 `matE` and `matF` matrices could be the results of previous operations. The 3 x 3 `matG` matrix is the product of the `matF` and `matE` matrices.

Rows and columns in the multiplied matrices

The number of *columns* in the *first* matrix and the number of *rows* in the *second* matrix must be the same. You can multiply a 2 x 3 and a 3 x 2 matrix, resulting in a 2 x 2 matrix, or a 3 x 2 and a 2 x 3 matrix, giving a 3 x 3 matrix, but you *cannot* multiply two 2 x 3 matrices.

Order of matrix multiplications

Chaining matrix multiplications is possible, but to get the correct result, the order of the matrices is *from right to left*. The product P of the matrices A, B, and C must be written as $P = C * B * A$.

Transposed and inverse matrices

Two other matrix operations will be used a lot in computer graphics: calculating the transpose of a matrix and the inverse of a matrix.

The transpose of a matrix

To transpose a matrix, the elements are swapped along the main diagonal. The best way to imagine the transposing operation is by swapping the index numbers of every element.

This example shows a matrix M and its transposed counterpart, M^T:

$$M = \begin{bmatrix} 3 & 5 & 1 \\ 7 & 9 & 0 \\ -1 & 2 & 1 \end{bmatrix}; M^T = \begin{bmatrix} 3 & 7 & -1 \\ 5 & 9 & 2 \\ 1 & 0 & 1 \end{bmatrix}$$

GLM has a separate operation to calculate the transpose of a matrix:

```
glm::mat3 m = glm::mat3(…);glm::mat3 mT = glm::transpose(m);
```

The 3 x 3 `m` matrix may be the result of some matrix-related calculation. The 3 x 3 `mT` matrix will contain the transpose of the `m` matrix.

The inverse of a matrix

The inverse matrix itself is defined as the matrix that must be multiplied by the current matrix to get the identity matrix. For the matrix *P*, we are searching for the matrix P^{-1}, so that the multiplication will result in the identity matrix *I*:

$$P * P^{-1} = I$$

The calculation of the inverse of a matrix requires a lot of mathematical operations. For the 2 x 2 matrix *P* in the following example, the **determinant** needs to be calculated first:

$$P = \begin{bmatrix} p_{11} & p_{12} \\ p_{21} & p_{22} \end{bmatrix}$$

The determinant is the product of the elements at the secondary diagonal subtracted from the product of the elements of the main diagonal:

$$det_P = p_{11}p_{22} - p_{12}p_{21}$$

As the next step, the elements of the main diagonal are swapped, and the sign of the elements of the secondary diagonal are inverted. Finally, the elements of the changed matrix are divided by the inverse of the determinant:

$$P^{-1} = \frac{1}{det_P} \begin{bmatrix} p_{22} & -p_{12} \\ -p_{21} & p_{11} \end{bmatrix}$$

For larger matrices, such as 3 x 3 or 4 x 4, the calculation is done recursively by dividing the large matrix into smaller matrices until only 2 x 2 matrices are left. The results are combined back to get the inverse of the larger matrices. You can look up the mathematics behind the inverse calculation of large matrices in a math book if you are interested in the exact details or use an online tool such as the *Wolfram Alpha* matrix calculator listed in the *Additional resources* section.

The inverse calculation is also available in GLM as a single command:

```
glm::mat4 p = glm::mat4(...);glm::mat4 pInverse = glm::inverse(p);
```

The 4 x 4 matrix, `p`, may again be a result of a previous matrix-related calculation. The 4 x 4 `pInverse` matrix will contain the inverse of the `p` matrix.

Matrix/vector multiplication

As the last operation, we will look at the multiplication of a matrix and a vector. This matrix/vector multiplication is done in the vertex shader. In the shader, the position vector for every vertex of every triangle is multiplied by the projection and view matrix. The position vector must be extended to a 4-element vector, as the number of elements must match the number of columns in the 4 x 4 `view` matrix:

```
gl_Position = projection * view * vec4(aPos, 1.0);
```

In mathematical terms, matrix/vector multiplication is like a matrix/matrix multiplication. The result is a vector with the same number of elements as before, as shown with the multiplication of the 2 x 2 matrix *J* and the vector *k*:

$$J = \begin{bmatrix} j_{11} & j_{12} \\ j_{21} & j_{22} \end{bmatrix} ; \vec{k} = \begin{pmatrix} k_1 \\ k_2 \end{pmatrix}$$

$$\vec{l} = J * \vec{k} = \begin{bmatrix} j_{11} & j_{12} \\ j_{21} & j_{22} \end{bmatrix} * \begin{pmatrix} k_1 \\ k_2 \end{pmatrix} = \begin{pmatrix} j_{11} k_1 + j_{12} k_2 \\ j_{21} k_1 + j_{22} k_2 \end{pmatrix}$$

For GLM, the multiplication operator is overloaded to support the matrix/vector multiplication:

```
glm::mat3 j = glm::mat3(…);
glm::vec3 k = glm::vec3(1.0f, 0.5, 3.0f);
glm::vec3 l = j * k;
```

Here, the 3 x 3 `j` matrix could be the result of some other matrix operation. The three-element `k` vector could be a vertex position. The resulting three-element `l` vector contains the result of the matrix/vector multiplication of `j` and `k`.

After all of this theoretical input, we will use some of the GLM vector and matrix operations to create a camera object for the renderers. Such a camera adds more "immersion" to the virtual worlds, as we can fly to objects and watch them from every angle.

Adding a camera to the renderer

To start with a free view in the renderer, we need these two additional variables:

- **Azimuth**: To store the view angle around the camera location in the virtual world, also known as **yaw**
- **Elevation**: For the up/down view of the camera, also called **pitch**

To visualize the two variables, let us use *Figure 6.3*:

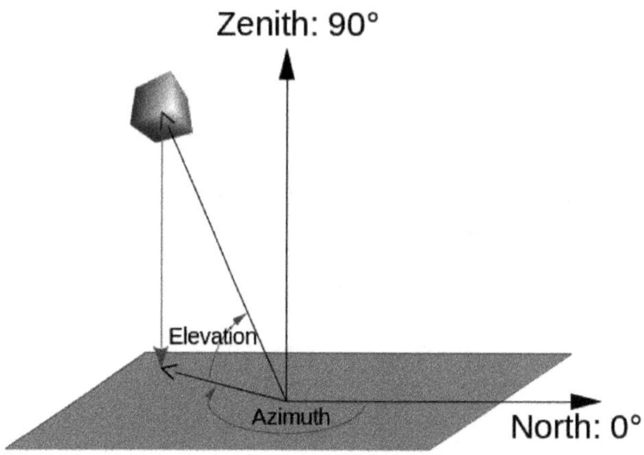

Figure 6.3: Elevation and azimuth of an object

The azimuth is the clockwise rotation around an imaginary vertical line pointing upward from the center of our coordinate system, and the elevation is the angle of the height of the object, as seen from the center of the coordinate system.

These two new variables go into the `OGLRenderData` struct of the `OGLRenderData.h` file in the `opengl` folder:

```
  float rdViewAzimuth = 320.0f;
  float rdViewElevation = -15.0f;
```

The initialization values are hand-picked to have the textured box placed in the middle of the screen when running the program.

Next, we will start the `Camera` class.

Creating the new Camera class

Create a new file called `Camera.h` in the `tools` folder:

```
#pragma once
#include <glm/glm.hpp>
#include "OGLRenderData.h"
```

After the `include` guard, we add the GLM header, as we use GLM functions and types, and `OGLRenderData.h` for the `OGLRenderData` struct with the new variables.

The `Camera` class has only a single `public` method:

```
class Camera {
  public:
    glm::mat4 getViewMatrix(OGLRenderData &renderData);
```

The `getViewMatrix()` method will use the view angles from the `OGLRenderData` struct to calculate a 4 x 4 matrix from the values and return this matrix.

We also need three `private` GLM vectors with three elements each to store some values:

```
  private:
    glm::vec3 mWorldPos = glm::vec3(0.5f, 0.25f, 1.0f);
    glm::vec3 mViewDirection = glm::vec3(0.0f, 0.0f, 0.0f);
    glm::vec3 mWorldUpVector = glm::vec3(0.0f, 1.0f, 0.0f);
};
```

The `mWorldPos` variable stores the position of the `Camera` class object in the virtual world, and the `mViewDirection` variable is used to represent the direction in which the camera is facing. It is calculated from the `Azimuth` and `Elevation` values. The last variable, `mWorldUpVector`, points straight up toward the *y* axis. We need an upward-pointing vector for the calculation of the `view` matrix using the camera values.

Now, we go for the implementation of the `Camera` class by adding the `Camera.cpp` file in the `tools` folder:

```
#include <glm/gtc/matrix_transform.hpp>
#include "Camera.h"
```

The GLM `matrix_transform.hpp` header is needed for the `glm::lookAt()` call to create the view matrix and `Camera.h` is required for the general `Camera` class declaration.

As the only method in the `Camera` class, `getViewMatrix()` is defined next:

```
glm::mat4 Camera::getViewMatrix(OGLRenderData &renderData){
  float azimRad = glm::radians(renderData.rdViewAzimuth);
  float elevRad = glm::radians(renderData.rdViewElevation);
```

First, the values for `Azimuth` and `Elevation` are converted to radians instead of degrees, as the `sin` and `cos` functions work with radians as parameters. GLM has the special `glm::radians()` function for this conversion, so we do not need to do it manually.

Next, we precalculate the `sin` and `cos` values of `Azimuth` and `Elevation`:

```
  float sinAzim = glm::sin(azimRad);
  float cosAzim = glm::cos(azimRad);
  float sinElev = glm::sin(elevRad);
  float cosElev = glm::cos(elevRad);
```

Defining these extra variables is not really required, but it shortens the parameters of the next call a lot:

```
  mViewDirection = glm::normalize(glm::vec3(
    sinAzim * cosElev,
```

```
    sinElev,
    -cosAzim * cosElev));
```

Here, we create a three-element GLM vector from the calculated `sin` and `cos` values:

- The first parameter is the *x* axis (left/right), the second parameter is the *y* axis (up/down), and the third parameter is the *z* axis (into the screen)
- We do a normal circle calculation from the azimuth angle of the camera position, where the `sin` value is used for the *x* axis and the `cos` value for the *z* axis
- The `cos` value is multiplied by `-1` as the *z* axis is negative toward the screen
- The cosine of the elevation is multiplied "on top," as the resulting value will be shorter if we look further up or down
- The *y* axis is calculated just by the sine of the elevation, as the up and the down view is independent of the rotation around the camera position

As the last step, we calculate and return the 4 x 4 `view` matrix:

```
  return glm::lookAt(mWorldPos,
    mWorldPos + mViewDirection, mWorldUpVector);
}
```

The call to `glm::lookAt()` creates a `view` matrix. This `view` matrix uses `mWorldPos` as the center position, the result of the addition of `mWorldPos` and `mViewDirection` as the direction to look at, and the *y* upward-pointing `mWorldUpVector` as the so-called "up vector." GLM needs this up vector to know the orientation of the camera in the virtual world.

As the preparations have been completed, we can implement the free view in the `OGLRenderer` class itself.

Integrating the new camera into the Renderer class

First, add the include for `Camera` to the `OGLRenderer.h` file in the `opengl` folder:

```
#include "Camera.h"
```

Next, the two `public` functions for the mouse callbacks called from the `Window` class must be declared in the `OGLRenderer` class:

```
    void handleMouseButtonEvents(int button, int action, int mods);
    void handleMousePositionEvents(double xPos, double yPos);
```

Then, add the mCamera object as a private data member:

```
    Camera mCamera{};
```

Finally, to store some internal values, add these three private data members:

```
    bool mMouseLock = false;
    int mMouseXPos = 0;
    int mMouseYPos = 0;
```

The mMouseLock variable is used to switch between two mouse modes. In the unlocked mode, moving the mouse pointer works normally (i.e., changing values in the ImGui settings). In locked mode, the mouse is used to move the view in the virtual world, and the mouse pointer is hidden. The position of the mouse pointer in the locked mode will be stored in the mMouseXPos and mMouseYPos variables.

Creating the free-view mouse mode

The implementation of the changes is done in the OGLRenderer.cpp file in the opengl folder. Start by adding the imgui GLFW header:

```
#include <imgui_impl_glfw.h>
```

We need the imgui_impl_glfw.h header to access an internal state of the ImGui, to avoid problems between the two mouse modes. Next, add the method to handle the mouse button events:

```
void OGLRenderer::handleMouseButtonEvents(int button,
    int action, int mods) {
```

At the start of the handleMouseButtonEvents() method, we have to forward the status of the mouse buttons to ImGui:

```
  ImGuiIO& io = ImGui::GetIO();
  if (button >= 0 && button < ImGuiMouseButton_COUNT) {
    io.AddMouseButtonEvent(button, action == GLFW_PRESS);
  }
```

The internal ImGuiIO struct knows where the ImGui windows are placed. So, clicking any mouse button must be handled by ImGui itself if the mouse pointer is above one of the windows and controls. After forwarding the mouse button status, ImGui sets an internal variable if the mouse is needed internally. We check this variable next:

```
  if (io.WantCaptureMouse) {
    return;
  }
```

If `WantCaptureMouse` in the `ImGuiIO` struct is set, we abort our mouse button handling to avoid interfering with the ImGui. If ImGui signals that it does not need to handle the mouse buttons, we continue to check for a right mouse button click:

```
  if (button == GLFW_MOUSE_BUTTON_RIGHT && action ==
      GLFW_PRESS) {
    mMouseLock = !mMouseLock;
```

On every right-button-click, we invert the value of the `mMouseLock` Boolean variable. The variable switches the mouse between the normal usage for ImGui and window property changes and the locked look-around mode.

Next, we check whether we are in the locked look-around mode:

```
    if (mMouseLock) {
      glfwSetInputMode(mRenderData.rdWindow,
        GLFW_CURSOR, GLFW_CURSOR_DISABLED);
```

To avoid confusion, we disable the mouse pointer when looking around. Disabling the mouse is the precondition to be able to switch the mouse to the "raw mode," which we do in the next lines:

```
      if (glfwRawMouseMotionSupported()) {
        glfwSetInputMode(mRenderData.rdWindow,
          GLFW_RAW_MOUSE_MOTION, GLFW_TRUE);
      }
```

We check whether the raw mode is supported and enable the raw mode if the platform supports the direct reading of the mouse data. The raw mode omits extra mouse features such as acceleration.

If we leave the look-around mode, we simply re-enable the mouse cursor:

```
    } else {
      glfwSetInputMode(mRenderData.rdWindow, GLFW_CURSOR,
        GLFW_CURSOR_NORMAL);
    }
  }
}
```

Implementing the relative mouse motion

Next, we go for the handling of the mouse motion. We must do this manually, as GLFW knows only the absolute position of the mouse pointer:

```
void OGLRenderer::handleMousePositionEvents(double xPos,
    double yPos){
```

The first lines are like the mouse button handling. We need to tell ImGui the current position of the mouse:

```
ImGuiIO& io = ImGui::GetIO();
io.AddMousePosEvent((float)xPos, (float)yPos);
```

Then, we check the internal `WantCaptureMouse` flag again:

```
if (io.WantCaptureMouse) {
  return;
}
```

We abort the mouse move handling again if ImGUI signals that it needs this event by itself. If ImGui is not interested in the mouse movement, we calculate the difference between the saved mouse position from the last event and the current event:

```
int mouseMoveRelX = static_cast<int>(xPos) -
  mMouseXPos;
int mouseMoveRelY = static_cast<int>(yPos) -
  mMouseYPos;
```

This calculation is required as ImGui only knows the absolute position of the mouse pointer in the window, but we need the relative movement for the view changes. The view will be changed only in the look-around mode when the mouse is locked:

```
if (mMouseLock) {
```

As the first operation, we update the `Azimuth` value:

```
  mRenderData.rdViewAzimuth += mouseMoveRelX / 10.0;
```

Scaling down to a tenth of the relative horizontal mouse movement is done to have better control over the amount of view movement. Next, we make sure the value is in the range between `0` and `360` degrees:

```
  if (mRenderData.rdViewAzimuth < 0.0) {
    mRenderData.rdViewAzimuth += 360.0;
  }
  if (mRenderData.rdViewAzimuth >= 360.0) {
    mRenderData.rdViewAzimuth -= 360.0;
  }
```

The `sin` and `cos` calculations can handle values outside the range, but as we want to show the value in the ImGui user interface, we should limit it here.

For the `Elevation` value, the vertical mouse movement is used, scaled to a tenth again:

```
  mRenderData.rdViewElevation -= mouseMoveRelY / 10.0;
```

The range check for the elevation is a bit different:

```
    if (mRenderData.rdViewElevation > 89.0) {
      mRenderData.rdViewElevation = 89.0;
    }
    if (mRenderData.rdViewElevation < -89.0) {
      mRenderData.rdViewElevation = -89.0;
    }
  }
```

Here, we limit the values to `89` degrees (nearly vertical upward) and `-89` degrees (nearly vertical downward). Skipping this check would also turn around the `Azimuth` calculation once we are over 90 or -90 degrees, making a proper mouse view impossible.

As the last operation, we store the current mouse position in the variables to have them available for the relative motion calculation in the next call:

```
  mMouseXPos = static_cast<int>(xPos);
  mMouseYPos = static_cast<int>(yPos);
}
```

Using the new camera

The `draw()` call of the `OGLRenderer` class also needs changes, as we moved some of the logic and properties into the `Camera` class. First, remove these three lines, as they are no longer needed in the `OGLRenderer` class:

```
  glm::vec3 cameraPosition = glm::vec3(0.4f, 0.3f, 1.0f);
  glm::vec3 cameraLookAtPosition = glm::vec3(0.0f, 0.0f,
    0.0f);
  glm::vec3 cameraUpVector = glm::vec3(0.0f, 1.0f, 0.0f);
```

Next, replace this line, which is mentioned in the next code snippet:

```
  mViewMatrix = glm::lookAt(cameraPosition,
    cameraLookAtPosition, cameraUpVector) * model;
```

This is the old calculation of the camera position. Use this line to replace the code line in the preceding code snippet:

```
  mViewMatrix = mCamera.getViewMatrix(mRenderData) * model;
```

We get the `view` matrix directly from the `mCamera` variable now, and all the calculations are done inside the `Camera` class.

Implementing mouse control in the Window class

We want to use the mouse to control the view, so two additional GLFW callbacks must be added to the `Window` class. Add these lines to the `init()` method of the `Window.cpp` file in the `window` folder, right after the other callbacks:

```
glfwSetMouseButtonCallback(mWindow, [](GLFWwindow *win,
    int button, int action, int mods) {
  auto renderer = static_cast<OGLRenderer*>
    (glfwGetWindowUserPointer(win));
  renderer->handleMouseButtonEvents(button, action, mods);
  }
);
glfwSetCursorPosCallback(mWindow, [](GLFWwindow *win,
    double xpos, double ypos) {
  auto renderer = static_cast<OGLRenderer*>
    (glfwGetWindowUserPointer(win));
  renderer->handleMousePositionEvents(xpos, ypos);
  }
);
```

The first call, `glfwSetMouseButtonCallback()`, reports any mouse button presses or releases, while the second call, `glfwSetCursorPosCallback()`, delivers the current position of the mouse pointer via callback to the renderer.

Next, we need to make sure that the values of `Azimuth` and `Elevation` are visible in the ImGui user interface.

Showing the camera values in the user interface

This task is done quickly, as the values are already in the `OGLRenderData` struct, by adding new text lines to the `createFrame()` method of the `UserInterface.cpp` file in the `opengl` folder. Place these lines between the timer section and the generic status output with the number of triangles and the window position:

```
ImGui::Text("View Azimuth:");
ImGui::SameLine();
ImGui::Text("%s", std::to_string
  (renderData.rdViewAzimuth).c_str());
ImGui::Text("View Elevation:");
ImGui::SameLine();
ImGui::Text("%s", std::to_string
  (renderData.rdViewElevation).c_str());
ImGui::Separator();
```

The complete code for this example is available in the `chapter06` folder, in the `01_opengl_view` subfolder for OpenGL and `03_vulkan_view` for Vulkan.

If you compile and start the program, you see the same scene with the rotating textured box we created at the end of *Chapter 5*. By clicking the right mouse button in the main window (but outside of the ImGui window), you can switch to the look-around mode:

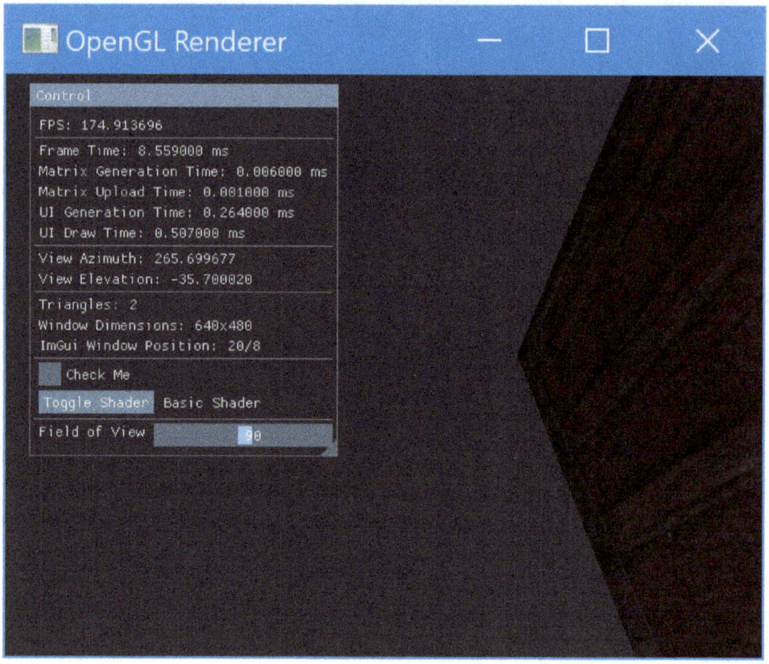

Figure 6.4: Altering the view using the locked mode in the OpenGL renderer

> **Important note**
>
> You may encounter sudden "jumping" view changes while moving the mouse in the look-around mode. This is a known bug in GLFW when working with a disabled cursor.

Changing the view of the scene is already quite nice, and the field-of-view slider also allows us to "zoom" in and out. But for a better examination of the future characters shown in the virtual world, we should be able to move the camera within the scene. Let us implement a freely movable camera object next.

Adding camera movement

A moving camera will enable us to "walk" through the virtual world, watching the objects from every angle. By using the usual *W-A-S-D* key pattern, we will be able to move forward and back, and left and right. We will also add the ability to move the camera up and down.

To signal the desired motion to the camera, we will check whether the movement keys are pressed, and adjust the Camera object depending on the keys that are pressed.

Using new variables to change the camera position

Start the implementation by adding these three variables to the OGLRenderData struct in the OGLRenderData.h file in the opengl folder:

```
int rdMoveForward = 0;
int rdMoveRight = 0;
int rdMoveUp = 0;
```

These three integer variables will store the directions of the camera movement. We don't need more variables; for rdMoveForward, we can use 1 to specify forward movement, -1 for backward movement, and 0 to have no movement at all in the forward/backward direction. The same goes for rdMoveRight and rdMoveUp.

Next, add another new variable in the OGLRenderData struct:

```
float rdTickDiff = 0.0f;
```

The rdTickDiff variable will store the difference between two rendered images. The difference is needed to allow steady movement, independent of the frame rate.

We also need a new private data member for the OGLRenderer class. Add this line to the OGLRenderer.h file in the opengl folder:

```
double lastTickTime = 0.0;
```

The lastTickTime variable stores the time given by glfwGetTime() at the start of the new draw() call of the OGLRenderer class. The difference between the current and the previous draw() calls will be stored in the rdTickDiff variable.

We also need a private method to check for the movement keys:

```
void handleMovementKeys();
```

The handleMovementKeys() method will be called during every draw() call to update the status of the three camera movement variables.

To implement the changes for the camera, we start with the new key handling method in the OGLRenderer.cpp file in the opengl folder:

```
void OGLRenderer::handleMovementKeys() {
  mRenderData.rdMoveForward = 0;
  if (glfwGetKey(mRenderData.rdWindow, GLFW_KEY_W) ==
      GLFW_PRESS) {
```

```
    mRenderData.rdMoveForward += 1;
  }
  if (glfwGetKey(mRenderData.rdWindow, GLFW_KEY_S) ==
      GLFW_PRESS) {
    mRenderData.rdMoveForward -= 1;
  }
```

At the start of the method, we set the forward movement variable to `0`. If the keys *W* or *S* are not pressed, the forward movement will remain at `0`. If the key *W* is pressed, we *add* one to the forward movement variable, and if the key *S* is pressed, we *subtract* one. This allows us to store both directions in the same variable. By adding and subtracting the same value, we also catch the case where both the *W* and *S* keys are pressed, resulting in `0` – no movement at all.

The variables for the right and up movements are set the same way:

```
  mRenderData.rdMoveRight = 0;
  if (glfwGetKey(mRenderData.rdWindow, GLFW_KEY_A) == GLFW_PRESS) {
    mRenderData.rdMoveRight -= 1;
  }
  if (glfwGetKey(mRenderData.rdWindow, GLFW_KEY_D) == GLFW_PRESS) {
    mRenderData.rdMoveRight += 1;
  }
  mRenderData.rdMoveUp = 0;
  if (glfwGetKey(mRenderData.rdWindow, GLFW_KEY_E) == GLFW_PRESS) {
    mRenderData.rdMoveUp += 1;
  }
  if (glfwGetKey(mRenderData.rdWindow, GLFW_KEY_Q) == GLFW_PRESS) {
    mRenderData.rdMoveUp -= 1;
  }
}
```

After the `handleMovementKeys()` method has finished execution, the three movement variables (`rdMoveForward`, `rdMoveRight`, and `rdMoveUp`) contain the desired motion directions of the camera.

Now, add these lines at the start of the `draw()` method:

```
  double tickTime = glfwGetTime();
  mRenderData.rdTickDiff = tickTime - lastTickTime;
```

We use the difference between the time of the current `draw()` invocation and the last one later in the `Camera` class to achieve a frame rate-independent movement.

Next, add the call to the `handleMovementKeys()` method to the `draw()` method:

```
  handleMovementKeys();
```

The best place is right after `mFrameTimer.start()`. This adds the key handling to the timing for the entire frame, still outside the other timers.

At the end of the `draw()` method, update the last `tick` time:

```
lastTickTime = tickTime;
```

The `lastTickTime` variable will be set with the time at the start of this `draw()` call execution, so we will have this time available in the next `draw()` call.

Moving the camera around

The `Camera` class also needs new variables. Add these two new GLM vectors in the `Camera.h` file in the `tools` folder, right below `mViewDirection`:

```
  glm::vec3 mRightDirection = glm::vec3(0.0f, 0.0f, 0.0f);
  glm::vec3 mUpDirection = glm::vec3(0.0f, 0.0f, 0.0f);
```

To be able to move in all directions, we have to calculate vectors for the left/right and up/down directions, and these two variables will hold the results.

We also remove the `mWorldPos` vector from the variables. The camera position will reside in the `mRenderData` struct of the `OGLRenderer` class.

The vector calculation itself is done in the `getViewMatrix()` method. Add these two lines to the `Camera.cpp` file, after `mViewDirection` has been set:

```
mRightDirection = glm::normalize
  (glm::cross(mViewDirection, mWorldUpVector));
mUpDirection = glm::normalize
  (glm::cross(mRightDirection, mViewDirection));
```

We use a little trick with cross products to get these two directions:

- `mRightDirection` is calculated as the cross product of the view direction and the *world up* vector. The resulting vector of the cross product has an angle of 90 degrees relative to both vectors; as the *world up* vector points toward the *y* axis, the resulting vector is created in the *x-z* plane of the virtual world, at a right angle to the view vector. The resulting right direction vector is independent of the `Elevation` value of our view, always pointing toward the right of our view vector.
- The `mUpDirection` upward vector for the camera is then calculated as the cross product of the view and the right vector. This calculation "tilts" the camera upward vector, and it will be at a right angle to the view vector, instead of just pointing straight up along the *y* axis, like the *world up* vector. The separate camera upward vector is used to avoid trouble when looking up or down. If the view direction is close to the *y* axis, up/down movement would be the same as forward/back when using the *world up* vector for the camera, losing one degree of our movement abilities.

After the calculation, the resulting vectors are normalized to have the same length. This way, we have now created a new local coordinate system for our camera, allowing us to use it to move the camera object relative to the current position.

As we store the movement key variables in the `OGLRenderData` struct, we can access these variables in the `Camera` class without any further parameter transfer. So, we can use the movement variables to update the position of the camera:

```
renderData.rdCameraWorldPosition += renderData.rdMoveForward *
      renderData.rdTickDiff * mViewDirection
  + renderData.rdMoveRight *
      renderData.rdTickDiff * mRightDirection
  + renderData.rdMoveUp *
      renderData.rdTickDiff * mUpDirection;
```

Here, we update the camera position with the three vectors: `mViewDirection`, `mRightDirection`, and `mUpDirection`. The vectors may be used in the direction they are pointing to (if multiplied by 1), in the opposite direction (if multiplied by -1), or not at all (if multiplied by 0). Adding all vectors up will move the camera in the direction specified by the movement keys. The scaling by the `rdTickDiff` value ensures the camera is always moved for the same amount per second, no matter how often the position update of the camera is called.

As the last step in the `getViewMatrix()` method, we create the `view` matrix for the camera with the `glm::lookAt()` call, using the new values for the world position and the view direction, and return the matrix:

```
    return glm::lookAt( renderData.rdCameraWorldPosition, renderData.
  rdCameraWorldPosition + mViewDirection,
      mUpDirection);
```

To see the camera position in the ImGui user interface, we have to add a new text line in the `UserInterface` class.

Adding the camera position to the user interface

Place these lines in the `UserInterface.cpp` file in the `opengl` folder, right before the display of the `Elevation` and `Azimuth` values:

```
ImGui::Text("Camera Position:");
ImGui::SameLine();
ImGui::Text("%s",glm::to_string
  (renderData.rdCameraWorldPosition).c_str());
```

The keys *W*, *A*, *S*, and *D*, and *E* and *Q* will move the camera in the virtual world, and locking the camera with the right mouse button gives us a free view. Using both methods together enables us to roam around in the virtual world, having the camera position and the `Azimuth` and `Elevation` values updated in the UI.

In the example code in the `02_opengl_movement` folder for OpenGL and `04_vulkan_movement` for Vulkan, the textured box in the `Model` class has been extended to a full textured cube with different colors on the sides, to have a real 3D object to explore. If you start the code and move and fly around the scene, you will get a screenshot like this:

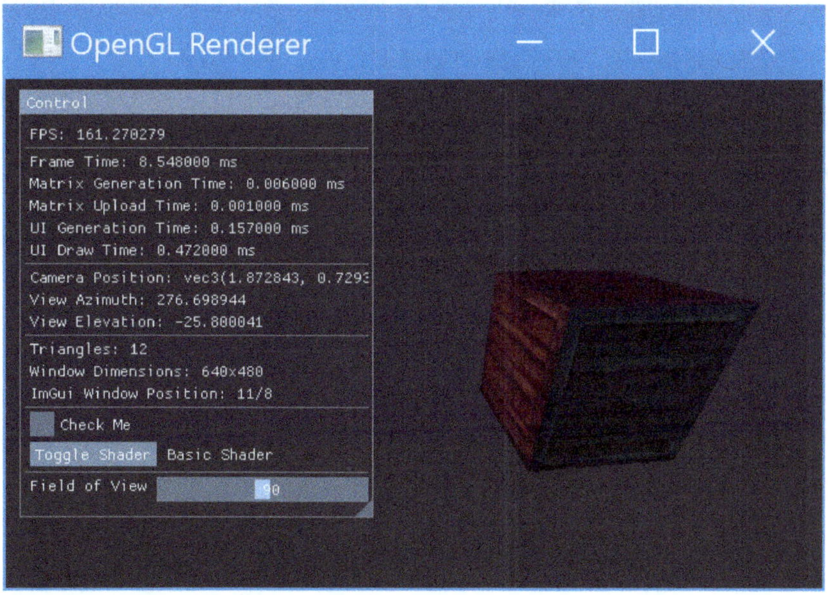

Figure 6.5: Free movement around a 3D textured cube in the OpenGL renderer

Summary

In this chapter, we checked some of the basic operations of vectors and matrices, plus the GLM functions used to get the results. Using GLM makes all the operations available for us, without having to implement each of them manually. This overview should also have given you some insights into how these data types are used in later chapters.

In addition to the basic operations, we also added a free view within the scene and, eventually, a free-moving camera object. The camera will become handy in the later chapters, as it enables us to get a perfect view of the character models on changes in the skinning method, animation details, or the results of the inverse kinematics.

In the next chapter, a couple more GLM operations are introduced, as we look at quaternions and spline curves. While quaternions help us to overcome some limitations of geometrical operations, splines will enable us to generate smooth curved lines out of a group of four points, without having to specify every segment of the curves manually.

Practical sessions

Here are some ideas for more code to add to the examples:

- Try to create the 3D crate box by yourself and add the remaining five sides to the `Model` class in the `01_opengl_view` and `03_vulkan_view` examples. This requires quite some imagination to get all the vertex positions, triangle outside faces, and texture coordinates right. Or you can use 3D tools such as Blender to create a cube and transfer the data to the `Model` class.
- Add the view and projection matrices to the user interface. This will give some more insights into how the changes in the position, view, or field-of-view parameters are reflected in the matrices.

Additional resources

- The GLM website: `https://glm.g-truc.net/0.9.9`
- Wolfram Alpha matrix inverse calculator: `https://www.wolframalpha.com/calculators/matrix-inverse-calculator`

7
A Primer on Quaternions and Splines

Welcome to *Chapter 7*! In the previous chapter, we had a deeper view of the vector and matrix mathematical elements and data types. Both types are important building blocks of every 3D graphical application, as the internal storage and the calculation of virtual objects rely to a large extent on vertices and matrices.

In this chapter, two other mathematical elements will be introduced: quaternions and splines, especially cubic Hermite splines. These two elements are heavily used in the **glTF** file format we use for the animated characters. The glTF file format will be explored in detail in *Part 3* of the book, starting with *Chapter 8*.

By the end of the chapter, you should have a basic understanding of what quaternions and splines are, and how to work with them. You should also know about their advantages in character animations. Having a picture in your mind of the two elements and their transformations will help you master the rest of the book.

In this chapter, we will cover the following main topics:

- What are quaternions?
- Exploring the vector rotation
- Using quaternions for smooth rotations
- A quick take on splines
- Constructing a Hermite spline

Technical requirements

For this chapter, you will need the OpenGL and Vulkan renderer code from *Chapter 6*.

Working with game character animations requires a basic knowledge of quaternions, but you will find them in many other places in computer graphics applications too. So, let us look at what a quaternion is.

In this chapter, we will focus on the graphical output of example applications and show and describe only the parts of the code that do all the calculations. You can check out the full source in the subfolders of the `chapter07` folder.

What are quaternions?

First, we need to check the mathematical elements that are required to describe and work with a quaternion. Without this, the quaternion is hard to understand.

Imaginary and complex numbers

If we try to solve this simple quadric equation, we are stuck if we are limited to the mathematical rules of the real numbers:

$$x^2 + 1 = 0 \mid -1$$

$$x^2 = -1$$

As the square of a number is always equal to or greater than zero and never negative, this equation has no result in the *default* mathematics world.

To be able to solve such equations, so-called imaginary numbers were introduced. The problem with equations like the one in the preceding formula is older than you may think: the basics of imaginary numbers have been known since the 15th century, and their usage was widely accepted in the 18th century.

To visualize the principle of imaginary numbers, a two-dimensional cartesian plane is used, as shown in *Figure 7.1*. The *normal* real numbers are on the horizontal *x* axis, while the imaginary numbers are on the vertical *y* axis:

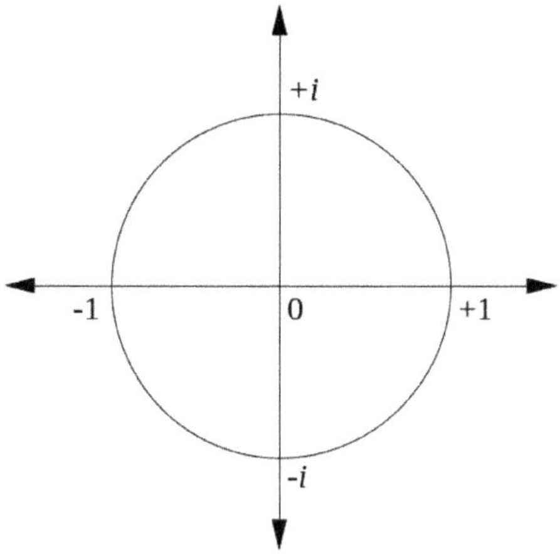

Figure 7.1: Complex cartesian plane with real and imaginary units

This extension to two dimensions allows us to work with imaginary numbers as we do with real numbers, with the exception of moving upward or downward instead of left and right on the cartesian plane:

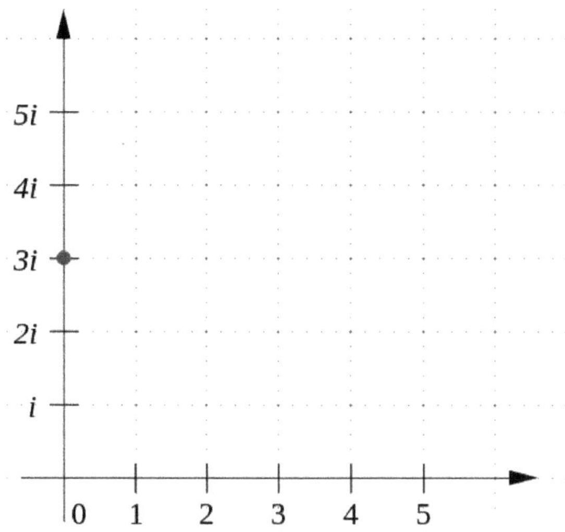

Figure 7.2: Real and imaginary numbers

In the end, this makes an imaginary number a real number multiplied by the **imaginary unit**, `i`. This imaginary unit, `i`, is defined by the single property $i^2 = -1$.

To give a simple example from *Figure 7.2*, `3i` is an imaginary number.

The concept of imaginary numbers was extended in the 16th century to a sum of a real and an imaginary number, creating so-called **complex numbers**. This creates a point in the two-dimensional complex cartesian plane, as shown in *Figure 7.3*.

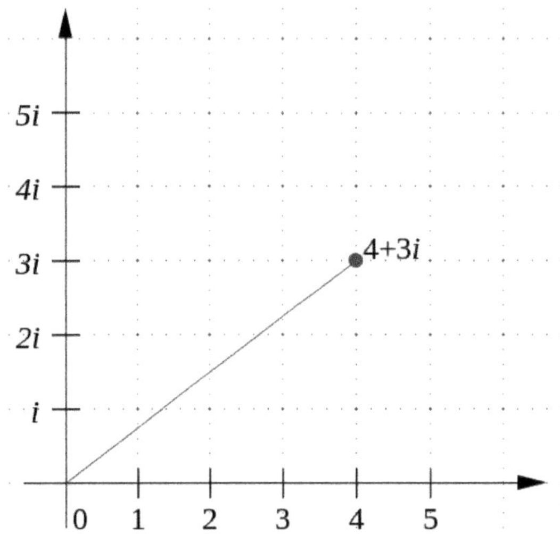

Figure 7.3: A complex number in the complex cartesian plane

Complex numbers consist of a real part and an imaginary part. As an example from *Figure 7.3*, `4+3i` is a complex number.

Doing calculations with complex numbers is the same as doing calculations with real numbers, the only difference is the special property $i^2 = -1$........, which must be considered. Here are some examples of adding and multiplying two complex numbers and calculating the square of a complex number:

$$1)\ (a + bi) + (c + di) = (a + c) + (b + d)i$$

$$2)\ r(a + bi) = ra + rbi$$

$$3)\ (a + bi)*(c + di) = (ac - bd) + (ad + bc)i$$

$$4)\ (a + bi)^2 = a^2 - b^2 + 2abi$$

Here are the details of all the examples in the preceding formulae:

- In the first example **(1)**, two complex numbers are added by adding the respective real and complex parts.
- In the second example **(2)** of the multiplication of a complex number with a real number, each part is multiplied by the real number.

- In the third example **(3)** of the multiplication of two complex numbers, the multiplication of two additions in braces is shown. The multiplication of `bi` and `di` uses the squared property of `i`, resulting in a negative product.
- In the final example **(4)**, squaring a complex number follows the same principle as that of multiplying in the third example, resulting in a negative b^2.

We need such calculation rules of complex numbers to work with the quaternions and their transformations. Next, let's see what quaternions are about.

The discovery of the quaternion

William Rowan Hamilton (1805 – 1865) tried to extend complex numbers even further, beyond a single imaginary part. After being unable to get two imaginary parts to work, he finally found, in 1843, an extension to three imaginary parts:

$$a + bi + cj + dk$$

The so-called quaternion in the preceding formula consists of the real part, `a`, and the three imaginary parts, `bi`, `cj`, and `dk`. Like the imaginary unit `i`, the square of the two imaginary units `j` and `k` is `-1`. And the product of all three imaginary units is also `-1`:

$$i^2 = j^2 = k^2 = ijk = -1$$

The three imaginary numbers `i`, `j`, and `k` can be interpreted as unit vectors, having a length of 1, pointing along the three axes of a three-dimensional coordinate system. The three factors `b`, `c`, and `d` define a 3D vector, *q*, and the real part `a` can be seen as the angle of a rotation around the virtual axis defined by the vector *q*:

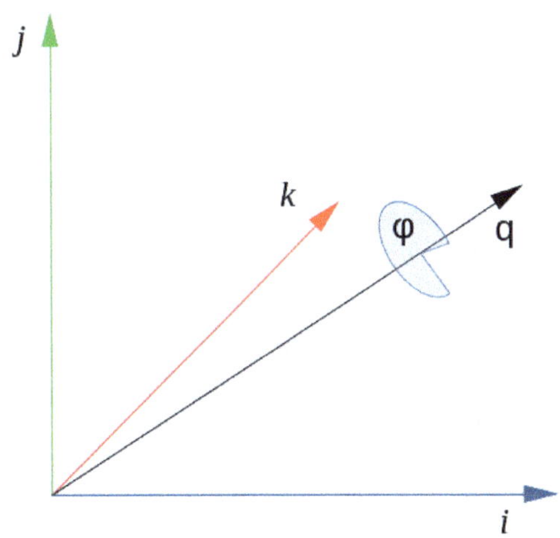

Figure 7.4: A graphical interpretation of a quaternion q as an axis and a rotation angle

An important phrase you will encounter with quaternions is **orientation**. This naming is the significant difference between a quaternion and a rotation matrix. A rotation matrix is the result of a rotation, or a combination of rotations, while a quaternion will rotate along an arbitrary axis.

We will come back to rotations and rotation matrices in the *The gimbal lock* section.

Now let us see how quaternions are created, and how mathematical operations are applied, such as additions and multiplications, both in math and code using GLM.

Creating a quaternion

The vector interpretation in the following formula allows us to use quaternions as a replacement for rotation matrices to rotate a given vector around an axis:

$$q(\phi) = \cos\left(\frac{\phi}{2}\right) + \sin\left(\frac{\phi}{2}\right)i + \sin\left(\frac{\phi}{2}\right)j + \sin\left(\frac{\phi}{2}\right)k$$

In mathematical terms, the preceding formula shows the creation of a quaternion with the angle of φ around the unit vectors facing in the direction of the three axes of the three-dimensional coordinate system.

To create a quaternion in GLM, three different approaches can be used:

- The first method is the conversion of a three-element vector into a quaternion. This conversion creates the orientation axis between the center of the coordinate system, which is the point (0, 0, 0), and the point of the vector:

  ```
  glm::quat q1 = glm::quat(0.0f, 3.0f, 2.0f, -1.0f);
    // order of elements: glm::quat(w, x, y, z)
  ```

  The real part, *w*, of the quaternion *must* be set to 0 for this to work. The other three parameters can be seen as the scaling of the *x*, *y*, and *z* unit vectors in the corresponding directions. The result is a standard GLM quaternion.

- The second method is the creation of a quaternion from the rotation angles around the *x*, *y*, and *z* axes:

  ```
  glm::quat q2 = glm::quat(glm::radians(30.0f),
  glm::radians(50.0f), glm::radians(10.0f));
    // order of elements: glm::quat(x, y, z)
  ```

  This method of creation of a quaternion is like the rotation of a vector in three-dimensional space. The three angles must be given in radians instead of degrees. We may convert them in place. The result is again a normal GLM quaternion.

- The last method is also like the rotation of a vector in three-dimensional space, but this time, we rotate only around one axis instead of all three at once:

  ```
  glm::vec3 xAxis = glm::vec3(1.0f, 0.0f, 0.0f);
  float angle = 30.0f;
  glm::quat qx = glm::angleAxis(glm::radians(angle), xAxis);
  ```

  For the full rotation around all three axes, we need to create three different quaternions and multiply them together to get the final quaternion with the correct orientation:

  ```
  glm::quat qRot = yAxis * zAxis * xAxis;
  ```

The second and third methods of creating a quaternion are handy, but they may also create a gimbal lock (see the *The gimbal lock* section for details).

Quaternion operations and transformations

Let us see how different operations and transformations are applied to a quaternion.

Calculating the length of a quaternion

The *length* of a quaternion is calculated like the length of a vector. We take the square root of the sum of the squared elements. But a quaternion length has a crucial difference – the real part is also used as an element under the square root:

$$q = a + bi + cj + dk$$

$$|q| = \sqrt{(a^2 + b^2 + c^2 + d^2)}$$

In GLM, we can use the `glm::length()` function to calculate the length of a quaternion:

```
float q1Length = glm::length(q1);
```

The `glm::length()` function is overloaded in C++ and detects the type of the parameter at compile time.

Normalizing a quaternion

Closely related to the length is the *normalization* of a quaternion. Normalizing a quaternion changes it to an overall length of 1. To normalize a quaternion, we take the length that we calculated in the *Calculating the length of a quaternion* section, and divide every quaternion element by it:

$$a' = \frac{a}{|q|}; b' = \frac{b}{|q|}; c' = \frac{c}{|q|}; d' = \frac{d}{|q|}$$

The real part, *a*, is also considered, and both the real and the imaginary parts are divided by the length of the quaternion.

Using GLM in our code, we can use the `glm::normalize()` function to normalize a quaternion:

```
glm::quat qNorm = glm::normalize(q1);
```

The resulting quaternion, `qNorm`, will have a length of 1.

Unit, null, and identity quaternions

Like vectors, quaternions have the special types of a *unit* and *null* quaternion. In addition, they also have an identity quaternion:

$$q_{unit} = \frac{q}{|q|}$$

$$q_{zero} = (0, 0, 0, 0)$$

$$q_{ident} = (1, 0, 0, 0)$$

A unit quaternion, denoted as q_{unit}, is a quaternion with a length of 1. So, any normalized quaternion is a unit quaternion. The null quaternion, q_{zero}, has all elements set to 0. You will not find this very often in code, as the null quaternion brings problems with the length calculation: you would divide the parts by 0. The identity quaternion, q_{ident}, stands for *no rotation* and has the imaginary parts set to 0. The real part is 1, which is the cosine of 0°, that is, no rotation at all.

Adding and subtracting quaternions

Quaternion addition is like the addition of complex numbers – we must simply add up the corresponding elements:

$$(a_1 + b_1 i + c_1 j + d_1 k) + (a_2 + b_2 i + c_2 j + d_2 k)$$

$$= (a_1 + a_2) + (b_1 + b_2)i + (c_1 + c_2)j + (d_1 + d_2)k$$

Subtraction is the same as addition – we just subtract the elements of the second quaternion from the corresponding elements of the first quaternion.

With GLM, we can use the overloaded `operator+` to add the quaternions:

```
glm::quat qa = glm::quat(a1, b1, c1, d1);
glm::quat qb = glm::quat(a2, b2, c2, d2);
glm::quat qResult = qa + qb;
  // same as glm::quat(a1 + a2, b1 + b2, c1 + c2, d1 + d2);
```

The addition of two quaternions seems to be strange at first view, because adding two orientations together may bring no real benefit. But quaternion addition is an uncomplicated way to create the average of two quaternions, thus finding the quaternion *in the middle* by adding up the two quaternions and normalizing the result afterward.

Calculating the conjugate of a quaternion

If we need the opposite orientation of a quaternion, we can calculate the so-called *conjugate*, written as q*. This is done by negating the imaginary parts of the quaternion, but keeping the real part unchanged:

$$q = a + bi + cj + dk$$

$$q^* = a - bi - cj - dk$$

The resulting conjugate is a quaternion of the same length, pointing from the center of the coordinate system to the exact opposite direction.

The GLM `glm::conjugate()` function can be used to obtain the conjugate:

```
glm::quat q3 = glm::quat(a, b, c, d);
glm::quat qConj = glm::conjugate(q3);
  // result equals: glm::quat(a, -b, -c, -d)
```

Calculating the inverse of a quaternion

In the quaternion world, there is a second operation for calculating the opposite orientation, the *inverse* q^{-1} of a quaternion. The inverse quaternion is the conjugate divided by the squared length of the quaternion:

$$q^{-1} = \frac{q^*}{|q|^2}$$

The inverse is identical to the conjugate for unit quaternions, as the square of length 1 is again 1.

> **Note**
>
> In math and code, we need an additional check for the inverse. If we have a *null quaternion*, we will divide the conjugate by 0.

In GLM, we can use the overloaded `glm::inverse()` function to calculate the inverse:

```
glm::quat gInverse = glm::inverse();
```

For the null quaternions, GLM returns a quaternion with all four elements set to *NaN* (*Not a Number*), stating that the result cannot be interpreted and is invalid.

Dot and cross products of quaternions

Quaternion calculations also know the *dot product* and the *cross product*. First, let us look at the dot product:

$$q_1 = a_1 + b_1 i + c_1 j + d_1 k$$

$$q_2 = a_2 + b_2 i + c_2 j + d_2 k$$

$$q_1 \cdot q_2 = a_1 a_2 + b_1 b_2 + c_1 c_2 + d_1 d_2$$

The dot product is the same as that for vectors. We multiply the corresponding scalar parts of the real and imaginary parts and sum up the products. If we use unit quaternions or divide the dot product by the lengths of the quaternions, the resulting number, like the vector dot product, is the *cosine* of the angle between the two quaternions:

$$\cos(\phi) = \frac{a_1 a_2 + b_1 b_2 + c_1 c_2 + d_1 d_2}{|q_1|\,|q_2|}$$

The cross product is a bit different, as it is only defined in three dimensions. A quaternion has four elements – the real part and the three imaginary parts, so the calculation needs to be adjusted:

$$q_1 \times q_2 = -a_1 \cdot a_2 + v_1 \times v_2$$

For a quaternion cross product, the imaginary parts of both quaternions are interpreted as vectors, and the normal vector cross product is calculated. The real part of the quaternion cross product is the negated dot product of the two quaternions.

Multiplying quaternions

The multiplication of two quaternions is a bit more complex, as all elements of the first quaternion must be multiplied with all other elements of the second quaternion:

$$\begin{aligned} q_1 * q_2 = {} & a_1 a_2 + a_1 b_2 i + a_1 c_2 j + a_1 d_2 k \\ & + b_1 a_2 i + b_1 b_2 i^2 + b_1 c_2 ij + b_1 d_2 ik \\ & + c_1 a_2 j + c_1 b_2 ji + c_1 c_2 j^2 + c_1 d_2 jk \\ & + d_1 a_2 k + d_1 b_2 ki + d_1 c_2 kj + d_1 d_2 k^2 \end{aligned}$$

For the calculation of some of the sub-products of the quaternion multiplication, the following rules are used, in addition to the imaginary number property $i^2 = -1$:

$$ij = -ji = k$$

$$jk = -kj = i$$

$$ki = -ik = j$$

After the simplification, the resulting quaternion looks as follows:

$$\begin{aligned} q_1 * q_2 = &\left(a_1 a_2 - b_1 b_2 - c_1 c_2 - d_1 d_2\right) \\ &+\left(a_1 b_2 - b_1 a_2 - c_1 d_2 - d_1 c_2\right) i \\ &+\left(a_1 c_2 - b_1 d_2 - c_1 a_2 - d_1 b_2\right) j \\ &+\left(a_1 d_2 - b_1 c_2 - c_1 b_2 - d_1 a_2\right) k \end{aligned}$$

This multiplication result is a *concatenation of the rotations*, equivalent to the rotation around the axis defined by q_2, followed by the rotation around the axis defined by q_1.

> **Note**
>
> Like matrix multiplication, quaternion multiplication is *not* commutative. We get a different result when we swap q_1 and q_2. However, like matrix multiplication, quaternion multiplication is applied *from right to left*. The first quaternion to rotate around is the rightmost, then the next to the left is multiplied.

In GLM, the multiplication of two quaternions is done with the overloaded multiplication operator:

```
glm::quat qMult = q1 * q2;
```

The resulting quaternion, `qMult`, contains the result of the multiplication of the quaternions, `q1` and `q2`, resulting in a rotation around the axis of `q2` as the first rotation and a rotation around the axis of `q1` as the second rotation.

Converting a quaternion to a rotation matrix and vice versa

As the last operations, let us look at the conversion of a quaternion to a rotation matrix and vice versa. This type of conversion may be required to get the data to the shaders if the application code uses quaternions to change the orientation of the vertices, as a shader can work only with a rotation matrix.

The first direction to look at is from a quaternion to a rotation matrix. If we convert the quaternion `q` to the 3x3 rotation matrix `Mq`, we get the following result:

$$q = a + bi + cj + dk; |q| = 1$$

$$M_q = \begin{bmatrix} 1 - 2c^2 - 2d^2 & 2bc - 2ad & 2bd + 2ac \\ 2bc + 2ad & 1 - 2b^2 - 2d^2 & 2cd - 2ab \\ 2bd - 2ac & 2cd + 2ab & 1 - 2b^2 - 2c^2 \end{bmatrix}$$

> **Note**
>
> The detailed calculation is left as an exercise for you, as it is beyond the scope of this book.

If we create a 4x4 matrix from the quaternion q, the remaining columns and rows are filled with a 0, except the bottom-right diagonal element, which is filled with a 1:

$$M_q = \begin{bmatrix} 1-2c^2-2d^2 & 2bc-2ad & 2bd+2ac & 0 \\ 2bc+2ad & 1-2b^2-2d^2 & 2cd-2ab & 0 \\ 2bd-2ac & 2cd+2ab & 1-2b^2-2c^2 & 0 \\ 0 & 0 & 0 & 1 \end{bmatrix}$$

In GLM, two separate functions exist to convert a quaternion into a rotation matrix:

```
glm::mat3 rotM3x3 = glm::mat3_cast(q1);
glm::mat4 rotM4x4 = glm::mat4_cast(q2);
```

The call to `glm::mat3_cast()` creates a 3x3 rotation matrix, while the call to `glm::mat4_cast()` returns a 4x4 rotation matrix.

The opposite conversion, that is, from a rotation matrix to a quaternion, requires several calculations and several extra checks. Both the real and the imaginary parts of the quaternion q from a 3x3 matrix or a 4x4 matrix, as shown in the preceding formulae of this section, could be recovered as follows:

$$a = \frac{1}{2}\sqrt{1+m_{11}+m_{22}+m_{33}}$$

$$b = \frac{1}{4a}(m_{32} - m_{23})$$

$$c = \frac{1}{4a}(m_{13} - m_{31})$$

$$d = \frac{1}{4a}(m_{21} - m_{12})$$

The indices of the rotation matrix are the same as those described in the *Matrix representation* section of *Chapter 6*: row number comes first, and column number is second.

> **Note**
>
> To be aware of numerical problems, that is, if the value for *a* comes close to zero, other formulas exist for the conversion. The details of the direction of conversion are also left as an exercise for you, as it is too out of scope for this book.

GLM has the overloaded `glm::quat_cast()` function, which automatically selects the proper conversion, from either a 3x3 or a 4x3 matrix to a quaternion:

```
glm::mat3 mMat3x3 = glm::mat3(...);
glm::mat4 mMat4x4 = glm::mat4(...);
glm::quat qM3x3 = glm::quat_cast(mMat3x3);
glm::quat qM4x4 = glm::quat_cast(mMat4x4);
```

After learning about all these basic mathematics and operations and transformations of quaternions, it is time to move on to the next topic. In the next section, we will look at another vector operation we will use a lot: rotations. In character animations, rotation is one of the most frequently used vector manipulations, as every move of a limb or bone involves potentially dozens of rotations.

Exploring vector rotation

Let us start with the most basic rotation we will have in the code, the *natural-feeling* rotation around the three axes in a three-dimensional cartesian space.

The Euler rotations

In the 18th century, the German mathematician Leonhard Euler (1707-1783) discovered the rule that a composition of two rotations in three-dimensional space is again a rotation, and these rotations differ only by the rotation axis.

We still use this rotation theorem today, to rotate objects around in virtual worlds. The final rotation of a three-dimensional object is a composition of rotations around the *x*, *y*, and *z* axis in three-dimensional cartesian space:

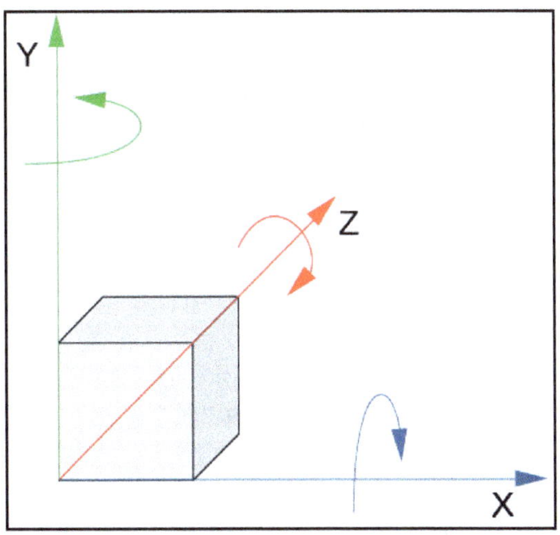

Figure 7.5: The three-dimensional cartesian space, plus the x, y, and z rotation axes

The rotations themselves are defined by the sine and cosine of the rotation angle:

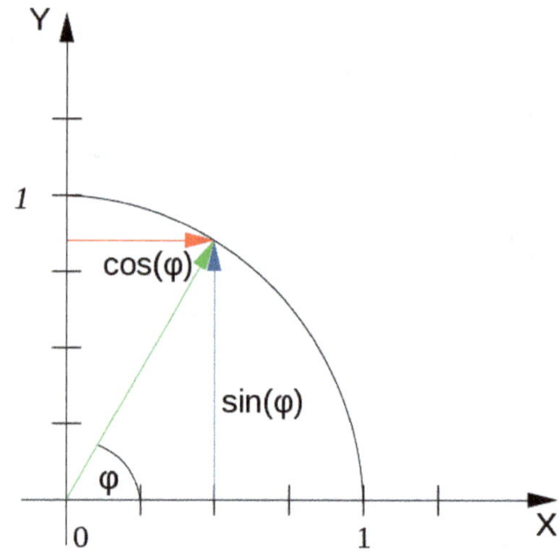

Figure 7.6: Definition of the sine and the cosine of an angle φ

We are using the inverse of the function we would normally use. Instead of calculating the sine and cosine values of the angle φ for a given point on the unit circle around the center of the coordinate system, we use the sine and cosine values to generate a rotation of the angle φ around the center.

To rotate our three-element vectors, consisting of x, y, and z coordinates, a 3x3 matrix is required to cover all three coordinate axes. Usually, we do not rotate around all three axes at once, but one axis after another. So, for every rotational step, we need a separate 3x3 matrix, covering only the rotation around this single axis.

The rotation matrices for rotations of an angle of ϕ around the x, y, and z axes are shown here:

$$R_x(\phi) = \begin{bmatrix} 1 & 0 & 0 \\ 0 & \cos(\phi) & -\sin(\phi) \\ 0 & \sin(\phi) & \cos(\phi) \end{bmatrix}$$

$$R_y(\phi) = \begin{bmatrix} \cos(\phi) & 0 & \sin(\phi) \\ 0 & 1 & 0 \\ -\sin(\phi) & 0 & \cos(\phi) \end{bmatrix}$$

$$R_z(\phi) = \begin{bmatrix} \cos(\phi) & -\sin(\phi) & 0 \\ \sin(\phi) & \cos(\phi) & 0 \\ 0 & 0 & 1 \end{bmatrix}$$

As shown in the preceding formula, the coordinate for the corresponding axis stays unchanged, while the other two coordinates will be rotated in a circular way.

Using GLM, we could do the three rotations around the unit vectors pointing toward the three directions and create a 3x3 *rotation matrix*. First, we need to define a three-element vector for every direction of the three-dimensional coordinate system:

```
glm::vec3 mRotXAxis = glm::vec3(1.0f, 0.0f, 0.0f); // X
glm::vec3 mRotYAxis = glm::vec3(0.0f, 1.0f, 0.0f); // Y
glm::vec3 mRotZAxis = glm::vec3(0.0f, 0.0f, 1.0f); // Z
```

Then, we rotate around an arbitrary angle on every axis. Here, we use the axis order YZX, and start with a rotation around the Y axis:

```
glm::mat4 mRotYMat = glm::rotate(glm::mat4(1.0f), glm::radians(30),
mRotYAxis);
```

We begin with a 4x4 identity matrix, created by `glm::mat4(1.0f)`, and create a rotation matrix that resembles a rotation of 30° around the Y axis. We need to convert the angle to radians using the `glm::radians()` function. If a vector were multiplied by the `mRotYMat` rotation matrix now, only a rotation around the vertical Y axis would occur.

The result of the `glm::rotate()` function is a 4x4 matrix, even if the rotation needs only the upper three rows and the first three columns. However, the generated 4x4 matrix may be used for other operations, such as translations or perspective corrections, which need the remaining elements of the matrix:

```
glm::mat4 mRotZMat = glm::rotate(mRotYMat, glm::radians(40),
mRotZAxis);
```

Next, a rotation of 40° around the *z* axis is done. We use the `mRotYMat` rotation matrix from the previous `glm::rotate()` call, altering it with the new rotation:

```
glm::mat3 mEulerRotMatrix = glm::rotate(mRotZMat, glm::radians(20),
mRotXAxis);
```

As the final step, the matrix is updated with a rotation of 20° around the *x* axis. As a result, a 3x3 matrix is generated here, as we are only using three-element vectors in the code, and no other operations are done with the matrix at this point.

> **Note**
>
> The YZX order of the rotation is one of the 12 possible rotations and has been chosen randomly. The rotations themselves can be divided into two groups. The first group, the *Eulerian*-type rotations, involve repeated rotations around one axis. This leads to the rotation orders XYX, XZX, YXY, YZY, ZXZ, and ZYZ. The second group is the *Cardanian*-type rotations, which involve all three axes: XYZ, XZY, YZX, YXZ, ZXY, and ZYX. The usage of those rotation orders differs among technical fields.

If we do the calculations by hand, the resulting rotation matrix would look as follows:

$$Y_\alpha Z_\beta X_\gamma = \begin{bmatrix} c_\alpha c_\beta & s_\alpha s_\gamma - c_\alpha s_\beta c_\gamma & s_\alpha c_\gamma + c_\alpha s_\beta s_\gamma \\ s_\beta & c_\beta c_\gamma & -c_\beta s_\gamma \\ -s_\alpha c_\beta & c_\alpha s_\gamma + s_\alpha s_\beta c_\gamma & c_\alpha c_\gamma - s_\alpha s_\beta s_\gamma \end{bmatrix}$$

The angles α, β, and γ denote the angles of the rotation per axis, the letter `s` in the matrix stands for the sine, and the letter *c* stands for the cosine of that angle.

The combined rotation matrix for all three angles is quite complex, using a lot of operations for every angle.

But there is a huge problem, called the gimbal lock, with the simple concatenation of rotations around the three axes, as we will see in the following section.

The gimbal lock

If we rotate exactly 90° around one of the axes, the matrix can be simplified. As the sine of 90° is 1 and the cosine of 90° is 0, a rotation angle of 90° removes some parts of the matrix elements. The resulting rotation matrix after 90° around the Z axis looks as follows:

$$Y_\alpha 90^\circ_\beta X_\gamma = \begin{bmatrix} 0 & -\left(c_\alpha c_\gamma - s_\alpha s_\gamma\right) & s_\alpha c_\gamma + c_\alpha s_\gamma \\ 1 & 0 & 0 \\ 0 & s_\alpha c_\gamma + c_\alpha s_\gamma & c_\alpha c_\gamma - s_\alpha s_\gamma \end{bmatrix}$$

Using trigonometric additions, we get back to the following matrix:

$$Y_\alpha 90^\circ_\beta X_\gamma = \begin{bmatrix} 0 & -\cos(\alpha + \gamma) & \sin(\alpha + \gamma) \\ 1 & 0 & 0 \\ 0 & \sin(\alpha + \gamma) & \cos(\alpha + \gamma) \end{bmatrix}$$

If we multiply a three-element vector by the obtained matrix, the resulting vector is as follows:

$$\begin{pmatrix} x' \\ y' \\ z' \end{pmatrix} = \begin{pmatrix} -y\cos(\alpha + \gamma) + z\sin(\alpha + \gamma) \\ x \\ y\sin(\alpha + \gamma) + z\cos(\alpha + \gamma) \end{pmatrix}$$

With the preceding matrix, a rotation around the global Y axis is done, regardless of any rotation angle using the `mRotXAxis` or `mRotZAxis` value. Now, we have a rotation with a gimbal lock and lose one degree of freedom of the three rotation axes.

You can check the gimbal lock in the `01_opengl_rotation` and `07_vulkan_rotation` examples in the `chapter07` folder.

Compiling and running the example code results in something like the screenshot in *Figure 7.7*:

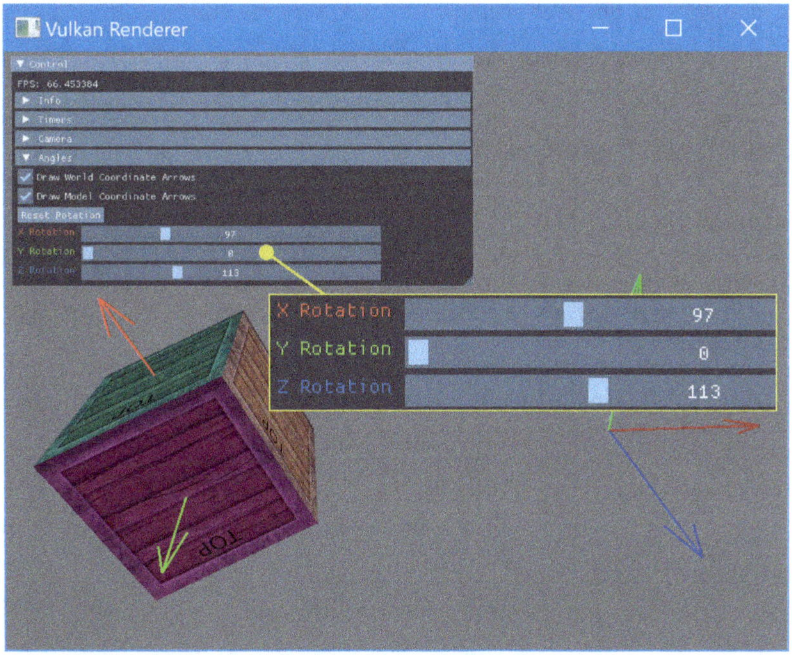

Figure 7.7: Rotation application to test the gimbal lock

You can use the three sliders to rotate the box around the three axes. To rotate an axis using a specific angle value, such as 90° or 270°, hold *Ctrl* while clicking the *left mouse button* on the slider for the Z rotation. Using *Ctrl* + *left mouse button*, the slider enters the input mode, and you can change the number in the slider field. By pressing *Enter*, or clicking outside the slider, you can leave the input mode.

If you change the angles, you will notice that some of the rotations no longer match the global rotation axis, shown on the right side, but rotate around the local axis of the box, or even around some arbitrary axis. This behavior is a result of the concatenation of the rotations, as the reference axis changes for each of the three rotations.

Now let us try the same rotations with quaternions. You may be surprised: by just using quaternions instead of the three rotations around the three axes, they *do not solve* the gimbal lock problem.

Rotating using quaternions

The reason for quaternions not solving the gimbal lock issue is simple: we need to construct the quaternion in the first place. We do this construction from Euler angles, using the same method: rotating around all three axes, one at a time.

The GLM `glm::quat()` function with three Euler angles hides the construction:

```
glm::quat orientation = glm::quat(glm::vec3(
  glm::radians(rotationXAngle),
  glm::radians(rotationYAngle),
  glm::radians(rotationZAngle));
```

Internally, GLM creates the quaternion using the cosine and the sine of the rotation angles from the rotation angles, as shown in the *Creating a quaternion* section. And that kind of creation is sadly also affected by the gimbal lock.

To compare the Euler and quaternion rotations, you can check the `02_opengl_quaternion` and `08_vulkan_quaternion` examples in the `chapter07` folder.

If you compile the example code, you will see something similar to *Figure 7.8*:

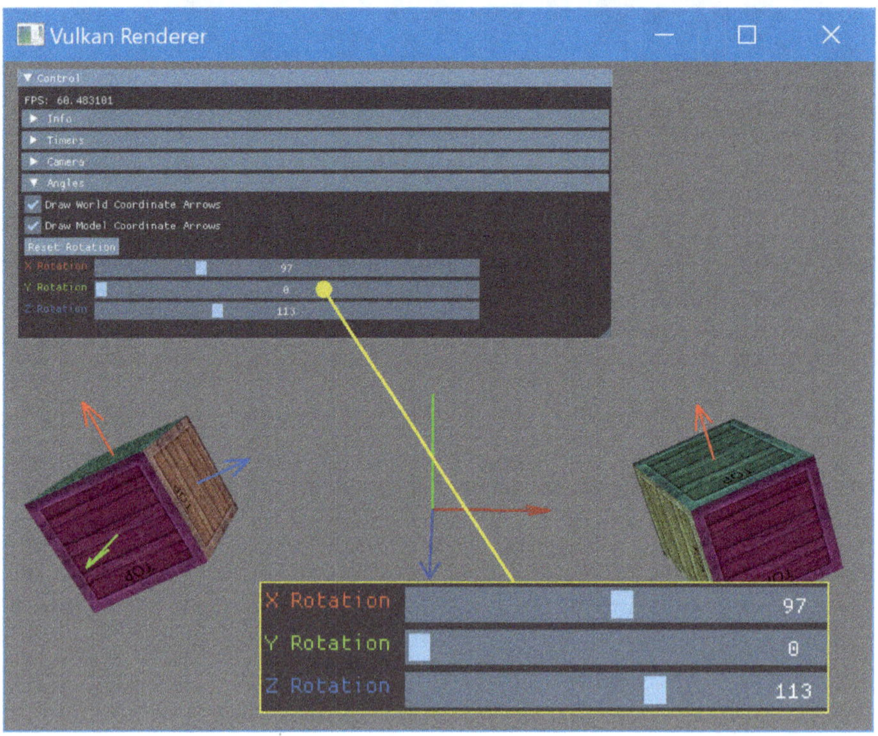

Figure 7.8: Rotating using a rotation matrix from Euler angles and a quaternion

You can try to set the rotation angle of one axis to 90° and move the other two sliders around to watch the resulting rotation of the boxes.

The left box, using Euler angles and a rotation matrix, loses the degree of freedom when rotated 90° around the Z axis, and the rotations around the X and Y axes are the same. The right box, using a quaternion to rotate the box, locks at a Y rotation of 90°.

The difference in the locking axis is the result of the different creation of the quaternion compared to the rotation matrix we are using.

> **Note**
>
> This gimbal lock *always* occurs, no matter which of the 12 rotation orders we choose. There will always be a rotation around 90° (and 270°) on one axis, which will cause the loss of one degree of freedom on the two other axes.

If we stay with quaternions after the initial rotation, there is no danger of getting to a gimbal lock. The same holds true for matrices. If we use only 4x4 matrices in the code, we cannot fall into a gimbal lock. But any construction of a rotation matrix or a quaternion by concatenating rotations from the three Euler angles will have the same side effects we already saw.

There is a solution to avoid the gimbal lock when creating a rotation matrix and a quaternion from rotations around the Euler angles, but this also comes with a price.

Incremental rotations

As the reason for the gimbal lock is a rotation of 90° or 270° around a critical axis, a simple question arises: *What if we try to avoid a rotation around 90°/270° altogether?*

This is indeed a valid question, and one of the proposed solutions when it comes to avoiding the gimbal lock is the usage of *incremental rotations*. Rotating around the axes in small steps minimizes the risk of having a 90° rotation, leading to a better solution when it comes to losing a degree of rotational freedom.

We can achieve the (almost) gimbal lock-free rotation with a rotation matrix and a quaternion. This quaternion in general is still vulnerable to produce a gimbal lock situation when we create it using the Euler angles, but we use only the differences of the rotation angles, compared to the previous `draw()` call. The update procedure with relative rotation angles is gimbal lock-free for the problematic rotation angles we have seen in the previous examples.

You can test the differences in the `03_opengl_relative_rotation` and `09_vulkan_relative_rotation` examples in the `chapter07` folder. Compiling the example code will show something similar to *Figure 7.9*:

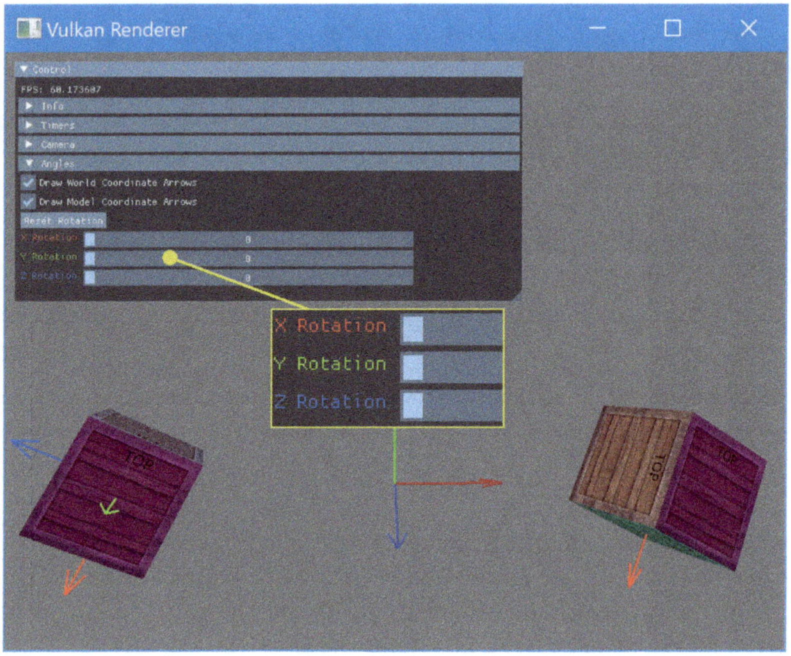

Figure 7.9: Incremental rotations with Euler angles and a quaternion

The incremental rotations allow you to rotate for any arbitrary angle around any of the axes, and the boxes nicely rotate around this – and only this – axis. No matter how hard you try, setting one of the rotation angles to 90° will never get the model into the gimbal lock, as the following rotation is relative to the current orientation.

But this solution comes with a price tag, as stated at the beginning of this section. As you can see in the application screenshot in *Figure 7.9*, all three rotation sliders are at zero, but the models are still in an odd position. There is no longer a direct connection between the local coordinate system of the boxes and the global axes. The local rotation around an arbitrary axis is summed up, making it hard or even impossible to go back to the initial orientation.

All these problems may sound like quaternions are useless for us, as they do not seem to help us with the rotations. But there is one point where quaternions are far superior, compared to the Euler angles: interpolation.

Using quaternions for smooth rotations

Spherical Linear Interpolation, or **SLERP** for short, uses mathematics to rotate from the position of one quaternion to the position of another quaternion. *Figure 7.10* shows an example of SLERP. The red line is the path for the interpolation between the quaternions with orientations φ_1 and φ_2.

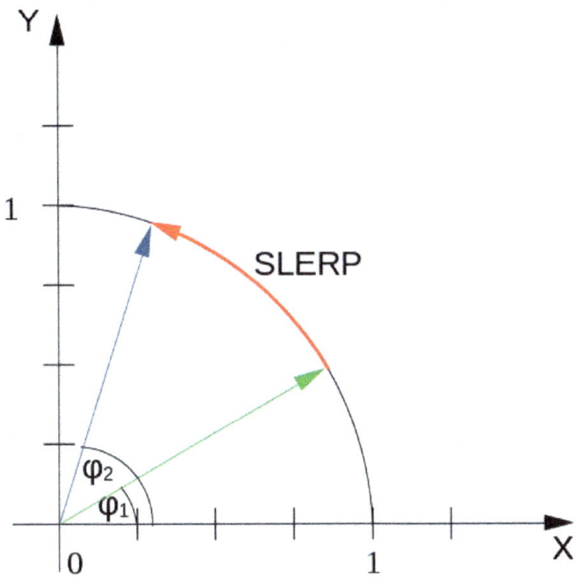

Figure 7.10: Spherical Linear Interpolation between two quaternions

Doing the same transition with Euler angles works in one dimension. But for a full three-dimensional path between two quaternions, there is no simple mathematical solution to go from one combined rotation to another while maintaining a steady path in all the directions of the movement.

> **Note**
>
> Rotating from orientation φ_1 and φ_2 has a second solution: the other way around the circle, starting on φ_1 and going "downward." It is not guaranteed that Spherical Linear Interpolation will use the shortest path between two quaternions; this must be checked in the implementation, that is, by checking the dot product.

You can test the result of SLERP in the `04_opengl_slerp` and `10_vulkan_slerp` examples in the `chapter07` folder.

Compiling and starting the code from the examples will show you something like *Figure 7.11*:

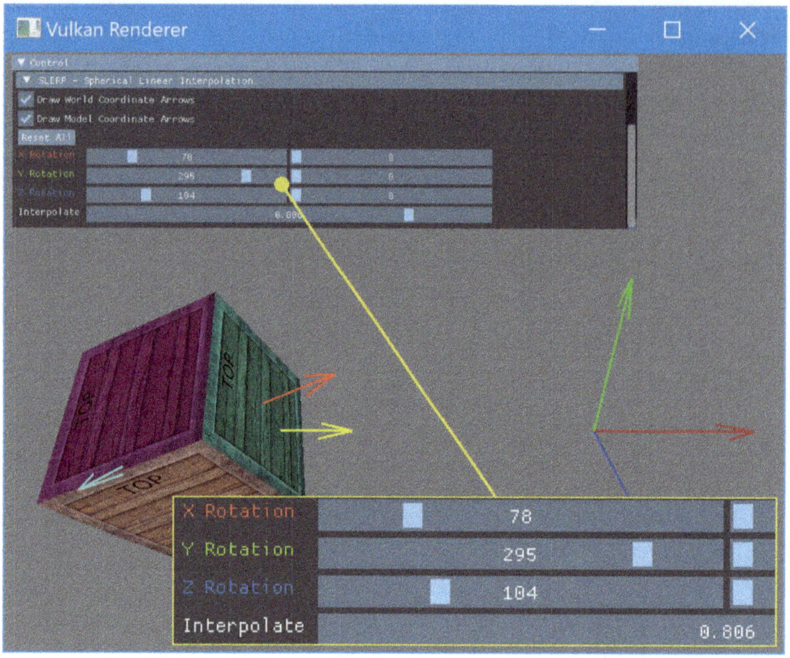

Figure 7.11: Spherical Linear Interpolation of two quaternions

The cyan arrow is changed with the first three rotation slides. This arrow shows the orientation of the box for the interpolation value of 0.000. The yellow arrow shows the position of the box at the end of the interpolation for the value 1.000. You can change the ending orientation with the second slider triplet. During the interpolation, the red arrow of the box shows the intermediate orientation.

When you move the interpolation slider, you will see the red arrow rotate and move between the orientations and positions of the cyan and yellow arrows. The box will rotate smoothly from the orientation of the start quaternion orientations to the orientation of the end quaternion.

In the application code, the interpolation between the two positions is done with the GLM `glm::slerp()` function:

```
glm::quat qInterpolated = glm::slerp(q1, q2, interpValue);
```

The function takes two quaternions and an interpolation value between 0 and 1 as input parameters and outputs a quaternion on the SLERP path between the two input quaternions. The output quaternions are rotated between 0% and 100%, according to the percentage of the interpolation value.

A second GLM function for the interpolation exists, called `glm::mix()`. While using `glm::slerp()` guarantees the shortest path between the two orientations, `glm::mix()` may generate an interpolation on the longer SLERP path.

A quaternion is perfect for rotating an object from one orientation to another, enabling us to animate any character parts, such as limbs or weapons, between two different rotational positions. But to move the hands, feet, or weapons from one position to another, a different mathematical element is used: a **spline**.

A quick take on splines

In computer graphics, a spline is a curve, defined piecewise by polynomials. A polynomial for splines is a formula, where a single variable is used with different exponents and the results are summed up:

$$h_{00}(t) = 2t^3 - 3t^2 + 1$$

In the preceding formula, the first of the four base polynomials of a cubic Hermite spline is shown. Here, the `t` variable is used in a cubic and a squared version, and a real number is added to the polynomial.

Different spline variants use different polynomials to generate the resulting curved lines. The plots for the basic functions of the usually used spline variants – B-splines, Bezier, and Hermite splines – are drawn in *Figure 7.12*:

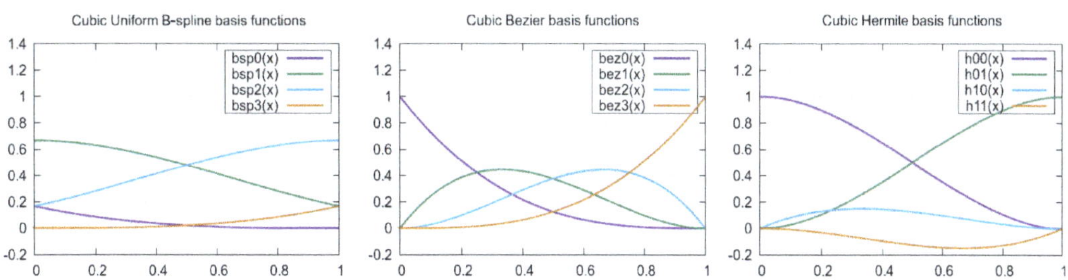

Figure 7.12: The basic functions for B-splines, Bezier, and Hermite splines

The construction of a spline can be done with numerical calculations, by solving all the polynomials for the given interpolation point between 0 and 1. Other splines can be created more easily by using geometrical means. For instance, the Bezier spline can be drawn faster using De Casteljau's algorithm compared to numerical calculations.

Examples of Bezier and Hermit splines are shown in *Figure 7.13*.

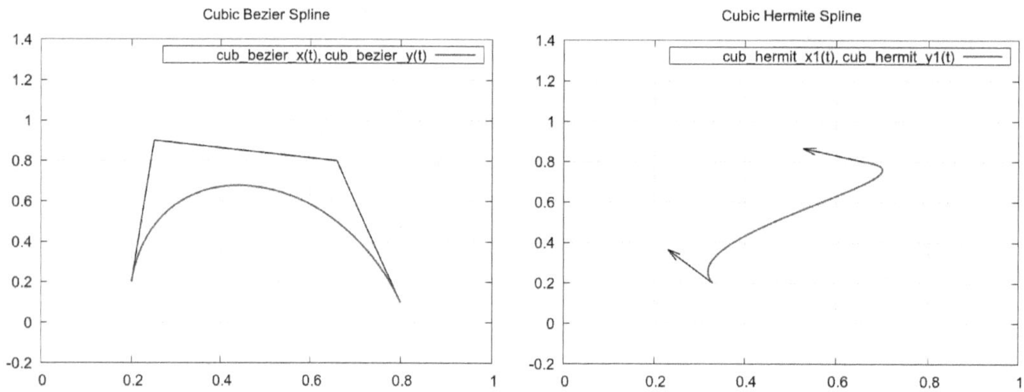

Figure 7.13: A Bezier spline and a Hermite spline

In this book, we will explore only the cubic Hermite splines. The exponent of the variable of a cubic spline is three or lower, hence the term *cubic* in the name. Cubic splines have four so-called *control points*, which control the appearance and shape of the curve.

> **Note**
>
> Any changes to the shape of a spline are indirect, as the control points only change the parameter for the polynomial calculations. These indirect changes can sometimes make the creation of a spline challenging.

The movement of object parts during the animation phases is stored in the **glTF** file format as a single point in time, as linear interpolations, as spherical linear interpolations for quaternions, or as Hermite spline interpolations to create curves. So, let us look at what these Hermite splines are and how they are constructed in math and code.

Constructing a Hermite spline

A Hermit spline consists of four control points, split into two groups:

- A starting and ending vertex
- An incoming and an outgoing tangent

The right side of *Figure 7.13* shows a Hermite spline. The two tangents start at the vertices: the incoming tangent begins at the start vertex, and the outgoing tangent starts at the end vertex.

> **Note**
>
> The incoming tangent of a Hermite spline points *toward* the direction of the spline path, and the outgoing tangent points *away* from the spline path.

The unequal directions of the two tangents may look a bit strange at first glimpse, as the Bezier spline on the left side of *Figure 7.13* is completely inside the polygon created by the four control points. But this definition has a significant impact on the continuity of Hermite splines.

Spline continuity

If we want to join two splines, we must take care of the continuity of the spline path. Just setting the location of the starting vertex of the second spline to the same value as the ending vertex of the first spline may give undesired results:

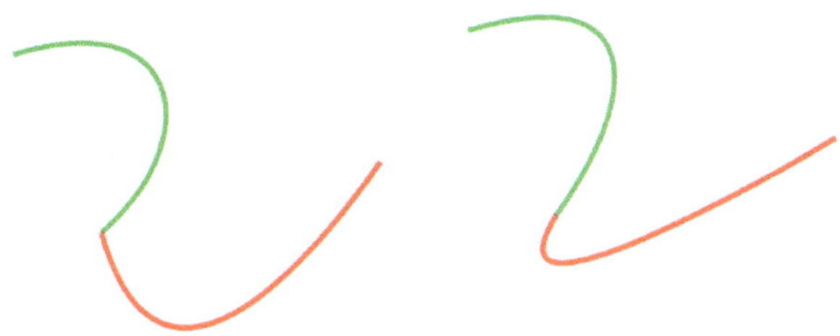

Figure 7.14: Two splines with different spline continuity

On the left side of *Figure 7.14*, the two splines are just joined in their vertices. The spline path is not interrupted, but an object moving along that path would have a sudden direction change. To achieve a continuous, smooth movement, various levels of continuity exist.

On the right side of *Figure 7.14*, we have the geometric continuity *Gn*. As an example, the continuity of *G0* stands for "both splines share the same point," while *G1* is "the outgoing tangent vector of spline one and the incoming tangent vector of spline two have the same directions."

The other kind of continuity is the parametric continuity *Cn*. The parametric continuity is stricter compared to the geometric continuity, so C^1 is already defined as "the outgoing tangent vector of spline one and the incoming tangent vector of spline two are identical."

> **Note**
>
> The definitions of *Gn* and *Cn* are out of scope for this book. You may look these up yourself if you want to know more details.

Due to the direction of the incoming and outgoing tangents of Hermite splines, we can easily achieve a high level of continuity. By using the ending vertex of the first spline as the starting vertex of the second spline and the outgoing tangent of the first spline as the incoming tangent of the second spline, both tangent vectors are already identical. Reaching the same level of continuity is a lot harder when using other cubic splines.

To construct a Hermite spline, we need to know the four base functions, plus a way to combine them to interpolate between the starting and the ending vertices.

Hermite polynomials

The base functions for a cubic Hermite spline are shown here:

$$h_{00}(t) = 2t^3 - 3t^2 + 1$$

$$h_{10}(t) = t^3 - 2t^2 + t$$

$$h_{01}(t) = -2t^3 + 3t^2$$

$$h_{11}(t) = t^3 - t^2$$

You do not have to memorize the four functions; it is okay just to know they exist. On the right side of *Figure 7.12*, the drawings of the functions can be seen.

To calculate the position of a point on the cubic Hermite spline, the following formula needs to be used:

$$p(t) = (2t^3 - 3t^2 + 1)v_0 + (t^3 - 2t^2 + t)m_0 + (-2t^3 + 3t^2)v_1 + (t^3 - t^2)m_1$$

The starting vertex is *v0* in the formula, the ending is vertex *v1*, and *m0* and *m1* are the incoming and outgoing tangents, respectively. The preceding formula is only valid if we use the closed interval of [0, 1], that is, a range between the values 0 and 1, including both values 0 and 1.

In GLM, the `glm::hermite()` function can be used to create interpolated points on a cubic Hermite spline.

We need to include the spline header to use the function:

```
#include <glm/gtx/spline.hpp>
```

Next, we need to define four three-element vectors for the start and end vertices and the incoming and outgoing tangents:

```
glm::vec3 startVec = glm::vec3(…);
glm::vec3 startTang = glm::vec3(…);
glm::vec3 endVec = glm::vec3(…);
glm::vec3 endTang = glm::vec3(…);
```

The tangents are also three-element vectors, storing the direction and length of the tangent vector relative to the origin of the coordinate system. For better visualization, the tangents are usually drawn from the corresponding vertex, and not from the origin.

To use the `glm::hermite()` function, we must supply five parameters:

```
glm::vec3 outPoint = glm::hermite(
  startVert, startTang, endVert, endTang, interpValue);
```

The order of the parameters is self-explanatory. First, the starting vector and tangent, then the ending vector and tangent, and, as the last parameter, the interpolation value in the interval between 0 and 1. The output is a three-element vector with the position of the interpolated point in three-dimensional space.

To experiment with a cubic Hermite spline, you can use the `05_opengl_spline` and `11_vulkan_spline` examples in the `chapter07` folder.

After compiling the code and starting the program, you should see something that looks like *Figure 7.15*:

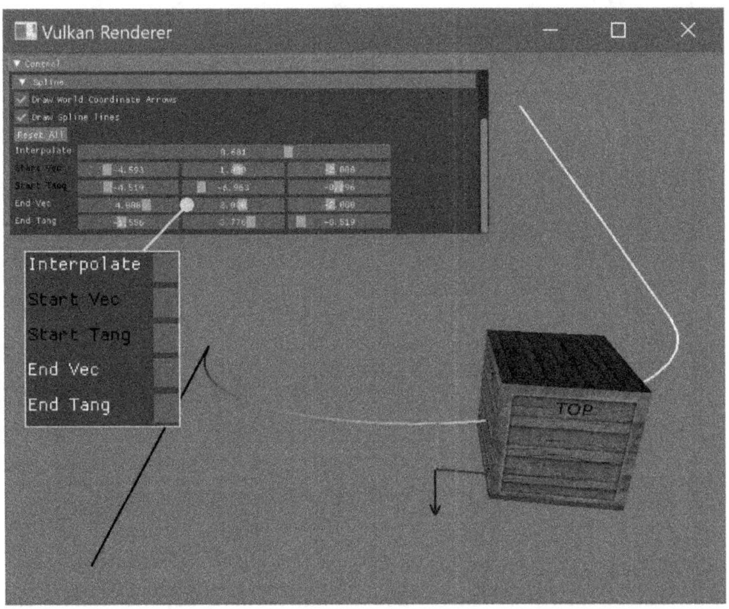

Figure 7.15: Moving a box along an interactive cubic Hermite spline

You may adjust the positions of the start and end vertex and both splines by using the sliders and playing with the direction and length of the two tangents. The interpolation slider will move the box along the spline created by the two vertices and the two tangents and follow the spline line if you change the values of the vertices and/or tangents in the middle of the interpolation.

At the end of this chapter, let us combine the two new elements in a single application and watch the effects of a quaternion and a spline in action.

Combining quaternions and splines

Using this chapter's knowledge, the combination of the interpolation of a quaternion and a spline is easy.

In the code, we use the GLM `glm::slerp()` function to get the interpolation between two quaternions and the `glm::hermite()` function to interpolate the point on a cubic Hermite spline. The resulting effect can be tested with the `06_opengl_quat_spline` and `12_vulkan_quat_spline` examples in the `chapter07` folder.

If you compile and start the example code, you will get something similar to *Figure 7.16*:

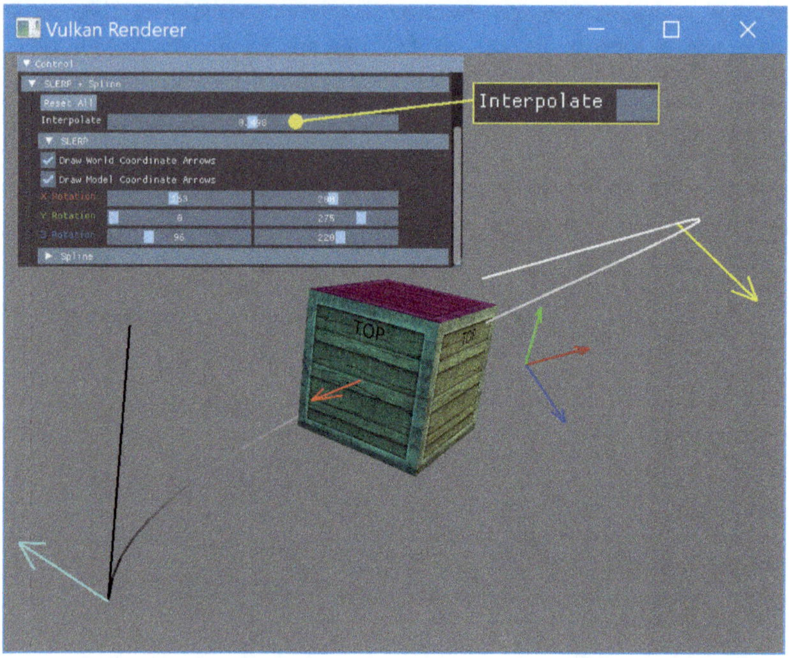

Figure 7.16: Combined example code with SLERP and cubic Hermite spline

As in the example in the *Using quaternions for smooth rotations* section, you can control the starting and ending orientations of a quaternion using sliders and interpolate between both orientations. And like in the example in the *Hermite polynomials* section, you can change the vertices and tangents of a cubic Hermite spline with the sliders.

The interpolation slider now controls both interpolations together, moving the box along the Hermite spline and rotating smoothly between the starting and the ending orientations.

With this combination of quaternions and splines, we have all the mathematical building blocks for the character animation in place. The quaternions are used to control the orientation of the various body parts of the characters in the three-dimensional space, allowing us to move from one orientation to another. And the splines are used to move the body parts along paths through the same three-dimensional space, giving us the ability to create natural-looking movements.

Summary

In this chapter, we introduced the two mathematical elements quaternion and spline, and the counterparts in GLM, ready to use in our code. After a brief discussion about the shortfalls of the usual three-dimensional rotation and the advantages of quaternions in character animations, we checked out splines and their usage in code.

All the steps from the first rotation to the quaternion/spline interpolation are accompanied by interactive code examples, ready to be tried out and to see the results of changing input values. These examples should have helped you to get a good insight into the possibilities of the two new data types.

In the next chapter, we start with the animation part of the book. The first step will be the exploration of the file format, the components inside it, what we need from the data, and which parts can be left out.

Practical sessions

Here are some ideas if you want to get a deeper insight into quaternions and splines:

- Join multiple Hermite splines in the `06_opengl_spline_quat` and/or `12_vulkan_spline_quat` examples to create a bigger spline and interpolate the moving box from the last example code along all of the splines. To continuously join two Hermite splines, the end vertex of the first spline needs to be the starting vertex of the second spline, and the output tangent of the first spline needs to be the input tangent of the second spline. Switching between the different splines may be a bit tricky though.
- Enhanced difficulty level: Assign different lengths of the overall interpolation range to the splines. This leads to different movement speeds of the box on the splines. One spline may take, say, 80% of the interpolation range, resulting in a slow-moving box along the path, while the others share the remaining 20%, and the box will move much faster along the path.
- Add some more points to the quaternion interpolation, either as in the `04_opengl_slerp` and `10_vulkan_slerp` examples or together with the Hermite spline extension of the `06_opengl_spline_quat` and `12_vulkan_spline_quat` examples. You may also add different ranges of interpolation, as in the second idea, to have varying movement speeds too.
- Add a cubic Bezier spline with its four control points. There is no GLM version, so you need to write the implementation yourself. By using De Casteljau's algorithm, the creation of the spline segments should be fairly easy.

Additional resources

- The quaternion explanation from 3D Game Engine Programming: `https://www.3dgep.com/understanding-quaternions/`
- Quaternions in the OpenGL tutorial: `http://www.opengl-tutorial.org/intermediate-tutorials/tutorial-17-quaternions/`
- An interactive demo of a 2D cubic Hermite interpolation: `http://demofox.org/cubichermite2d.html`

Part 3: Working with Models and Animations

In this part, you will explore the glTF file format and learn how to load a 3D model from a glTF file. You will be also introduced to the basic components of a glTF model: the skeleton and the vertex skin. In addition, the different parts of the animations of the model are explored, and you will learn how to draw animated models on a screen. Finally, you will get an overview of how to blend a model on the screen between animation clips.

In this part, we will cover the following chapters:

- *Chapter 8, Loading Models in the glTF format*
- *Chapter 9, The Model Skeleton and Skin*
- *Chapter 10, About Poses, Frames, and Clips*
- *Chapter 11, Blending between Animations*

8
Loading Models in the glTF Format

Welcome to *Chapter 8*! In the previous two chapters, we explored the mathematical elements and GLM data types of Vector, Matrix, Quaternion, and Spline.

In this chapter, you will learn how to use these four data types to transform the data from the glTF model description in a file into a C++ model class, storing the first parts of the glTF data to display a static, non-animated model on the screen. We will progressively expand the C++ model class in the upcoming chapters, incorporating additional data from the glTF model we utilize.

At the end of the chapter, you will know the basic elements of the glTF format, how to load it into a C++ class using a glTF loader library, and how to display the loaded model on the screen in the OpenGL and Vulkan renderer.

In this chapter, we will cover the following topics:

- An analysis of the glTF file format
- Exploring an example glTF file
- Using a C++ glTF loader to get the model data
- Adding new glTF shaders
- Organizing the loaded data into a C++ class

Technical requirements

For this chapter, you will need the example code from *Chapter 6*, `02_opengl_movement`, or *Chapter 7*, `02_opengl_quaternion` or `03_opengl_relative_rotation`, as a basis for the new code.

For a better understanding of the internal data for the models we will use for the remaining part of the book, we will start with a broad overview of the file format.

An analysis of the glTF file format

The glTF file format was created with efficiency in the transmission and loading of 3D scenes and models in mind. The file format is an open standard, supports external files and embedded, Base64-encoded data, and can be easily extended to adopt new features.

Figure 8.1 shows the general hierarchy of the glTF file format. Even if it contains only a small number of object types, loading and interpreting a file can be a complex task.

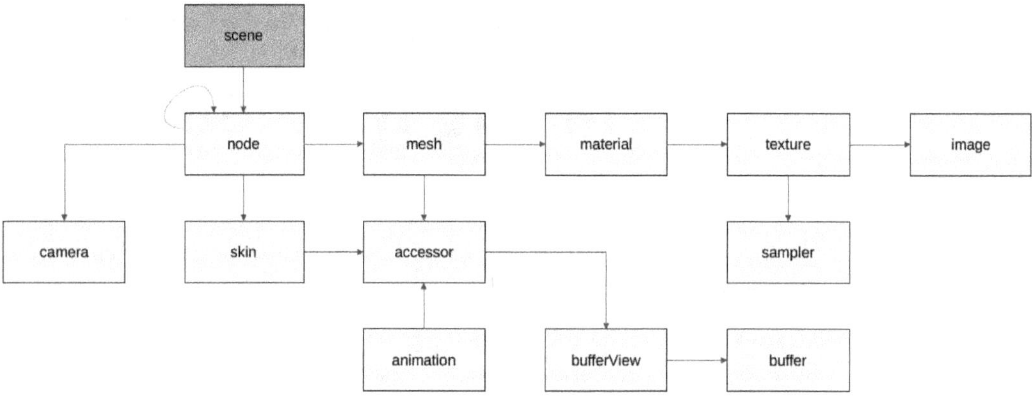

Figure 8.1: An overview of the glTF 2.0 file format

We will take a closer look at these objects and their function in the file format. Some of the descriptions may sound abstract, but these will be clarified once we look at an glTF example file in the *Exploring an example glTF file* section.

The following list describes the main elements of a glTF file:

- **Scene**: The top element of every glTF file is the **scene**. The scene is the anchor for all other elements, creating a hierarchical structure. A glTF file may contain more than one scene definition, plus an extra property indicating the default scene to show. Every scene contains an array of root nodes in the scene.
- **Nodes**: A **node** in the glTF file usually describes something such as an arm or a leg of a human model, or a mechanical part of a machine model. The node definition contains various information about a single node, including the data for the position, rotation, or scaling, and the child nodes attached to it. A node is also the smallest part of the model, which can be displayed as a single unit and animated.
- **Camera**: The **camera** is a separate object type, enabling the creator of the glTF model to define fixed view positions for the contained model. The camera also allows other properties to be set, such as the camera type, to have an orthographic or perspective-distorted view of the model. A camera can be attached to a node, allowing animated camera paths.

- **Skin**: To allow proper vertex modifications during animations, so-called vertex skinning is used. A **skin** defines the parameters for the vertex skinning. The skin object can be attached to a node, which will change during the animations. Any values used for the vertex skinning are obtained from an accessor.
- **Mesh**: The **mesh** is a property of a node, defining the object geometry and the primitives to draw when displaying that specific node. An accessor is used to gather the actual geometric data, and, in addition, a material can be set here to define the appearance of the object.
- **Animation**: An **animation** defines the changes of one or more nodes over a specific amount of time. The node changes can include transformations and rotations, creating the movement of the parts of the model.
- **Buffer**: A **buffer** is a block of binary data, either embedded in the glTF file or pointing to an external file. As it consists of binary data instead of text, the following two elements, `bufferView` and `accessor`, are required to interpret the contents.
- **bufferView**: Reading a buffer first requires a **bufferView**. The `bufferView` slices the buffer data into parts of defined starting offsets and lengths in bytes, plus a "magic number" that represents the type of data this slice contains.
- **Accessor**: The **accessor** can be seen as a kind of abstract data source for mesh, skin, or animations. An `accessor` defines the type, layout, and alignment of the data inside a `bufferView`. Examples of the type and layout are single integer values for index buffers, describing the vertex number to draw, or collections of float values to create a three-element vector for a position or color data.
- **Material**: A **material** contains definitions about the appearance of the model, or parts of it. The glTF file format uses **Physically Based Rendering** (**PBR**) for the object appearance. The PBR model uses a base color for the main surface color, a so-called metallic value for reflection, and a so-called roughness, defining the smoothness or roughness of the surface. More properties are supported, such as light emission or transparency values. Materials also may refer to textures.
- **Texture**: To allow a natural appearance of a gLTF model, **textures** can be used inside materials. The textures are the same as the ones we used for the basic textured box in both the OpenGL and the Vulkan renderers. A texture in glTF refers to one image and one sampler object.
- **Image**: The **image** for a texture points to the filename of an image file, or to some data embedded into the glTF file. Usually, JPEG or PNG files are used for images.
- **Sampler**: A **sampler** of a texture defines the properties of an image when applied to object(s), such as the minification or magnification filters, or the wrapping of the texture.

After this broad overview of the main elements, let's dive into an example now to explore the meanings of the different object types and their relations.

Exploring an example glTF file

The glTF format uses **JSON** to store data. JSON is a well-known format; readers and writers are available for all kinds of operating systems and programming languages. A second format type, binary glTF, contains the textual description and all referred data in a single file. The binary type avoids the overhead for the Base64 encoding of the file data and the management of several separate files for the model description, texture images, and other buffer data.

We will now walk through the basic glTF file using the official glTF tutorial. The link to this glTF file is available in the *Additional resources* section.

Understanding the scenes element

The first part of the file defines the scene, or scenes:

```
{
  "scene": 0,
  "scenes" : [
    {
      "nodes" : [ 0 ]
    }
  ],
```

The `scene` field contains the index of the default scene in this file. The default scene can be used to create a generic starting point after loading the model file. The following `scenes` part defines an array with all scenes in the file. In most cases, you will see only one scene, but be aware that multiple scenes can be found here. For every entry of the `scenes` array, an array containing all the root nodes for this scene is set. In this example, the only node in the file is used.

> **Note**
>
> The indices in the array of the JSON file are *implicitly* numbered. The order is the same as they are defined in the file, starting with the index 0. There is no explicit index inside one of the JSON arrays; in the worst-case scenario, you need to count the number of entries if you try to analyze a glTF file manually.

Finding the nodes and meshes

Now, the nodes are defined:

```
  "nodes" : [
    {
      "mesh" : 0
    }
  ],
```

We have only a single node here, implicitly numbered as node `0`. This node references just a mesh; it has no child nodes. The child nodes would be defined by a separate children block, and no further translations, such as a rotation or scaling. Another field is a `name` field, which adds a human-readable description to the nodes of a model.

The mesh of the node is defined as shown in the following code block:

```
"meshes" : [
  {
    "primitives" : [ {
      "attributes" : {
        "POSITION" : 1
      },
      "indices" : 0
    } ]
  }
],
```

The `primitives` field of a mesh element is the only mandatory one; all other fields are optional. The `attributes` dictionary inside of `primitives` defines the type of data stored in the accessors. In this example, we have `POSITION`-type data in the accessor with the index `1`. The positional data could be added directly to a vertex buffer.

An alternative way of drawing the vertices in the vertex buffer is called **indexed geometry**. To draw a polygon using indexed geometry, an additional buffer is used, containing the indices of the vertices. If the glTF model uses indexed geometry, the optional `indices` field is set, pointing to the accessor with the index data. In this example, the vertex indices are stored in the buffer and are referenced by the accessor with index `0`. In glTF files using non-indexed geometry models, the `indices` field is omitted.

Decoding the raw data in the buffers element

The data to draw is defined in the `buffers` element:

```
"buffers" : [
  {
    "uri" : "data:application/octet-stream;base64,AAABAAIAAAAAAAAAAA
AAAAAAAAAAAIA/AAAAAAAAAAAAAAAAAACAPwAAAAA=",
    "byteLength" : 44
  }
],
```

In this example, the `buffers` field contains a **data URI**, and the **base64**-encoded data is embedded into the file. Also, we have the (mandatory) length of the data in bytes. The length can be used to allocate the proper amount of memory for the data if an external file needs to be loaded.

After decoding the buffer data back to its binary format by using the online converter linked in the *Additional resources* section, we will get this result:

```
00 00 01 00 02 00 00 00  00 00 00 00 00 00 00 00
00 00 00 00 00 00 80 3f  00 00 00 00 00 00 00 00
00 00 00 00 00 00 80 3f  00 00 00 00
```

These numbers look like some arbitrary data – just a lot of zeros and some other numbers. To give the buffer data more structure, the values in the sub elements of the `bufferViews` elements are used:

```
"bufferViews" : [
  {
    "buffer" : 0,
    "byteOffset" : 0,
    "byteLength" : 6,
    "target" : 34963
  },
  {
    "buffer" : 0,
    "byteOffset" : 8,
    "byteLength" : 36,
    "target" : 34962
  }
],
```

These two example `bufferViews` definitions contain two different views of the same buffer, with the index `0`. The first `bufferView` starts at byte position `0` and has a length of `6` bytes. The second `bufferView` starts at byte position `8`, having a length of `36` bytes. There is a gap left of two bytes between the two `bufferView` definitions. Such unused data may be needed to create a proper alignment for the second `bufferView`.

The "magic numbers" in the `target` fields are from the glTF standard definition and used to identify the type of data inside the buffer view. The first number, `34963`, stands for `ELEMENT_ARRAY_BUFFER`, containing the vertex indices for indexed geometry rendering. The second number, `34962`, is the magic number for the `ARRAY_BUFFER` buffer type, a buffer that stores the vertex data, such as the position or color.

We previously used a similar definition in the `VertexBuffer` class in the OpenGL renderer code in the *Vertex buffers and vertex arrays* section of *Chapter 2*:

```
glBindBuffer(GL_ARRAY_BUFFER, mVertexVBO);
```

Also, in the Vulkan renderer, the vertex buffer type was defined during the initialization of the `VertexBuffer` class, when filling the `VkBufferCreateInfo` struct:

```
bufferInfo.usage = VK_BUFFER_USAGE_VERTEX_BUFFER_BIT …
```

All the buffer types in the glTF file have a respective counterpart in the OpenGL and Vulkan standards, allowing easy mapping between the glTF `bufferView` target and the buffer type in the renderer code.

Splitting the buffer data according to the `bufferView` information, we get this data part for the first `bufferView`:

```
00 00 01 00 02 00
```

And then we get this data part for the second `bufferView`:

```
00 00 00 00 00 00 00 00  00 00 00 00 00 00 80 3f
00 00 00 00 00 00 00 00  00 00 00 00 00 00 80 3f
00 00 00 00
```

However, there is still little meaning in the data without knowing the data types and structure.

Understanding the accessor element

The missing pieces are delivered by the accessor element:

```
"accessors" : [
  {
    "bufferView" : 0,
    "byteOffset" : 0,
    "componentType" : 5123,
    "count" : 3,
    "type" : "SCALAR",
    "max" : [ 2 ],
    "min" : [ 0 ]
  },
  {
    "bufferView" : 1,
    "byteOffset" : 0,
    "componentType" : 5126,
    "count" : 3,
    "type" : "VEC3",
    "max" : [ 1.0, 1.0, 0.0 ],
    "min" : [ 0.0, 0.0, 0.0 ]
  }
],
```

We have two `accessors` elements in the example file, one for every `bufferView` instance. The first accessor references `bufferView` at index `0`, and the second accessor references `bufferView` with index `1`.

The `componentType` and `type` fields are used to specify the exact type of single data element inside `bufferView` (and with it, the referenced part of the buffer object). In the first accessor, the magic number `5123` stands for `UNSIGNED_SHORT`, a scalar type of `2` bytes in length each. The `SCALAR` type simply means this data type is not composed of other data types. In the second accessor, the number `5126` defines a `FLOAT` data type for the data, a 4-byte-long floating-point type. By using the `VEC3` as a type, the second accessor data type is a 3-element float vector. In the code of the OpenGL renderer in *Chapter 2* and the code of the Vulkan renderer in *Chapter 3*, we used this data type, using GLM as `glm::vec3`.

The `count` field states how many elements of the previously defined data type are in the accessor. Combined with `byteOffset`, `count` allows multiple accessors to get different parts of the data from the same `bufferView`. In this example, we have three integer values and three 3-element float vectors.

Translating data using the buffer views

Now, let's check the data of the `bufferViews` elements with the additional information we got from the `accessors` data. The first `bufferViews` instance contains three unsigned short values. The binary data in the buffer is stored with the lower value first, resulting in these three integers:

```
0 1 2
```

For the second `bufferViews` instance, the translation is more complex. We have the binary representation of float values, and the lowest bits first. By reversing the bytes in groups of four bytes and sorting them into 3-element groups, we get these results:

```
00000000 00000000 00000000
3f800000 00000000 00000000
00000000 3f800000 00000000
```

The hex value of `0x3f800000` converted to a float is `1.0`. The mathematical way to get the float value from the hexadecimal value is left as an exercise for you.

The three groups now look like this:

```
0.0  0.0  0.0
1.0  0.0  0.0
0.0  1.0  0.0
```

In `accessors`, the data type for the second `bufferViews` instance is set to `VEC3`. We could use GLM to write the values, as it has a 3-element vector data type:

```
glm::vec3(0.0f, 0.0f, 0.0f);
glm::vec3(1.0f, 0.0f, 0.0f);
glm::vec3(0.0f, 1.0f, 0.0f);
```

We need to combine the resulting data with the information from the `attributes` fields of the `primitives` element, of the `meshes` array in the file. According to these `attributes`, the accessor with index `0` contains the indices of the vertices to draw to the framebuffer. These attributes match perfectly with the data type of an `unsigned short int` and the data we found, the integer numbers 0, 1, and 2. The accessor with index `1` contains the positional data of the vertices as a `VEC3` data type, and we found three vertices of the 3-element vectors. The vertices are placed on the origin of the coordinate system, one unit away from the origin on the *x* axis and one unit away on the *y* axis. If we imagine drawing these three points, it looks like a simple triangle.

However, before we check that assumption, let's continue with the rest of the glTF file.

Checking the glTF version in the asset element

The last block of the file contains the `asset` definition:

```
  "asset" : {
    "version" : "2.0"
  }
}
```

`asset` is not a separate object type and, therefore, not listed in *Figure 8.1*. Inside the `asset` block, various metadata is stored. The only mandatory element is `version` – defining the version of the glTF file format, and allowing us to switch the reading application to the correct implementation.

Additional fields include copyright, a field showing the person or company who created and/or owns the model data, and a field showing the program that generated the file, which is useful for debugging purposes.

So, what is in the glTF file we just examined? If we open the file with the glTF viewer from the *Additional resources* section, we can see that our interpretation of the data is correct – the example glTF defines a simple triangle. The result is shown in *Figure 8.2*:

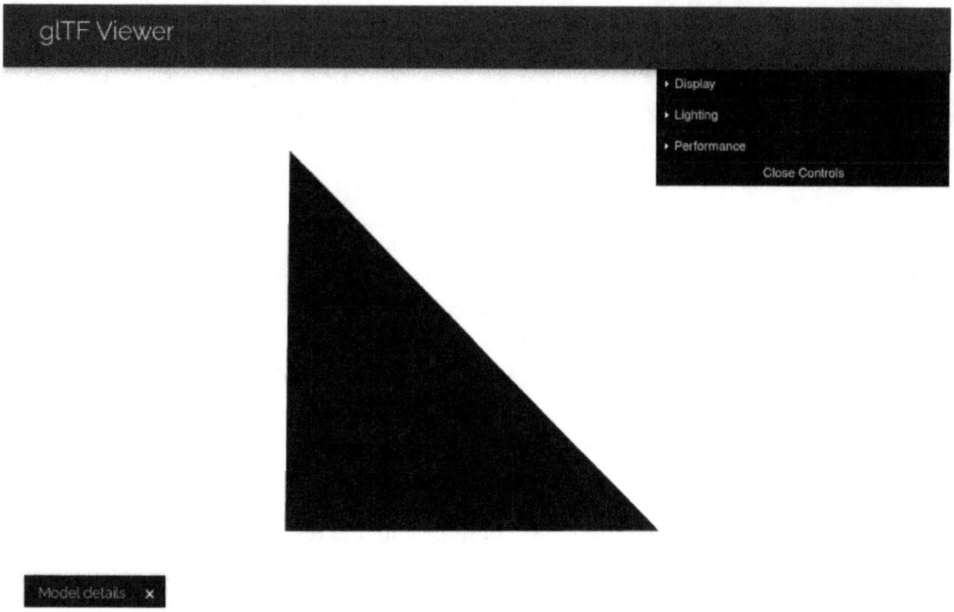

Figure 8.2: The graphical result of the glTF example

Now that we have stepped through a basic glTF file example file, it is time to load a model file into a renderer. The example code in the `chapter08` folder contains a simple model, named `Woman.gltf`, inside the `assets` subfolder of the `01_opengl_gltf_load` and `02_vulkan_gltf_load` folders.

Using a C++ glTF loader to get the model data

An uncomplicated way to load a glTF model into a structured data model can be achieved by using a glTF loader library. For this book, we will use the `tinygltf` library.

The repository for the project is available at GitHub: `https://github.com/syoyo/tinygltf`.

We need to add a couple of files to our project. Create a new folder called `tinygltf`, download the following files, and move them into the new folder:

- `tiny_gltf.h`
- `tiny_gltf.cc`
- `json.hpp`

The `tiny_gltf.h` file contains the glTF loader implementation itself; this is the file we will have to include to the classes loading the model file. The next file on the list, `tiny_gltf.cc`, has some additional C-style `#define` directives that are required for the loader. The last file, `json.hpp`, is required to read and write JSON files.

In addition to these three files, we need to get two other files. Download these two files to the `include` folder:

- `stb_image.h`
- `stb_image_write.h`

The first file may be already known to you, as we have already used it in the `Texture` classes of the OpenGL renderer in the *Buffer types* section of *Chapter 2*, and in the Vulkan renderer in the *Fitting the Vulkan nuts and bolts together* section of *Chapter 3*. The `tinygltf` loader also uses the STB image to read and write image files.

We must *remove* the first line of the `Texture.cpp` file of both renderers, located in the case of the OpenGL renderer in the `opengl` folder, and in the case of the Vulkan renderer in the `vulkan` folder, helping us avoid problems due to a duplicate C-style definition:

```
#define STB_IMAGE_IMPLEMENTATION
```

Without removing the line, the code compilation would fail, as the symbol is defined in the new `tinygltf` code and the existing `Texture` classes.

To be able to use the new `tinygltf` code files, the `CMakeLists.txt` file needs some adjustments. The first change is the list of folders containing the C++ files:

```
file(GLOB SOURCES
  ...
  tinygltf/*.cc
)
```

Appending the line enables us to find the `tiny_gltf.cc` file with the C-style definitions in the new `tinygltf` subfolder.

Then, the header `include` directive must be extended:

```
target_include_directories(Main PUBLIC include … tinygltf)
```

Add the new `tinygltf` folder as a last entry to get the two new files, `tiny_gltf.h` and `json.hpp`. The two SBT header files reside in the `include` folder, which is already part of the list.

As a final, *optional* change, we can add a custom `CMake` command to copy the asset files to the correct place. The alternative solution would be the adjustment of the path to the glTF model. The first part of this change adds the files in the `assets` subfolder of the project to a new `CMake` variable:

```
file(GLOB ASSET_FILES
  assets/*
)
```

Here, a new variable called ASSET_FILES is created, containing all files in the subfolder.

The next step is the definition of a custom target:

```
add_custom_target(
  Assets DEPENDS ${ASSET_FILES}
)
```

The new CMake target, Assets, now depends on the files of the asset subfolder.

Now, add the Assets target as a dependency to our Main executable target:

```
add_dependencies(Main Assets)
```

This line triggers the Assets target before the Main target is run, thus before the compilation of the executable.

Finally, define a new custom command:

```
add_custom_command(TARGET Assets POST_BUILD
  COMMAND ${CMAKE_COMMAND} -E copy_directory
  "$<TARGET_PROPERTY:Main,SOURCE_DIR>/assets"
  "$<TARGET_PROPERTY:Main,BINARY_DIR>/$<CONFIGURATION>/assets"
)
```

The new custom command runs a copy command as a post-build dependency of the new Assets target. There is nothing to compile in the Assets target, so this command will be run every time we run cmake, creating the files required to compile the executable of the project. The asset files will now be copied before the executable is compiled and linked, avoiding missing files when we start the program after the build.

Now, let's implement the code to load the glTF model. We will start with a new set of shaders.

Adding new glTF shaders

Most of the glTF models contain a normal vector for every vertex, in addition to the color and the position we used for the textured box in the *Loading and compiling shaders* section of *Chapter 2*. The normal vector will be used to calculate the angle between every triangle and a light vector in the scene. We will then use a simple lighting model to make the final color brighter or darker, depending on the angle between the normal of the vertex and the light source.

To support the changed format for the vertex data, we must create a new pair of shaders. The first shader is the vertex shader. Create a new file, gltf.vert, in the shaders folder:

```
#version 460 core
layout (location = 0) in vec3 aPos;
```

```
layout (location = 1) in vec3 aNormal;
layout (location = 2) in vec2 aTexCoord;
```

The shader uses GLSL 4.6, like the other renderer shaders in the *Loading and compiling shaders* section of *Chapter 2*, and the *Fitting the Vulkan nuts and bolts together* section of *Chapter 3*. We will define three input vectors per vertex – the position vector in `aPos`, the normal vector in `aNormal`, and the texture coordinate as a vector in `aTexCoord`.

Now, we will define two output variables to hand over to the fragment shader:

```
layout (location = 0) out vec3 normal;
layout (location = 1) out vec2 texCoord;
```

We will transfer the normal data in the `normal` vector and the texture coordinates in the `texCoord` vector.

The uniform block is the same as in the other shaders; we need to have the `view` and the `projection` matrices available:

```
layout (std140, binding = 0) uniform Matrices {
  mat4 view;
  mat4 projection;
};
```

The `main()` function is also simple, like in the basic shader:

```
void main() {
  gl_Position = projection * view * vec4(aPos, 1.0);
  normal = aNormal;
  texCoord = aTexCoord;
}
```

We multiply the position vector of every vertex with the `view` and the `projection` matrices to get the final position in the perspective distorted image.

We also need a new fragment shader. Create a file called `gltf.frag` in the `shaders` folder:

```
#version 460 core
layout (location = 0) in vec3 normal;
layout (location = 1) in vec2 texCoord;
```

The two input vectors `normal` and `texCoord` match the outgoing vectors of the vertex shader, as required by GLSL.

The output colour will be stored again in a variable named `FragColor`:

```
out vec4 FragColor;
```

And the `tex` texture uniform is also used, like in the basic shader:

```
uniform sampler2D tex;
```

Now comes an important difference – the light calculation. First, we will define two new vectors, a light position in the scene called `lightPos` and the color of this light source, `lightColor`:

```
vec3 lightPos = vec3(4.0, 5.0, -3.0);
vec3 lightColor = vec3(0.5, 0.5, 0.5);
```

Both vectors are currently hardcoded; it is left as an exercise listed in the *Practical session* section for you to change them to `uniform` variables.

In the `main()` function, the light calculation is done:

```
void main() {
  float lightAngle = max(dot(normalize(normal),
    normalize(lightPos)), 0.0);
  FragColor = texture(tex, texCoord) *
    vec4((0.3 + 0.7 * lightAngle) * lightColor, 1.0);
}
```

To get the cosine of the angle between the light and the normal vectors, we calculate the dot product of the normalized normal vector of the normalized vertex and light vector. It is required to normalize the vector, as you may remember from *Chapter 6*. To avoid negative values if the normal vector points in the opposite direction of the light vector, which makes the angle larger than 90°, the light angle is limited to a minimum value of `0.0`.

The final color per fragment is taken from the texture and then multiplied by the light angle and the light color. The value of `0.3` is used to create some ambient light, instead of a complete black color if the vertex normal points away from the light. The light angle is also scaled down slightly to avoid "overshooting" the color to a value larger than `1.0` when adding the values from the ambient light and light angle.

We use the calculated light value to control the color and the brightness of the pixel we read from the model texture with the `texture()` call. If the light vector and the vertex normal point in the same direction, the light value is at its maximum of `1.0`, and the pixel is modified fully by the color of the light source. The larger the angle between the light vector and the vertex normal becomes, the lower the influence of the light color.

The result of this shader is a rough-shaded glTF model, as you will see in *Figure 8.3* at the end of the *Learning about the design and implementation of the C++ class* section.

Now, create the new class to load and display the glTF model. We will include the logic to decode the data in this class, load the texture, and draw the vertices in the class too. Following these steps allows us an easier extension of the class, as the details are completely hidden from the renderer.

There is one exception – the newly created gITF shader will still be loaded in the renderer class, so we can reuse the shader for multiple models, instead of loading and compiling the same shader in every model instance we create.

> **Note**
>
> This model class is tailored to show the basics of loading and drawing a glTF model, and it may work only with the asset for this book. Any other glTF model "in the wild" could be drawn incompletely, distorted, or not drawn at all.

Organizing the loaded data into a C++ class

As we have now explored the glTF file format and an example glTF file, extending the shader code in preparation to draw a glTF model in previous sections of this chapter, we will use this new-found knowledge to create a new C++ model class. The new class will encapsulate all functionality and code to load a glTF file from the filesystem, drawing the model defined by the file on the screen.

Learning about the design and implementation of the C++ class

Our new model class will have two purposes:

- **Loading a glTF model**: To load the model, we need the filename for the model and the texture; plus, we will update the user interface to show the number of triangles that the glTF model is made of
- **To draw a glTF model**: Drawing the model needs to be split into the creation of the vertex and index buffer, the upload of the vertex and index data, and the call to draw the model itself

Finally, a cleanup method will be implemented to delete the OpenGL objects we created.

We will begin by creating the new `Model` class.

Creating the new Model class

To make the new class, create the `GltfModel.h` file in the `model` folder:

```
#pragma once
#include <string>
#include <vector>
#include <memory>
#include <glad/glad.h>
#include <tiny_gltf.h>
#include "Texture.h"
#include "OGLRenderData.h"
```

We will start with the usual set of headers to make various data types and functions of C++, OpenGL, and `tinygltf` available, as well as our own `Texture` class and the `OGLRenderData` struct, containing values that need to be shared across classes.

Now, we have the class definition:

```
class GltfModel {
  public:
    bool loadModel(OGLRenderData &renderData,
      std::string modelFilename,
      std::string textureFilename);
    void draw();
    void cleanup();
```

The first of the `public` methods, `loadModel()`, loads the model data of a specified glTF file and a single texture for that model into an instance of the `Model` class. Once the data has been loaded, we can use the `draw()` call to draw the vertices to the currently bound framebuffer. Finally, we can remove the saved data with the `cleanup()` method.

Two more methods are responsible for the OpenGL buffer creation:

```
    void uploadVertexBuffers();
    void uploadIndexBuffer();
```

We have seen in the example file that we always need a vertex buffer, and probably also a second buffer for the vertex indices. To upload the extracted model data to the graphics card, these two methods, `uploadVertexBuffers()` and `uploadIndexBuffer()`, will be used.

We will continue with three `private` methods and the internal data elements:

```
  private:
    void createVertexBuffers();
    void createIndexBuffer();
    int getTriangleCount();
```

The three methods do what their names suggest. The first one, `createVertexBuffers()`, creates an OpenGL vertex buffer object for every primitive attribute. The second one, `createIndexBuffer()`, creates the buffer to store the vertex indices. Finally, the `getTriangleCount()` method updates the `OGLRenderData` field with the number of triangles in the model.

We will also store some internal data in the class. The first data element is the `tinygltf` model we loaded:

```
  std::shared_ptr<tinygltf::Model> mModel = nullptr;
```

We will use a smart pointer here to move the loaded data to the heap memory and offload the memory management to the compiler.

Working with OpenGL values

Now, we will save the OpenGL values for the buffers:

```
    GLuint mVAO = 0;
    std::vector<GLuint> mVertexVBO{};
    GLuint mIndexVBO = 0;
```

In the `mVAO` variable, we will save the generated vertex array object, making the drawing easier later on, as we only need to bind this single object. The vertex buffer objects for the vertex data itself are stored in the `mVertexVBO` vector, and the OpenGL index buffer object will be saved in `mIndexVBO`.

The following `std::map` requires a brief explanation:

```
    std::map<std::string, GLint> attributes =
      {{"POSITION", 0}, {"NORMAL", 1}, {"TEXCOORD_0", 2}};
```

Here, we create a relation between the attribute type of the glTF model's primitive field and the vertex attribute position. The order matches the input variables in the shader – the position first, the normal second, and the texture coordinate as third element. We could also do this by using a dynamic lookup of the input variables in the shader, but for the sake of simplicity, we will hardcode the order here.

Finally, we will store the model texture in a `Texture` object:

```
    Texture mTex{};
};
```

Implementing the methods

We also need to implement the methods. Create the `GltfModel.cpp` class file in the `model` folder:

```
#include "GltfModel.h"
#include "Logger.h"
```

We will need the header files from the `GltfModel` class, plus the custom `Logger` class, as we will output messages to the console.

Creating the vertex buffers from the primitives

The first method we will implement creates the vertex buffers:

```
void GltfModel::createVertexBuffers() {
  const tinygltf::Primitive &primitives =
    mModel->meshes.at(0).primitives.at(0);
  mVertexVBO.resize(primitives.attributes.size());
```

As a first step, we get a reference to the `primitives` data structure of our model's mesh. We hardcode the first mesh at index position `0` here because our test model contains only a single mesh. For more complex models, a loop over all meshes found would be required here; you could try this as part of the exercises listed in the *Practical sessions* section. Then, we will resize the C++ vector storing the OpenGL vertex buffer object, according to the size of the `attributes` vector we find in the file.

Then, we loop over all the attributes of the `primitives` element for the mesh. The general format of the `attributes` field was shown in the *Exploring an example glTF file* section:

```
for (const auto& attrib : primitives.attributes) {
  const std::string attribType = attrib.first;
  const int accessorNum = attrib.second;
```

Saving the attribute type and the index number of the accessor in separate variables is done to simplify access to the data. Using the accessor index, we will walk through the glTF model data to find the buffer that is associated with the current accessor:

```
  const tinygltf::Accessor &accessor =
    mModel->accessors.at(accessorNum);
  const tinygltf::BufferView &bufferView =
    mModel->bufferViews[accessor.bufferView];
  const tinygltf::Buffer &buffer =
    mModel->buffers[bufferView.buffer];
```

This triple indirection is required every time we need to find the buffer containing the data. Starting from the `accessor` element found in the `attributes` field of the `primitives` element, we must use `bufferViews` to finally get the correct buffer index.

Right now, we only need a subset of the attributes, so we will filter here:

```
  if ((attribType.compare("POSITION") != 0) &&
      (attribType.compare("NORMAL") != 0) &&
      (attribType.compare("TEXCOORD_0") != 0)) {
    continue;
  }
```

If we find an attribute not pointing to an accessor containing position, normal, or texture coordinates, we can skip the rest of the method.

The data types in the accessors need to be analyzed, ensuring the correct number of elements for the OpenGL vertex buffers. We will do this with a small `switch/case` statement:

```
  int dataSize = 1;
  switch(accessor.type) {
    case TINYGLTF_TYPE_SCALAR:
      dataSize = 1;
```

```
      break;
    case TINYGLTF_TYPE_VEC2:
      dataSize = 2;
      break;
    case TINYGLTF_TYPE_VEC3:
      dataSize = 3;
      break;
    case TINYGLTF_TYPE_VEC4:
      dataSize = 4;
      break;
    default:
      Logger::log(1, "%s error: accessor %i uses
    data size %i\n", __FUNCTION__, accessorNum,
     dataSize);
      break;
  }
```

The SCALAR type stands for a single element; the three different VEC types are for 2-, 3-, or 4-element vectors. We will save the value in the dataSize variable.

Like the data size, we also need the data type to create the OpenGL buffer:

```
  GLuint dataType = GL_FLOAT;
  switch(accessor.componentType) {
    case TINYGLTF_COMPONENT_TYPE_FLOAT:
      dataType = GL_FLOAT;
      break;
    default:
      Logger::log(1, "%s error: accessor %i uses
        unknown data type %i\n", __FUNCTION__,
        accessorNum, dataType);
      break;
  }
```

This switch/case may look useless, as we just check for the float type. It is shown in the preceding code block as an example of the basic principles to choose the correct data type.

After we have collected all the data we need, we are finally able to create the OpenGL vertex buffer objects:

```
  glGenBuffers(1, &mVertexVBO[attributes[attribType]]);
  glBindBuffer(GL_ARRAY_BUFFER,
    mVertexVBO[attributes[attribType]]);
```

Here, the std::map attributes variable is used to retrieve the vertex buffer number for the current attribute type. We will create a new vertex buffer and also bind it as the active vertex buffer.

Configuring newly created buffer

The newly created vertex buffer will be configured next:

```
      glVertexAttribPointer(attributes[attribType], dataSize,
        dataType, GL_FALSE, 0, (void*) 0);
      glEnableVertexAttribArray(attributes[attribType]);
      glBindBuffer(GL_ARRAY_BUFFER, 0);
    }
  }
```

Using the correct data size and data type of the buffer, we will create a new OpenGL vertex attribute pointer and enable it. Again, the attributes map is used to gather the correct index values. As a last step, we unbind the vertex buffer to prevent unwanted changes.

Creating the index buffer for the vertices is done faster than doing the same for Vulkan because we need just two OpenGL calls:

```
void GltfModel::createIndexBuffer() {
  glGenBuffers(1, &mIndexVBO);
  glBindBuffer(GL_ELEMENT_ARRAY_BUFFER, mIndexVBO);
}
```

The format of the index buffer is well defined and needs no further configuration, as we use the default unsigned short integers as the data type in the glTF model. So, we only need to generate a new index buffer and bind it as the active one.

> **Note**
>
> Do *not* unbind the element buffer during the vertex array object creation. The index buffer must be in the bound state; unbinding it will lead to a crash during the `draw()` call.

To upload the vertex and index data of the loaded glTF model, the following two methods are used. We will start with `uploadVertexBuffers()`:

```
void GltfModel::uploadVertexBuffers() {
  for (int i = 0; i < 3; ++i) {
    const tinygltf::Accessor& accessor = mModel->accessors.at(i);
    const tinygltf::BufferView& bufferView =
      mModel->bufferViews[accessor.bufferView];
    const tinygltf::Buffer& buffer =
      mModel->buffers[bufferView.buffer];
```

We will loop over the first three accessors to get the buffer from the corresponding accessor data. For our glTF example model, accessor `0` points to the buffer with the vertex position data, accessor `1` points to the normal data, and accessor `2` points to the texture coordinates. In a real-world application, we would need to do additional steps to assure we take the correct accessors.

Uploading data to the graphics card

After we have the right buffer, we will upload the data to the graphics card:

```
      glBindBuffer(GL_ARRAY_BUFFER, mVertexVBO[i]);
      glBufferData(GL_ARRAY_BUFFER, bufferView.byteLength,
        &buffer.data.at(0) + bufferView.byteOffset,
        GL_STATIC_DRAW);
      glBindBuffer(GL_ARRAY_BUFFER, 0);
    }
  }
```

The vertex buffer with the current indices is bound, and by using the `byteLength` and the `byteOffset` values of the `bufferView` variable, the corresponding part of the data in the `tinygltf` buffer is copied to the GPU.

For the `uploadIndexBuffer()` method, the upload is easier, compared to the upload of the vertex buffer data:

```
void GltfModel::uploadIndexBuffer() {
  const tinygltf::Primitive& primitives =
    mModel->meshes.at(0).primitives.at(0);
  const tinygltf::Accessor& indexAccessor =
    mModel->accessors.at(primitives.indices);
  const tinygltf::BufferView& indexBufferView =
    mModel->bufferViews[indexAccessor.bufferView];
  const tinygltf::Buffer& indexBuffer =
    mModel->buffers[indexBufferView.buffer];
```

First, we will get the accessor for the index data from the primitives of the mesh and search the buffer. Then, we will also copy the index data to the GPU:

```
  glBindBuffer(GL_ELEMENT_ARRAY_BUFFER, mIndexVBO);
  glBufferData(GL_ELEMENT_ARRAY_BUFFER,
    indexBufferView.byteLength, &indexBuffer.data.at(0) +
    indexBufferView.byteOffset, GL_STATIC_DRAW);
}
```

We use again the `byteLength` and the `byteOffset` values, this time from the `indexBfferView` variable, to let OpenGL copy the corresponding part of the `indexBuffer` data to the GPU. To get the number of triangles of the loaded glTF model, the `getTriangleCount()` method is used:

```
int GltfModel::getTriangleCount() {
  const tinygltf::Primitive &primitives =
      mModel->meshes.at(0).primitives.at(0);
```

```
    const tinygltf::Accessor &indexAccessor =
        mModel->accessors.at(primitives.indices);
    return indexAccessor.count;
  }
```

The number of indices can be read from one of the accessors containing the indices of the vertices. Using the position data for the triangle count may get the wrong results, as not all triangles may be drawn, or some of the vertices may be used in multiple triangles.

Loading model data from a file

Now, the model loading method, `loadModel()`, can be implemented:

```
  bool GltfModel::loadModel(OGLRenderData &renderData,
      std::string modelFilename,
      std::string textureFilename) {
    if (!mTex.loadTexture(textureFilename), false) {
      return false;
    }
```

We will try to load the texture given by the `textureFilename` parameter, aborting the model loading process entirely if the texture loading fails. If we were to continue without a texture, the result of the drawing would be undefined.

After loading the texture, the smart pointer for the model is populated with a newly constructed `tinygltf` model:

```
    mModel = std::make_shared<tinygltf::Model>();
```

Now, the glTF model will be loaded, using the `tinygltf` code. In addition, some helper variables are required to catch a warning or error that may occur:

```
    tinygltf::TinyGLTF gltfLoader;
    std::string loaderErrors;
    std::string loaderWarnings;
    bool result = false;
    result = gltfLoader.LoadASCIIFromFile(mModel.get(),
      &loaderErrors, &loaderWarnings, modelFilename);
```

The `gltfLoader` contains the loading methods, filling the data structures of the model data. We use the `ASCII` loading call here, loading a model from a textual representation file, like the example in the *Exploring an example glTF file* section. `tinygltf` also supports loading the pure binary format, containing all required data in a single file.

Any errors during the load will be stored in the `loaderErrors` string, and any warning in the `loaderWarnings` string. The overall status of the model loading call is stored in `result`, signalling success or failure.

After the loading has finished, we will check for warnings and errors:

```
if (!loaderWarnings.empty()) {
  Logger::log(1, "%s: warnings while loading glTF
    model:\n%s\n", __FUNCTION__, loaderWarnings.c_str());
}
if (!loaderErrors.empty()) {
  Logger::log(1, "%s: errors while loading glTF
    model:\n%s\n", __FUNCTION__, loaderErrors.c_str());
}
```

If there is any data in the strings, we will output the contents to the console that the program was started from. Showing the data to the user may help to debug invalid data in the model file.

A check of the loading `result` follows the warning and error output:

```
if (!result) {
  Logger::log(1, "%s error: could not load file '%s'\n",
    __FUNCTION__, modelFilename.c_str());
  return false;
}
```

Checking the success or failure after printing the error is intentional. The opposite order would just stop the program, without showing any information about what may have caused the loading process to abort.

Creating OpenGL objects

At this point, we have some valid model data loaded, and it is time to create the OpenGL objects to store it:

```
glGenVertexArrays(1, &mVAO);
glBindVertexArray(mVAO);
createVertexBuffers();
createIndexBuffer();
glBindVertexArray(0);
```

To store the vertex buffers and the index buffer, we will create and bind a vertex array object. The vertex array object will encapsulate the other buffers. Then, we will call the creation functions for the buffers, and we will unbind the vertex array object again.

Finally, we will update the variable for the triangle count shown in the user interface, returning `true` to signal a successful model load:

```
    renderData.rdTriangleCount = getTriangleCount();
    return true;
  }
```

Using the cleanup() method

Once we no longer need the model, we can remove all OpenGL-specific data with the `cleanup()` method:

```
  void GltfModel::cleanup() {
    glDeleteBuffers(mVertexVBO.size(), mVertexVBO.data());
    glDeleteBuffers(1, &mVAO);
    glDeleteBuffers(1, &mIndexVBO);
    mTex.cleanup();
    mModel.reset();
  }
```

`cleanup()` deletes the vertex buffers, the vertex array, and the index buffer. We will also use the `cleanup()` call to the texture here to remove the created OpenGL texture object. As a last cleanup step, we will free the memory used by the model.

Finally, the `draw()` method for the `GltfModel` class is implemented:

```
  void GltfModel::draw() {
    const tinygltf::Primitive &primitives =
      mModel->meshes.at(0).primitives.at(0);
    const tinygltf::Accessor &indexAccessor =
      mModel->accessors.at(primitives.indices);
```

At the top of the `draw()` method, we will get the `primitives` element and `accessor` containing the index data for the model's first mesh. We need `accessor` at the end of the `glDrawElements()` method, as it contains the data type of the index buffer and the correct number of triangles to draw. In the `primitives` element, the drawing mode for the model is set. In our example, we will draw triangles.

Getting the drawing mode for the model

The next step is reading out the drawing mode of the first mesh's primitives:

```
    GLuint drawMode = GL_TRIANGLES;
    switch (primitives.mode) {
      case TINYGLTF_MODE_TRIANGLES:
        drawMode = GL_TRIANGLES;
        break;
      default:
```

```
        Logger::log(1, "%s error: unknown draw mode %i\n",
          __FUNCTION__, drawMode);
        break;
    }
```

The mode variable of the primitives contains the drawing mode for the model. This mode can be set to draw triangles but also for other draw modes, such as lines. Like the data type and size, this switch/case is shown as an example.

Now, we will prepare the objects we need to draw the model:

```
    mTex.bind();
    glBindVertexArray(mVAO);
```

We will bind the texture and the vertex array object, making both available for the OpenGL draw call. The vertex array object contains the vertex buffers and the index buffer, so we do not need to bind the buffers separately.

After all buffers are created and filled, we can hand over the index data to OpenGL to draw the triangles of the model to the framebuffer:

```
    glDrawElements(drawMode, indexAccessor.count,
      indexAccessor.componentType, nullptr);
```

As we have indexed geometry in the model, we need to call glDrawElements() instead of glDrawArrays(). The drawMode element has been set in a switch/case statement, and the count variable contains the number of primitives of this type to draw – in our case, this is the number of triangles. componentType is defined with the same internal value as in OpenGL, so we can use it directly here, without an extra conversion.

At the end of the draw() method, we will unbind the vertex array object and the texture again, avoiding trouble if the following calls in the renderer continue to draw:

```
    glBindVertexArray(0);
    mTex.unbind();
  }
```

With the completion of the draw() method, the new GltfModel class is ready to be used. So, let's add the new class to the renderer.

Adding the new model class to the renderer

You can use the example code from *Chapter 6* (02_opengl_movement), or *Chapter 7* (02_opengl_quaternion or 03_opengl_relative_rotation), as a basis here, as it already contains all the code to move the camera around. Feel free to remove the code for the shader switching from the code of *Chapter 6*, or the boxes and rotations from the code of *Chapter 7*. The example code for *Chapter 8* is based on the code of the `02_opengl_quaternion` example from *Chapter 7*.

To load and show the model in the OpenGL renderer, we have to include the new header file. Add this line to the `OGLRenderer.h` file in the `opengl` folder:

```
#include "GltfModel.h"
```

Then, add these two `private` data members of the `OGLRenderer` class to the `OGLRenderer.h` file:

```
    Shader mGltfShader{};
    std::shared_ptr<GltfModel> mGltfModel = nullptr;
```

We added the shader code in *Adding new glTF shaders* section; therefore, the `mGltfShader` variable will hold the OpenGL shader. The second variable, `mGltfModel`, will point to the data of the glTF model. We will also use a smart pointer here to simplify the memory handling, like we already did for the `tinygltf` model file in the `GltfModel` class in the *Creating the new Model class* section.

Now, we will add the implementation of the `OGLRenderer` class. Include the following lines within the `init()` method of the `OGLRenderer.cpp` file, located in the `opengl` folder, alongside the other shader loading code:

```
  if (!mGltfShader.loadShaders("shader/gltf.vert",
    "shader/gltf.frag")) {
    return false;
  }
```

We will load the new shaders and store them in the `mGltfShader` variable, aborting the renderer initialization if anything went wrong.

A bit below the shader loading in the `init()` method, where the other models are initialized, add these new lines:

```
  mGltfModel = std::make_shared<GltfModel>();
  std::string modelFilename = "assets/Woman.gltf";
  std::string modelTexFilename = "textures/Woman.png";
```

The first line creates a shared smart pointer for the new `GltfModel` object, and the other two lines add temporary strings, containing the filename of the example glTF model data and the texture for the model.

Now, we can load the glTF model into the `GltfModel` object:

```
if (!mGltfModel->loadModel(mRenderData, modelFilename,
  modelTexFilename)) {
  return false;
}
mGltfModel->uploadIndexBuffer();
```

As with the shader loading at the start of this section, we will abort the `init()` renderer if the model cannot be loaded successfully, and we will upload the indices of the vertices right after the model was loaded. The index buffer data never changes during the lifetime of the glTF model, so this needs to be done only once.

Once the glTF data has been loaded, the `mGltfModel` object contains the vertex data. To upload the data to the GPU, add this line to the `draw()` method, inside the calls to `mUploadToVBOTimer.start()` and `mUploadToVBOTimer.stop()`:

```
mGltfModel->uploadVertexBuffers();
```

Uploading the vertex buffer data in every frame is required for the code of *How (not) to apply a skin to a skeleton* section in *Chapter 9*, as the vertices of the model will change if we use CPU-based vertex skinning. After we moved the vertex skinning process to the GPU in *Implementing GPU-based skinning* section of *Chapter 9*, the vertex buffer data must be uploaded only once.

Still in the `draw()` method, between the drawing of the rotating boxes and the unbinding of the framebuffer, add these two lines:

```
mGltfShader.use();
mGltfModel->draw();
```

Here, the glTF shader, `mGltfShader`, will be bound, and `mGltfModel` is instructed to draw itself to the framebuffer.

The last addition for the `OGLRenderer` class will be in the `cleanup()` method, freeing the resources we used:

```
mGltfModel->cleanup();
mGltfModel.reset();
mGltfShader.cleanup();
```

The `cleanup()` method of the `mGltfModel` releases the resources of our model object, and the following `reset()` releases the shared pointer, leading to the destruction of the `mGltfModel` object. In addition, the glTF shader will be released.

Some other, smaller changes are also required, to show the triangle count of the mode in the user interface and to fix the wrong vertical flipping of the texture for our glTF model.

First, we need to add the new triangle counter to the `OGLRenderData` struct. Add this line to the definition of `OGLRenderData` in the `OGLRenderData.h` file in the `opengl` folder:

```
unsigned int rdGltfTriangleCount = 0;
```

Then, we must add this triangle counter to the user interface so that we can see the overall number of the triangles. Adjust the line that displays the number of drawn triangles in the `UserInterface.h` file in the `opengl` folder:

```
ImGui::Text("%s",
  std::to_string(renderData.rdTriangleCount +
  renderData.rdGltfTriangleCount).c_str());
```

We will simply add the `rdTriangleCount` variables for the boxes and the new `rdGltfTriangleCount` for the glTF model.

The last change needs to be done in the `Texture` class. After loading the textures using the STB image, we flipped all images vertically. The texture for the example glTF model is already flipped, so we need an additional switch to prevent the double flip, resulting in wrong colors.

Adjust the definition of the `loadTexture()` method to the `Texture.h` file in the `opengl` folder:

```
bool loadTexture(std::string textureFilename,
  bool flipImage = true);
```

We will add an additional Boolean parameter, named `flipImage`, and set the default to `true`.

The new `flipImage` parameter for the `loadTexture()` method also needs to be added to the implementation. Change this line in the `Texture.cpp` file in the `opengl` folder:

```
bool Texture::loadTexture(std::string textureFilename,
  bool flipImage) {
```

Inside the `loadTexture()` method, the new `flipImage` variable is simply given to the STB loading call, instead of all images being flipped:

```
stbi_set_flip_vertically_on_load(flipImage);
```

After these changes, we can control the image flipping. For the original box model, we will need to flip the texture, due to the opposite *x* axis definition in normal images and the OpenGL coordinate system.

Compiling and starting the program will result in a picture similar to *Figure 8.3*:

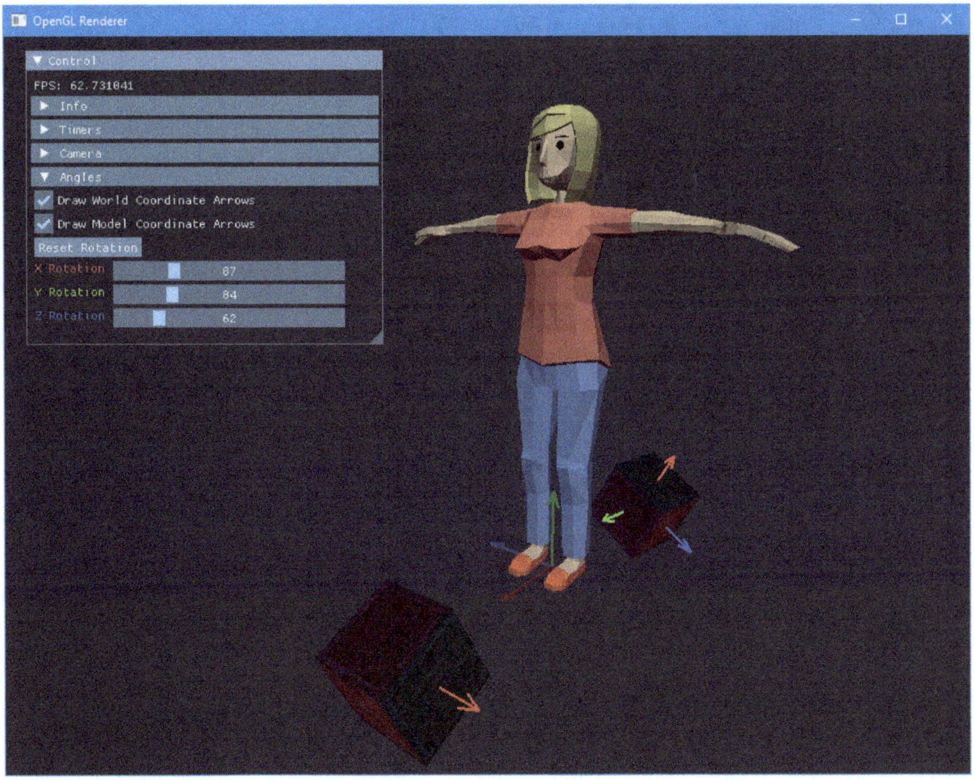

Figure 8.3: The loaded glTF model

The picture on your screen could look different, the reason was explained at the start of the *Adding the new model class to the renderer* section – the outcome depends on the previous example code you used as starting point, and whether you used the unchanged example code, or if you cleaned the code up and removed additional items like the boxes.

To add the glTF loader and the new `GltfModel` class to Vulkan, things become more complex, compared to OpenGL.

Adding the glTF loader and model to the Vulkan renderer

Here, the part where we get the buffers of the glTF model using the accessors is similar, but everything else is quite different. You can check the resulting code in the example code, `02_vulkan_gltf_load`, in the `chapter08` folder.

The following list summarizes the differences between the changes made to the Vulkan renderer and the OpenGL renderer:

- The Vulkan pipeline is immutable after creation, so we need a new pipeline for the new glTF model shaders. This new pipeline has been moved to an entirely new class, as the handling of the input variables in the new vertex shader is entirely different.
- We need more `VertexBuffer` objects – one for the boxes, and one for every glTF attribute. The data required to manage the vertex buffers has been moved to a new struct called `VkVertexBufferData`.
- The glTF model uses indexed geometry, so we need a new `IndexBuffer` class. The new class manages all objects required to create the buffer type for the indices and also uploads data to the index buffer. All data related to the index buffer management has been added to a new struct called `VkIndexBufferData`.
- Uploading and drawing the vertex data must happen inside a Vulkan command buffer recording. The upload of these command buffer needs to be done outside the render pass, and the draw inside the render pass.
- The variables for the Vulkan objects containing the data of the glTF model were moved to a separate struct. A new struct called `VkGltfRenderData` has been created, containing the data for the glTF model in one place.
- Multiple textures also need multiple buffers, samplers, and memory allocation objects. These have been moved to another new struct, called `VkTextureData`.

Essentially, we perform the same operations as in the OpenGL renderer. The differences in data handling are caused by cross-usages of different Vulkan objects across the renderer.

At this point, we have the tools ready to read the data from a glTF model file, extract the vertex data, upload the vertices to the GPU, and display the model on the screen. Being able to draw a glTF model is an important milestone on our way to controlling a fully animated model in our application.

Summary

In this chapter, we explored the structure of a glTF model file format by using a simple example. Other glTF model files will be much more complex, so we just focused on the important parts. You can try out the suggestions in the *Practical sessions* section; they will enable you to load and draw even more complex models.

The theoretical knowledge gained from the analysis of the glTF file format and the exploration of the example file has been used to create a C++ class, containing the vertex data of the model and the vertex indices to draw the model. Our focus here was to encapsulate the model data and create independent objects that can be drawn to the screen using a couple of simple commands in the renderer.

In the following chapter, we will continue with the fundamental parts of a character in a game. You will learn the basic steps to animate a game character, how animation data is stored in the glTF model file, and how to extract and interpret this data.

Practical sessions

Here are some ideas if you want to get a deeper insight into the glTF format:

- Change the `lightPos` and `lightColor` fragment shader variables into uniform variables, and make them adjustable via sliders in the user interface. You could use two `SliderFloat3` ImGui elements – one for the color, and the other one for the position.
- Load a binary glTF model. A link to sample models is included in the *Additional resources* section. The `tinygltf` loader has a function to load binary models, called `LoadBinaryFromFile();` you should use the filename extension to switch between textual (`.gltf`) and binary (`.glb`) model format loading.
- Try to load the textures of the binary models. The textures are not stored as separate files but included in the binary model file. Compared to the normal file-based method, this should be easier, as you will get the texture data to upload to the GPU as part of one of the glTF buffers – no need to load from files.
- Add support for non-indexed geometry rendering. If the `indices` field of the primitives' part of the mesh is not set, you could just draw the vertices in the vertex buffers from start to end, using the already known functions `glDrawArrays()` for OpenGL and `vkCmdDraw()` for Vulkan.
- Load models with more than one mesh. The official sample models linked in the *Additional resources* section are a good start to find models containing multiple meshes.

Additional resources

- The tinygltf loader: `https://github.com/syoyo/tinygltf`
- The official glTF tutorial: `https://github.com/KhronosGroup/glTF-Tutorials/tree/master/gltfTutorial`
- Sample glTF models: `https://github.com/KhronosGroup/glTF-Sample-Models`
- The glTF website of the Khronos® Group Inc: `https://www.khronos.org/gltf/`
- A browser-based glTF model viewer: `https://gltf-viewer.donmccurdy.com`
- A tutorial on building a glTF viewer: `https://gltf-viewer-tutorial.gitlab.io`
- Convert Base64 to hexadecimal: `https://cryptii.com/pipes/base64-to-hex`

9

The Model Skeleton and Skin

Welcome to *Chapter 9*! In the previous chapter, we examined the glTF file format, its elements, and the relations between these elements. We also added a simple C++ class for reading data from an example file and displaying the character model on the screen.

In this chapter, we will explore the glTF format in more depth. Every character model has a skeleton, like a human. The skeleton is required to animate the parts of the character independently. You will learn how to extract the model's skeleton and store the skeleton data in a tree structure.

Next, we will look at how to apply a skin to a character – the triangles that define the model. For the animations in the next chapter to appear correctly, the skin must follow the motion of the skeleton. Special attention must be paid to the joints between the bones of the model to ensure that the model's skin behaves like human skin.

At the end of the chapter, we will look at another method of applying skin using **dual quaternions**. Dual quaternions help to retain the volume of the model's body when joints move, which may be lost when using the default skinning method.

In this chapter, we will cover the following topics:

- These skeletons are not spooky
- How (not) to apply a skin to a skeleton
- Implementing GPU-based skinning
- Using dual quaternions for skinning

Technical requirements

To follow along with this chapter, you will need the OpenGL and Vulkan renderer code from *Chapter 8*.

If we want to animate our game character model, we must extract the skeleton. This first step requires some work to complete, which we will cover in this chapter. As an example, we need to construct a tree structure of the model's nodes and extract the so-called **inverse bind matrices**.

These skeletons are not spooky

If you think of a skeleton, the first picture in your mind will most probably be the one on the left side of *Figure 9.1*. But the type of skeleton we are talking about in this section is the one on the *right* side of the picture:

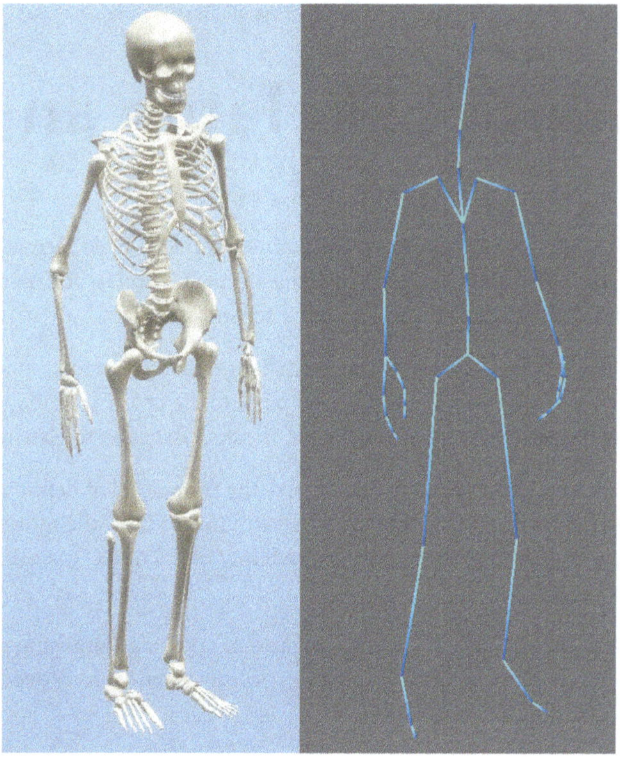

Figure 9.1: A human skeleton and the glTF example model skeleton

The skeleton in our example glTF model file looks surprisingly like a human skeleton. We can identify the hips, legs and feet, spine and neck, shoulders, and arms and hands.

Our first step on the way to creating the model's skeleton is the creation of a hierarchical structure of all the nodes in the model. The hierarchy will let us propagate changes to one of the bones to the remaining parts of the skeleton connected to that bone.

Why do we create a node tree of the skeleton?

When you stretch out your left arm and raise it upward or to the side, you will automatically move all the parts of your arm with it. Your upper and lower arm bones, your hand, and the fingers of that hand will all remain the same distance from your shoulder as before.

The same behavior needs to be implemented for our game character models to allow natural-looking movement during the animations. An effortless way to achieve this is by connecting all the bones using a tree as a data structure. A simple list would not be enough because we have two shoulders, two legs, and multiple fingers on every hand, and they must be attached to the right places. Even if a binary tree is enough for our example model file, we use a general tree, allowing multiple child nodes for every node.

In *Figure 9.2*, a simple general tree is shown:

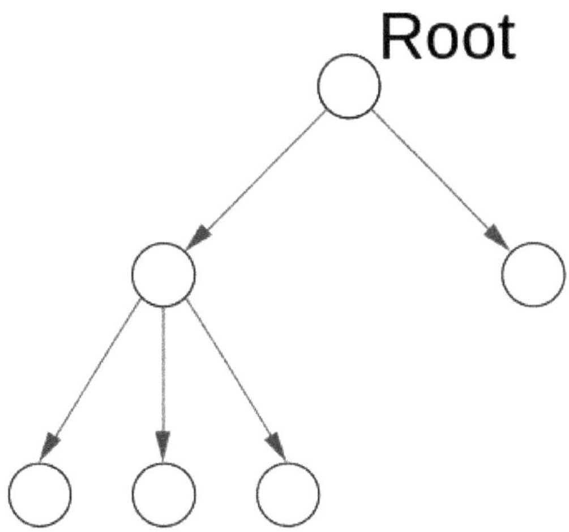

Figure 9.2: A simple general tree

The general tree has a root node, and for every node, any number of child nodes is possible. Every node has only a single parent, except the root node, which has no parent. And every child node can be a parent for more child nodes. Circular dependencies are not allowed. This tree is the so-called **Directed Acyclic Graph** (**DAG**).

By using a tree as a data structure, any changes to a node can be propagated simply down to all child nodes, the child's child nodes, and so on. This limits the effect of changes to a part of the tree, exactly what we need for skeletal behavior.

We will only walk through the basic parts of the node class here; you can follow the complete code changes and additions in the `01_opengl_gltf_bindpose` example in the `chapter09` folder.

Adding the node class

The `GltfNode` class is declared in the `GltfNode.h` file in the `model` folder. Every node uses a `std::vector` to store all of its (possible) child nodes, added as a `private` data member of the class:

```
  private:
    std::vector<std::shared_ptr<GltfNode>> mChildNodes{};
```

The elements are of the same type as our class, allowing us to traverse the tree recursively.

The most important data elements are the per-node transformation information:

```
glm::vec3 mScale = glm::vec3(1.0f);
glm::vec3 mTranslation = glm::vec3(0.0f);
glm::quat mRotation = glm::quat(1.0f, 0.0f, 0.0f, 0.0f);
```

The values for scale, translation, and rotation will be used for the values read by **tinygltf** from the model file. The values are initialized with default values that do not affect the transformation if the respective field for this node is not set in the glTF model file.

Finally, we store three 4x4 matrices:

```
glm::mat4 mLocalTRSMatrix = glm::mat4(1.0f);
glm::mat4 mNodeMatrix = glm::mat4(1.0f);
glm::mat4 mInverseBindMatrix = glm::mat4(1.0f);
```

`mLocalTRSMatrix` contains the transformation matrix, which is calculated from the values of the **Translation**, **Rotation**, and **Scale**, hence the name **TRS matrix**. TRS also denotes the order for the matrix multiplication of the three values:

```
TRS: Translation * Rotation * Scale;
```

`mNodeMatrix` contains the matrix product of the node matrix of the parent node matrix and the node local TRS matrix:

```
mNodeMatrix = parentNodeMatrix * mLocalTRSMatrix;
```

As the root matrix has no parent, the parent node matrix is replaced by the identity matrix, retaining only the TRS matrix.

Combining the parent node and local matrices in this way propagates the changes from every node down to the child nodes:

```
Structure:             local transform       global transform
root                   R                     R
 +- nodeA              A                     R*A
     +- nodeB          B                     R*A*B
     +- nodeC          C                     R*A*C
```

The last matrix of the class, `mInverseBindMatrix`, will be discussed in depth in the *The inverse bind matrices and the binding pose* section.

For the implementation in the `GltfNode.cpp` file in the `model` folder, we look only at the calculation of the TRS matrix because it may require an explanation:

```
void GltfNode::calculateLocalTRSMatrix() {
  glm::mat4 sMatrix = glm::scale(glm::mat4(1.0f), mScale);
  glm::mat4 rMatrix = glm::mat4_cast(mRotation);
  glm::mat4 tMatrix = glm::translate(glm::mat4(1.0f),
    mTranslation);
  mLocalTRSMatrix = tMatrix * rMatrix * sMatrix;
}
```

We generate a 4x4 matrix for every one of the transformations using `glm::scale()` to create a scaling matrix, `glm::mat4_cast()` to create a rotation matrix from the quaternion used for rotation, and `glm::translate()` to create a translation matrix. As the last step, we multiply these three temporary matrices in the correct order, creating the local TRS matrix for the node.

Now we are ready to create a tree containing the hierarchical structure of the glTF model skeleton.

Filling the skeleton tree in the Gltf model class

In the `GltfModel.h` file in the `model` folder, we need to include the header for the `GltfNode` class, and we need to add a smart pointer for the root node of the skeleton tree as a `private` element:

```
#include "GltfNode.h"
...
    std::shared_ptr<GltfNode> mRootNode = nullptr;
```

The tree filling happens in the `loadModel()` method of the `GltfModel` class, in the `GltfModel.cpp` file in the `model` folder:

```
  int rootNode = mModel->scenes.at(0).nodes.at(0);
  mRootNode = GltfNode::createRoot(rootNode);
```

First, we create the root node and populate it with the number of the root node of the scene data from the glTF file. Then, we fill the node with the transformation data using the `getNodeData()` method:

```
  getNodeData(mRootNode, glm::mat4(1.0f));
```

The `getNodeData()` method sets the node values for translation, rotation, and scale and triggers the calculation of the local TRS matrix and the node matrix.

As the last step, we call the `getNodes()` method with the root node:

```
  getNodes(mRootNode);
```

The `getNodes()` method reads the children from the corresponding node in the glTF model file and adds the correct number of – as yet empty – child nodes. Next, it reads the node matrix from the node given as a parameter and calls `getNodeData()` and `getNodes()` for every created child. This recursive call traverses the glTF nodes and creates a tree of the `GltfNode` nodes.

To verify the successful creation of the skeleton tree, we can use the `printTree()` method of the `GltfNode` class:

```
mRootNode->printTree();
```

The method will print out the structure of the created tree, using a greater indent every time it finds a new child. Children of the same depth share the same indent:

```
printTree: ---- tree ----
printTree: parent : 42 (Armature)
printNodes:  - child : 40 (Hips)
printNodes:   - child : 29 (Spine)
printNodes:    - child : 28 (Spine1)
printNodes:     - child : 27 (Spine2)
printNodes:      - child : 2 (Neck)
printNodes:       - child : 1 (Head)
printNodes:        - child : 0 (HeadTop_End)
printNodes:      - child : 14 (LeftShoulder)
printNodes:       - child : 13 (LeftArm)
...
printNodes:     - child : 37 (RightFoot)
printNodes:      - child : 36 (RightToeBase)
printNodes:       - child : 35 (RightToe_End)
printTree: -- end tree -
```

After we create the model skeleton, we need to explore inverse bind matrices next. Inverse bind matrices are required to apply the model skinning in the *How (not) to apply a skin to a skeleton* section.

The inverse bind matrices and the binding pose

The inverse bind matrices are the connection between the **T-pose**, as seen in *Figure 8.3* in *Chapter 8*, and the so-called **binding pose**, as shown in *Figure 9.3*:

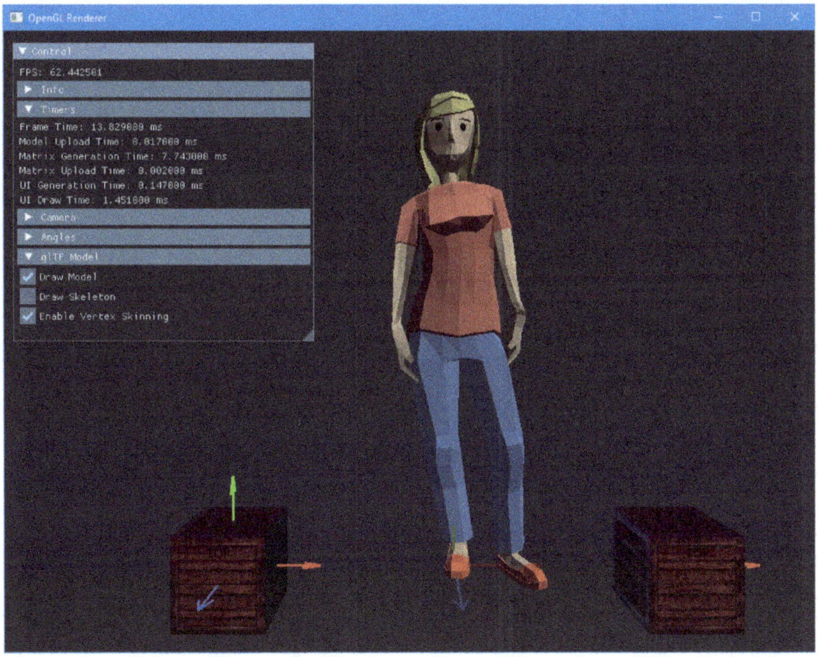

Figure 9.3: The glTF model standing in the binding pose

In glTF model format, the vertices in the position buffer are stored in the T-pose, as seen in *Figure 8.3* in *Chapter 8*, where we simply display the vertices from the buffers. But the root of the animations in *Chapter 10* is the binding pose because all the transformations in the animation data start with the binding pose.

To calculate the binding pose of the model, the transformation matrices for each node are stored as inverse matrices, transforming the node positions from the T-pose to the binding pose. Storing inverse matrices is useful in terms of optimization. The calculation of the inverse of a matrix is expensive, and using the inverse matrix for the translation of every node in every frame will save a lot of CPU or GPU power.

The `inverseBindMatrices` element is defined in the `skins` section of a glTF file:

```
"skins" : [
    {
        "inverseBindMatrices" : 6,
...
```

The number referenced by the `inverseBindMatrices` entry is the index number of the corresponding `accessors` entry.

By moving downward to `bufferViews` and `buffers`, we can copy the inverse bind matrices into `std::vector<glm::mat4>`:

```
mInverseBindMatrices.resize(skin.joints.size());
std::memcpy(mInverseBindMatrices.data(),
  &buffer.data.at(0) + bufferView.byteOffset,
  bufferView.byteLength);
```

Now that we have the inverse bind matrices in place, we can start vertex skinning.

How (not) to apply a skin to a skeleton

To create a character for a game, we need to apply a body structure that fits the intended role in the game. For example, a male wizard has a different body than a female elf, and both are completely different to a human blacksmith. Therefore, the skin needs to reflect the amount of muscle and fat on the body of the model to appear plausible.

Naive model skinning

The naive way of applying a skin to a character skeleton is by using constant distances from the start and end of a node. This works if the entire model moves, but if individual nodes are rotated or translated, the character body will be distorted in an unwanted manner. In *Figure 9.4*, you can see the effect of the rotation of the middle and right nodes of a part of a functional character:

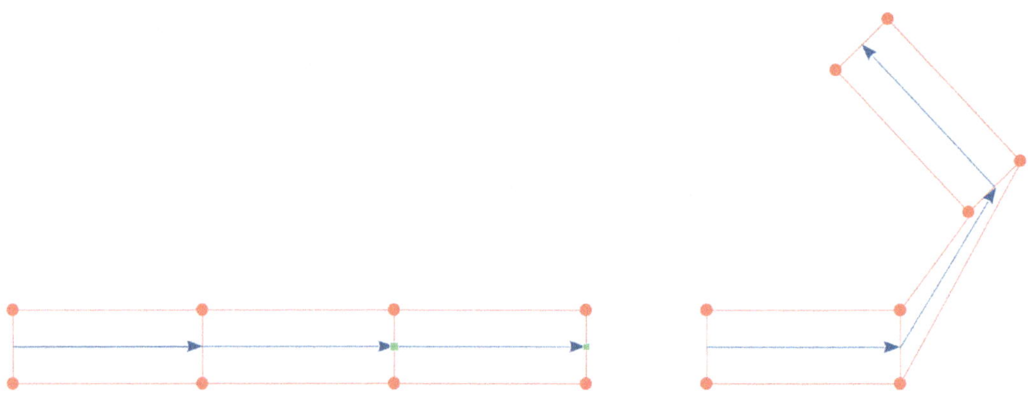

Figure 9.4. Naive idea of applying the skin to moving nodes gone wrong

Nodes are shown as blue arrows, vertices are red dots, and the skin is depicted by the red lines between the vertices. As shown on the right in *Figure 9.4*, the skin of the middle node will be squashed unnaturally, leading to artifacts in the animated character model.

Vertex skinning in glTF

The authors of the glTF file format added a solution to the deformation shown in *Figure 9.4*: if a node changes its position, rotation, or scale, then the position of the vertices belonging to the node can be moved too. In addition, the vertices of adjacent nodes can also be changed, leading to proper movement of the skin, just as if there were muscles below the skin.

Figure 9.5 shows a simple example of moving the vertices upon rotating the middle and right nodes:

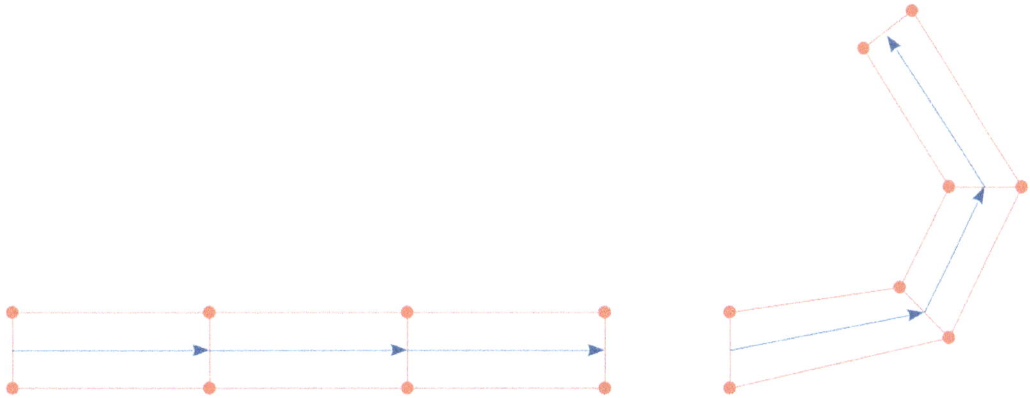

Figure 9.5: Better vertex skinning by moving the vertices with the nodes

The basic structure of the middle node stays intact. The vertices of all three nodes move during the rotation, and the vertices of the left node are also changed upon the movement of the right node to minimize the overall distortion.

In glTF, two elements are used to store the movement of the vertices: up to four nodes that affect a vertex and a weight for every of these up to four nodes. The nodes used for the vertex skinning have another name: joints.

Connecting joints and nodes

In many glTF models, nodes and joints will be the same; they may even have a 1:1 relationship. But the reason for the differentiation between nodes and joints is simple: not all nodes need to be part of the vertex skinning process. A glTF model may contain static nodes; these nodes could be used without needing to change in every frame during an animation. And, instead of adding a separate property for the nodes, a new `joints` array can be created, containing only the nodes affected by transformations.

The `joints` are defined in the `skins` section of a glTF file:

```
"skins" : [
    {
        "joints" : [
```

```
        40,
        29,
        28,
        ...
```

The `joints` array does an implicit numbering by the index, creating a connection between the joint index number and the node at that index. The following table explains the connections between the joints and the nodes for the first three joints in the array:

Joint	Node
0	40
1	29
2	28
...	...

Figure 9.6: Connections of the first three joints with nodes in the array

This mapping between joints and nodes is important for the model skinning process, as the nodes affecting the movement of a vertex are identified by their joint number instead of the node number.

Figure 9.6 shows the first three mappings between joints and nodes. As an example for the mapping, all vertex skinning entries referencing joint number 1 (as shown on the left side of the table in *Figure 9.6*) will affect the vertices of node 29 (as shown on the right side of the table in *Figure 9.6*). A lookup table is the best way to handle this mapping. In the `GltfModel.h` file in the `model` folder, a new `private` data element will be added:

```
    std::vector<int> mNodeToJoint{};
```

We use the node number as the index in the vector and store the joint number in the position of the corresponding node in the `mNodeToJoint()` vector. This inverse mapping of nodes and joints allows a fast lookup to get the joint number from the node number, as the lookup direction from the node to the joint is used most frequently:

```
  mNodeToJoint.resize(mModel->nodes.size());
  const tinygltf::Skin &skin = mModel->skins.at(0);
  for (int i = 0; i < skin.joints.size(); ++i) {
    int destinationNode = skin.joints.at(i);
    mNodeToJoint.at(destinationNode) = i;
  }
```

The next step in achieving vertex skinning is reading the joints affecting every vertex position, and the weight of the joints.

Joints and weights for the vertices

The joint and weight data is stored along with the vertex position, the vertex normal, and the vertex texture coordinates under `attributes` in the `primitives` part of the `meshes` section:

```
...
    "meshes" : [
        {
            "name" : "WomanMesh",
            "primitives" : [
                {
                    "attributes" : {
                        "POSITION" : 0,
                        "NORMAL" : 1,
                        "TEXCOORD_0" : 2,
                        "JOINTS_0" : 3,
                        "WEIGHTS_0" : 4
                    },
...
```

The joints are stored in the accessor of the `JOINTS_0` attribute, here in accessor number `3`, and the weights are stored in the accessor of the `WEIGHTS_0` attribute, here in accessor number `4`.

To get the data out of the buffers for both attributes, we have to follow the chain from the `accessors` via `bufferViews` to `buffer`. From the `accessors`, we can get the number of elements, the component, and the type of the data:

```
...
        {
            "bufferView" : 3,
            "componentType" : 5123,
            "count" : 5718,
            "type" : "VEC4"
        },
        {
            "bufferView" : 4,
            "componentType" : 5126,
            "count" : 5718,
            "type" : "VEC4"
        },
...
```

The joints are stored as a four-element vector of either an unsigned short int, or as an unsigned int. In our example model file, we have a `componentType` of `5123`: this is the magic number for the unsigned short int, both in tinygltf and OpenGL. The weights are usually stored as a four-element float vector. Both joints and weights contain 5,718 elements each: this is also the number of vertices in the model.

The buffer number, the offset in the buffer, and the data length can be taken from the `bufferView` number defined in the accessor. To store the joints and weights, we add two new `private` data members in the `GltfModel.cpp` file in the `model` folder:

```
std::vector<glm::tvec4<uint16_t>> mJointVec{};
std::vector<glm::vec4> mWeightVec{}
```

> **Note on data sizes**
>
> The `mJointVec` vector will be hardcoded to use `glm::ivec4`, with unsigned short int as the internal type. For the sake of simplicity, we tailor the `GltfModel` class to the model files we use in this book. In a real-world data reader, you need to check the `componentType` field and convert the joint data to the data type used in your shader during model creation.

For the `mWeightVec` vector, we use a `glm::vec4` to store the four `float` weight values.

By using the raw data of the `mJointVec` vector, we can copy the buffer data directly to the vector and do an implicit type conversion:

```
int jointVecSize = accessor.count;
mJointVec.resize(jointVecSize);
std::memcpy(mJointVec.data(), &buffer.data.at(0) +
  bufferView.byteOffset, bufferView.byteLength);
```

First, we need to resize the vector to the number of data elements. After copying the data with `std::memcpy()`, we can access each of the joint data elements by simply using the index of the `mJointVec` vector.

The same copy behavior happens for the weight data:

```
int weightVecSize = accessor.count;
mWeightVec.resize(weightVecSize);
std::memcpy(mWeightVec.data(), &buffer.data.at(0) +
  bufferView.byteOffset, bufferView.byteLength);
```

Again, we resize the `mWeightVec` vector to ensure there is enough space for the copy process, and then we copy the data by using a `memcpy` call.

As the last step on the path to vertex skinning, we need to combine the propagated node matrix and the inverse bind matrix for every node.

Creating the joint transformation matrices

By multiplying the node matrix and the inverse bind matrix, we create the final transformation matrix for the positional change of every vertex of a node appearing in the `joints` array.

To create the matrix, we must add a new `private` variable in the `GltfModel` class. Add the following line to the `GltfModel.h` file in the `model` folder:

```
std::vector<glm::mat4> mJointMatrices{};
```

The `mJointMatrices` vector will contain a 4x4 transformation matrix for each joint, and to simplify access to the matrices, the index in the vector will be the same index as in the `joints` array of the glTF model file.

We also need to resize the vector before we add the data. This resize operation should be done while getting the inverse bind matrices. Add the new line to the `getInvBindMatrices()` method in the `GltfModel.cpp` file in the `model` folder:

```
mInverseBindMatrices.resize(skin.joints.size());
mJointMatrices.resize(skin.joints.size());
```

Filling the `mJointMatrices` vector is done by the `getNodeData()` method. Add the new line right after the local TRS matrix and the node matrix are created in the `getNodeData()` method of the `GltfModel.cpp` file:

```
treeNode->calculateNodeMatrix(parentNodeMatrix);
mJointMatrices.at(mNodeToJoint.at(nodeNum)) =
  treeNode->getNodeMatrix() *
  mInverseBindMatrices.at(mNodeToJoint.at(nodeNum));
```

Here, we use the `mNodeToJoint` mapping to place the resulting matrix in the position of the corresponding joint.

Now we are ready to create the skin of our character model.

Applying vertex skinning

In the first example, we use the CPU to calculate the final vertex positions. The vertex calculation is done in every `draw()` call of the renderer. We do this to demonstrate the amount of time that would be required if we used the processor for this part of the rendering process.

The altered vertex positions are stored in the `std::vector` of three-element GLM vectors, which is added as a `private` data element in the `GltfModel` class:

```
std::vector<glm::vec3> mAlteredPositions{};
```

We resize the vector before using it in the `createVertexBuffers()` method because we know the number of vertices:

```
    if (attribType.compare("POSITION") == 0) {
      int numPositionEntries = accessor.count;
      mAlteredPositions.resize(numPositionEntries);
    }
```

The entire calculation is done in the `applyVertexSkinning()` method of the `GltfModel` class:

```
  std::memcpy(mAlteredPositions.data(),
    &buffer.data.at(0) + bufferView.byteOffset,
    bufferView.byteLength);
```

As the first step, we copy the original position data to our `mAlteredPositions` vector. In the `draw()` call of the renderer, the `mAlteredPositions` vector will be uploaded to the vertex buffer containing the position data.

Next, we check whether we want to enable vertex skinning at all:

```
  if (enableSkinning) {
    for (int i = 0; i < mJointVec.size(); ++i) {
      glm::ivec4 jointIndex =
        glm::make_vec4(mJointVec.at(i));
      glm::vec4 weightIndex =
        glm::make_vec4(mWeightVec.at(i));
```

Disabling vertex skinning in the user interface results in the model remaining in the T-pose. If we enable vertex skinning, we loop through the vector containing the joint data. Inside the loop, we extract the joint indices and weights for the current vertex.

By using the weight and the joint index, we can calculate the vertex skinning matrix:

```
      glm::mat4 skinMat =
        weightIndex.x * mJointMatrices.at(jointIndex.x) +
        weightIndex.y * mJointMatrices.at(jointIndex.y) +
        weightIndex.z * mJointMatrices.at(jointIndex.z) +
        weightIndex.w * mJointMatrices.at(jointIndex.w);
```

For every one of the four joint entries, the corresponding joint matrix is scaled by the weight given in the weight index. All four matrices are added together to create the skinning matrix, `skinMat`.

Finally, the position data is multiplied by the skinning matrix to calculate the new position for every vertex:

```
        mAlteredPositions.at(i) = skinMat *
        glm::vec4(mAlteredPositions.at(i), 1.0f);
      }
    }
```

In the `draw()` call of the `OGLRenderer` class, the vertex skinning could be added inside the timing for the matrix generation, or a new timer for the model skin generation:

```
    mGltfModel->applyVertexSkinning(
        mRenderData.rdEnableVertexSkinning);
```

Running the program will result in the picture shown in *Figure 9.3*. The timings should be as shown in *Figure 9.7*:

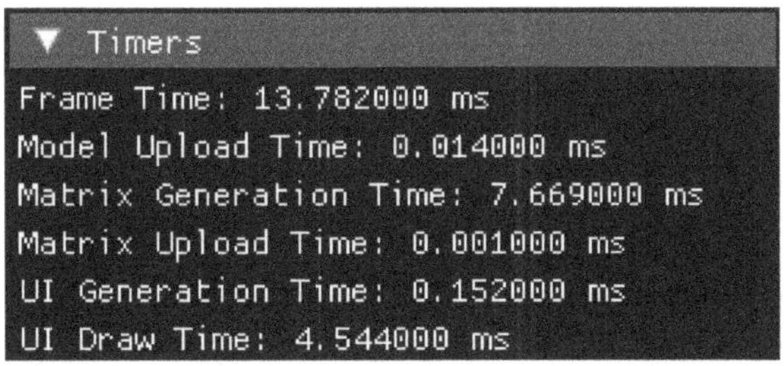

Figure 9.7: Timings for CPU-based vertex skinning

Even with our single, small character model, CPU-based calculation of the vertex positions costs several milliseconds in every frame. Much larger character models, or more characters on the screen, would lead to a bottleneck in the CPU.

So, let's move the expensive parts of the vertex skinning to the graphics card. You can find the full code in the `02_opengl_gltf_gpu_skinning` folder.

Implementing GPU-based skinning

The huge advantage of GPU-based calculations is the sheer amount of parallel execution achieved using shaders. We usually use only one CPU core to calculate the vertex position because multi-threading in code is complex and not easy to implement. In contrast, a GPU can run dozens or hundreds of shader instances in parallel, depending on the model and driver. The shader units are also specialized to do vertex and matrix operations, generating even more speed in the vertex position calculation.

Moving the joints and weights to the vertex shader

To move the calculation to the vertex shader, a new shader pair needs to be created. We can use the `gltf.vert` vertex shader and the `gltf.frag` fragment shader as the basis and copy the files to new files called `gltf_gpu.vert` and `gltf_gpu.frag`.

While the fragment shader can be used without changes, the vertex shader needs a couple of additions:

```
layout (location = 3) in vec4 aJointNum;
layout (location = 4) in vec4 aJointWeight;
```

First, we add two new input attributes. The first new attribute is the four-element float vector containing the joints that alter the current vertex. The joints are stored as integer values, but the transport to the shader is easier as a float vector. The second new attribute is another four-element float vector, storing the weights for every joint.

To access the pre-calculated joint matrices created from the node matrices and the inverse bind matrices, we are using a second uniform buffer:

```
layout (std140, binding = 1) uniform JointMatrices {
  mat4 jointMat[42];
};
```

The `JointMatrices` uniform buffer will be uploaded in the `draw()` call of the renderer, but as it only contains a 4x4 matrix for every joint, the size is small.

A uniform buffer has a huge drawback when using it as an array: we must define the number of elements at shader compile time. Without the size, shader compiling will fail. We set a fixed size here, according to the number of joints in our model. The fixed index will be removed in the following *Getting rid of the fixed UBO array size* section.

In the `main()` method of the `gltf_gpu.vert` vertex shader, the calculation of the skin matrix is added:

```
  mat4 skinMat =
    aJointWeight.x * jointMat[int(aJointNum.x)] +
    aJointWeight.y * jointMat[int(aJointNum.y)] +
    aJointWeight.z * jointMat[int(aJointNum.z)] +
    aJointWeight.w * jointMat[int(aJointNum.w)];
  gl_Position = projection * view * skinMat *
    vec4(aPos, 1.0);
```

If we compare the calculation of `skinMat` with the matrix created in the `applyVertexSkinning()` method, the only difference we see is the casting of the joint number from `float` to `int`. All other parts are identical, and the calculation will be done on the GPU now.

The new shader pair needs to be loaded and compiled in the `OGLRenderer` class. In the `draw()` function of the renderer, we simply select the shader to be used with the `rdGPUVertexSkinning` variable set in the user interface:

```
if (mRenderData.rdGPUVertexSkinning) {
  mGltfGPUShader.use();
} else {
  mGltfShader.use();
}
mGltfModel->draw();
```

On the CPU side, our only task left is the calculation of the joint matrices. And, as our model does not change now, this calculation must be done only once, during the creation of the model skeleton. Once we start the model animations, we must recalculate the joint matrices in every frame.

We also do not need to upload the vertex data of the model in every `draw()` call, as the vertices themselves never change.

If we use the GPU for vertex skinning, we see virtually no impact on the timing, as shown in *Figure 9.8*:

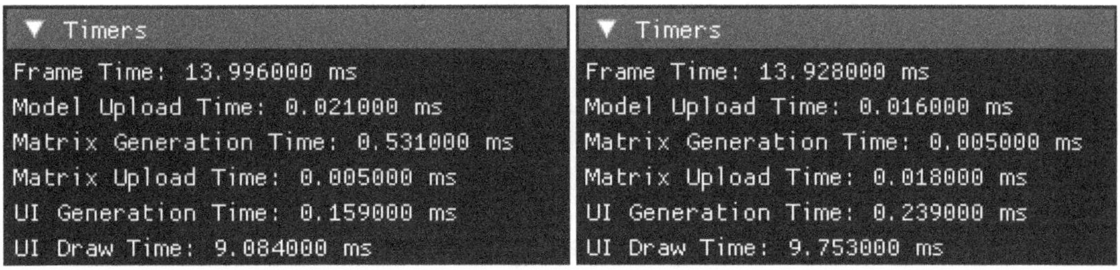

Figure 9.8: Timings for the T-pose in example 01_opengl_gltf_bindpose (left) versus GPU-based vertex skinning in example 02_opengl_gltf_gpu_skinning (right)

The CPU no longer has to work on the expensive task of calculating the positions for every vertex in every frame, and the amount of extra work for the GPU is negligible.

After we move the calculation to the vertex shader, there is one annoying problem left: we need to add the array size to the joint matrix uniform buffer data. For our example model, we can hardcode the array size according to the glTF model data, but for other or more models, a more flexible solution would be nice.

This solution comes is **Shader Storage Buffer Objects** (**SSBOs**). The example code can be found in the `03_opengl_gltf_ssbo` folder.

Getting rid of the UBO fixed array size

OpenGL has used SSBOs since version 4.3, and Vulkan has had SSBOs since version 1.0. An SSBO can be seen as a mix between a uniform buffer and a texture. SSBOs have some advantages compared to UBOs, as follows:

- SSBOs can be much larger; the minimum guaranteed size is 128 MB (UBO: 16 KB)
- SSBOs are writable (UBOs are read-only)
- SSBOs can store arrays of arbitrary length (UBOs have a fixed size)

Changing a uniform buffer into a shader storage buffer is astonishingly easy.

First, we need to create a new C++ class for the shader storage buffer. We call the class `ShaderStorageBuffer` and store the files in the `opengl` folder. The files can be simply copied from the `UniformBuffer` class, the class must be renamed in both files, and every occurrence of the `GL_UNIFORM_BUFFER` element needs to be replaced by `GL_SHADER_STORAGE_BUFFER`. And we should rename the upload method `uploadSsboData()`.

Next, we must find the following uniform buffer in the `OGLRenderer` class:

```
UniformBuffer mGltfUniformBuffer{};
```

We need to replace it with the new shader storage buffer class:

```
ShaderStorageBuffer mGltfShaderStorageBuffer{};
```

The usages of these buffer types are 100% compatible, so all the calls in the renderer can remain as they are, despite the method renaming.

Finally, we need to find the uniform buffer definition in the `gltf_gpu.vert` vertex shader:

```
layout (std140, binding = 1) uniform JointMatrices {
  mat4 jointMat[42];
};
```

It needs to be replaced by the SSBO definition, changing `uniform` to `buffer`:

```
layout (std430, binding = 1) readonly buffer JointMatrices{
  mat4 jointMat[];
};
```

The new SSBO will use the new memory layout while keeping the same binding spot. And we set the buffer to `readonly`, because we do not need to write to it. Telling the graphics driver that we never write the data could also be useful for memory access optimizations.

Removing the fixed array size enables us to use any joint matrix size now, and we do not have to care about the number of joints in our model. We will use a dynamic number of joint matrices in *Chapter 14*, where we add multiple models to the screen.

Having the vertex position calculations on the GPU results in a fast method for our model's vertex skinning.

But, in some cases, using weighted joint matrices may lead to unexpected results. Correcting these results can be achieved by using **dual quaternions**. The full example code is available in the `04_opengl_gltf_dual_quat` folder.

Identifying linear skinning problems

To get an idea of the problem, *Figure 9.9* shows a simple box, twisted in the middle:

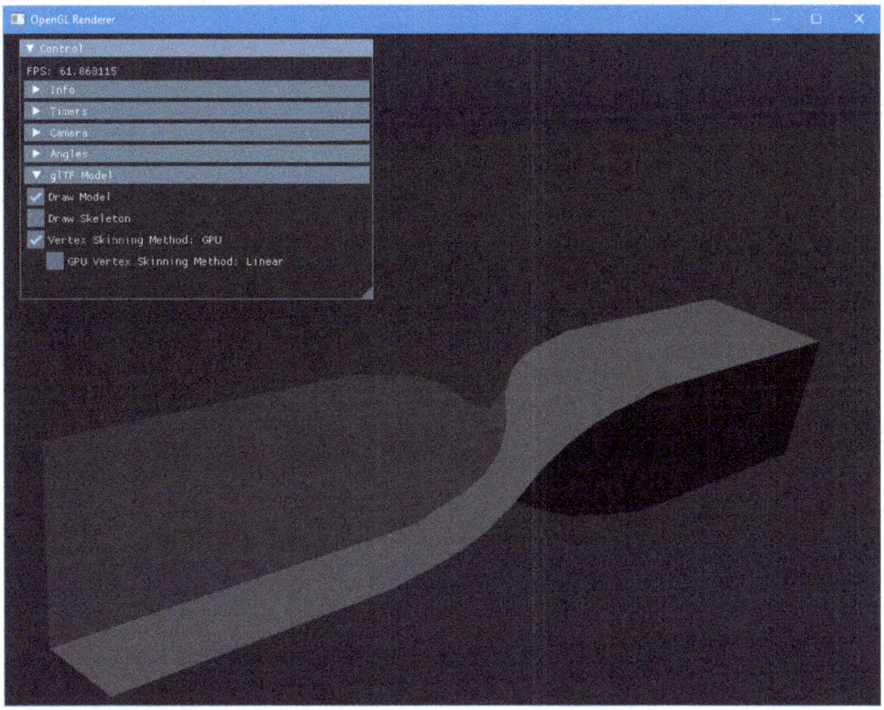

Figure 9.9: A noticeable volume loss in the middle when twisting the model

We can see that the twist leads to volume loss, a phenomenon we thought we had solved by using the joints affecting the vertices, and the weights of the joints per vertex. Apparently, something in the calculation is still going wrong.

Particularly on a *sharp* bend or twist, the linear interpolation may lead to wrong results. This is because linear interpolation uses the shortest path between the vertices:

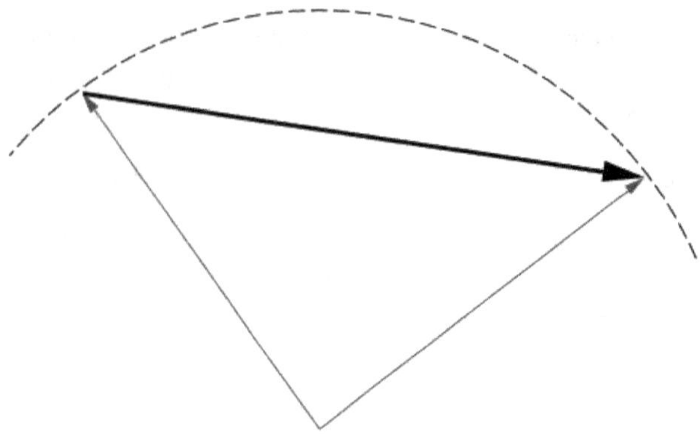

Figure 9.10: Shortest path for linear interpolation using matrices

If we use quaternion interpolation instead of linear interpolation, the paths of the connection between the vertices will be located on an arc between the two locations, keeping the virtual volume of the model in this place:

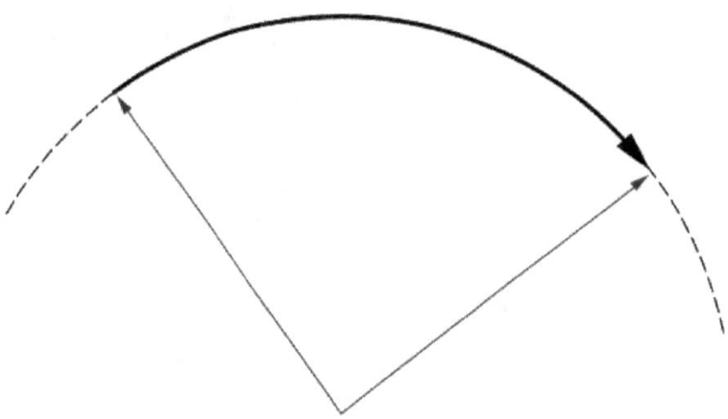

Figure 9.11: Shortest path for spherical interpolation using quaternions

For the full explanation of quaternion interpolation, you could go back to the *Using quaternions for smooth rotations* section in *Chapter 7*.

Quaternions still have a shortcoming: a quaternion can store only a rotation around an arbitrary axis. But for the vertex skinning process, the vertices also need to be translated to the new positions. What if we just take two normal quaternions and "glue" them together?

The dual quaternion

Dual quaternions have been known since the end of the 19th century, only a couple of decades after the discovery of the quaternion itself. Similar to the imaginary number scheme for complex numbers, dual quaternions use **dual numbers**.

While imaginary numbers use the symbol *i*, dual numbers use the Greek epsilon, ε. And this ε has only one property:

$$\varepsilon^2 = 0 \; with \; \varepsilon \neq 0$$

Luckily, we do not have to deal with the mathematical details of ε. In our case, it is just a placeholder for telling apart the two quaternions inside. If you are interested in the mathematical background of dual numbers, you will find a link in the *Additional resources* section.

A dual quaternion, *dq*, consisting of the quaternions *p* and *q* can be written as follows:

$$dq = p + \varepsilon q$$

The only operation we need to know for the vertex skinning is addition:

$$dq_1 = p_1 + \varepsilon q_1$$

$$dq_2 = p_2 + \varepsilon q_2$$

$$dq_1 + dq_2 = (p_1 p_2) + \varepsilon (q_1 + q_2)$$

Here, the real and the dual parts of the dual quaternions are added for each component.

But why don't we need more dual quaternion operations?

Using dual quaternions as data storage

For character vertex skinning, we are "abusing" the general idea of dual quaternions and use them only as a simple data storage element, enabling to store both the rotation and the translation values for the vertex transformations. Having two separate quaternions in a single data structure also gives us the mathematical operations we need to transform the vertices of the skin:

- Adding two quaternions and normalizing the result will create the average between the two quaternions. This operation is perfect for the vertex rotation.
- Adding two quaternions without normalization is equal to a four-element vector addition, like the addition of two elements of type `glm::vec4`. This operation is perfect for vertex translation.

As we only have two quaternions, one for rotation and one for translation, there is no space to store changes in model scales. You will find a link in the *Additional resources* section on how to handle scaling with dual quaternions.

To store a rotation in a dual quaternion *dq*, we use the real quaternion *p*:

$$p(\phi) = \cos\left(\frac{\phi}{2}\right) + \sin\left(\frac{\phi}{2}\right)i + \sin\left(\frac{\phi}{2}\right)j + \sin\left(\frac{\phi}{2}\right)k$$

This is the same formula as in the *Creating quaternions* section of *Chapter 7*. We do a normal quaternion operation here. Extracting the rotation from the quaternion p can be done by converting the quaternion back to a rotation matrix, as seen in *Converting a quaternion to a rotation matrix and vice versa* section of *Chapter 7*. After the rotation matrix has been created, the three Euler angles can be computed by using inverse trigonometric functions. You can find a link in the *Additional resources* section with the detailed formulas.

Saving the translation in the dual quaternion part q requires a different approach:

$$q(t) = \left(\frac{t_x}{2}i + \frac{t_y}{2}j + \frac{t_z}{2}k\right)*p$$

Because we want to store a translation instead of a rotation in the quaternion q, the real part of the quaternion, which would normally contain a rotation angle, is not used and remains zero. The translation vector t is then divided by 2, and the three elements of the halved translation vector t are saved as the three axis values of the quaternion. Then, the resulting translation quaternion is multiplied by the real quaternion part p (containing the rotation) to calculate the dual quaternion part q.

Extracting the translation value from the quaternion part q can be done by reversing the store operations:

$$t = 2*q*p$$

First, the conjugate of the real quaternion part p must be created. Then, the dual quaternion part q and the conjugate of p are multiplied to undo the quaternion multiplication, and the result is doubled. The multiplication by 2 reverses the division by 2 when the dual quaternion part q was created – a multiplication of a quaternion by a scalar factor is just the multiplication of each of the four quaternion elements by the scaling factor. Finally, the three elements of the original translation vector t can be directly read from the imaginary part of the resulting quaternion.

Note on dual quaternion normalization

You should normalize a dual quaternion after all operations to prevent unwanted side-effects such as the model skewing, twisting, scaling, or even vanishing from the screen, caused by the additional length change of the quaternion.

In GLM, a separate data type exists, which simplifies the handling of dual quaternions for us.

Dual quaternions in GLM

The dual quaternions are defined in the extension header, `dual_quaternion.hpp`; we must include the header to use the data type:

```
#include <glm/gtx/dual_quaternion.hpp>
```

A dual quaternion, `dq`, is declared just like all the other GLM data types:

```
glm::dualquat dq;
```

Accessing the real and the dual parts of the dual quaternion can be achieved by using a C-style array index on `glm::dualquat`:

```
glm::quat p = dq[0];
glm::quat q = dq[1];
```

Since GLSL shaders don't support quaternions or dual quaternions, we must use a 2x4 matrix to transport the data to the shader. GLM has the `glm::mat2x4_cast` function to convert a dual quaternion to a 2x4 matrix:

```
glm::mat2x4 dqMat = glm::mat2x4_cast(dq);
```

After we have stepped through the basics we need, let's implement vertex skinning with dual quaternions in code.

Adding dual quaternions to the glTF model

The dual quaternions should replace the joint matrices, so we must add them to the `GltfModel` class. The `GltfModel.h` header in the `model` folder gets a new `private` data element to store the dual quaternions:

```
    std::vector<glm::mat2x4> mJointDualQuats{};
```

We are using a `std::vector` of 2x4 matrices here to simplify the data upload, as the shader can only work with matrices instead of quaternions.

In the `GltfModel.cpp` file, we have to resize the vector before we can use it. This could happen in the `getInBindMatrices()` method:

```
mJointDualQuats.resize(skin.joints.size());
```

Now, in the `getNodeData()` method in the `GltfModel.cpp` file, we convert the joint matrices to dual quaternions and store the values in the `mJointDualQuats` vector. We do this by using GLM to *decompose* the joint matrix into its components.

First, we add temporary variables for all the elements the decomposing returns:

```
glm::quat orientation;
glm::vec3 scale;
glm::vec3 translation;
glm::vec3 skew;
glm::vec4 perspective;
glm::dualquat dq;
```

We will only use the orientation quaternion and the translation vector, but we need to add the correct data types for the GLM call, `glm::decompose`:

```
if (glm::decompose(
  mJointMatrices.at(mNodeToJoint.at(nodeNum)), scale,
  orientation, translation, skew, perspective)) {
```

Here, we set the joint matrix of the current node as the input parameter and get all the separate parts of the composed transformation in the joint matrix back. If the decomposition fails, we don't try to use the values.

Then, we fill the dual quaternion as explained in the *Using dual quaternions as data storage* section:

```
dq[0] = orientation;
dq[1] = glm::quat(0.0, translation.x, translation.y,
  translation.z) * orientation * 0.5f;
```

The rotation is at index zero, and we can simply copy the quaternion data to it. The translation needs to be converted to the correct value.

As the last step in the model code, we convert the dual quaternion to a 2x4 matrix:

```
mJointDualQuats.at(mNodeToJoint.at(nodeNum)) =
  glm::mat2x4_cast(dq);
```

We use the `mNodeToJoint` mapping vector again to save the 2x4 matrix representing the dual quaternions for the node at the correct location in the `joints` array.

To use the dual quaternions on the GPU, we have to add a new set of shader files.

Adding a dual quaternion shader

The new shaders could be copied from the existing GPU shaders in the `shaders` folder to have the best starting point. Name the new shader files `gltf_gpu_dquat.vert` and `gltf_gpu_dquat.frag` to make clear they use dual quaternions instead of the joint matrices. The fragment shader does not need to be changed here, so we can fully concentrate on the vertex shader.

First, change the matrix type and name of the SSBO:

```
layout (std430, binding=2) readonly buffer JointDualQuats {
  mat2x4 jointDQs[];
};
```

We will use 2x4 matrices in the shader, and the SSBO needs to be changed to reflect the correct spacing between the entries.

Then, the new `getJointTransform()` GLSL function is added to get the weighted and interpolated dual quaternion. We must return a 2x4 matrix again due to the lack of quaternion support in GLSL:

```
mat2x4 getJointTransform(ivec4 joints, vec4 weights) {
  mat2x4 dq0 = jointDQs[joints.x];
  mat2x4 dq1 = jointDQs[joints.y];
  mat2x4 dq2 = jointDQs[joints.z];
  mat2x4 dq3 = jointDQs[joints.w];
```

Here, we do a lookup in the SSBO array to get the dual quaternions for the joints affecting the vertex.

The next step is a shortcut to get the shortest rotation path:

```
  weights.y *= sign(dot(dq0[0], dq1[0]));
  weights.z *= sign(dot(dq0[0], dq2[0]));
  weights.w *= sign(dot(dq0[0], dq3[0]));
```

We use the sign of the dot product of the angles between different quaternions to adjust the rotation weight, possibly conjugating some quaternions if we could rotate the longer path instead of the shorter one.

Now, we do the same as with the joint matrices:

```
  mat2x4 result =
      weights.x * dq0 +
      weights.y * dq1 +
      weights.z * dq2 +
      weights.w * dq3;
```

By summing up the weighted quaternions, we do a hidden interpolation between the four dual quaternions.

As the final step, we normalize the resulting quaternion:

```
  float norm = length(result[0]);
  return result / norm;
}
```

Rather than directly calculating the skinning matrix, we incorporate a call to a new GLSL function called `getskinMat()` into the computation of the final position for the current vertex:

```
void main() {
  Mat4 skinMat = getSkinMat();
  gl_Position = projection * view * skinMat *
    vec4(aPos, 1.0);
  normal = aNormal;
  texCoord = aTexCoord;
}
```

The new `getSkinMat()` function retrieves the weighted dual quaternion from the `getJointTransform()` function by using the joints and weights for the current vertex as parameters:

```
mat4 getSkinMat() {
  mat2x4 bone = getJointTransform(ivec4(aJointNum),
    aJointWeight);
```

Then, the function extracts the real part containing the rotation (r) and the dual part containing the translation (t) from the 2x4 matrix mimicking the dual quaternion:

```
  vec4 r = bone[0];
  vec4 t = bone[1];
```

As the last step, the shader converts the rotation and translation quaternions to a 4x4 transformation matrix, containing a rotation part and a translation part:

```
  return mat4(
  ...
  );
}
```

The transformation matrix is created in the GLSL column-major format, resulting in a matrix that looks like this:

$$T = \begin{bmatrix} & R & & t_x \\ & & & t_y \\ & & & t_z \\ 0 & 0 & 0 & 1 \end{bmatrix}$$

The 3x3 submatrix R is created matching to the rotation matrix, as seen in the *Converting a quaternion to a rotation matrix and vice versa* section of *Chapter 7*, and the translation parts are in the last column.

To see the new shader in action, we also need to update the renderer.

Adjusting the renderer

In the `OGRenderer` class, we must create a new `Shader` called `mGltfGPUDualQuatShader` and load the newly created shader file pair, `gltf_gpu_dquat.vert` and `gltf_gpu_dquat.frag`. We also must create a new SSBO called `mGltfDualQuatSSBuffer` and upload the joint dual quaternions from `GltfModel` in every `draw()` call. `OGLRenderData` also needs to be extended by a new Boolean called `rdGPUDualQuatVertexSkinning`.

In the `UserInterface` class, the new Boolean value is added to a check box, granting the ability to change it at runtime.

Finally, we need to hitch the shader according to the value of the new `rdGPUDualQuatVertexSkinning` between the normal GPU-based skinning and the dual quaternion skinning:

```
if (mRenderData.rdGPUVertexSkinning) {
  if (mRenderData.rdGPUDualQuatVertexSkinning) {
    mGltfGPUDualQuatShader.use();
  } else {
    mGltfGPUShader.use();
  }
} else {
  mGltfShader.use();
}
```

Running the code of the `04_opengl_gltf_dual_quat` example and switching in the dual quaternion skinning will result in the picture shown in *Figure 9.12*:

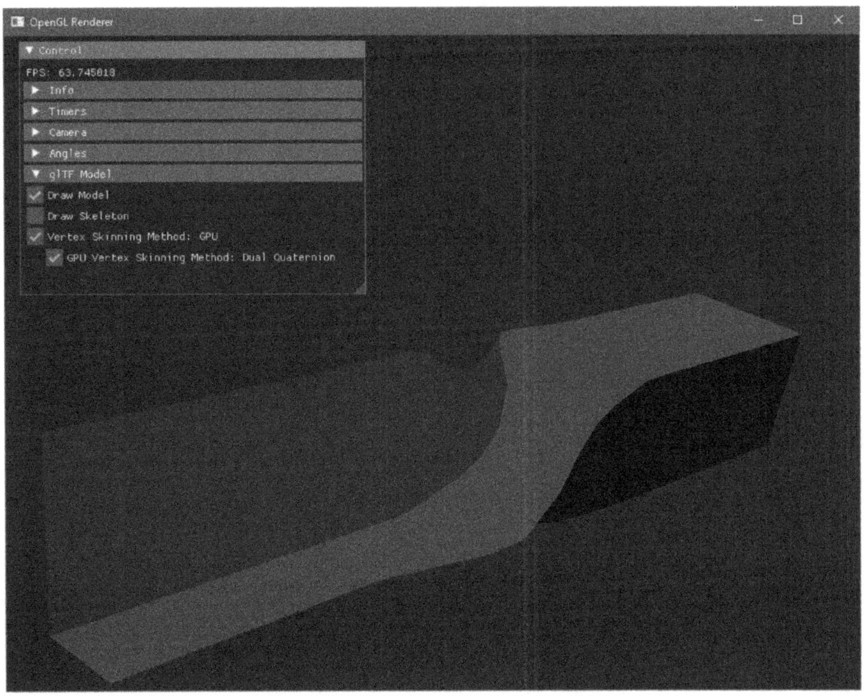

Figure 9.12: A much better volume handling of the middle part using dual quaternions

You can see a significant difference compared to *Figure 9.8*. The bottleneck in the middle of the box has vanished, it was replaced by a better volume-retaining form of the model. By switching between different vertex skinning mechanisms at runtime, you can easily compare the advantages and drawbacks of every method.

Summary

In this chapter, we explored the skeleton of the glTF model and different methods of applying the vertex skin to the character model.

First, we created a tree structure for the skeleton. This step is required for the vertex skinning process, as we need the transformation matrices of the nodes to alter the vertex positions properly.

Next, we extracted all the data elements from the glTF file required to apply the vertex skinning. The CPU-based skinning was done to show the basic principle of the process. Then, we switched to GPU-based vertex skinning, moving the calculations from the processor to the vertex shader. Using the GPU instead of the CPU leads to a huge performance boost, as the massive parallel shader calculation is much faster than our single CPU core.

Finally, we added dual quaternion vertex skinning as a GPU skinning variant. Using dual quaternions enables a better, volume-retaining transformation behavior than linear blending. The dual quaternion approach prevents skin-collapsing artifacts that may happen in some cases with the weighted joint matrix summing.

In the next chapter, we eventually start with the main topic of the book: game character animations. We will analyze how animation data is stored in glTF data format and add a new class so that the relevant data is easily accessible.

Practical sessions

Try out these ideas to get a deeper insight into vertex skinning:

- Implement dual quaternion skinning also on the CPU side. This is simpler than the GLSL variant because you can use the quaternion and dual quaternion data types of GLM in the code, and do not have to convert them to 2x4 matrices. Compare the timings with the normal CPU vertex skinning.
- Adjust the vector normals in the shader to follow the changes in the vertices. Right now, the vertex normals are copied unchanged to the fragment shader, and the normals are not altered when the model triangles are rotated. This leads to incorrect lighting on the model as the direction of the normal and the direction of the triangle no longer match. Hint: use the transpose of the inverse matrix.
- Clean up the renderers and remove the box model data. In the next chapter, we will fully concentrate on character animations, and the boxes will most probably obstruct the exploration of the animations.

Additional resources

- Introduction to dual numbers: `https://en.wikipedia.org/wiki/Dual_number`
- Dual quaternion skinning overview: `https://users.cs.utah.edu/~ladislav/dq/index.html`
- Dual quaternion skinning paper: `https://users.cs.utah.edu/~ladislav/kavan08geometric/kavan08geometric.pdf`
- Dual quaternion skinning with scale: `http://rodolphe-vaillant.fr/entry/78/dual-quaternion-skinning-with-scale`
- Dual quaternion bulge fix: `http://rodolphe-vaillant.fr/entry/72/bulge-free-dual-quaternion-skinning-trick`
- Extracting the Euler angles from a rotation matrix: `https://en.wikipedia.org/wiki/Euler_angles#Conversion_to_other_orientation_representations`

10
About Poses, Frames, and Clips

Welcome to *Chapter 10*! In the previous chapter, we introduced the model skeleton and the process of vertex skinning on the CPU and GPU. We also explored vertex skinning using dual quaternions as an alternative to linear interpolation to achieve better volume retention.

In this chapter, we will discuss the main topic of the book: game character animations. The steps taken in the previous chapters and the code we created were just the prerequisites for creating the animations in this chapter.

We start with a general definition of the terms used for various parts of the animations in the rest of the book. Next, we will examine how the animation data is stored in the glTF file format, how to extract the data, and how the glTF model will be altered during the animations.

At the end of the chapter, we will use the knowledge we have gained to create C++ classes for the animations and integrate these new classes into the renderers and the user interface. You will be able to control some aspects of the animations and watch the glTF model from every angle and from different distances during the animation.

In this chapter, we will cover the following topics:

- A brief overview of animations
- What is a pose and how do we represent it?
- From a single frame to an entire animation clip
- Pouring the knowledge into C++ classes

Technical requirements

To follow along in this chapter, you will need the OpenGL and Vulkan renderer code from *Chapter 9*.

Before we start examining the animations in the glTF file format, let's take a quick look at the parts of the animations, their names, and how they relate to each other.

A brief overview of animations

Today's game character animations are completely different from the 2D animations from cartoons created about 100 years ago, such as the famous cartoons by Walt Disney in the 1930s. But there are still a lot of similarities between modern computer animations and the hand-drawn animations of the past.

glTF animations are based on **key poses**. Every animation has at least a starting and an ending key pose, and most animations also have many key poses at specific points in time. If the starting and the ending key poses are the same, or similar, the animation can be played in a continuous loop. But if these two key poses are too different, another animation must follow at the end, or the direction of the animation must be reversed.

To fill the time between the key poses, **intermediate frames** are calculated. While intermediate frames had to be drawn by hand in the past, the calculations in modern 3D animations are done by interpolating the vertex positions between two adjacent key poses. Using interpolation, a smooth transition from one key pose to the next is done.

If we play the animation from the starting key pose to the ending key pose, including all intermediate frames, we create an **animation clip**. In a clip, we can add additional controls, such as the playback speed or the looping from the ending key pose back to the starting key pose.

Multiple animation clips could be arranged to create an **animation track**. A track could simply append two or more clips to create the illusion of a longer animation or add transitions such as blending between the animations in different clips.

This book will cover everything from poses to clips – creating additional classes to manage animation tracks is left as an exercise for you. See the *Practical sessions* section at the end of the chapter.

Let's start with the first element of the animations: the pose.

What is a pose and how do we represent it?

At the end of *Chapter 8*, we saw the T-pose, the initial pose of the glTF model after drawing the vertices from the unaltered position buffer. After applying the inverse bind matrices, joints, and joint weights to the vertices in *Chapter 9*, the glTF model was drawn in the binding pose.

Both poses are entirely static poses, unrelated to any of the model animations. But it is possible for the T-pose and binding pose to be the starting pose for model animations. It depends on the animator to define the poses in the animation program.

Let's take a look at a simplified view of poses.

The pose for the exact time point of the key pose is created simply: we extract the values specified for a node from the buffer at the time point and overwrite the corresponding value of our glTF model. There is no further vector addition or interpolation from the original values; the node properties for translation, scale, and position are just overwritten with the value from the corresponding time point.

The skeleton for a pose must be adjusted too. The changes to the node matrix must be propagated from the root node to all child nodes. This may be the most expensive step as it includes a lot of matrix multiplications.

As the last step, vertex skinning with the changed node (joint) values must be applied to the updated skeleton. The vertex skinning will create the key pose now.

This is an extremely simple overview of how a key pose is created. We will now explore the detailed process of getting from the glTF model file to an entire animation clip.

From a single frame to an entire animation clip

The glTF file uses a separate element type to adjust the position, scaling, and rotation of the nodes to create the key poses for an animation, the `channel`. Combined with some points in time for the key poses, accessible via the `sampler` element, and the interpolation between the key poses at fixed time points, the final animation frame can be calculated. Showing all the animation frames in a consecutive order finally creates the animation clip, bringing our glTF model to life.

We will start with an explanation of the elements of the glTF file format.

Animation elements in the glTF file format

The animations in glTF are defined inside the `animations` array:

```
    "animations" : [
```

The order of the `animations` array is not important because the fields are not referenced in the other parts of a glTF file. Every array element contains the definitions for a separate animation clip.

For every animation clip entry, one or more `channels` are defined:

```
        {
            "channels" : [
                {
                    "sampler" : 0,
                    "target" : {
                        "node" : 40,
                        "path" : "rotation"
                    }
                },
...
```

The `sampler` field of every channel points to the corresponding index in the `samplers` array of the same animation entry. This link between the channel and the sampler index is relative to the current animation clip only. So, every animation clip starts with a `channels` entry that has an implicit index number zero, and in every channel of an animation clip, there can be a `sampler` pointing to the first entry of the `samplers` array for this animation clip (index `0`). But the data inside the `channels` and `samplers` entries is related to the owning animation clip, and not shared across different clips.

Inside the `target` element of each channel, two other elements are defined. The first element, `node`, is the number of the node to manipulate whenever this channel of the animation clip is applied. The node can be found by a lookup in the `GltfModel` object for the glTF model we loaded.

Once we find the right node, we must alter the correct property of that specific node. The `path` element of the `target` tells us if we must apply the change found in the sampler to the scale, translation, or rotation property of this node. As we change only one of the three node properties per channel, the animation clip array may have multiple channels for a single node.

Next, an optional `name` for the animation clip may be defined:

```
"name" : "Running",
```

You should not rely on a human-readable name for the animation clip, as many files do not name the animation, and use the index number instead, or an empty field.

The connection between the time points of the key poses and the node property changes for that pose is realized in the `samplers` elements:

```
"samplers" : [
    {
        "input" : 7,
        "interpolation" : "LINEAR",
        "output" : 8
    },
...
```

The `input` field points to an index in the `accessors` array of the file. By traversing the path to `bufferViews` and `buffers`, we are able to extract the data for the time points of the key poses. The time points are saved as an array of floats, ascending from zero to an arbitrary maximum time, depending on the animation clip.

A list of time points for an animation may look like this:

Time	0.00	0.25	0.50	0.75	1.00

Figure 10.1: Example animation time points

The buffer referenced by the `input` accessor in *Figure 10.1* contains five float values, arranged in ascending order.

Any values between two of the time points need to be interpolated according to the value in the `interpolation` field. Three interpolations for a sampler are defined: `STEP`, `LINEAR`, and `CUBICSPLINE`:

- The `STEP` interpolation is not a real interpolation; it just uses the data for the time point equal to or smaller than the current time in the animation clip.
- A `LINEAR` interpolation does a standard linear interpolation between the values for time points smaller than and the time points greater than the current time of the animation for translation and scale, and a spherical linear interpolation for rotation.
- The third interpolation type, `CUBICSPLINE`, uses the cubic Hermite spline interpolation, optimized for storage density.

Finally, the `output` field contains the accessor index with the new data for the target `node` and `path`. The data type of the `output` buffer depends on the values of the target path and the interpolation. Step and linear interpolation use three-element vectors for translation and scale changes, and a four-element quaternion for rotation changes. In contrast, the cubic spline interpolation stores three separate elements per time point: an in-tangent value, a property value, and an out-tangent value. In addition, cubic spline interpolation needs at least two time points for key poses.

Optimizing Spline storage in glTF

We talked about the splines in the *Constructing a Hermite spline* section of *Chapter 7*. Here, we can see the difference between storing standard cubic Hermite splines, defined by two points and two tangents, and the optimized cubic spline interpolation of the glTF file format.

For the perfect continuity of two cubic Hermite splines, the first point of the second spline must be the same as the second point of the first spline, and the starting tangent of the second spline must be equal to the ending tangent of the first spline.

By reordering the points and tangents, we can only store three values per spline and "borrow" the second point and the outgoing tangent from the following data entry to reconstruct the spline. Accessing the next data entry in the buffer to reconstruct a cubic Hermite spline also explains why at least two time point entries are needed for the cubic spline interpolation of a node in the glTF specification.

The order of a single entry for the `CUBICSPLINE` interpolation is as follows:

- The in-tangent value
- The property value
- The out-tangent value

The data type for each of these values is a three-element vector for the scaling and the translation, and a quaternion for the rotation.

But how do we interpolate the values from the `output` buffer?

Connecting the input time points and the output node values

The `sampler` element of the glTF file format has an important constraint: the number of data elements in the buffer referenced by the `output` field *must* match the number of elements in the buffer of the `input` field. There is a 1:1 relationship between time points/key frames and target node changes, required for interpolation.

As an example, we take the five time points as input and add a separate three-element vector containing a translation value for every time point:

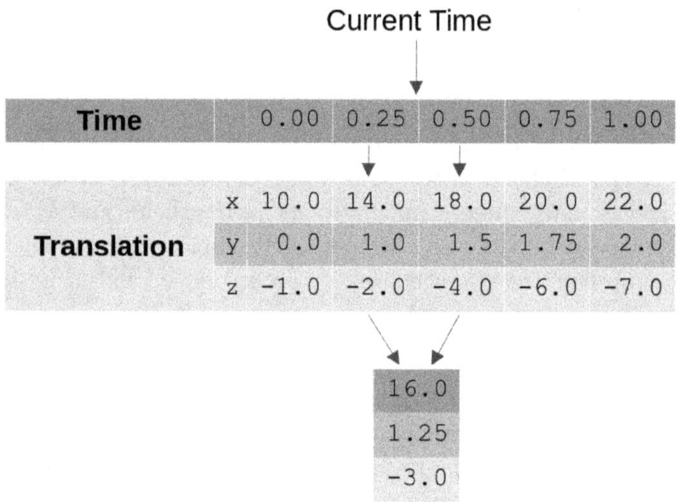

Figure 10.2: Translation interpolation example

The time in *Figure 10.2* may be `0.375`, right in the middle between the two time points `0.25` and `0.50`.

For `STEP` interpolation, we would simply take the values from the `0.25` time point. But if the animation should use the `LINEAR` interpolation instead, we need to calculate the interpolated time value between the next time point and the previous time point. The next and previous time points are chosen relative to the current animation replay time.

We can do this by using the following formula:

$$interpolationValue = \frac{(currentTime - previousTime)}{(nextTime - previousTime)}$$

Here, we calculate the ratio between the time we are in the current time point and the distance to the next time point in our list. The result will be a value between `0`, if we are exactly at the first time point, and close to `1`, if we are just before the next time point.

Having the interpolated time value, we can calculate the interpolated translation vector using the following formula:

$$currentVec = previousVec + interpolationValue^{*}(nextVec - reviousVec)$$

The difference between the three-element vectors `nextVec`, at the index of the next time point, and `previousVec` from the previous time point, is again a three-element vector. We scale this vector by the interpolated time value, that is, between `0` and `1`, and add it to the vector from the previous time point.

The result is the translation position between the values for the two time points, smoothly interpolated between the two values of the previous time and the next time.

For `LINEAR` interpolation of rotation, spherical linear interpolation between two quaternions must be done (see the *Using quaternions for smooth rotations* section of *Chapter 7*).

And for `CUBICSPLINE` interpolation, the default formula for cubic Hermite splines could be used, with respect to the modified data structure (see *Chapter 7*, *Figure 7.41*).

So far, we have explored a single entry of the `channels` array, changing one path of a single node. What needs to be done for a complete animation frame?

Creating a single animation frame

As stated in the glTF file format exploration in the *Animation elements in the glTF file format* section, one channel is responsible for one of the three paths of a target node. This means that to change all three properties of translation, scaling, and rotation of a single node, we need three separate channel entries. Plus, up to three channel entries for every node that is part of the animation are required, with each `sampler` also having a different interpolation type. This means we must calculate up to three different interpolated values for all nodes taking part in one animation clip for every frame of the animation.

As we saw in the *Adding the Node class* section of *Chapter 9*, the local TRS matrix of every node is multiplied by the node matrix of the parent node, creating a chain of matrix multiplications up to the root node. To calculate the final position of all the nodes for a single animation frame, the skeleton must be adjusted too. Starting from the root node, all property changes must be propagated down to the child nodes of every node.

After all the nodes have their new position, the vertex skinning process from *Chapter 9* must be applied, either CPU-based or GPU-based. Only with all these steps in the correct order will our glTF model be rendered correctly in the desired animation frame.

By doing the frame-rendering based on an advancing time value, we can finally create the animation clip from the glTF model's `animations` array slot.

Now that we have the theoretical knowledge about glTF animations in place, let's create two C++ classes for our glTF animations. You can find the full code for this chapter in the `chapter10` folder. Look in the `01_opengl_animations` subfolder for the code that uses the OpenGL renderer, and use `02_vulkan_animations` for the Vulkan renderer.

> **Code cleanup note**
>
> If you read the *Practical sessions* section in *Chapter 9*, you may have cleaned up the renderers as part of the tasks in that section. Even if you skipped the task, it is a good idea to remove the drawing of the boxes before you add the new code, or at least to move the boxes farther away from the center of the screen to prevent overlaps with the glTF model.

Pouring the knowledge into C++ classes

We will split the code for the animations into two separate classes to follow the structure of the glTF file format. In a glTF file, the animation clips and the animation channels are stored in different elements because one animation clip uses data from multiple animation channels.

The first class, named `GltfAnimationChannel`, will contain the data of a glTF animation channel. We will store all data of a single `channels` entry and the corresponding `samplers` entry in this class: the time points from the `input` buffer, the new data for the target node from the `output` buffer, the interpolation type from the sampler, plus the target path and the target node from the channel definition.

The second class, `GltfAnimationClip`, manages the animation clips and uses the `GltfAnimationChannel` class to store the animation channel data per clip.

Storing the channel data in a class

We start the animation channel class, `GltfAnimationChannel`, with the header file, `GltfAnimationChannel.h`, in the `model` folder. The first lines are the headers we need to include:

```
#pragma once
#include <string>
#include <vector>
#include <memory>
#include <tiny_gltf.h>
#include <glm/glm.hpp>
#include <glm/gtx/quaternion.hpp>
```

As well as the `string`, `vector`, and `memory` headers for the respective C++ data types, we also need the `tiny_gltf.h` header to extract data from the model file, and the standard GLM plus GLM quaternion headers to manipulate the model data.

Next, we define two enumeration classes:

```
enum class ETargetPath {
  ROTATION,
  TRANSLATION,
  SCALE
};
enum class EInterpolationType {
  STEP,
  LINEAR,
  CUBICSPLINE
};
```

By using the `ETargetPath` enum, we store which of the three node properties (translation, rotation, or scale) will be changed. The second enum, `EinterpolationType`, will be used to signal if the interpolation type of the sampler is step, linear, or cubic spline.

Using enumerations instead of the original strings will simplify the selection of the correct path or interpolation because we can use a `switch/case` instead of an `if/else` chain with multiple string comparisons.

The `GltfAnimationChannel` class starts with the `public` method for extracting the channel data from the glTF model file:

```
class GltfAnimationChannel {
  public:
    void loadChannelData(
      std::shared_ptr<tinygltf::Model> model,
      tinygltf::Animation anim,
      tinygltf::AnimationChannel channel);
```

Here, we hand over the smart pointer to the already loaded model file, plus the animation number and the animation channel this class instance will contain.

The remaining `public` methods will return data from the animation channel:

```
    int getTargetNode();
    ETargetPath getTargetPath();
```

The first two methods, `getTargetNode()` and `getTargetPath()`, deliver the number of the target node and the enum value for the target path. In the animation clip class, we need to alter the target node number and the property path. These two methods enable us to locate the specific node and node property effectively.

The `getScaling()`, `getTranslation()`, and `getRotation()` methods will return the respective properties of the target node for the specified time:

```
    glm::vec3 getScaling(float time);
    glm::vec3 getTranslation(float time);
    glm::quat getRotation(float time);
```

The value will be interpolated using the interpolation method from the sampler.

Finally, the last `public` method gives the maximum time of the `input` time points:

```
    float getMaxTime();
```

We will use this time value to find the correct end point of the animation clip.

Next, we have the `private` methods and member variables:

```
  private:
    int mTargetNode = -1;
    ETargetPath mTargetPath = EtargetPath::ROTATION;
    EInterpolationType mInterType =
      EInterpolationType::LINEAR;
```

The `mTargetNode` member variable stores the target node, the `mTargetPath` enum stores the target path value, and the `mInterType` enum saves the interpolation value.

We also need to store the data from the input and output buffer of the sampler:

```
    std::vector<float> mTimings{};
    std::vector<glm::vec3> mScaling{};
    std::vector<glm::vec3> mTranslations{};
    std::vector<glm::quat> mRotations{};
```

The data for every property and the timings are stored in a `std::vector` to allow easy and fast access to the values.

Finally, the setter methods for the buffer data are declared:

```
    void setTimings(std::vector<float> timinings);
    void setScalings(std::vector<glm::vec3> scalings);
    void setTranslations(std::vector<glm::vec3> tranlations);
    void setRotations(std::vector<glm::quat> rotations);
```

The `setTimings()`, `setScalings()`, `setTranslations()`, and `setRotations()` methods are used to fill the internal member variables of the channel with the extracted animation data of the glTF model. We only need these methods during the data extraction. So, they can remain in the `private` part of the class.

The implementation of the `GltfAnimationChannel` class will be done in the `GltfAnimationChannel.cpp` file inside the `model` folder.

The first line in the file is, as always, the header of the `GltfAnimationChannel` class declaration:

```
#include "GltfAnimationChannel.h"
```

Let's fill the `loadChannelData` method with the implementation:

```
void GltfAnimationChannel::loadChannelData(
    std::shared_ptr<tinygltf::Model> model,
    tinygltf::Animation anim,
    tinygltf::AnimationChannel channel) {
```

Then, we store the target node number in the `mTargetNode` member variable:

```
  mTargetNode = channel.target_node;
```

We will need the target node later in the animation clip class to set the saved data for the correct model node.

The next part is well-known; it's the traversal from the input accessor to the buffer:

```
  const tinygltf::Accessor& inputAccessor = model->accessors.
    at(anim.samplers.at(channel.sampler).input);
  const tinygltf::BufferView& inputBufferView = model->bufferViews.
    at(inputAccessor.bufferView);
  const tinygltf::Buffer& inputBuffer = model->buffers.
    at(inputBufferView.buffer);
```

Here, we extract the buffer and the buffer view for the `input` field of the sampler, which contains the time values.

After we extract the required data, we fill a temporary `std::vector` with the raw time values and hand over the vector data to the member variable:

```
  std::vector<float> timings;
  timings.resize(inputAccessor.count);
  std::memcpy(timings.data(), &inputBuffer.data.at(0) +
    inputBufferView.byteOffset,
    inputBufferView.byteLength);
  setTimings(timings);
```

Next, we set the enum value for the interpolation type:

```
  const tinygltf::AnimationSampler sampler =
    anim.samplers.at(channel.sampler);
```

```
if (sampler.interpolation.compare("STEP") == 0) {
  mInterType = EinterpolationType::STEP;
} else if (sampler.interpolation.compare("LINEAR") == 0)  {
  mInterType = EinterpolationType::LINEAR;
} else {
  mInterType = EinterpolationType::CUBICSPLINE;
}
```

The interpolation enum will make the node data update a lot easier.

Now, as with the input accessor, we do the same traversal with the output accessor of the sampler data:

```
const tinygltf::Accessor& outputAccessor = model->accessors.
  at(anim.samplers.at(channel.sampler).output);
const tinygltf::BufferView& outputBufferView = model->bufferViews.
  at(outputAccessor.bufferView);
const tinygltf::Buffer& outputBuffer = model->buffers.
  at(outputBufferView.buffer);
```

Choosing the right member variable to update requires a bit more work.

The first `if` checks whether the channel contains rotation data:

```
if (channel.target_path.compare("rotation") == 0) {
  mTargetPath = EtargetPath::ROTATION;
  std::vector<glm::quat> rotations;
  rotations.resize(outputAccessor.count);
  std::memcpy(rotations.data(), &outputBuffer.data.at(0) +
    outputBufferView.byteOffset,
    outputBufferView.byteLength);
  setRotations(rotations);
}
```

The check for the rotation data is essentially the same as for the timing values, but with quaternions. We also set the `mTargetPath` enum to the corresponding value for the desired update action here, saving another string comparison with the channel's target path when we update the node data in the `setAnimationFrame()` method of the `GltfAnimationClip` class in the *Adding the class for the animation clips* section.

The next check is done for a translation, including the extraction of the translation data:

```
else
  if (channel.target_path.compare("translation") == 0) {
  mTargetPath = EtargetPath::TRANSLATION;
  std::vector<glm::vec3> translations;
  translations.resize(outputAccessor.count);
```

```
      std::memcpy(translations.data(),
        &outputBuffer.data.at(0) +
        outputBufferView.byteOffset,
        outputBufferView.byteLength);
      setTranslations(translations);
    }
```

The last `else` branch extracts scale data if we had no rotation or translation:

```
  else {
      mTargetPath = EtargetPath::SCALE;
      std::vector<glm::vec3> scale;
      scale.resize(outputAccessor.count);
      std::memcpy(scale.data(), &outputBuffer.data.at(0) +
        outputBufferView.byteOffset,
        outputBufferView.byteLength);
      setScalings(scale);
    }
  }
```

> **A note on the target path**
>
> There is a fourth target path: the `weight` path. `weight` is used for **morph targets**, a special target type that adds displacements to the mesh. The demo models do not contain the morph properties, so we will skip the morph target here. You can check out the glTF sample models if you want to implement the morphing feature by yourself.

The animation clip class needs the channel data at a specific time in the animation to change the scaling, translation, and rotation properties of the nodes. The calculation of the exact changes for the properties at a given point in time is handled by the `getScaling()`, `getRotation()`, and `getTranslation()` methods.

As the principle is the same for all three methods, we only need to look at the `getScaling()` method:

```
glm::vec3 GltfAnimationChannel::getScaling(float time) {
  if (mScaling.size() == 0) {
    return glm::vec3(1.0f);
  }
```

The first check returns a scaling factor of `1.0` if we do not have any scaling data in the member variable. Even though this should not happen, a sanity check such as this may prevent the application from crashing because of accessing elements of an empty member variable.

Another simple check is made for the timing values:

```
if (time < mTimings.at(0)) {
  return mScaling.at(0);
}
if (time > mTimings.at(mTimings.size() - 1)) {
  return mScaling.at(mScaling.size() - 1);
}
```

If the requested `time` is lower than the value of the first time point in the `mTimings` member variable, we return the value of the first time point. And if the value of the `time` parameter is higher than the value of the last time point in `mTimings`, we return the value of the last time point. Now, let's find the two time points that are just above and below the requested time:

```
int prevTimeIndex = 0;
int nextTimeIndex = 0;
for (int i = 0; i < mTimings.size(); ++i) {
  if (mTimings.at(i) > time) {
    nextTimeIndex = i;
    break;
  }
  prevTimeIndex = i;
}
```

We loop over the array containing the time points and compare the time points in the vector position with the `time` parameter to find the two time point indexes right before and directly after the requested time.

If we manage to get the same value for both indexes, we can simply return the scaling value to one of the index positions:

```
if (prevTimeIndex == nextTimeIndex) {
  return mScaling.at(prevTimeIndex);
}
```

At this point, we should have two different time point index values: one for the previous time point and one for the next time point.

Then, we initialize a temporary scale value with a default value of `1.0f`:

```
glm::vec3 finalScale = glm::vec3(1.0f);
```

Scaling the model by a factor of `1.0f` does not change the size of the model at all. For a rotation, we will use a quaternion initialized with `glm::quat(1.0f, 0.0f, 0.0f, 0.0f)`, and, for translations, the initial value will be `glm::vec3(0.0f)`. These values will never make changes to the model.

The following `switch/case` statement contains the logic that returns the correct value, depending on the interpolation type set:

```
switch(mInterType) {
  case EinterpolationType::STEP:
      finalScale = mScaling.at(prevTimeIndex);
    break;
```

`STEP` is the simplest type of interpolation, and, as stated before, is not really interpolation. We just return the scaling value of the `mScaling` vector at the index of the time point that lies chronologically before the requested time.

The `LINEAR` type uses normal linear interpolation:

```
  case EinterpolationType::LINEAR:
    {
      float interpolatedTime =
        (time - mTimings.at(prevTimeIndex)) /
        (mTimings.at(nextTimeIndex) -
         mTimings.at(prevTimeIndex));
```

We calculate the location of the time between the two time points we found in the `for` loop over the `mTimings` vector. The formula was introduced in the *Connecting the input time points and the output node values* section, and it returns a value between `0.0` and `1.0`.

Then, we get the scaling values from the two time point indexes:

```
      glm::vec3 prevScale = mScaling.at(prevTimeIndex);
      glm::vec3 nextScale = mScaling.at(nextTimeIndex);
```

And then do linear interpolation between the two scaling values:

```
      finalScale = prevScale +
        interpolatedTime * (nextScale - prevScale);
    }
    break;
```

For the third interpolation type, `CUBICSPLINE`, an extra step is required:

```
  case EinterpolationType::CUBICSPLINE:
    {
      float deltaTime = mTimings.at(nextTimeIndex) -
        mTimings.at(prevTimeIndex);
      glm::vec3 prevTangent = deltaTime *
        mScaling.at(prevTimeIndex * 3 + 2);
      glm::vec3 nextTangent = deltaTime *
        mScaling.at(nextTimeIndex * 3);
```

To calculate the correct index for the `mScaling` vector, we must multiply the two index variables, `prevTimeIndex` and `nextTimeIndex`, by `3`. As explained in the *Optimizing spline storage in glTF* section, each element of the `mScaling` vector contains three consecutive values if the `CUBICSPLINE` interpolation is used – the in-tangent, the data value, and the out-tangent.

For the `prevTangent` variable, we read the out-tangent of the previous time index by adding a value of `2` after the multiplication by `3`, and for the `nextTangent`, we use the in-tangent of the next time index.

Also, all tangent values are stored as normalized vectors or normalized quaternions in glTF file format. To calculate the correct tangent for the spline, the unit vector or the unit quaternion must be scaled according to the time difference, `deltaTime`, between the two time points.

Calculating the interpolated time value is the same as for the `LINEAR` interpolation:

```
float interpolatedTime =
  (time - mTimings.at(prevTimeIndex)) /
  (mTimings.at(nextTimeIndex) -
   mTimings.at(prevTimeIndex));
```

A cubic Hermite spline needs the square and the cube of the interpolated time, so let's calculate the two extra values to keep the final calculation short:

```
float interpolatedTimeSq =
  interpolatedTime * interpolatedTime;
float interpolatedTimeCub =
  interpolatedTimeSq * interpolatedTime;
```

Before we can calculate the spline, we must also extract the two spline points:

```
glm::vec3 prevPoint =
  mScaling.at(prevTimeIndex * 3 + 1);
glm::vec3 nextPoint =
 mScaling.at(nextTimeIndex * 3 + 1);
```

Here, the multiplication by factor `3` is also required to calculate the correct index in the `mScaling` vector. After the multiplication by `3`, we must add a value of `1` to access the data property for a given time index. For the `CUBICSPLINE` interpolation, we read the two 3D vectors containing the spline points for the previous and the next time index from the `mScaling` vector.

After we have extracted the two tangent vectors and the two spline points, we can reconstruct the cubic Hermite spline and use the value of the `InterpolatedTime` variable to calculate the interpolated point by using the cubic Hermite formula from *Figure 7.42* in *Chapter 7*:

```
finalScale =
  (2 * interpolatedTimeCub -
```

```
          3 * interpolatedTimeSq + 1) * prevPoint +
         (interpolatedTimeCub -
          2 * interpolatedTimeSq + interpolatedTime) *
          prevTangent +
         (-2 * interpolatedTimeCub +
          3 * interpolatedTimeSq) * nextPoint +
         (interpolatedTimeCub - interpolatedTimeSq) *
          nextTangent;
    }
    break;
  }
```

As a result, we have cubic Hermite spline interpolated scaling. The same formula also works for the translation vector, and even for the rotation quaternion.

Finally, we return the calculated value and end the method:

```
  return finalScale;
}
```

The remaining methods of the `GltfAnimationChannel` class in the example code only set or get the data of the member variables. We can omit those trivial methods here.

The second class will collect all the channel data for a single animation clip, enabling simple management of the clips.

Adding the class for the animation clips

We start with the header of the new class, `GltfAnimationClip`. Create the new file called `GltfAnimationClip.h` in the `model` folder and add the following headers:

```
#pragma once
#include <string>
#include <vector>
#include <memory>
#include <tiny_gltf.h>
#include "GltfNode.h"
#include "GltfAnimationChannel.h"
```

The headers are straightforward: `string`, `vector`, and `memory` for the C++ data types and smart pointers, `tiny_gltf.h` to hand over the model data to the channel class, and the `GltfNode` and the `GltfAnimationChannel` class headers because we will use both types here.

The `public` part of the class declaration starts with a custom constructor, taking the clip name as the only parameter:

```
class GltfAnimationClip {
  public:
    GltfAnimationClip(std::string name);
```

Calling the constructor with the class name is the easiest way to initialize the instance.

The `addChannel()` method has the same signature as the `loadChannelData()` method of the `GltfAnimationChannel` class:

```
    void addChannel(std::shared_ptr<tinygltf::Model> model,
      tinygltf::Animation anim,
      tinygltf::AnimationChannel channel);
```

We will simply store the loaded channels in a `std::vector` and forward the parameters to the new channel object.

To update the model nodes with data from a specific time point, we create a method called `setAnimationFrame()`:

```
    void setAnimationFrame(
      std::vector<std::shared_ptr<GltfNode>> nodes,
      float time);
```

Instead of the entire model, we just pass a `std::vector` of `GltfNodes` here. Using a vector makes the update easier because we do not need to parse the node tree.

The last two methods, `getClipEndTime()` and `getClipName()`, return the time of the last time point and the name of the clip:

```
    float getClipEndTime();
    std::string getClipName();
```

In the `private` part of the class, we store the animation channels and the clip name:

```
  private:
    std::vector<std::shared_ptr<GltfAnimationChannel>>
      mAnimationChannels;
    std::string mClipName;
};
```

The implementation of the `GltfAnimationClip` class is in the `GltfAnimationClip.cpp` file in the `model` folder. The file starts with the class header and the custom constructor:

```
#include "GltfAnimationClip.h"

GltfAnimationClip::GltfAnimationClip(std::string name) :
  mClipName(name) {}
```

The constructor uses a member initialization list to fill in the clip name, but a simple assignment in the body would also be possible.

Filling the channel vector is done in the `addChannel()` method:

```
void GltfAnimationClip::addChannel(
    std::shared_ptr<tinygltf::Model> model,
    tinygltf::Animation anim,
    tinygltf::AnimationChannel channel) {
  std::shared_ptr<GltfAnimationChannel> chan =
    std::make_shared<GltfAnimationChannel>();
  chan->loadChannelData(model, anim, channel);
  mAnimationChannels.push_back(chan);
}
```

We simply create a new instance using a smart pointer, let the instance load the data itself by handing over the `tinygltf` data, and append the filled channel to the `mAnimationsChannel` vector.

The `setAnimationFrame()` method updates the model to a specified point in time with the data of the current channel:

```
void GltfAnimationClip::setAnimationFrame(
    std::vector<std::shared_ptr<GltfNode>> nodes,
    float time) {
  for (auto &channel : mAnimationChannels) {
    int targetNode = channel->getTargetNode();
```

Here, we loop through all channels of the clip and extract the target node number first.

Using the target path of the current channel, we then update the node property specified in the channel in another `switch/case` block:

```
    switch(channel->getTargetPath()) {
      case ETargetPath::ROTATION:
        nodes.at(targetNode)->setRotation(
          channel->getRotation(time));
        break;
      case ETargetPath::TRANSLATION:
```

```
        nodes.at(targetNode)->setTranslation(
          channel->getTranslation(time));
        break;
      case ETargetPath::SCALE:
        nodes.at(targetNode)->setScale(
          channel->getScaling(time));
        break;
    }
  }
```

After the new rotation, translation, or scale property of the node has been set, we must update the local translate/rotate/scale matrices of all nodes:

```
  for (auto &node : nodes) {
    if (node) {
      node->calculateLocalTRSMatrix();
    }
  }
}
```

At the end of the `setAnimationFrame()` method, all nodes taking part in the current animation clip have new properties, and the TRS matrix is also updated.

The implementations of the `getClipEndTime()` and `getClipName()` methods are trivial, so we will omit them here.

To extract the animation data from the glTF model file and store the animation clips, we need to adjust the `GltfModel` class.

Loading the animation data from the glTF model file

Implementing the animation loading part is a quick task.

First, we add the header for the `GltfAnimationClip` class to the `GltfModel.h` header file in the `model` folder:

```
#include "GltfAnimationClip.h"
```

The `private` member variable for storing the animation clips is a `std::vector`:

```
    std::vector<GltfAnimationClip> mAnimClips{};
```

We store the animation clips in the `mAnimClips` vector in the same order as they appear in the glTF model file. It is not a good idea to use a map to store the name as the clip name is optional, and a map cannot have an empty value as the key.

Next, we add a `private` method to extract the animation data from the model file:

```
void getAnimations();
```

We will only call `getAnimations()` in the `loadModel()` method; there is no need to make this method public.

Four other new `public` methods are also needed to manage and play the animations:

```
void playAnimation(int animNum, float speedDivider);
void setAnimationFrame(int animNumber, float time);
float getAnimationEndTime(int animNum);
std::string getClipName(int animNum);
```

The `playAnimation()` method will play the animation frame by frame. The replay speed can be adjusted by the `speedDivider` parameter to slow down or accelerate the animation. A single animation frame could be drawn by calling the `setAnimationFrame()` method. The parameter is the time point inside the animation that should be used. The remaining two methods, `getAnimationEndTime()` and `getClipName()`, are used in the `UserInterface` class to show more information about the current animation clip.

The implementation of these methods goes into the `GltfModel.cpp` file in the `model` folder. We must add the `chrono` header in the `include` statements at the top because we use the system time to replay the animations, and we need the `cmath` header for the `fmod` C function:

```
#include <chrono>
#include <cmath>
```

Filling the `mAnimClips` vector is done in the `getAnimations()` method:

```
void GltfModel::getAnimations() {
  for (const auto &anim : mModel->animations) {
    GltfAnimationClip clip(anim.name);
    for (const auto& channel : anim.channels) {
      clip.addChannel(mModel, anim, channel);
    }
    mAnimClips.push_back(clip);
  }
}
```

We are looping over the animations of the glTF model file and adding a channel for every animation found. The `addChannel()` method reads the `channels` and `samplers` data from the `animations` element, and the extracted clip is appended to the `mAnimClips` vector.

To draw the frames of an animation, the `playAnimation()` method uses the current time to determine the right frame to show:

```
void GltfModel::playAnimation(int animNum,
    float speedDivider) {
  double currentTime =
    std::chrono::duration_cast<std::chrono::milliseconds>(
    std::chrono::steady_clock::now().time_since_epoch()
    ).count();
  setAnimationFrame(animNum,
    std::fmod(currentTime / 1000.0 * speedDivider,
    mAnimClips.at(animNum).getClipEndTime()));
}
```

First, we get the current system time in milliseconds. Using seconds here would not work because we need to draw several frames every second to achieve the illusion of an animated character. Then, we use the `std::fmod()` function to calculate the modulo of the current time and the overall time of the animation clip.

The modulo operation results in the clip time running from zero to the end time, and starting again at zero, creating an endless loop. We divide the current time by `1000.0` (a double!) to go back from milliseconds to seconds, and we can adjust the playback speed with the `speedDivider` parameter to speed up or slow down the animation.

A single frame of the clip is drawn by the `setAnimationFrame()` method:

```
void GltfModel::setAnimationFrame(int animNum, float time) {
  mAnimClips.at(animNum).setAnimationFrame(mNodeList, time);
  updateNodesMatrices(mRootNode, glm::mat4(1.0f));
}
```

The `setAnimationFrame()` method is also used by the `playAnimation()` method to display a frame at the calculated time. To draw a frame, we call the `setAnimationFrame()` method of the clip to update the TRS matrices of the nodes and update the node matrices using the `updateNodesMatrices()` call.

The node matrix update method traverses the model skeleton tree from the top to all children and updates all node matrices. After this update, the positions of the nodes of the model are according to the time parameter of the animation clip.

Getting the overall time and the name of the clip for the user interface is done by the remaining two methods, `getAnimationEndTime()` and `getClipName()`:

```
float GltfModel::getAnimationEndTime(int animNum) {
  return mAnimClips.at(animNum).getClipEndTime();
}
```

```
std::string GltfModel::getClipName(int animNum) {
  return mAnimClips.at(animNum).getClipName();
}
```

Here, we just extract the end time and the name of the animation clip from the `mAnimClips` vector.

As the last step, we add the extraction of the animations at the end of the `loadModel()` method in the `GltfModel` class and update the `rdAnimClipSize` variable:

```
  getAnimations();
  renderData.rdAnimClipSize = mAnimClips.size();
```

The `rdAnimClipSize` variable of the `OGLRenderData` struct will be used to set the correct limit for the slider showing the number of animation clips.

Finally, we will update the renderer and user interface classes to show and manage the animations of the glTF model.

Adding new control variables for the animations

First, some new variables must be added to the `OGLRenderData.h` file in the `opengl` folder:

```
  bool rdPlayAnimation = true;
  std::string rdClipName = "None";
  int rdAnimClip = 0;
  int rdAnimClipSize = 0;
  float rdAnimSpeed = 1.0f;
  float rdAnimTimePosition = 0.0f;
  float rdAnimEndTime = 0.0f;
```

The `rdPlayAnimation` variable is used to toggle the animation replay on or off. We will also use the variable to switch between the replay speed, controlled by the `rdAnimSpeed` variable, and the time position in the current animation clip, controlled by the `rdAnimTimePosition` variable.

In the `rdAnimClip` variable, the number of the current clip is stored, accompanied by the `rdClipName` variable with the clip name and the `rdAnimEndTime` variable with the maximum time for the clip. We have already seen the last new variable, `rdAnimClipSize`, in the `GltfModel` class.

The animations will be managed by new elements of the `UserInterface` class.

Managing the animations in the user interface

First, we add a new collapsed header for the new controls:

```
  if (ImGui::CollapsingHeader("glTF Animation")) {
```

Now, a slider to select one of the available animation clips will be drawn in the new part of the user interface:

```
ImGui::Text("Clip No");
ImGui::SameLine();
ImGui::SliderInt("##Clip", &renderData.rdAnimClip, 0,
  renderData.rdAnimClipSize - 1);
```

The upper limit of the slider is the number of animation clips minus one, as the values start at zero. This number of clips is extracted from the glTF model at loading time. In *Chapter 12*, we will add more control types to the user interface, such as a **list box** containing all animation clip names. For now, the selection will be done using a simple slider.

We also set the clip name here:

```
ImGui::Text("Clip Name: %s",
  renderData.rdClipName.c_str());
```

Next, the checkbox to control the animation replay is added:

```
ImGui::Checkbox("Play Animation",
  &renderData.rdPlayAnimation);
```

We will use the `rdPlayAnimation` variable in the `UserInterface` class to control the availability of UI elements, and we will use it in the `renderer` class to switch between animation replay and single-frame display.

If we activate the **Play Animation** checkbox to play an animation clip, the `rdPlayAnimation` variable is set to `true` and we enable the `ClipSpeed` slider (we do not disable the text field and the slider). The `ClipSpeed` slider allows us to control the factor of the animation clip replay speed:

```
if (!renderData.rdPlayAnimation) {
  ImGui::BeginDisabled();
}
ImGui::Text("Speed  ");
ImGui::SameLine();
ImGui::SliderFloat("##ClipSpeed",
  &renderData.rdAnimSpeed, 0.0f, 2.0f);
if (!renderData.rdPlayAnimation) {
  ImGui::EndDisabled();
}
```

We limit the speed factor to values between `0` and `2`. A value of `0` freezes the animation in the current frame , a value of `1` plays the animation at the default speed, and a value of `2` doubles the animation replay speed. Setting the speed factor to `0` does not disable the animation replay, only the time point inside the animation clip remains unchanged.

Clearing the **Play Animation** checkbox sets the `rdPlayAnimation` variable to `false`, and we enable the `ClipPos` slider instead of the `ClipSpeed` slider:

```
    if (renderData.rdPlayAnimation) {
      ImGui::BeginDisabled();
    }
    ImGui::Text("Timepos");
    ImGui::SameLine();
    ImGui::SliderFloat("##ClipPos",
      &renderData.rdAnimTimePosition, 0.0f,
      renderData.rdAnimEndTime);
    if (renderData.rdPlayAnimation) {
      ImGui::EndDisabled();
    }
  }
```

If the animation replay is disabled, we can use the `ClipPos` slider to set the time position in the animation to an arbitrary value between zero and the end time of the animation clip.

Finally, to animate the model, some lines must be added to the `OGLRenderer` class.

Adding the animation replay to the renderer

Add the following new lines to the `draw()` method of the `OGLRenderer.cpp` file in the `opengl` folder, right after the call to `mMatrixGenerateTimer.start()`:

```
  mRenderData.rdClipName =
    mGltfModel->getClipName(mRenderData.rdAnimClip);
```

The first line updates the clip name from the currently played clip. Doing the clip name update every frame seems to be overkill, but for the sake of simplicity, this is the best place to set the name of the current animation clip.

Next, we switch between the animation replay and the single frame control:

```
  if (mRenderData.rdPlayAnimation) {
    mGltfMode->playAnimation(mRenderData.rdAnimClip,
      mRenderData.rdAnimSpeed);
  } else {
    mRenderData.rdAnimEndTime =
      mGltfModel->getAnimationEndTime(
      mRenderData.rdAnimClip);
    mGltfModel->setAnimationFrame(mRenderData.rdAnimClip,
      mRenderData.rdAnimTimePosition);
  }
```

If we play the animation clip, the `playAnimation()` method of the model will be called in every `draw()` call, updating the frame according to the modulo of the system time and the clip end time, and the speed factor set by the `ClipSpeed` slider. And, if we do not play the animation, the frame of the animation clip at the time specified by the `ClipPos` slider will be drawn.

Compiling the code and running the executable produces an enhanced version of the model viewer application. A single frame of the jumping animation clip is shown in *Figure 10.3*:

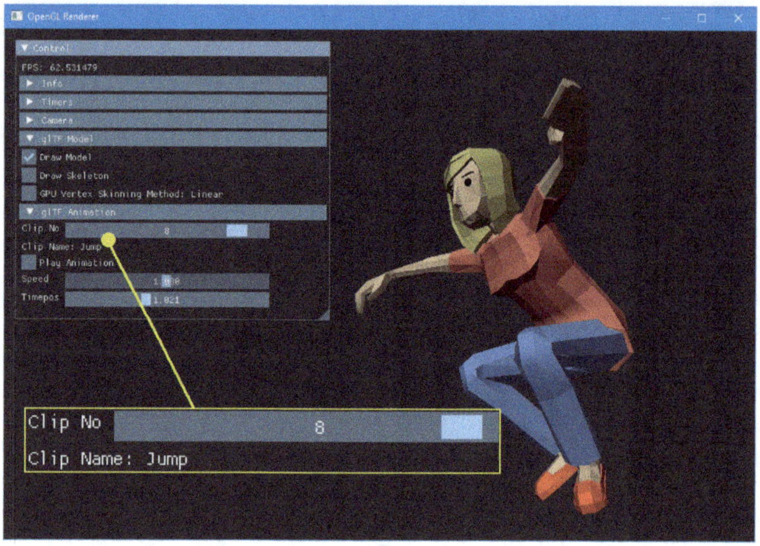

Figure 10.3: A single frame of the jumping animation with the unfolded animation controls

We can now select which animation clip we want to play using the slider, and the name of the current clip is shown in the text field below the slider. In addition, we can control whether the animation is played or not. If the animation replay is enabled, the slider to control the speed of the animation is activated, or, if the replay is disabled, we can select a point in time for the selected animation to be shown.

Summary

In this chapter, we finally arrived at the point where we were able to animate our loaded glTF model in the renderers we started in *Chapter 2* and *Chapter 3*.

First, we got a broad overview of the different elements of animations and the model poses. Then, we analyzed the animation elements of the glTF file format, the sub-element channels and samplers, and the relations of these elements to the other parts of the glTF model, such as the joints and nodes.

Finally, we created two new C++ classes for managing the glTF channels and the animation clips and included these classes in the renderer. We also added new UI elements to the application, allowing fine-grained control of various parameters of the animations.

In the next chapter, we will dive deeper into the realms of game character animations. We will explore different forms of animation blending, such as the blending between the binding pose as a "still pose", where the model does not move, and the full animation clip, or crossfading between two different animations.

Practical sessions

Try out the following ideas to enhance the code for the animation playback:

- Add a class to append multiple animation clips to a longer animation track. You could join the running and jumping clips to create the illusion of a long-running glTF model by playing jump animation clips between a couple of running animation clips.
- Add the ability to control the looping of an animation, such as not only switching the loop on and off, but also controlling the number of loops to play in a row. The animation should stop after the last loop has finished.
- Add a UI control and the logic to play the clips backward. For many clips, this will result in quite interesting behavior of the model, but animations such as sitting and leaning will become more meaningful. The model will stand up from a sitting position and lean back to the upright position.

Additional resources

- The official glTF tutorial: `https://github.com/KhronosGroup/glTF-Tutorials/tree/master/gltfTutorial`
- The tinygltf loader: `https://github.com/syoyo/tinygltf`

11
Blending between Animations

Welcome to *Chapter 11*! In the previous chapter, we took our first steps in character animations. We explored the way animations are stored in the glTF file format, extracted the data, and were finally able to watch our character become animated.

In this chapter, we push the envelope even further. We will start with an overview of animation blending, and dive into the first part of character animations: blending between the binding pose and any animation clip. You will learn how to extend the current code to change the blending by adjusting a slider in the user interface.

Next, we will upgrade our work to feature crossfading between two animations. Crossfading is like simple blending, but instead of blending from the binding pose as the starting point, we play an animation clip and blend it into another animation clip.

At the end of the chapter, we will look at additive animation blending. Additive blending is different from simple blending and crossfading in that it allows us to animate only some nodes of the model skeleton. We can also play two different animations for different nodes.

In this chapter, we will cover the following main topics:

- Does it blend?
- Blending between the binding pose and animation clip
- Crossfading animations
- How to do additive blending

Technical requirements

To follow along with this chapter, you will need the OpenGL and Vulkan renderer code from *Chapter 10*.

Let us start with a brief overview of the types of animation blending.

Does it blend?

In *Chapter 10*, we did our animations by simply overwriting the translation, rotation, and scale node properties with the values taken from the `channels` and `samplers` entries. If we did not hit the exact time of one of the time points that are stored in the `mTimings` vector of the `GltfAnimationChannel` class, the values were interpolated using linear, spherical linear, or spline interpolation. But we never had the chance to choose any option other than the animation clip.

In animation blending, we can adjust the extent of the node property changes. The adjustment can be made between the binding pose and any animation clip, between two different animation clips, and be limited to parts of the character model.

As we will cover all three variants, let us take a quick look at these animation blending types and their characteristics.

Fading animation clips in and out

In the simplest form, animation blending changes only the amount of the node property changes. We do linear interpolation between a value of `0`, where only the binding pose is drawn, and a value of `1`, where the full animation is played. Using linear interpolation for scaling and translation and spherical linear interpolation for rotation, we can control the amount of property changes between *nothing at all* and the full animation.

Crossfading between animation clips

The second blending type, crossfading, uses linear interpolation for scaling, and translation operations and spherical linear interpolation for the rotations to blend between two different animation clips. In this type of blending, we determine the extent of the node property changes taken from the first animation clip vis-à-vis the second clip. A blending value of `0` uses only the node property changes from the first clip, and a blending value of `1` only from the second clip. Any value in between will result in animation frames with node property changes between both clips.

Technically, we can also blend between two instances of the same animation clip, but this will just play the single animation clip, as we will be trying to blend between the same values.

Adding multiple animation clips into one clip

Additive animation blending is a bit different from the preceding two types as blending does not happen between the binding pose and the animation clip or between two animation clips. We add multiple animations to a final clip, but we create a *mask* for the parts of the model skeleton that should be changed (or not changed) using the values of a specific animation clip. The masked-out parts of the model skeleton will not receive node property changes from a given animation clip, limiting the animation to a subset of nodes. For the non-masked nodes, node property changes from another animation clip could be applied, resulting in a "mix" of two different animation clips.

As an example, we could play a running animation for the character model but mask out the right arm from this animation. For the right arm, we then play a completely different animation, such as a hand waving, balancing some artifact, or throwing a weapon.

A more complex animation could be composed of gesturing arms and hands, head movements in the up/down and left/right directions, facial animations to express different moods, and a speech animation applied to the mouth. When added carefully, we would be able to create a character model that can move its head to follow our position when explaining quest details while having the mouth animation synchronized to the spoken text. To deepen the immersion, the model could also use its arms and hands during the speech animation and express different moods such as anger and joy via animation of its face.

It is also possible to sum up the property changes from different animation clips. To achieve this kind of addition, the animation properties must be carefully crafted during creation and blending. Just adding up the values of properties will result in a distorted model, as translations or scaling are summed, while the quaternion rotations are interpolated.

We will start with an implementation of the most basic type of animation blending, just blending between the standing-still binding pose and one animation clip. You can find the full source code for this section in the folder for `chapter11`. The example code inside the `01_opengl_blending` subfolder uses the OpenGL renderer, while the example code inside the `04_vulkan_blending` subfolder uses the Vulkan renderer.

Blending between the binding pose and animation clip

To blend from the binding pose to an animation clip, we add three new variables for the translation, scale, and rotation to every node. While the original variables store the node properties for the binding pose, the new variables will be used to save the node property changes that occur during the animation clips. By interpolating the translation, scale, and rotation values between the binding pose and the animation clip, we can control the amount of influence of the animation clip over the binding pose.

Let's start by adding some new variables to the node class.

Enhancing the node class

The data type of the new variables must be the same as for the original values, so we just add three new variables with the prefix `Blend` as new `private` data members of the `GltfNode` class to the `GltfNode.h` file in the `model` folder:

```
glm::vec3 mBlendScale = glm::vec3(1.0f);
glm::vec3 mBlendTranslation = glm::vec3(0.0f);
glm::quat mBlendRotation =
  glm::quat(1.0f, 0.0f, 0.0f, 0.0f);
```

All three variables, mBlendScale, mBlendTranslation, and mBlendRotation, will be initialized with values that do not change the node properties.

We also need public setter methods for the new variables, prefixed by the word blend in the method name to keep the purpose clear:

```
    void blendScale(glm::vec3 scale, float blendFactor);
    void blendTranslation(glm::vec3 translation,
      float blendFactor);
    void blendRotation(glm::quat rotation,
      float blendFactor);
```

The implementation of these three new methods, blendScale(), blendTranslation(), and blendRotation(), will be added to the GltfNode.cpp file in the model folder after we've extended the existing methods.

First, the C++ algorithm header must be added in the top area of the GltfNode.cpp file, as follows:

```
#include <algorithm>
```

We will use the std::clamp() C++ function from the algorithm header in the blending methods.

The new variables, mBlendScale, mBlendTranslation, and mBlendRotation, will be set in the default setters for the property variables, along with the existing variables. We simply add them as the second line in every method:

```
void GltfNode::setScale(glm::vec3 scale) {
  mScale = scale;
  mBlendScale = scale;
}
void GltfNode::setTranslation(glm::vec3 translation) {
  mTranslation = translation;
  mBlendTranslation = translation;
}
void GltfNode::setRotation(glm::quat rotation) {
  mRotation = rotation;
  mBlendRotation = rotation;
}
```

The new Blend variables must be set to reasonable values, as we will use them instead of the normal, non-blending variables when we calculate the TRS matrix. So, we need to replace the member variables with the Blend ones in the calculateLocalTRSMatrix() method:

```
void GltfNode::calculateLocalTRSMatrix() {
  glm::mat4 sMatrix = glm::scale(glm::mat4(1.0f),
    mBlendScale);
```

```
    glm::mat4 rMatrix = glm::mat4_cast(mBlendRotation);
    glm::mat4 tMatrix = glm::translate(glm::mat4(1.0f),
      mBlendTranslation);
    mLocalTRSMatrix = tMatrix * rMatrix * sMatrix;
}
```

We have declared three new, short blending methods in the header file and will implement them now. Let us examine one of the methods, for instance, `blendScale()`:

```
void GltfNode::blendScale(glm::vec3 scale,
    float blendFactor) {
```

We use a clamping operation as the first line to keep the incoming blend factor in the valid range between the values `0.0` and `1.0`:

```
    float factor =
      std::clamp(blendFactor, 0.0f, 1.0f);
```

The `std::clamp()` function first compares the value in the `blendFactor` variable and the lower limit of `0.0f`, given as the second parameter, and continues with the higher of the two values, ensuring that the blending factor will not fall below `0`. Then, `std::clamp()` compares the result of the first comparison with the upper limit of `1.0f`, given as the third parameter. Here, the lower of the two values is taken, making sure that the blending factor will not be bigger than `1`. After the call to `std:clamp()`, the value of the resulting `factor` variable is always somewhere in the range between `0` and `1`.

Next, we apply standard linear interpolation between the incoming `scale` parameter and the `mScale` member variable, using the `factor` variable containing the clamped `blendFactor`:

```
    mBlendScale = scale * factor +
      mScale * (1.0f - factor);
}
```

The preceding line sets the `mBlendScale` member variable to a smoothly blended three-element vector between the `mScale` value of the node and the incoming `scale` value.

For translation, the implementation is identical:

```
void GltfNode::blendTranslation(glm::vec3 translation,
  float blendFactor) {
    float factor =
      std::clamp(blendFactor, 0.0f, 1.0f);
      mBlendTranslation = translation * factor +
      mTranslation * (1.0f - factor);
}
```

The only difference for the rotation is the usage of SLERP instead of normal linear interpolation, as we always use spherical linear interpolation for quaternions:

```
void GltfNode::blendRotation(glm::quat rotation,
    float blendFactor) {
  float factor =
    std::clamp(blendFactor, 0.0f, 1.0f);
    mBlendRotation = glm::normalize(glm::slerp(mRotation,
    rotation, factor));
}
```

Every one of the tree methods, namely `blendScale()`, `blendTranslation()`, and `blendRotation()`, allows us to blend the respective node property value between the value set during node initialization and the incoming parameter.

The new blending functions will be used in the `GltfModel` class, but with some minimal changes applied.

Updating the model class

To be able to blend the amount of property changes in the model, we must add the blending factor as a new parameter to two `public` methods.

First, we change the signature of the `playAnimation()` method in the `GltfModel.h` file inside the `model` folder:

```
    void playAnimation(int animNum, float speedDivider,
      float blendFactor);
```

Here, we append the `blendFactor` parameter. `blendFactor` will allow us to interpolate the animation clip between the binding pose and the full clip movements.

Next, we *rename* the `setAnimationFrame()` method using the new name, `blendAnimationFrame()`, and appending `blendFactor` as the new parameter:

```
    void blendAnimationFrame(int animNumber, float time,
      float blendFactor);
```

Keeping the old `setAnimationFrame()` method around makes no sense. We can achieve the same functionality in `blendAnimationFrame()` if we set the `blendFactor` parameter to `1.0`.

The implementation of the new `playAnimation()` method in the `GltfModel.cpp` file in the `model` folder changes only the blending method to be called:

```
void GltfModel::playAnimation(int animNum,
    float speedDivider, float blendFactor) {
  double currentTime =
```

```
    std::chrono::duration_cast<std::chrono::milliseconds>(
    std::chrono::steady_clock::now().time_since_epoch()
    ).count();
    blendAnimationFrame(animNum, std::fmod(
      currentTime / 1000.0 * speedDivider,
      mAnimClips.at(animNum)->getClipEndTime()),
      blendFactor);
}
```

We simply call `blendAnimationFrame()` instead of `setAnimationFrame()` to make use of the new `blendFactor` parameter.

The new `blendAnimationFrame()` method calls the same named method on the current animation clip and updates the node matrices afterward:

```
void GltfModel::blendAnimationFrame(int animNum,
    float time, float blendFactor) {
  mAnimClips.at(animNum)->blendAnimationFrame(mNodeList,
    time, blendFactor);
  updateNodesMatrices(mRootNode, glm::mat4(1.0f));
}
```

A new blending method in `GltfAnimationClip` must be created, and will be similar to `setAnimationFrame()`. Let us implement the new method in the next section.

Adding the blend to the animation clip class

We define the new `public` method, `blendAnimationFrame`, in the `GltfAnimationClip.h` file in the `model` folder:

```
    void blendAnimationFrame(
      std::vector<std::shared_ptr<GltfNode>> nodes,
      float time, float blendFactor);
```

This signature is similar to the one already defined `setAnimationFrame()` method, but we also added the `blendFactor` parameter in the newly added method.

Also, the implementation of the `blendAnimationFrame()` method in the `GltfAnimationClip.cpp` file in the `model` folder is nearly identical to that of the `setAnimationFrame()` method:

```
void GltfAnimationClip::blendAnimationFrame(
    std::vector<std::shared_ptr<GltfNode>> nodes,
    float time, float blendFactor) {
  for (auto &channel : mAnimationChannels) {
    int targetNode = channel->getTargetNode();
```

We iterate again over our animation channels and extract the target node.

Next, we select the proper property path to update on the node in a `switch/case`:

```
    switch(channel->getTargetPath()) {
      case ETargetPath::ROTATION:
        nodes.at(targetNode)->blendRotation(
          channel->getRotation(time), blendFactor);
        break;
      case ETargetPath::TRANSLATION:
        nodes.at(targetNode)->blendTranslation(
          channel->getTranslation(time), blendFactor);
        break;
      case ETargetPath::SCALE:
        nodes.at(targetNode)->blendScale(
          channel->getScaling(time), blendFactor);
        break;
    }
  }
```

The same `switch/case` is also present in the `setAnimationFrame()` method, but in the `blendAnimationFrame()` method, we call the blending functions instead of the setters.

After all nodes that are part of the animation clip are updated, we recalculate the TRS matrices of all nodes:

```
  for (auto &node : nodes) {
    if (node) {
      node->calculateLocalTRSMatrix();
    }
  }
}
```

We do a simple, brute-force loop here, regardless of the node that was updated. Keeping track of the updates to the local TRS matrix in every single node is also possible, but this would require additional flags to signal to the `calculateLocalTRSMatrix()` method if the properties changed during the last update. We will look at these changes in the *Moving computations to different places* section of *Chapter 15*.

As the last step, we must update the renderer to enable us to control the simple animation blending type.

Implementing animation blending in the OpenGL renderer

The first step for the renderer is the creation of a new `rdAnimBlendFactor` variable in the `OGLRenderData.h` file in the `opengl` folder:

```
float rdAnimBlendFactor = 1.0f;
```

This new variable will hold the factor for blending.

Next, we adjust the animation part in the `OGLRenderer.cpp` file in the `opengl` folder:

```
  if (mRenderData.rdPlayAnimation) {
    mGltfModel->playAnimation(mRenderData.rdAnimClip,
      mRenderData.rdAnimSpeed,
      mRenderData.rdAnimBlendFactor);
  } else {
    mRenderData.rdAnimEndTime =
       mGltfModel->getAnimationEndTime(
       mRenderData.rdAnimClip);
    mGltfModel->blendAnimationFrame(
      mRenderData.rdAnimClip,
      mRenderData.rdAnimTimePosition,
      mRenderData.rdAnimBlendFactor);
}
```

If the animation is played, we use the new `playAnimation()` method with the additional `blendFactor` parameter.

Finally, we create a slider to the `UserInterface` class. We add the following code block to the existing animation block in the `createFrame()` method, in the `UserInterface.cpp` file located inside the `opengl` folder:

```
  if (ImGui::CollapsingHeader("glTF Animation Blending")) {
    ImGui::Text("Blend Factor");
    ImGui::SameLine();
    ImGui::SliderFloat("##BlendFactor",
      &renderData.rdAnimBlendFactor, 0.0f, 1.0f);
  }
```

The slider will be in a separate collapsing header, allowing us to hide this part of the user interface if we want to control other parts of the animation.

> **Note on the Vulkan renderer**
>
> For the Vulkan renderer, the changes are identical. The new variable has to be added to the `VkRenderData.h` file, and the animation part must be changed in the `VkRenderer` file. Both files can be found in the `vulkan` folder.

Compiling and running the code will result in an output as shown in *Figure 11.1*. You can use the slider to adjust the amount of blending between the binding pose and the full animation clip.

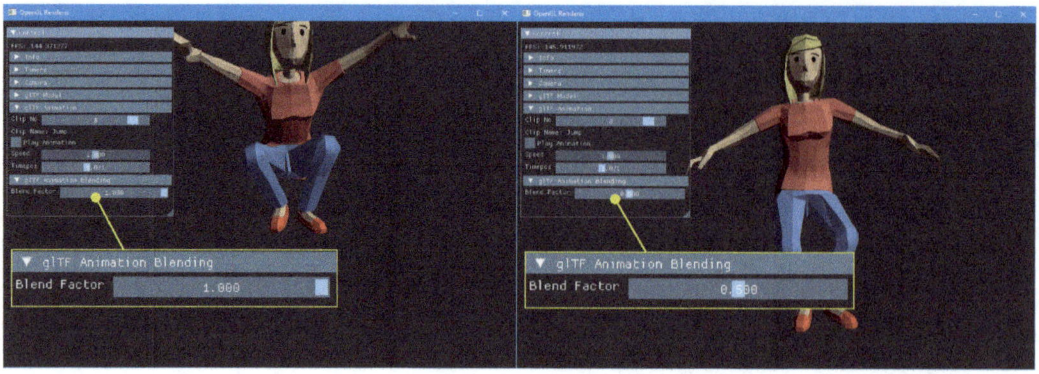

Figure 11.1: Blending the Jump animation clip

On the left side of *Figure 11.1*, the Jump animation clip is played with full blending. This result is the same as in the code from the *Pouring the knowledge into C++ classes* section in *Chapter 10*. On the right side, the same Jump animation is played, but the node property changes are interpolated down to 50% between the blending pose and the animation.

Having the basic animation blending in place, we can extend the code to allow us to cross-blend between two different animations. The source code for this section is in the `chapter11` folder, in the `02_opengl_crossblending` subfolder for the OpenGL renderer and the `05_vulkan_crossblending` subfolder for Vulkan.

Crossfading animations

While the default animation blending uses the binding position with the joint weights as the starting point, crossfading interpolates between two animation clips. We could use the same animation clip as both the source and destination, but this would just play the animation, regardless of the position of the crossfading slider.

We will enhance the `GltfModel` class to store the values for two animation clips, instead of only the binding pose and one animation clip. For the renderer, new shared variables are needed, containing the second clip name and the percentage of blending between the two clips. The user interface must also reflect the new blending mode and new controls, like the selected destination clip, or a slider to adjust the percentage of the blending between the two clips. As the first step, we'll update the model class.

Upgrading the model classes

To set the starting point of the glTF model to an animation, we will *abuse* the default model properties for translation, scale, and rotation for the first animation clip. This also means that we have to reset the glTF model data every time we switch away from the crossfading animation and restore the data for the binding pose. Extending the code to avoid the model reset is left to you as a task in the *Practical sessions* section.

We start by adding four new methods to the `GltfModel` class. We append these three methods to the `public` declaration in the `GltfModel.h` file in the `model` folder:

```
    void playAnimation(int sourceAnimNum, int destAnimNum,
      float speedDivider, float blendFactor);
```

The new `playAnimation()` method has the source and destination animation clip numbers as parameters.

The `crossBlendAnimationFrame()` method is where the real crossfading between the source and the destination clip will occur:

```
    void crossBlendAnimationFrame(int sourceAnimNumber,
      int destAnimNumber, float time, float blendFactor);
```

To reset the node data to the default values, the generic `resetNodeData()` method can be called:

```
    void resetNodeData();
```

As the node data reset must be done for all nodes along the node skeleton tree, a second `private` method is added:

```
    void resetNodeData(std::shared_ptr<GltfNode> treeNode,
      glm::mat4 parentNodeMatrix);
```

The private `resetNodeData()` method with the pointer to the node and the parent node matrix as parameters has been created, as it will be called recursively on every node. Splitting the methods allows us to expose the simple version without parameters as a `public` method, hiding details such as the skeleton tree from other classes.

All these new methods are implemented in the `GltfMode.cpp` file in the `model` folder. The new `playAnimation()` method is similar to the original `playAnimation()` method for the simple animation blending:

```
void GltfModel::playAnimation(int sourceAnimNumber,
    int destAnimNumber, float speedDivider,
    float blendFactor) {
  double currentTime =
    std::chrono::duration_cast<std::chrono::milliseconds>(
    std::chrono::steady_clock::now().time_since_epoch())
    .count();
```

Like in the previous `playAnimation()` method, we calculate the elapsed time in the animation clip by using the modulo of the running time of the application and the length of the animation clip.

Next, we blend between the source clip and the destination clip:

```
    crossBlendAnimationFrame(sourceAnimNumber,
      destAnimNumber,
      std::fmod(currentTime / 1000.0 * speedDivider,
      mAnimClips.at(sourceAnimNumber)->getClipEndTime()),
      blendFactor);
    updateNodesMatrices(mRootNode, glm::mat4(1.0f));
  }
```

While the `playAnimation()` method with a single clip as its parameter uses `blendAnimationFrame()`, the two-parameter version calls `crossBlendAnimationFrame()` to set the data for the animation clip at the previously calculated time. At the end of the method, the node matrices are updated to make the changes available to the renderer.

The `crossBlendAnimationFrame()` method requires a bit more explanation as it is responsible for the proper blending between the frames of two different animation clips:

```
void GltfModel::crossBlendAnimationFrame(
    int sourceAnimNumber, int destAnimNumber, float time,
    float blendFactor) {
```

As the first step, we get the lengths of the source and destination animation clips:

```
  float sourceAnimDuration = mAnimClips.at(
    sourceAnimNumber)->getClipEndTime();
  float destAnimDuration = mAnimClips.at(
    destAnimNumber)->getClipEndTime();
```

Next, we scale the current time for the destination clip by the quotient of the destination and source clip lengths:

```
  float scaledTime = time *
    (destAnimDuration / sourceAnimDuration);
```

This time scaling is done to equalize the clip lengths for the source and destination animations. Without the time adjustment, the shorter animation clip will end suddenly, resulting in a possible gap in the model movement.

Now, it is time to set the node properties of the model to the data of the first animation clip:

```
  mAnimClips.at(sourceAnimNumber)->setAnimationFrame(
    mNodeList, time);
```

The data of the second animation clip will be blended by `blendFactor`, but the time point for the frame is `scaledTime` instead of the original `time` parameter:

```
    mAnimClips.at(destAnimNumber)->blendAnimationFrame(
      mNodeList, scaledTime, blendFactor);
```

As the last step, we recalculate the node matrices:

```
    updateNodesMatrices(mRootNode, glm::mat4(1.0f));
  }
```

Using the preceding implementation, the original model data will be overwritten. The model data can be restored using the two `resetNodeData()` methods:

```
  void GltfModel::resetNodeData() {
    getNodeData(mRootNode, glm::mat4(1.0f));
    resetNodeData(mRootNode, glm::mat4(1.0f));
  }
```

We are using the `getNodeData()` method of the `GltfModel` class to reset the values for translation, scaling, and rotation back to the original values from the glTF model file.

And, as we must do the reset for the entire skeleton tree, we call `getNodeData()` in a recursive way for all child nodes too:

```
  void GltfModel::resetNodeData(
      std::shared_ptr<GltfNode> treeNode,
       glm::mat4 parentNodeMatrix) {
    glm::mat4 treeNodeMatrix = treeNode->getNodeMatrix();
    for (auto &childNode : treeNode->getChilds()) {
      getNodeData(childNode, treeNodeMatrix);
      resetNodeData(childNode, treeNodeMatrix);
    }
  }
```

The model classes are ready for crossfading now. Let us adjust the renderer to use the new blending capabilities.

Adjusting the OpenGL renderer

Like in simple blending, we need new variables to control cross-blending. Add the following lines to the `OGLRenderData.h` file in the `opengl` folder:

```
    bool rdCrossBlending = false;
    int rdCrossBlendDestAnimClip = 0;
    std::string rdCrossBlendDestClipName = "None";
    float rdAnimCrossBlendFactor = 0.0f;
```

Using the `rdCrossBlending` Boolean, we can enable or disable crossfading. The `rdCrossBlendDestAnimClip` variable stores the number of the animation clip that will be used as the blending destination. The `rdCrossBlendDestClipName` string is filled with the name of the destination animation clip. Finally, the value for the blending between the two animation clips is saved in the new variable named `rdAnimCrossBlendFactor`.

The OpenGL renderer needs only a few updates. First, we must add the setting of the destination clip name variable, `rdCrossBlendDestClipName`, of the `mRenderData` struct to the `OGLRenderer` class. Add the following line to the `draw()` method in the `OGLRenderer.cpp` file in the `opengl` folder, and right below this line we set `rdClipName`:

```
mRenderData.rdClipName =
  mGltfModel->getClipName(mRenderData.rdAnimClip);
mRenderData.rdCrossBlendDestClipName =
  mGltfModel->getClipName(
  mRenderData.rdCrossBlendDestAnimClip);
```

We will also update the destination clip name in every `draw()` call. An extra check could be added for whether the clip name has changed since the last frame, but the code will most probably not be faster than this "brute-force" method of overwriting, as we would need an expensive string comparison operation to determine whether the clip name needs to be changed, along with an extra Boolean variable that will be checked. By contrast, copying the string to the destination is only a simple memory copy.

To reset the model data to the original values, we add a `static` Boolean variable:

```
static bool blendingChanged = mRenderData.rdCrossBlending;
```

A variable declared as `static` will keep the current value across method invocations, and we will make use of this feature to save the current state of cross-blending:

```
if (blendingChanged != mRenderData.rdCrossBlending) {
  blendingChanged = mRenderData.rdCrossBlending;
  mGltfModel->resetNodeData();
}
```

Whenever we enable or disable the cross-blending feature, a reset of the model data will be done. Without a reset, the model nodes may use the values of the source clip for cross-blending, resulting in a distorted animation clip.

Next, we add the cross-blending to the existing part of the model matrix creation:

```
if (mRenderData.rdPlayAnimation) {
  if (mRenderData.rdCrossBlending) {
    mGltfModel->playAnimation(mRenderData.rdAnimClip,
      mRenderData.rdCrossBlendDestAnimClip,
      mRenderData.rdAnimSpeed,
```

```
        mRenderData.rdAnimCrossBlendFactor);
  } else {
    mGltfModel->playAnimation(mRenderData.rdAnimClip,
      mRenderData.rdAnimSpeed,
      mRenderData.rdAnimBlendFactor);
  }
```

In the preceding code, we add a check for the state of the cross-blending. The `rdCrossBlending` variable determines whether we call the `playAnimation()` method for normal blending, or the cross-blending variant with the source and destination clip numbers is used.

The same decision must be made in the `else` part of the `rdPlayAnimation` test:

```
} else {
  mRenderData.rdAnimEndTime =
    mGltfModel->getAnimationEndTime(
    mRenderData.rdAnimClip);
  if (mRenderData.rdCrossBlending) {
    mGltfModel->crossBlendAnimationFrame(
      mRenderData.rdAnimClip,
      mRenderData.rdCrossBlendDestAnimClip,
      mRenderData.rdAnimTimePosition,
      mRenderData.rdAnimCrossBlendFactor);
  } else {
    mGltfModel->blendAnimationFrame(
      mRenderData.rdAnimClip,
      mRenderData.rdAnimTimePosition,
      mRenderData.rdAnimBlendFactor);
  }
}
```

We use the same check for the cross-blending state as before to switch between the rendering of a normal blended animation frame and a cross-blended animation frame. The `rdAminTimePosition` parameter sets the time point for the frame of the animation clip that will be created.

As the last step, we will add some new control elements to the `UserInterface` class, allowing us to control the cross-blending using sliders and checkboxes.

Adding new controls to the user interface

The changes in the user interfaces are a bit bigger. We could just add the sliders as we did before, but a selection box to enable or disable the cross-blending will help us to disable the unused control elements.

Update the `createFrame()` method in the `UserInterface.cpp` file in the `opengl` folder to include the following highlighted lines:

```
  if (ImGui::CollapsingHeader("glTF Animation Blending")) {
    ImGui::Checkbox("Blending Type:",
      &renderData.rdCrossBlending);
    ImGui::SameLine();
    if (renderData.rdCrossBlending) {
      ImGui::Text("Cross");
    } else {
      ImGui::Text("Single");
    }
```

We add an `ImGui` checkbox to enable or disable the cross-blending. In addition, we create a text field next to the checkbox to show the current state of blending.

Now a code section is defined where the `ImGui` controls are disabled if the `rdCrossBlending` Boolean is set to `true`:

```
    if (renderData.rdCrossBlending) {
      ImGui::BeginDisabled();
    }
```

The original blend factor slider is added to this section of the code:

```
    ImGui::Text("Blend Factor");
    ImGui::SameLine();
    ImGui::SliderFloat("##BlendFactor",
      &renderData.rdAnimBlendFactor, 0.0f, 1.0f);
    if (renderData.rdCrossBlending) {
      ImGui::EndDisabled();
    }
```

If cross-blending is enabled, we activate the control elements for the new blending type in the user interface:

```
   if (!renderData.rdCrossBlending) {
      ImGui::BeginDisabled();
   }
```

First, a slider to select the destination animation clip is created:

```
    ImGui::Text("Dest Clip    ");
    ImGui::SameLine();
    ImGui::SliderInt("##DestClip",
```

```
    &renderData.rdCrossBlendDestAnimClip, 0,
    renderData.rdAnimClipSize - 1);
```

The slider range is set from zero to the total number of animation clips minus one to allow the selection of all the animation clips from the model.

Below the slider, a text field containing the name of the destination animation clip is added:

```
  ImGui::Text("Dest Clip Name: %s",
    renderData.rdCrossBlendDestClipName.c_str());
```

Finally, the cross-blending factor can be set with another slider:

```
  ImGui::Text("Cross Blend ");
  ImGui::SameLine();
  ImGui::SliderFloat("##CrossBlendFactor",
    &renderData.rdAnimCrossBlendFactor, 0.0f, 1.0f);
```

The cross-blending factor slider has a range from `0.0`, which will play only the source clip, and `1.0` for the destination clip only. Any value in between will blend between the two animation clips.

We also need to close the disabled controls code section:

```
  if (!renderData.rdCrossBlending) {
    ImGui::EndDisabled();
  }
}
```

If you compile and run the updated code, you will get a result like that shown in *Figure 11.2*:

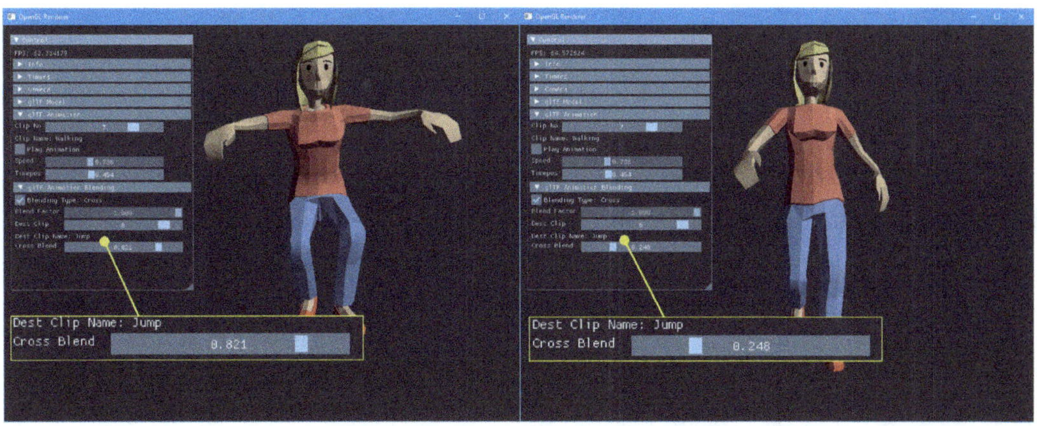

Figure 11.2: Crossfading between the Walking and Jump animation clips

Both outputs shown in *Figure 11.2* use the same source and destination animation clips: Walking as the source clip and Jump as the destination clip. The only difference is the amount of blending between the clips.

In the left output, the slider for the cross-blending factor is near the value of `1.0`, resulting in a mostly full Jump animation frame. The cross-blending factor in the right output has been moved more toward the value of `0.0`, and the animation frame looks more like that of the Walking animation.

> **Note on the Vulkan renderer**
>
> The node from the *Implementing animation blending in the OpenGL renderer* section is also valid for this section. All variable names and methods are the same for the Vulkan renderer; all that differs is the files in which we need to apply the changes and new values. The shared variables go in the `VkRenderData.h` file instead of `OGLRenderData.h`, and the renderer changes need to be done in the `VkRenderer.cpp` and `VkRenderer.h` files, instead of `OGLRenderer.cpp` and `OGLRenderer.h`. The changes in the `GltfModel` and `UserInterfaces` classes are identical.

The final animation blending type, additive blending, takes a different approach to the node property changes. So, let us now explore the steps involved in implementing this type of blending. You can find the full source code for the following section in the `chapter11` folder. The code for the OpenGL renderer is in the `03_opengl_additive_blending` subfolder, and the code for the Vulkan renderer in the `06_vulkan_additive_blending` subfolder.

How to do additive blending

The basic principle of additive animation blending has already been outlined in the *Does it blend?* section. We must split our model into two distinct parts and animate both parts using different animation clips. Let's see how.

Splitting the node skeleton – part I

The first change is for convenience, as it allows us to print the name of the current node in the user interface. Add the following `public` method to the `GltfNode.h` file in the `model` folder:

```
std::string getNodeName();
```

In the implementation in the `GltfNode.cpp` file, also in the `model` folder, we return the saved node name:

```
std::string GltfNode::getNodeName() {
  return mNodeName;
}
```

Splitting the model will be done in the `GltfModel` class. We add the two `public` methods, `setSkeletonSplitNode()` and `getNodeName()`, to the `GltfModel.h` file in the `model` folder:

```
void setSkeletonSplitNode(int nodeNum);
std::string getNodeName(int nodeNum);
```

The first `setSkeletonSplitNode()` method allows us to specify the node of the skeleton where the split will start. The other method, `getNodeName()`, returns the name of the node number given as the parameter. We will use the returned node name in the *Finalizing additive blending in the OpenGL renderer* section to show the selected skeleton split node in the user interface.

We manage the nodes that are (or are not) part of the current animation with an array of Booleans. Add the following `private` data members to the `GltfModel` class:

```
std::vector<bool> mAdditiveAnimationMask{};
std::vector<bool> mInvertedAdditiveAnimationMask{};
```

In the `mAdditiveAnimationMask` vector, we store a value for every node, indicating whether the node is part of the animation (`true`) or not (`false`). We also save the inverted mask, allowing us to use a second animation clip for the remaining part of the skeleton.

The `updateAdditiveMask()` method to update the mask is also `private`, as it will be called from `setSkeletonSplitNode()`:

```
void updateAdditiveMask(
  std::shared_ptr<GltfNode> treeNode, int splitNodeNum);
```

Before we implement the new methods of the `GltfModel` class, some of the existing methods must be adjusted or extended.

First, the node count will be made part of the `OGLRenderData` struct. Add the following line to the `OGLRenderData.h` file in the `opengl` folder:

```
int rdModelNodeCount = 0;
```

Back in the `model` folder, *remove* the following lines of the `loadModel()` method in the `GltfModel.cpp` file:

```
int nodeCount = mModel->nodes.size();
mNodeList.resize(nodeCount);
```

The following *new* lines to be added use the node count variable of the `OGLRenderData` struct:

```
renderData.rdModelNodeCount = mModel->nodes.size();
mNodeList.resize(renderData.rdModelNodeCount);
```

If you use the `nodeCount` variable in a `Logger` output, do not forget to change those corresponding lines too.

At the end of the `loadModel()` method of the `GltfModel` class, the mask vectors will be initialized:

```
mAdditiveAnimationMask.resize(
  renderData.rdModelNodeCount);
mInvertedAdditiveAnimationMask.resize(
  renderData.rdModelNodeCount);
```

The vector needs a valid field for every node, so we must resize the two `std::vector` instances using the node count from the model. Then, we use the `std::fill()` method to populate the normal mask vector:

```
std::fill(mAdditiveAnimationMask.begin(),
  mAdditiveAnimationMask.end(), true);
```

Finally, we copy the mask to the inverted mask and calculate the inverted mask:

```
mInvertedAdditiveAnimationMask = mAdditiveAnimationMask;
mInvertedAdditiveAnimationMask.flip();
```

The `flip()` C++ method for Boolean vectors swaps the `true` and `false` values. The STL `flip()` function spares a manual `for` loop over the vector.

To use the new node mask, we adjust the `blendAnimationFrame()` method of the `GltfModel` class:

```
mAnimClips.at(animNum)->blendAnimationFrame(mNodeList,
  mAdditiveAnimationMask, time, blendFactor);
```

We add the mask as a new second parameter between the node list and the `time` parameter. The same change must be done in the `crossBlendAnimation()` method:

```
mAnimClips.at(sourceAnimNumber)->setAnimationFrame(
  mNodeList, mAdditiveAnimationMask, time);
mAnimClips.at(destAnimNumber)->blendAnimationFrame(
  mNodeList, mAdditiveAnimationMask, scaledTime,
  blendFactor);
```

We also add two new calls to the `crossBlendAnimation()` method, using the inverted additive mask:

```
mAnimClips.at(destAnimNumber)->setAnimationFrame(
  mNodeList, mInvertedAdditiveAnimationMask, scaledTime);
mAnimClips.at(sourceAnimNumber)->blendAnimationFrame(
  mNodeList, mInvertedAdditiveAnimationMask, time,
  blendFactor);
```

Here, we swap the numbers of the source and destination animation clip, and also `time` and `scaledTime`. Combined with the usage of the inverted mask, the second (destination) animation clip will be applied to the nodes that are not part of the first (source) animation clip.

Now it is time to implement the new methods in the `GltfMode` class.

Splitting the node skeleton – part II

Let us start with the update of the node skeleton mask. Add the following method to the `GltfModel.cpp` file in the `model` folder:

```
void GltfModel::updateAdditiveMask(
    std::shared_ptr<GltfNode> treeNode, int splitNodeNum) {
  if (treeNode->getNodeNum() == splitNodeNum) {
    return;
  }
  mAdditiveAnimationMask.at(treeNode->getNodeNum()) = false;
  for (auto &childNode : treeNode->getChilds()) {
    updateAdditiveMask(childNode, splitNodeNum);
  }
}
```

The `updateAdditiveMask()` method calls itself recursively to traverse the node skeleton tree. If the current node number equals the requested split node number, we return immediately, stopping the node tree traversal.

If the current node is above the split node, it will no longer be part of the animation clip. We set the mask for the current node to `false`, removing it from the animation.

To set the split node of the model, the `setSkeletonSplitNode()` method must be called. The method is short and simple:

```
void GltfModel::setSkeletonSplitNode(int nodeNum) {
  std::fill(mAdditiveAnimationMask.begin(),
    mAdditiveAnimationMask.end(), true);
  updateAdditiveMask(mRootNode, nodeNum);
```

First, we call `updateAdditiveMask()` to calculate the mask for the desired split node:

```
  mInvertedAdditiveAnimationMask = mAdditiveAnimationMask;
  mInvertedAdditiveAnimationMask.flip();
}
```

Then, we copy the new mask to the inverted mask and flip the values in the inverted mask, keeping both mask vectors synchronized.

As the last new method, we need the getter for the node name:

```
std::string GltfModel::getNodeName(int nodeNum) {
  if (nodeNum >= 0 && nodeNum < (mNodeList.size()) &&
      mNodeList.at(nodeNum)) {
    return mNodeList.at(nodeNum->getNodeName();
  }
  return "(Invalid)";
}
```

After some sanity checks, the name of the node is returned. If any of the checks fails, we return the `"(Invalid)"` string to populate the text field in the user interface with a value.

The additive node mask will be used in the `GltfAnimationClip` class. So, let us also adjust that class.

Updating the animation clip class

Using the node mask for additive animation blending requires only two minor changes in the `GltfAnimationClip.cpp` file in the `model` folder. The first change is in the `setAnimationFrame()` method:

```
void GltfAnimationClip::setAnimationFrame(
    std::vector<std::shared_ptr<GltfNode>> nodes,
    std::vector<bool> additiveMask, float time) {
  for (auto &channel : mAnimationChannels) {
    int targetNode = channel->getTargetNode();
    if (additiveMask.at(targetNode)) {
      switch(channel->getTargetPath()) {
...
      }
    }
...
```

Here, we add the `std::vector` array of Booleans with the mask as the second parameter. Within the loop that iterates through all animation channels in this animation clip, we perform updates to the node properties only when the mask value in the `additiveMask` variable for the corresponding node is set to `true`. If the node is not part of the current animation clip, the node properties will remain unchanged, which resembles the binding pose of the model.

In the `blendAnimationFrame()` method, the same two changes are required:

```
void GltfAnimationClip::blendAnimationFrame(
    std::vector<std::shared_ptr<GltfNode>> nodes,
    std::vector<bool> additiveMask, float time,
    float blendFactor) {
```

```
for (auto &channel : mAnimationChannels) {
  int targetNode = channel->getTargetNode();
  if (additiveMask.at(targetNode)) {
    switch(channel->getTargetPath()) {
...
    }
  }
...
```

These signature adjustments must be made in the header declarations of the class. Change the two methods in the `GltfAnimationClip.h` file in the `model` folder and add the new parameter to the `setAnimationFrame()` and `blendAnimationFrame()` methods:

```
  void setAnimationFrame(
    std::vector<std::shared_ptr<GltfNode>> nodes,
    std::vector<bool> additiveMask, float time);
  void blendAnimationFrame(
    std::vector<std::shared_ptr<GltfNode>> nodes,
    std::vector<bool> additiveMask, float time,
    float blendFactor);
```

With these changes, the model update is complete, and the renderer can now be updated.

Finalizing additive blending in the OpenGL renderer

To control additive blending in the renderer, three more values must be added to the `OGLRenderData.h` file in the `opengl` folder:

```
bool rdAdditiveBlending = false;
int rdSkelSplitNode = 0;
std::string rdSkelSplitNodeName = "None";
```

The `rdAdditiveBlending` variable enables or disables additive blending, and `rdSkelSplitNode` stores the desired node number of the splitting point in the model skeleton tree. To display the name of the split node in the user interface, we will set the node name in the `rdSkelSplitNodeName` variable.

The `init()` and `draw()` methods of the `OGLRenderer.cpp` file in the `opengl` folder must also be adjusted to implement the new additive blending feature.

In the `init()` method, add the following line before `mFrameTimer.start()` is called:

```
mRenderData.rdSkelSplitNode =
  mRenderData.rdModelNodeCount - 1;
```

We initialize the desired split node number of the skeleton tree with the highest node of our model. In our glTF example model, this node is the root node for all other nodes, resulting in the entire model being part of the source animation clip. However, note that this initialization of the default split node is model-specific because the nodes of other glTF models may be ordered differently in the file. So, you will most probably get different results if you load other models.

Next, an addition to the check for a change of the cross-blending state is made:

```
static bool blendingChanged =
  mRenderData.rdCrossBlending;
if (blendingChanged != mRenderData.rdCrossBlending) {
  blendingChanged = mRenderData.rdCrossBlending;
  if (!mRenderData.rdCrossBlending) {
    mRenderData.rdAdditiveBlending = false;
  }
  mGltfModel->resetNodeData();
}
```

The new line, highlighted in the preceding code snippet, is called when we disable both cross-blending and additive blending. Having additive blending enabled while cross-blending is disabled makes no sense, as we use the control elements for the destination clip and also the crossfading factor for the additive blending, so we disable both animation types here.

A similar check as that for cross-blending is then done for additive blending:

```
static bool additiveBlendingChanged =
  mRenderData.rdAdditiveBlending;
if (additiveBlendingChanged !=
    mRenderData.rdAdditiveBlending) {
  additiveBlendingChanged =
    mRenderData.rdAdditiveBlending;
```

We create another `static` Boolean to track the state of the additive blending across multiple `draw()` calls in the renderer. And, if the `rdAdditiveBlending` variable changes, we update the `static` variable too.

Disabling additive blending also resets the split node number:

```
  if (!mRenderData.rdAdditiveBlending) {
    mRenderData.rdSkelSplitNode =
      mRenderData.rdModelNodeCount - 1;
  }
```

Not resetting the split node will cause side effects when rendering the model, as the last-calculated node mask will still be active.

Finally, we also reset the node data on any change in the additive blending state:

```
    mGltfModel->resetNodeData();
  }
```

A third `static` variable, `skelSplitNode`, will take care of the currently set split node, enabling us to respond to any changes in the node number:

```
  static int skelSplitNode = mRenderData.rdSkelSplitNode;
```

The next check is just like the two preceding blending state checks:

```
  if (skelSplitNode != mRenderData.rdSkelSplitNode) {
    mGltfModel->setSkeletonSplitNode(
      mRenderData.rdSkelSplitNode);
    skelSplitNode = mRenderData.rdSkelSplitNode;
    mRenderData.rdSkelSplitNodeName =
      mGltfModel->getNodeName(mRenderData.rdSkelSplitNode);
    mGltfModel->resetNodeData();
  }
```

We update the `static` variable, set the name for the new split node, and reset the node data to the default values. These three steps will result in a fresh start after every change of the split node.

The definite last step for this chapter is the addition of control elements for the new additive blending variables to the `UserInterface` class.

Exposing the additive blending parameters in the user interface

To create control elements for additive blending, add the following lines to the `UserInterface.cpp` file in the `opengl` folder. Make sure to add them below the lines added to the cross-blending in the *Adding new controls to the user interface* section:

```
  if (ImGui::CollapsingHeader("glTF Animation Blending")) {
...
    ImGui::Checkbox("Additive Blending",
      &renderData.rdAdditiveBlending);
```

We add a new checkbox that enables and disables additive blending. We also use the value of the `rdAdditiveBlending` variable to enable or disable the control elements:

```
    if (!renderData.rdAdditiveBlending) {
      ImGui::BeginDisabled();
    }
```

When additive blending is disabled, the controls will be grayed out.

The slider for the split node is next:

```
ImGui::Text("Split Node  ");
ImGui::SameLine();
ImGui::SliderInt("##SplitNode",
  &renderData.rdSkelSplitNode, 0,
  renderData.rdModelNodeCount - 1);
```

We create the slider with a range of zero to the last element of the node mask, calculated by taking the node count and decreasing the value by one. The split node name is updated here too:

```
ImGui::Text("Split Node Name: %s",
  renderData.rdSkelSplitNodeName.c_str());
```

Finally, we close the controls that will be disabled without additive blending:

```
if (!renderData.rdAdditiveBlending) {
  ImGui::EndDisabled();
}
```

For the Vulkan renderer, the note at the end of the *Crossfading animations* section applies here too: the renderer changes must be made in the Vulkan renderer source files in the `vulkan` folder, instead of those of the OpenGL renderer code in the `opengl` folder.

Compiling and running the code will show you a window with the new controls, as depicted in *Figure 11.3*:

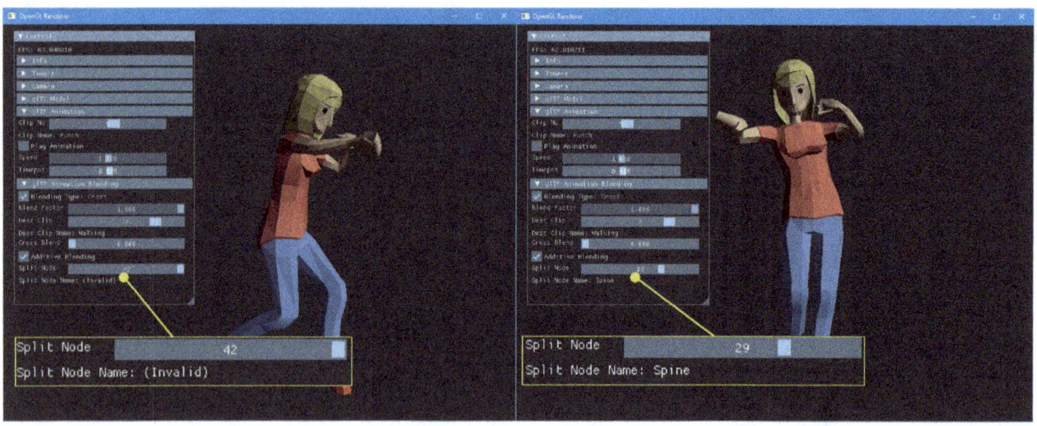

Figure 11.3: Additive blending by splitting the glTF model skeleton in two parts

On the left side of *Figure 11.3*, a frame of the Punch animation clip for the entire model is shown. The split node is the root node of the entire model. If we choose a split node of the skeleton using the slider, one part of the model will still show the Punch animation clip frame, while the rest of the model changes to the destination clip frame. In the right-hand output of *Figure 11.3*, the feet will do the Walking animation.

With this new understanding of additive animation blending under your belt, we have now completed the three types of animation blending we wanted to explore.

Summary

In this chapter, we moved from pure animation replays to animation blending.

We started with a brief overview of the three animation blending types that are part of this chapter. Then, we added simple blending between the binding pose and one animation clip, and worked on an example of cross-blending between two animation clips.

As the last step, we added the code for additive animation blending. Additive blending works differently compared to the other two blending types, and requires adding the ability to split the skeleton tree into two parts.

In the next chapter, we switch the topic entirely, and add new control element types to the `UserInterface` class. Some of the new elements will help us to clean up the user interface, while others will allow us to show more information about the internals of the renderer.

Practical sessions

You may try out the following ideas to explore more features of animation blending:

- Update the `GltfNode` class to include another set of properties storing the translation, rotation, and scaling values, and use them to apply cross-blending to two animations. Adding a third property set should enable you to get rid of the model reset in the renderer class, which is currently required after changing the blending type to reload the original data from the model file.
- Blend between three different animation clips. This technique is perfect for a transition between the idle animation clip to the running clip and back, using the walking animation as the connection between the two movements.
- Add a speed adjustment for clips of different lengths. In the current code, the time for the second animation clip is stretched or compressed to match the length of the first clip, resulting in faster or slower playback. Adjusting the playback speed in the opposite direction of the time change could create a smoother transition between the two clips.

Part 4: Advancing Your Code to the Next Level

In the final part, you will update the user interface with more complex Dear ImGui control elements. In addition, you will get an overview of inverse kinematics and how it can make the animations of 3D models appear more natural. You will also learn how to draw a large amount of 3D models on a screen, instead of only one model. Finally, you will explore methods to measure the performance of a created application, learn how to find bottlenecks and hotspots on the CPU and GPU, and understand methods to apply further code optimizations.

In this part, we will cover the following chapters:

- *Chapter 12, Cleaning Up the User Interface*
- *Chapter 13, Implementing Inverse Kinematics*
- *Chapter 14, Creating Instanced Crowds*
- *Chapter 15, Measuring Performance and Optimizing the Code*

12

Cleaning Up the User Interface

Welcome to *Chapter 12*! In the previous chapter, we integrated three different kinds of animation blending into the existing code. We also added some control elements for easy manipulation of the blending types and properties.

In this chapter, we will clean up the user interface by using more ImGui elements. We will start with an overview of various types of UI controls and their intended usage. Then, two ImGui elements, a combo box and a radio button, will be introduced. The function of these two elements is well known, and we will look at how to use them in code.

Then, we will check the drawing of the so-called ImGui plots. Plots are graphical diagrams and are perfect for visualizing a short, graphical history of numerical values, such as the FPS counter or the timer values.

At the end of the chapter, we will have a cleaner user interface for our tool, using more appropriate elements to simplify the usage of the character animation program.

In this chapter, we will cover the following main topics:

- UI controls are cool
- Creating combo boxes and radio buttons
- Drawing time series with ImGui
- The sky is the limit

Technical requirements

To follow along with this chapter, you will need the OpenGL and Vulkan renderer code from *Chapter 11*.

Before we examine the new ImGui control elements in detail, we will take a short detour to look at some of the element types, their functions, and the advantages and disadvantages of using them for specific tasks.

UI controls are cool

In *Chapter 5*, we added a slider to control the field of view of the renderer output. For such a task, a slider is great, as it shows visual feedback of the range and the selected value within that range. However, using a slider to select the animation clip or skeleton node has a major drawback – it lacks the visible mapping between the numerical value of the clip or node and the clip or node name itself. Selecting a specific clip or a node is a try-and-error process, resulting in you having to remember or write down the most important numbers.

By changing the slider to a list box or a combo box, the names of the animation clips and nodes will be shown instead of just the numbers of the clips and nodes. Internally, the currently selected entry of the combo box is identified by its index in the array of all elements in the combo box, resulting in an implicit mapping between a numerical value and name. So, we do not need any additional control structure, making it a perfect replacement to simplify the selection of clips or nodes.

Moreover, in *Chapter 5*, the checkbox was introduced. In *Chapter 7*, a checkbox was used to toggle the rendering of the spline lines and the coordinate arrows, and in *Chapter 9*, we switched the vertex skinning between the CPU and the GPU. In that chapter, we also gave the user the ability to disable the model skeleton overlay rendering, using a checkbox. However, for many tasks, a checkbox is not the best solution. Enabling and disabling the model skeleton is perfect for a checkbox, but switching between different states, such as in the vertex skinning, already has disadvantages, such as the nested checkboxes we used in *Chapter 9* to enable the dual quaternion skinning, which could only be done if the vertex skinning was calculated on the GPU. Also, a checkbox becomes a less ideal option if we must select between more than two alternatives, as we would have to track and adjust the state of every checkbox to avoid illegal combinations.

Choosing a set of radio buttons makes such a selection task easier. The user will get a list of all alternatives and give clear feedback on which of the options is active. In addition, the selection of an illegal combination is impossible, and we do not need to check for invalid combinations of options in code.

In ImGui, we can use not only integer values but also the types `enum` and `enum class`. A selection for three or more alternatives becomes easy using the `enum` variant, as the result could be checked by the name instead of just a number.

In the *Drawing time series with ImGui* section, we will add a graphical ImGui element – that is, a 2D plot – to our user interface. The source of the plot is a simple array. During the ImGui draw call, the index of the array is used for the *X* dimension, and the stored value at that index position in the array is taken for the *Y* dimension. The result is a two-dimensional graph, visualizing the values of the array.

Such a graph is a great solution to show the timeline of changes in numerical values. Our brain can handle a line with peaks or dips much better than just some arbitrary numbers "jumping around." Drawing a line for the frames per second, or for some or all the timer values, gives a much better overall picture of what an application does. Also, if we find some recurring peaks or dips in a graph, we may have a chance to find a correlation between anomalies and calculations in the code.

On a somehow loosely related topic, we will also aim to replace many of the `BeginDisabled()` and `EndDisabled()` sections in the code. Disabling a control element is important to stop input and changes, but the element itself remains visible. Having a lot of elements will pollute the user interface, requiring the user to scroll up and down to access all the controls.

Sometimes, it can be a better solution to hide the control elements that should not be used on a specific selection of other elements, such as radio buttons or checkboxes. If only the valid controls for a selection are presented to the user, they will not become overwhelmed by the sheer number of options, knobs, and sliders. A clean user interface is the key to a great user experience.

After this theoretical overview, let us start switching from sliders to combo boxes and replacing some of the checkboxes with radio buttons. The full source code for this example can be found in the `chapter12` folder, in the `01_opengl_combobox` subfolder for OpenGL and the `04_vulkan_combobox` subfolder for Vulkan.

Creating combo boxes and radio buttons

ImGui has two different widget variants that allow you to select an element from a list of options – list boxes and combo boxes.

A **list box** usually displays a configurable number of list elements on the screen, using a larger amount of screen space compared to a combo box. In contrast, the **combo box** only shows a preview of the currently selected list element and unfolds to enable the user to select an element. On the left-hand side in *Figure 12.1*, you can see a list box, which is permanently shown with a configurable height. A combo box is initially drawn as a folded single line, as shown in the middle of *Figure 12.1*, and is only expanded upon user interaction. An expanded combo box can be seen in *Figure 12.1* on the right-hand side:

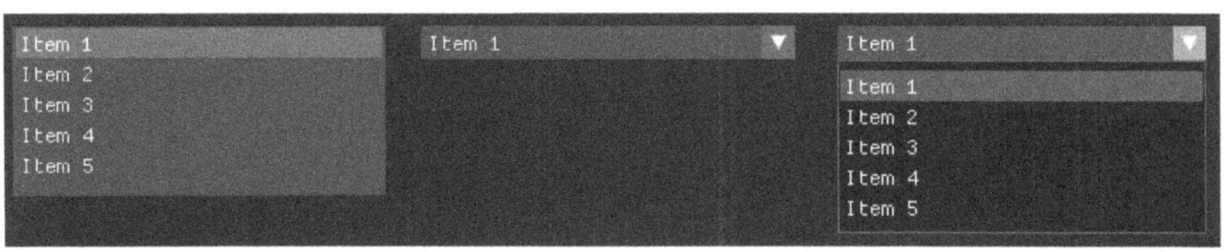

Figure 12.1: A list box (left), a folded combo box (middle), and an expanded combo box (right)

We will use the combo box in our example code, as the single-line display avoids extending the user interface vertically. We can even reduce the vertical size by replacing the slider and the text display below the slider with a single combo box.

Using ImGui in combination with C++ brings some interesting problems with data types, which must be solved to have a working combo box.

Implementing a combo box the C++ way

In the ImGui demo code, you will find a line like the following. The number of elements in the `items` C-style array has been reduced, but the general idea should be apparent:

```
const char* items[] = { "AAAA", "BBBB", "CCCC", "DDDD"};
static int currentItem = 0;
ImGui::Combo("combo", &currentItem, items, IM_ARRAYSIZE(items));
```

The `ImGui::Combo()` function takes a widget ID, the number of the currently selected element, the C-style array of elements, plus the size of the array as parameters.

The element array must be made from the C-style character array, terminated by a `NULL` character. Switching the array to a C++ variant and using a vector of `std::strings` elements will *not* work:

```
std::vector<std::string> items{ "AAAA", "BBBB", "CCCC"};
static int currentItem = 0;
ImGui::Combo("combo", &currentItem, items.data(), items.size());
```

`std::string` is not compatible with `char*`; a conversion is not available, and compiling the code will fail:

```
no known conversion for argument 3 from
'std::__cxx11::basic_string<char>*' to 'const char* const*'
```

Luckily, a configurable version of the ImGui combo box exists. By using the `ImGui::BeginCombo()` and `ImGui::EndCombo()` functions, we have full control of the list elements inside the combo box.

Let us check the code that is required to create an ImGui combo box in a C++-compatible way. The following code can be found in the `UserInterface.h` file in the `opengl` folder:

```
std::string curVal =
  renderData.rdClipNames.at(renderData.rdAnimClip);
```

As the first step, we will create `std::string` with the animation clip name of the currently selected clip. Then, we will call `ImGui::BeginCombo()`, with the widget name and the animation clip name as parameters:

```
if (ImGui::BeginCombo("##ClipCombo", curVal.c_str())) {
```

Using the double hashtags in front of the name, the widget name will be hidden from the user interface. The second parameter – in this case, `curVal.c_str()`, the C-type string of the currently set option, is the text shown in the collapsed combo box. To use the animation clip name as the second parameter, we must convert the string into a C-compatible `char*` pointer by calling `c_str()` on it.

We will put the call into an `if` block because ImGui returns the `collapsed` or `expanded` status of the combo box as a Boolean. If the function returns `false`, the combo box is closed, and if `true` is returned, the box has been expanded by the user.

We will enter the body of `if` block but only if the box was opened by the user:

```
    for (int i=0; i<renderData.rdClipNames.size();++i) {
```

In the body of the `if` block, we will loop over all the values of the `std::vector` containing the animation clip names. First, we will check whether we have reached the currently selected element:

```
      const bool isSelected = (renderData.rdAnimClip == i);
```

We will set a Boolean variable called `isSelected` to `true` if we are working on the current selection. The Boolean is also made `const` to select the correct overload of the `ImGui::Selectable()` function. Then, we will extract the current animation clip name into a string called `selVal`:

```
      std::string selVal = renderData.rdClipNames.at(i);
```

We will use the converted clip name as the first parameter of the `ImGui::Selectable()` function, and the `const` variable, `isSelected`, as the second parameter:

```
      if (ImGui::Selectable(selVal.c_str(), isSelected)) {
        renderData.rdAnimClip = i;
      }
```

The `ImGui::Selectable()` function returns `true` if the currently highlighted entry has been clicked with the mouse to select it. In this case, we will change the animation clip number to the current value of our loop variable, `i`.

To visualize the currently selected element, the text line with the current selection is shown in a different color by calling `ImGui::SetItemDefaultFocus()`:

```
      if (isSelected) {
        ImGui::SetItemDefaultFocus();
      }
```

Finally, we will close the ImGui combo box:

```
    }
    ImGui::EndCombo();
  }
```

Note on the curVal and selVal variables

The two `curVal` (for the *current value*) and `selVal` (for the *selected value*) variables are inserted into the listing to keep the lines short. In the example code on GitHub, the variables are omitted, and the animation clip names are used directly in the functions.

The preceding code block is used in the example code for the animation clip name, replacing the slider and the `ImGui::Text()` line below the slider with a combo box. We can *remove* the following two lines from the `createFrame()` method in the `UserInterface.cpp` file in the `opengl` folder:

```
ImGui::SliderInt("##Clip", &renderData.rdAnimClip, 0,
  renderData.rdAnimClipSize - 1);
ImGui::Text("Clip Name: %s",
  renderData.rdClipName.c_str());
```

For the destination animation clip names and the skeleton node names, the sliders are replaced the same way – instead of the `ImGuiI::SliderInt()` slider and the `ImGui::Text()` field, `ImGui::BeginCombo()/ImGui::EndCombo()` with the `std:.string` vector and the value from the `OGLRenderData` struct are used.

Two other changes are required to complete the slider swap. We must adjust the data type of the animation clip and skeleton node names from a string to a vector of strings, and these vectors of strings must be filled with the names of the animation clips and skeleton node names.

Swapping the data types

The clip and node names are defined in the `OGLRenderData.h` file in the `opengl` folder. Therefore, *remove* the following string variables in the `OGLRenderData struct`:

```
std::string rdClipName = "None";
std::string rdSkelSplitNodeName = "None";
```

Replace them with the following vectors of strings:

```
std::vector<std::string> rdClipNames{};
std::vector<std::string> rdSkelSplitNodeNames{};
```

In both variable names, the letter `s` has been appended, stating that the variables now may contain multiple elements.

Also, *remove* the following line from the `OGLRenderData struct`, as the separate destination clip name is no longer needed:

```
std::string rdCrossBlendDestClipName = "None";
```

Then, *remove* the following lines from the `draw()` method in the `OGLRenderer.cpp` file, also in the `opengl` folder:

```
mRenderData.rdClipName =
  mGltfModel->getClipName(mRenderData.rdAnimClip);
mRenderData.rdCrossBlendDestClipName = mGltfModel->getClipName(
  mRenderData.rdCrossBlendDestAnimClip);
```

Both the preceding lines were responsible for setting the animation clip names for the currently running clip as a string value, shown in the user interface. The `ImGui::Text()` call using these variables will be removed, so we will also remove the calls to fill the strings.

The skeleton node name has been set in the same way, but we no longer have the variable in the `OGLRenderData struct`. Also, *remove* the bold printed line that sets the skeleton node name from the `draw()` method in the `OGLRenderer.cpp` file:

```
if (skelSplitNode != mRenderData.rdSkelSplitNode) {
  mGltfModel->setSkeletonSplitNode(mRenderData.rdSkelSplitNode);
  mRenderData.rdSkelSplitNodeName =
    mGltfModel"->getNodeName(mRenderData.rdSkelSplitNode);
  skelSplitNode = mRenderData.rdSkelSplitNode;
  mGltfModel->resetNodeData();
}
```

At this point, the new vectors of string variables will be created, and the renderer and the user interface will be updated. Let us proceed to the next step and fill in the name arrays.

Filling the arrays for the combo boxes

The best place to populate name arrays is in the `GltfModel` class. The model class knows all the animation clips and their names, along with all the node names. To fill the arrays, add the following two blocks to the end of the `loadModel()` method of the `GltfModel.cpp` file in the `model` folder:

```
for (const auto &clip : mAnimClips)
  renderData.rdClipNames.push_back(clip->getClipName());
}
```

In the preceding block, we will loop over all animation clips, extract the clip name, and append the name to the newly created `rdClipNames` vector of the `OGLRenderData struct`. This appending results in a direct mapping between the clip number in the `mAnimClips` vector and the clip names in the `rdClipNames` vector.

For the node names, a more cautious `for` loop will be used:

```
for (const auto &node : mNodeList) {
  if (node) {
    renderData.rdSkelSplitNodeNames.push_back(
      node->getNodeName());
  } else {
    renderData.rdSkelSplitNodeNames.push_back(
      "(invalid)");
  }
}
```

We removed the node containing only the skin metadata, as it does not contribute anything to the model data, and this node confuses the skeleton display. So, we must check whether the node is valid before extracting the node name. In addition, we are not allowed to skip the node name append. Such a skip would create a mismatch between the node numbers and the node names for all the nodes that follow.

After all the updates have been done, compiling and running the code will bring up a screen like the one shown in *Figure 12.2*:

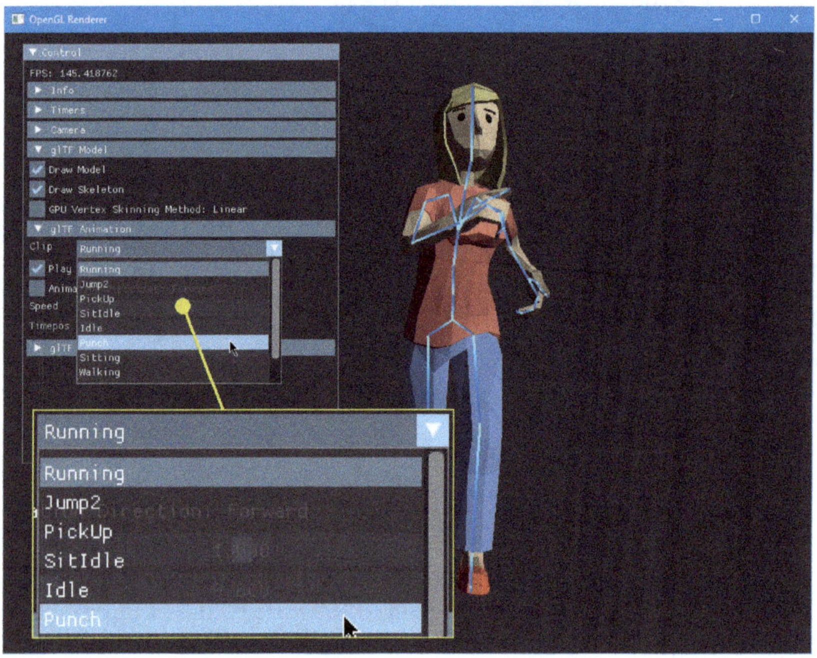

Figure 12.2: The sliders are replaced by combo boxes

The three sliders to select the main animation clip of the model, the destination clip of the cross-fading blending type, and the skeleton node names for the additive blending type have been replaced by shiny combo boxes. The combo boxes simplify the selection process of the animation clips and the split node by a large amount, and we can now see and select the clip name in the element list.

Moving from sliders to combo boxes was the first part of the change of the UI control elements of this section. The second part is the replacement of some of the checkboxes with radio buttons. The updated code for this part of the section can be found in the `02_opengl_radiobutton` subfolder for the OpenGL renderer and the `05_vulkan_radiobutton` subfolder for the Vulkan renderer.

Fine-tuning selections with radio buttons

Radio buttons come in groups of at least two, and they have an important property – all the radio buttons in a group are mutually exclusive. You do not have to worry about checking for conflicting selections, as a user can only select one of the given options per group. As you can see in *Figure 12.3*, you are unable to select two of the options at the same time:

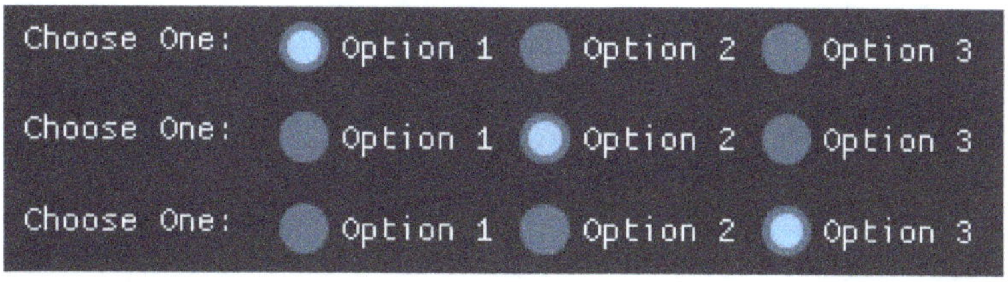

Figure 12.3: Radio buttons allow only a single option to be selected

In ImGui, you can use the `ImGui::RadioButton()` function with any arbitrary kind of data type. There is no built-in limitation to use only `int` values, or `enum`, and strings or entire C++ classes can also be used.

The reason for the unlimited usage is simple – you must manage the state tracking of the options by yourself. The ImGui radio button only helps you with the display of the active button of the group and reacts to a click:

```
bool ImGui::RadioButton(const char* label, bool active);
```

Usually, the `active` check will be done by comparing the state and the option that the current radio button is responsible for. If this check results in `true`, the given radio button is shown as active in the user interface.

If the user clicks on the radio button, the function returns `true`. Using the call to `ImGui::RadioButton()` as an `if` condition, like the `ImGui::ComboBox()` call we used in the previous part of this section, allows you to react to the mouse click. You just need to set the state to the value that the given radio button represents inside the `if` block, and then the new state is recorded.

We will use an `enum class` per radio button group, as this is a simple and efficient way to compare the state of the group in other parts of the code.

Adjusting the renderer code

To create the `enum` definitions for the three radio button groups we will use, add the following lines to the `OGLRenderData.h` file in the `opengl` folder. Make sure to add these lines above the `OGLRenderData struct` definition:

```
enum class skinningMode {
  linear = 0,
  dualQuat
};
enum class blendMode {
  fadeinout = 0,
  crossfade,
  additive
};
enum class replayDirection {
  forward = 0,
  backward
};
```

The first `enum` will replace the checkbox, allowing us to select the desired vertex skinning mode, either the linear mode using the joint matrices, or the dual quaternion skinning. The second `enum` will combine the selection of the different blending modes into a single group.

> **Note on the replayDirection enum**
>
> If you completed the third task of the *Practical session* section in *Chapter 10*, you will have added an option to play the animation clip in a forward or backward direction.
>
> A possible implementation for this task has been added to the example code, as the control of the playback direction is another good example of using a radio button group.

In the `OGLRenderData struct` of the `OGLRenderData.h` file, we must also adjust the data types of some of the variables. These variables will use the new `enum` classes instead of the previous Booleans.

To change the variables, *remove* the following lines from the `OGLRenderData struct`:

```
  bool rdGPUDualQuatVertexSkinning = false;
  bool rdCrossBlending = false;
  bool rdAdditiveBlending = false;
  bool rdPlayAnimationBackward = false;
```

Then, *add* the following lines to the `OGLRenderData struct`:

```
  skinningMode rdGPUDualQuatVertexSkinning = skinningMode::linear;
  blendMode rdBlendingMode = blendMode::fadeinout;
  replayDirection rdAnimationPlayDirection = replayDirection::forward;
```

Due to the reorganization of the blending mode, the `rdAdditiveBlending` variable needs no replacement. We will include the selection of the additive blending mode to the radio buttons, using the `blendMode` enum class.

All variable type changes must be made in the remaining parts of the code too, so we will adjust the `OGLRenderer` class next.

First, we can get rid of parts of the variable and check for the blending modes. Because we had two separate variables for the general blending mode and additive blending, two separate code blocks with checks were needed.

The complex, nested check for the cross-blending and the additive blending is no longer needed, so you can *remove* all these lines from the `draw()` call in the `OGLRenderer.cpp` file in the `opengl` folder:

```
static bool blendingChanged = mRenderData.rdCrossBlending;
if (blendingChanged != mRenderData.rdCrossBlending) {
  ...
}
static bool additiveBlendingChanged =
  mRenderData.rdAdditiveBlending;
if (additiveBlendingChanged != mRenderData.rdAdditiveBlending) {
  ...
}
```

Then, *add* the following lines for the blend mode change check:

```
static blendMode lastBlendMode = mRenderData.rdBlendingMode;
if (lastBlendMode != mRenderData.rdBlendingMode) {
  lastBlendMode = mRenderData.rdBlendingMode;
  if (mRenderData.rdBlendingMode != blendMode::additive)
     mRenderData.rdSkelSplitNode = mRenderData.rdModelNodeCount - 1;
  }
  mGltfModel->resetNodeData();
}
```

The new code is much simpler. We only need one block now instead of two, and the reset of the split node is included in the preceding block.

To complete the renderer changes, the other checks for the blending mode must also be replaced. Search for the following line in the `draw()` method of the `OGLRenderer` class (you should find two occurrences):

```
  if (mRenderData.rdCrossBlending) {
```

Then, *replace* the preceding line with the following two lines:

```
  if (mRenderData.rdBlendingMode == blendMode::crossfade ||
  mRenderData.rdBlendingMode == blendMode::additive) {
```

Both code snippets perform the same functionality, but again, the new lines state explicitly when to use cross-blending and additive blending.

For the vertex skinning type, the same replacement must be done too. *Remove* the following line in the `draw()` method of the `OGLRenderer` class:

```
    if (mRenderData.rdGPUDualQuatVertexSkinning) {
```

Replace it with this one:

```
    if (mRenderData.rdGPUDualQuatVertexSkinning ==
      skinningMode::dualQuat) {
```

Finally, the playback direction is also controlled by a Boolean, so we change the type to `enum` and rename the variable. In the `draw()` method of the `OGLRenderer` class, *remove* the following line:

```
mRenderData.rdPlayAnimationBackward
```

Replace it with this one:

```
mRenderData.rdAnimationPlayDirection
```

Changing the data type for the playback direction requires an additional action, so we must also adjust the data type in the `GltfModel` class.

Updating the model class

Luckily, the model class changes are small. We must swap the variable type in the signature of the two `playAnimation()` methods, in the `GltfModel.h` and `GltfModel.cpp` files in the `model` folder, replacing the `bool` type of the last parameter with the `replayDirection` type. Also, we should change the name of the parameter variable to reflect its purpose.

As an example, we will change the following signature:

```
void playAnimation(int animNum, float speedDivider,
  float blendFactor, bool playBackwards);
```

The preceding signature will be changed to the following:

```
void playAnimation(int animNum, float speedDivider,
  float blendFactor, replayDirection direction);
```

Moreover, inside the two `playAnimation()` definitions in the `GltfModel.cpp` file, the check of the playback direction must be adjusted. Therefore, *remove* the following line:

```
  if (playBackwards) {
```

Replace it with this one:

```
if (direction == replayDirection::backward) {
```

Now, the renderer and model code use the new variables. It's time for the last step – replacing the control element in the `UserInterface` class.

Switching the control elements in the user interface

To complete this implementation, we must remove the old checkboxes and add the logic for the radio buttons. This change is also an easy task.

Let us add a set of radio buttons for the vertex skinning mode as an example. First, we must *remove* the ImGui checkbox and the line of text that shows the selected method in the UI:

```
ImGui::Checkbox("GPU Vertex Skinning Method:",
  &renderData.rdGPUDualQuatVertexSkinning);
ImGui::SameLine();
if (renderData.rdGPUDualQuatVertexSkinning) {
  ImGui::Text("Dual Quaternion");
} else {
  ImGui::Text("Linear");
}
```

Then, we will *add* the radio button logic:

```
ImGui::Text("Vertex Skinning:");
ImGui::SameLine();
```

For the label of the radio button group, we will add a normal `ImGui::Text()` call. The radio buttons should follow on the same line as the label, so `ImGui::SameLine()` is used to avoid the line skip.

Now, the first radio button for the linear vertex skinning is created, using the joints and matrices:

```
if (ImGui::RadioButton("Linear",
    renderData.rdGPUDualQuatVertexSkinning ==
      skinningMode::linear)) {
  renderData.rdGPUDualQuatVertexSkinning = skinningMode::linear;
}
```

The radio button for the linear vertex skinning will be shown as active if the current vertex mode is set to `skinningMode::linear`. On any other mode, the radio button will be drawn as inactive. Also, if the user clicks on the radio button, the vertex skinning mode will be set to linear skinning. Even if the mode was already set to the linear vertex skinning, the variable will be set here.

We can add the second radio button with a similar line; we will only change the check for the mode and the variable assignment if the radio button was clicked:

```
    ImGui::SameLine();
    if (ImGui::RadioButton("Dual Quaternion",
        renderData.rdGPUDualQuatVertexSkinning ==
          skinningMode::dualQuat)) {
      renderData.rdGPUDualQuatVertexSkinning = skinningMode::dualQuat;
    }
  }
```

The same changes must be made to the playback direction and the blending mode checkboxes, and we will eventually replace all three checkboxes with radio button groups.

If we compile and run the code from the radio button example, the user interface looks like the screen shown in *Figure 12.4*:

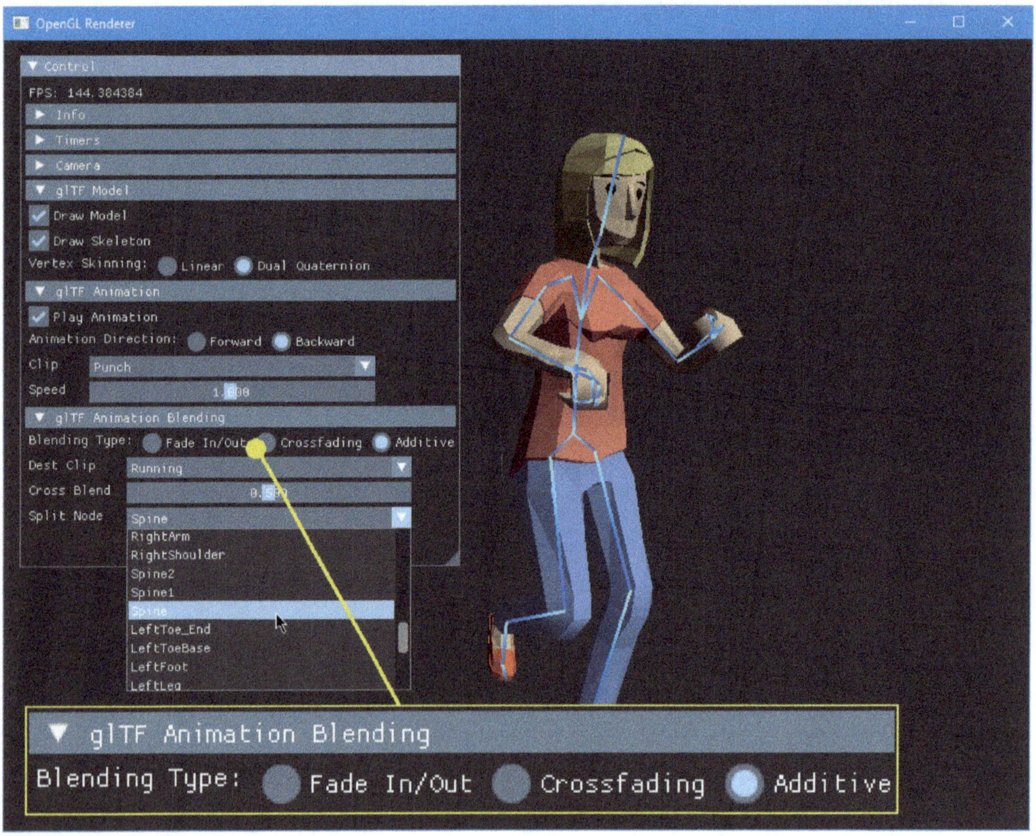

Figure 12.4: Using radio buttons instead of checkboxes in the user interface

Our new user interface is less ambiguous for the vertex skinning, the playback direction, and the blending type. The radio buttons give a user the ability to select one of several options, which is preferable to just setting an activating checkbox and explaining the change in separate text.

As preparation for *Chapter 15*, we will now add a third control type, plots. These plots will help you to get a better understanding of where an application spends its computation or waiting times. The full source code for the following section can be found in the `03_opengl_plots` subfolder for OpenGL and the `06_vulkan_plots` subfolder for Vulkan.

Drawing time series with ImGui

You will find charts with two-dimensional time series in many places. A graphical drawing is easier to understand, compared to a table of numbers. In *Figure 12.5*, a simple example of a time series chart is shown:

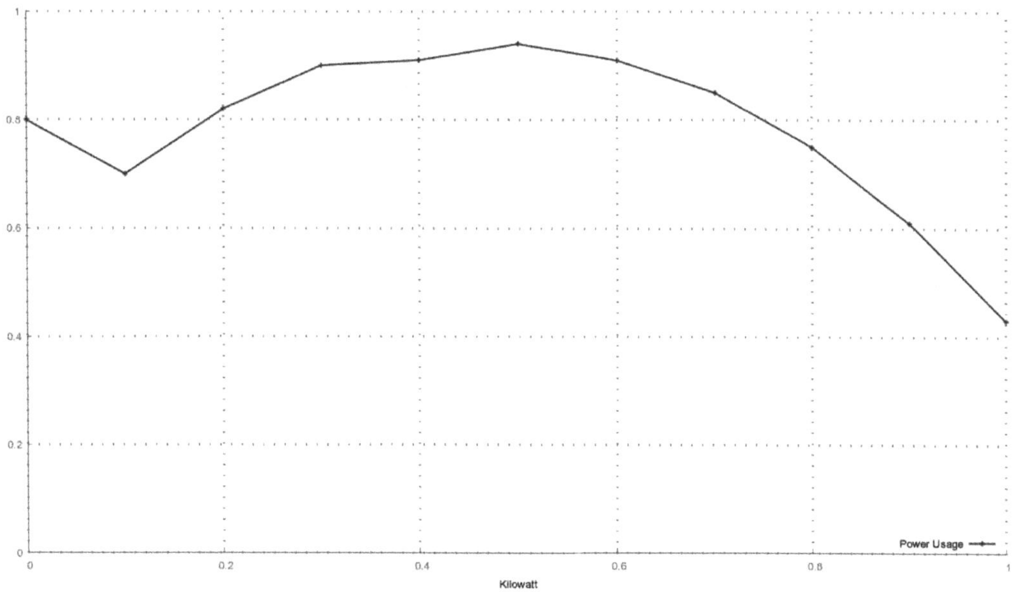

Figure 12.5: An example of a time series chart

For the *X* axis of the chart, an ascending time will be used. On the *Y* axis, the value for a specific time is drawn as a point, and all the points are connected by lines thereafter. The result is a single line from left to right, enabling us to detect possible correlations between different time points, which is easier than just having a column of numbers.

Figure 12.6 shows a plot of a sine wave made in ImGui. The basic principle is the same as for the preceding time series – the horizontal *X* axis of the chart is the time value, and for every point in time, a value on the vertical *Y* axis can be set:

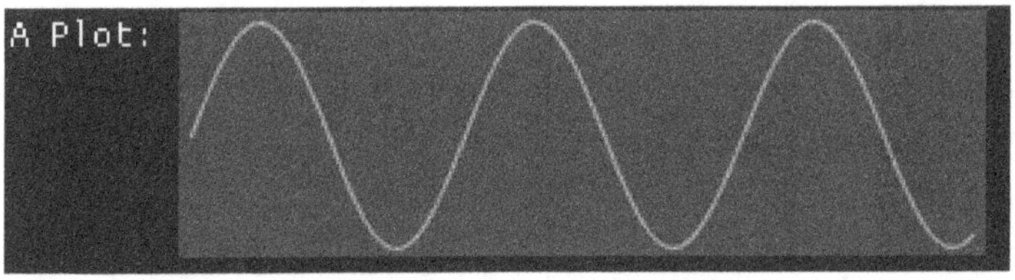

Figure 12.6: A plot of a sine wave made in ImGui

However, to draw time series for timers, or the FPS values, we must check another data type first – the ring buffer.

One ring buffer to rule them all

To display a time series, the drawing of the points usually starts at the first data point. As an example, in `std::vector`, the first data point would be the element with the index `0`. All other data points follow until the last element is shown and the time series chart is fully drawn.

This procedure is perfect for static data, or data that barely changes. For frequently changing data, we run into a performance trap – any newly arrived data must be inserted at one of the ends of our data structure, and all the data already recorded must be moved one index up or down before the insertion of the new data. This means that we would have to copy the entire buffer every time we get a new data element. For a larger, frequently updated buffer, such a copy operation binds a lot of CPU cycles for every data update. The removal of the last element on the opposite side of the insertion process is simple. The data element will not be copied – that is, it *falls out* of the buffer.

Moving data around for every data point is an expensive operation, so we need a solution to avoid moving data to create a free spot for the new data.

A so-called **ring buffer**, or **circular buffer**, is an elegant way to deal with the addition of new data without moving the existing data in the memory. In a ring buffer, the write pointer wraps around to the first buffer element when the pointer is moved forward after reaching last element of the buffer. This wraparound creates a virtual circle, as we always pass the elements endlessly in the same order.

Reading from a ring buffer works like writing. The read pointer also wraps around at the end, virtually appending the buffer part before the read pointer position at the end. As long as both pointers are identical, or the read pointer does not *overtake* the write buffer, we can insert new data without any movement operation, reading the existing data like a normal buffer.

The ImGui plot widget also supports a ring buffer as a data source. We have now found a perfect solution to draw the time plots for our application timers.

Creating plots in ImGui

Due to the default values in the declaration of the `ImGui::PlotLines()` function, the number of parameters to use a ring buffer as a data source is quite small:

```
void ImGui::PlotLines(const char* label,
  const float* values, int values_count, int values_offset);
```

As the first parameter, we will pass the label to be shown on the screen. Like for all other ImGui widget labels, a double hashtag will hide the label text from the user interface. The second parameter is a pointer to an array of `float` values where the data points to plot to the screen are stored, and the number of values to plot from the array are given as the third parameter. As the fourth parameter, the offset into the ring buffer is given to the function call. Internally, `ImGui::PlotLines()` wraps around the pointer to the first element of the `values` array if it accesses a position greater than `values_count` in the array.

All we must deliver to the `ImGui::PlotLines()` function is a C-style array and the array size. By using `std::vector` to store the values, we can get both the raw pointer and the array size from the vector:

```
std::vector<float> values{};
const float* valuePtr = values.data();
int valueSize = values.size();
```

That is all we need to know to implement ImGui plots. Now, let's look at the `UserInterface` class files.

Adding plots to the user interface

The logic of the plots resides entirely in the user interface, allowing easy and quick implementation. We will use the plot for the FPS counter to walk through the required changes and additions. The plots for the timers are created the same way as they are for the FPS counter, so an explanation of the timer plots will be skipped here.

Using `std::vector` to store data requires the inclusion of the correct header. As the first step, we will add the `<vector>` header to the `UserInterface.h` file in the `opengl` folder:

```
#include <vector>
```

In the same file, we will add two new `private` data members, the vector and the size:

```
    std::vector<float> mFPSValues{};
    int mNumFPSValues = 90;
```

Using a numerical value for the number of data elements will allow an easier adaptation of the amount of data collected for the timer. In the *Practical sessions* section, one of the tasks involves making the data sources for plots adjustable.

Before storing values in the `mFPSValues` vector, we must allocate memory in the underlying data storage. This allocation is done in the `init()` method in the `UserInterface.cpp` file, also in the `opengl` folder:

```
mFPSValues.resize(mNumFPSValues);
```

Then, we need a helper variable to limit the update frequency of the plot data. Doing a data update in every user interface drawing call would make the plot depend on the frame rate. By skipping some user interface updates, we can create a stable update rate for the plot data.

Add the new `static` variable, `updateTime`, at the beginning of the `createFrame()` method:

```
static double updateTime = 0.0;
```

The `updateTime` variable will hold a timestamp of the last update of the plot data.

A `static` variable will keep its value across all invocations of the method, and the initialization part is done only in the first method call. As we will never need the data of the `updateTime` variable outside the `createFrame()` method, using a static variable is *perfectly* fine here. In general, "polluting" the class with lots of member variables can be avoided by using `static` variables for values that are only needed inside one method, and the method has to retain its value after the current execution of the method ends.

We have to initialize the variable on the first run of `createFrame()`:

```
if (updateTime < 0.000001) {
  updateTime = ImGui::GetTime();
}
```

Comparing the variable with a small value instead of using the == operator should always be done for floating point numbers. An exact match may never occur for some values, caused by the internal representation of floating-point numbers.

Now, we will add the ring buffer offset for the plot data:

```
static int fpsOffset = 0;
```

The `fpsOffset` variable is also `static`, like the `updateTime` variable. Then, we will store the current FPS value and advance the offset:

```
while (updateTime < ImGui::GetTime()) {
  mFPSValues.at(fpsOffset) = mFramesPerSecond;
  fpsOffset = ++fpsOffset % mNumFPSValues;
```

```
    updateTime += 1.0 / 30.0;
  }
```

Here, we will wrap around the offset variable by using the modulo operator. Once we exceed the configured number of values, we will jump back to the start. We will also update the updateTime variable here, advancing the next plot data update about 33 **milliseconds** (**ms**) into the future (1/30 of a second). By doing this, the next new data element will be added 33 ms later, and we will add a total of 30 new data elements every second. With the configured mNumFPSValues value of 90, the FPS plot will show the data from the last three seconds. You can adjust updateTime and the number of values stored in the mFPSValues vector as required.

Having the plot data values updated regularly leaves the display of the plot left. Instead of adding plots to the existing user interface, we will make them pop up as tooltips when a user hovers over the FPS counter. This saves a lot of vertical space in the user interface and some CPU calculation time, as the plot will be drawn only if the tooltip is shown.

Popping up a tooltip with the plot

To create a usable tooltip, we must create a virtual ImGui widget group:

```
  ImGui::BeginGroup();
  ImGui::Text("FPS:");
  ImGui::SameLine();
  ImGui::Text("%s",
    std::to_string(mFramesPerSecond).c_str());
  ImGui::EndGroup();
```

By adding ImGui::BeginGroup() and ImGui::EndGroup() around the FPS counter text, the two text lines will be grouped internally into a single widget. This new widget group is used to check the widget against the mouse position. *If* the mouse pointer is placed over the widget group, the call to ImGui::IsItemHovered() returns true:

```
  if (ImGui::IsItemHovered()) {
```

The first step when the mouse is placed over the widget group is starting a tooltip:

```
    ImGui::BeginTooltip();
```

The tooltip will be placed as a semi-transparent window above the user interface, next to the position of the mouse pointer. Also, if we leave the widget group with the mouse pointer, the tooltip window will automatically be removed.

Inside the plot, we will show two values – the current FPS values, and an average calculated across all values of the plot data. To create the average value, we will define a new `float` variable called `averageFPS` and sum up all the plot data elements in it:

```
float averageFPS = 0.0f;
for (const auto value : mFPSValues) {
  averageFPS += value;
}
```

Then, we will divide the summed value by the number of values, creating the average:

```
averageFPS /= static_cast<float>(mNumFPSValues);
```

We will cast the `mNumFPSValues` variable to a floating-point value here to avoid making an integer division. For small values, the integer division will give the wrong results.

For the overlay text, we will create a string with the calculated values:

```
std::string fpsOverlay = "now:      " +
  std::to_string(mFramesPerSecond) + "\n30s avg: " +
  std::to_string(averageFPS);
```

Appending strings and the converted values may not be the fastest method to create data. However, as this will be done only once for every user interface update, it is good enough to create a string befitting our needs.

After all the values are available, we will fill the tooltip widget:

```
ImGui::Text("FPS");
ImGui::SameLine();
ImGui::PlotLines("##FrameTimes", mFPSValues.data(),
  mFPSValues.size(), fpsOffset, fpsOverlay.c_str(),
  0.0f, FLT_MAX, ImVec2(0, 80));
```

The `FPS` text will be shown on the left of the plot, at the same height as the start of the plot. After skipping the line break, the plot itself will be drawn.

We will hide the label again, as it would appear on the right side of the plot. Then, we set the pointer to the array containing the data elements, the size of the data array, and the offset of the first element we want to plot from the array. The data array will be accessed as a ring-buffer by ImGui, so the full array content is plotted, starting at the offset. After the offset, we will add the C-style string with the current and average timer values, by calling `c_str()` on the `fpsOverlay` string.

The last three parameters are the minimum and maximum values for the *y*-axis of the plot to show on the screen, and the position of the overlay text, given as a two-dimensional ImGui vector.

By passing `FLT_MAX` as the value for the maximum value, we will instruct ImGui to adjust the plot dynamically. If we were to use a fixed value here, any data greater than the maximum value would clamp larger plot data values to this maximum, resulting in a flat line at the top in the worst-case scenario.

Finally, we can close the tooltip widget:

```
    ImGui::EndTooltip();
}
```

Adding tooltip plots for the timers, compiling, and running the code will show a window like the one shown in *Figure 12.7*:

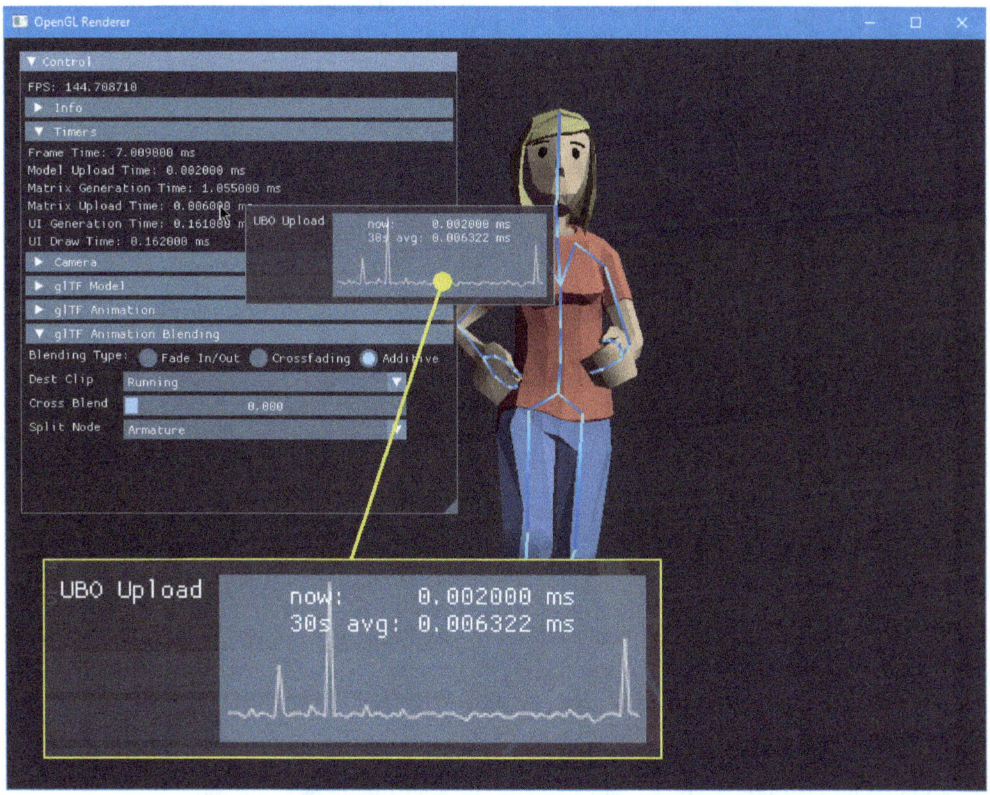

Figure 12.7: Hovering over the timer shows an ImGui plot diagram in a tooltip

Once you hover with the mouse over the FPS value or any timer, a tooltip will appear, showing you the plot for the last seconds, the current value, and the average across all stored values. You can see some spikes in the plot in *Figure 12.7*, telling us that the update of the matrices took a lot longer at certain points in time. Such a plot is a good starting point for debugging, a topic that we will cover in *Chapter 15*.

The widgets we used in this chapter and *Chapter 5* are only a small subset of all the widgets available in ImGui. A lot of other built-in widgets are available, most of them having adjustable properties. Also, many custom-made extensions have been built, aiming to deliver extra functionality for various purposes.

The sky is the limit

If you look at the message thread behind the **Gallery** link in the ImGui repository on GitHub, you will find many amazing user interfaces that have been created using ImGui. See the *Additional resources* section for the link, and make sure to follow the links in the first comment to the older tickets.

ImGui offers many other widget types that may be useful for your programming. You can do the following:

- Open extra settings in separate, closeable windows
- Display dialogs to a user
- Create modal dialogs that must be acted on
- Add menus to the control window
- Let the user choose colors by implementing a color picker widget
- Group settings in tabs instead of collapsed headers
- Organize controls and text in tables
- Show images in your windows, even create 2D animations
- Adjust parameters, such as colors, fonts, and the layout of widgets

To explore the ImGUI widgets and options, check out the *live demo* link in the *Additional resources* section. The demo is made using WebAssembly and shows the demo page included in the ImGui GitHub repository in a browser.

There are also a lot of ImGui extensions available, such as a file browser, text editors, or graphical tools, to build an ImGui user interface using the mouse. Follow the *extensions* link in the *Additional resources* section, and check out the extensions mentioned on that website.

If you want to create a cool-looking and feature-rich user interface, available for many operating systems and graphics backends, you should strongly consider ImGui as an option.

Summary

In this chapter, we explored how to create a cleaner user interface by replacing some of the currently used widgets with new ones.

After a quick overview of the widgets, we removed the sliders we used to select the animation clips and skeleton nodes, adding combo boxes instead. Then, we removed some ambiguous checkboxes and added radio button groups as replacements.

In the last part of the chapter, we added ImGui plots to draw time series of the FPS counter and the timers, and we created tooltips to show the plotted charts whenever a user hovers a mouse over the FPS counter and timer widgets.

In the following chapter, we will refocus on the animation part. You will learn the basics of **inverse kinematics**, a method that allows us to create and limit the movement of model nodes in a natural-looking way.

Practical sessions

You can try out the following ideas to get a deeper insight into the creation of user interfaces using ImGui elements:

- Add tooltips to a user interface. You can add a (disabled) question mark on the same line as the text field and explain the purpose of the control if the mouse hovers over the question mark. Adding explanations allows more accessibility for users without detailed knowledge of character animation.
- Add a confirmation dialog before closing a window. Create a modal dialog in the center of the window, requesting a user to confirm the end of the current renderer session.
- Add two sliders to a user interface to control the number of data points and the update frequency of the timer plots. The slider values do not need to be exposed to other components in the `OGLRenderData struct`; you can keep the logic inside the `createFrame()` method of the `UserInterface` class.
- **Advanced difficulty**: Search for an ImGui-based file browser extension and add it to the code. Some ready-to-use implementations are available "in the wild"; you do not have to do all the work by yourself. If you have a file browser available, you can try to adjust the model loading process, allowing a model swap at runtime.

Additional resources

- The ImGui website: `https://github.com/ocornut/imgui`
- ImGui examples: `https://github.com/ocornut/imgui/labels/gallery`
- ImGui extensions: `https://github.com/ocornut/imgui/wiki/Useful-Extensions`
- An ImGui live demo: `https://jnmaloney.github.io/WebGui/imgui.html`

13
Implementing Inverse Kinematics

Welcome to *Chapter 13*! In the previous chapter, the user interface was modified to a much cleaner state by adding new types of controls. We will use the new combo boxes and radio buttons in this chapter too, allowing fine-grained control of the parameters of the new algorithms.

In this chapter, we will deep dive into an advanced technique for more natural-looking animations. Being able to easily move the hand or foot of the animated character to a specific point in space helps to create better animations, without us having to precalculate every possible motion and store them in animation clips.

First, we will clarify what Inverse Kinematics is and how it differs from the motion of the bones we used in the previous chapters. Then, we will explore the basics of the **Cyclic Coordinate Descent** algorithm (**CCD**) and add a solver class by implementing CCD.

At the end of the chapter, we will look at the **Forward and Backward Reaching Inverse Kinematics** algorithm (**FABRIK**). We will also add the code for it to the solver class and adjust the remaining code, allowing us to choose between CCD and FABRIK.

In this chapter, we will cover the following topics:

- What is Inverse Kinematics, and why do we need it?
- Building a CCD solver
- Building a FABRIK solver

First, we want to clarify the meaning of **Inverse Kinematics**, and why the usage of these kinds of algorithms is a basic requirement of a natural-looking character animation.

Technical requirements

For this chapter, you will need the OpenGL and Vulkan renderer code from *Chapter 12*.

What is Inverse Kinematics, and why do we need it?

The word "kinematics" is defined as the mechanics behind the motion of an object but without referencing the forces that cause this motion. So, every part of our daily motion can be described, in kinematic terms, as the movement of our bones.

The two types of Kinematics

If we look at the character animations in *Chapters 10–12*, the kinematics definition also holds true. The type of animation of our character is called **Forward Kinematics**. An example of Forward Kinematics is shown in *Figure 13.1*:

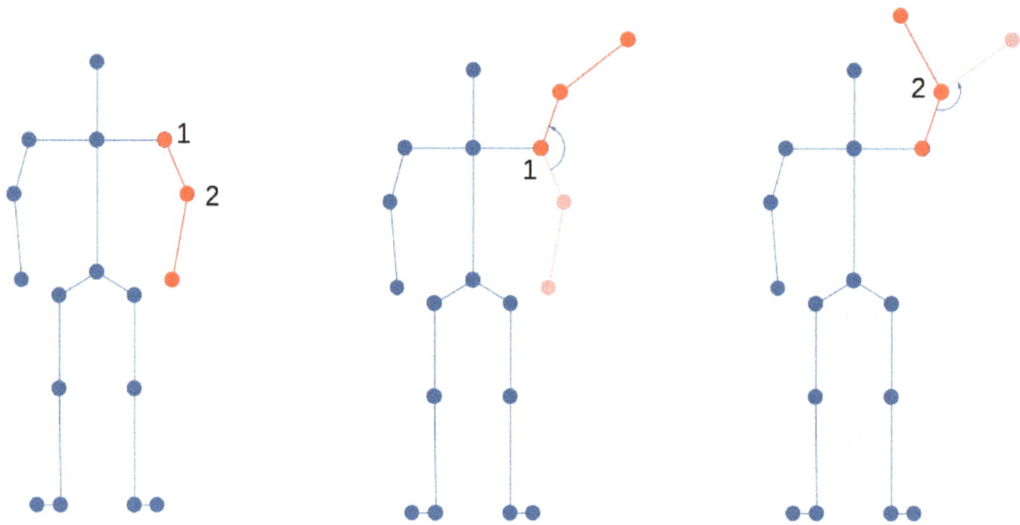

Figure 13.1: Raising the hand of the simple skeleton by using Forward Kinematics

The skeleton in *Figure 13.1* raises its simplified hand by rotating the arm at the shoulder (**1**), and the elbow (**2**).

During the movement or rotation of the skeletal bone, all the other nodes attached to it are also affected. Rotating the arm around the shoulder does not change the elbow or the forearm, as we only change one bone at a time. Then, the forearm itself is rotated around the elbow, bringing the hand to the final position. This final position of the hand is defined by the concatenation of the changes of all the bones from the shoulder to the hand.

However, what happens if we only know the desired final position of the hand?

If we want to move the hand of the skeleton in *Figure 13.2* to the green target point, or we want to put the foot onto the green target block, our only chance with Forward Kinematics would be "trial and error."

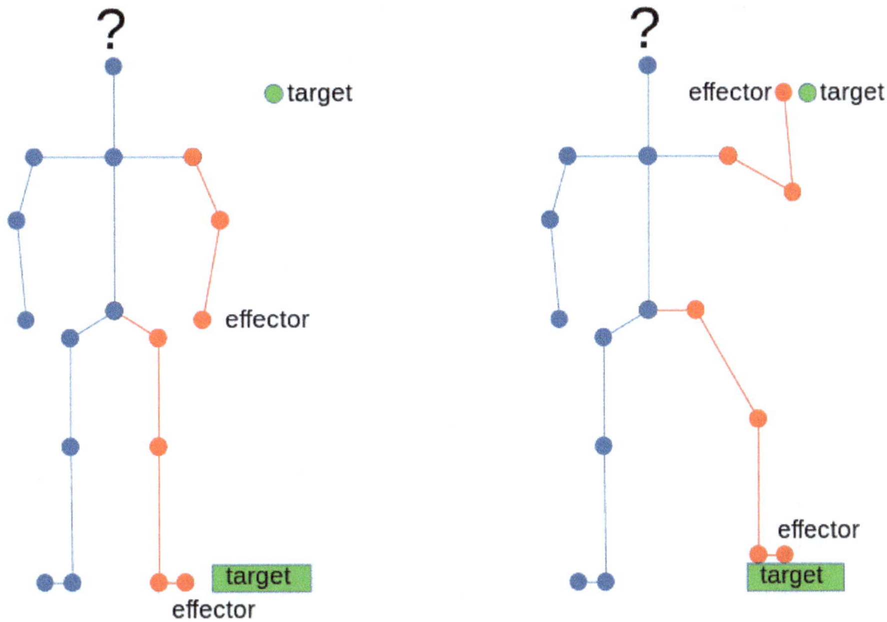

Figure 13.2: How to move the hand to the target, or put the foot on the box

We would have to adjust all the nodes on the arm or the leg over and over, until we reach a matching position. This is where Inverse Kinematics comes into play, and instead of randomly trying to reach the desired target, we can use well-known methods and algorithms to speed up the process of finding desirable positions for the bones of the skeleton.

In computer games, Inverse Kinematics is often used to place the feet of a character on top of a terrain, enabling the natural behavior of the feet and legs when the character stands, walks, or runs around. In robotics, Inverse Kinematics is used to calculate the motion of a robotic arm from an initial position to the destination position – that is, to reach an object and take or modify it.

Choosing a path to reach the target

To reach the target, we need a way to calculate the motion and/or rotation of the nodes. This motion must start at a given node (such as the shoulder, or the hips) and end with the hand touching the green target point, or the foot standing on the green box, as shown on the right-hand side of *Figure 13.2*.

In Inverse Kinematics, the term **effector** is used to describe the part of the skeleton that should reach the **target**. If the target is too far away to be reached by the effector, we should at least try to find a position as close as possible to the target.

To have the nodes reach the desired target, two main solution types exist.

First, we can try to calculate the movements for every node in an **analytical** or **numerical** solution. For a small number of nodes, an analytical solution can be formulated, but for the Inverse Kinematics calculation of a skeleton with many nodes, a numerical solution becomes easier, compared to the analytical solving. The numerical solving gives reliable results, but the complexity of the solution still rises with every node and every degree of freedom we have for the joints. If we use the Jacobian matrix solution, we may end up with a large, non-square matrix that needs to be inverted to be solved in a numerical way. You can check the link in the *Additional resources* section to get a detailed explanation of solving the target-reaching problem using the Jacobian matrix solution.

Conversely, we can stick with the "trial and error" option and try a **heuristic** method, finding a node movement that is "good enough" for us to use. These heuristic methods will not give exact solutions, like the numerical solution, but the complexity will be drastically reduced.

Instead of inverting and solving a big matrix on every frame, we simply iterate a couple of times over all the nodes that should be changed, moving the nodes closer to the target. In most cases, we can live with the trade-off of a faster and cheaper solution that may not bring perfect results.

In this book, we will explain two of the most used heuristic methods to solve the target-reaching movements, CCD and FABRIK. Let us look at the CCD algorithm first.

Building a CCD solver

CCD is a simple and popular Inverse Kinematics method to solve the motion of nodes to reach a target.

We start with an overview of the CCD algorithm, and after the CCD basics have been explored, we will add a new Inverse Kinematics solver class and enhance the existing classes, enabling the model to use the CCD solver.

Understanding the CCD basics

The basic idea of CCD is to rotate every bone of the skeleton limb in an iterative way to get closer to the target. To explain the steps involved, we will use a simplified robotic arm. A sample CCD iteration is shown in both *Figure 13.3* and *Figure 13.4*:

1. We can see the initial position of the three nodes in *Figure 13.3* (**1**). Here, three bones, the target, and the effector are drawn. The blue node is attached to the ground, and the outer red node is used as the effector.

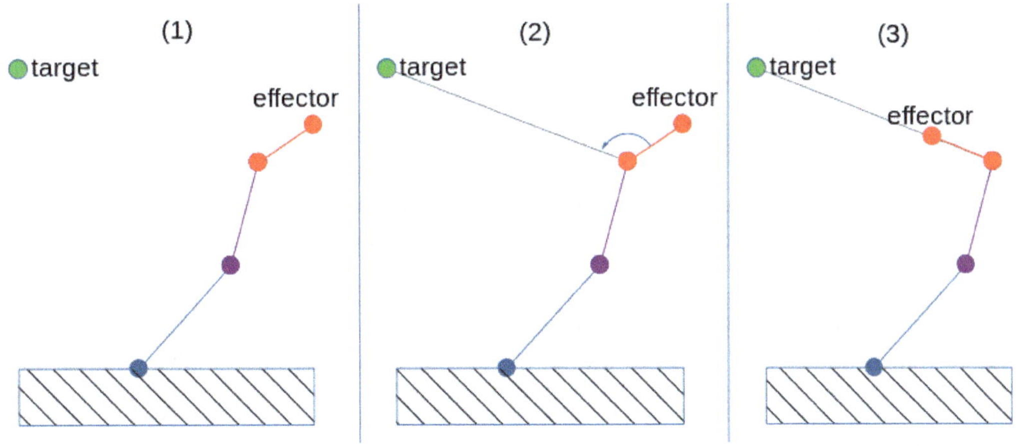

Figure 13.3: Solving Inverse Kinematics using CCD – part 1

2. Then, we will draw a virtual line between the lower joint of the red bone and the target, as shown in *Figure 13.3* (**2**). This "line of sight" defines the shortest path of the lower joint and the target.
3. Now, we will rotate the red bone to make the effector cut the virtual line. In this case, the entire red bone will be aligned with the virtual line. *Figure 13.3* (**3**) shows the result of the rotation.
4. After the rotation of the red bone, we will draw a new virtual line from the target to the lower joint of the next purple bone. The new line is shown in *Figure 13.4* (**4**).

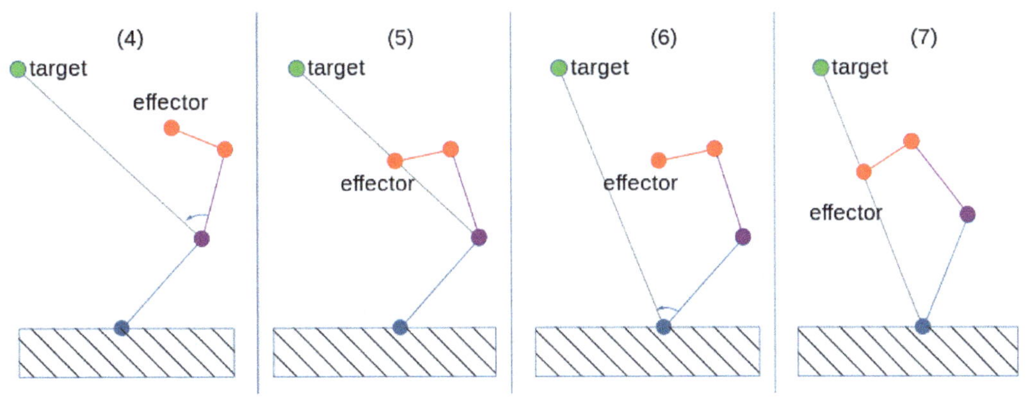

Figure 13.4: Solving Inverse Kinematics using CCD – part 2

5. In *Figure 13.4* (**5**), we rotate around the purple bone's lower joint, stopping again once the effector cuts the virtual line.
6. Then, the rotation around the fixed blue joint will be complete. We will draw another virtual line from the target to the joint we rotate around, as shown in *Figure 13.4* (**6**).

7. The bone is rotated until the effector cuts the line between the target and the blue joint. The result of the rotation is shown in *Figure 13.4* (**7**).

After all the bones are rotated once, the first CCD iteration is finished.

If the effector is not yet in close range to the target, or has reached the target, we start over from *step 2*. We will draw the virtual line to the lower joint of the red bone and rotate it until the effector cuts the virtual line, and so on. *Steps 2* to *7* will be repeated until the effector touches the target, or if the maximum number of iterations are reached.

Using this knowledge of a single CCD iteration and the exit conditions, we can start with the implementation of an Inverse Kinematics solver in C++, including CCD as the first solving algorithm.

We will cover only the important parts of the solver class for the sake of brevity. You can check the complete source code for the following section in the folder for `chapter13`. The `01_opengl_ccd` subfolder contains the source code for the OpenGL renderer, and the code for the Vulkan renderer is in the `03_vulkan_ccd` subfolder. Let us start with the extension of the `GltfNode` class.

Updating the code of the node class

To update the `GltfNode` class, we must adjust the header file, `GltfNode.h`, in the `model` folder.

The first change involves adding the ability to create a `std::shared_ptr` smart pointer of the current object inside a class method. We will accomplish this ability by deriving the `GltfNode` class from the special `std::enable_shared_from_this` class:

```
class GltfNode : public
  std::enable_shared_from_this<GltfNode> {
```

Then, we will add the `public` declaration of the `getParentNode()` method to retrieve the parent node from a node:

```
    std::shared_ptr<GltfNode> getParentNode();
```

We will also add the public method declarations, `getLocalRotation()` and `getGlobalRotation()`, to read out the local and the respective global rotations of the node, plus the `getGlobalPosition()` method to retrieve the global position of the node:

```
    glm::quat getLocalRotation();
    glm::quat getGlobalRotation();
    glm::vec3 getGlobalPosition();
```

Finally, to descend down the nodes of the skeleton tree from the root node and update all the node matrices on the path, the new `updateNodeAndChildMatrices()` method is added:

```
    void updateNodeAndChildMatrices();
```

As we will add the ability of a node to get its parent node directly, we can adjust the `calculateNodeMatrix()` method to calculate the node matrix from the parent node matrix, and the `parentNodeMatrix` parameter is no longer needed:

```
void calculateNodeMatrix(glm::mat4 parentNodeMatrix);
```

Simply *remove* the `parentNodeMatrix` parameter from the definition of the `calculateNodeMatrix()` method.

To save the pointer to the parent node, the `private` member variable, `mParentNode`, will be used:

```
std::weak_ptr<GltfNode> mParentNode;
```

We will use a "weak pointer" here to avoid circular dependencies – the parent node stores its child nodes already as a smart pointer, and if we use `std::shared_ptr` for the parent node too, the reference counter of both smart pointers can never reach zero, as each node waits for its counterpart to be destroyed first. A weak pointer breaks such a circular dependency by not counting toward the shared reference counter. Check out the *Additional resources* section for a link to a detailed explanation of how a weak pointer works.

The implementations of the five new methods – `getParentNode()`, `getLocalRotation()`, `getGlobalRotation()`, `getGlobalPosition()`, and `updateNodeAndChildMatrices()` – will be created in the `GltfNode.cpp` file in the `model` folder. We will start by adding a new header right below the existing `#include` lines:

```
#include <glm/gtx/matrix_decompose.hpp>
```

GLM has the built-in `glm::decompose()` function to break down a 4x4 transformation matrix into its components. To use this function, we must include the `matrix_decompose.hpp` header.

Now, in the `addChilds()` method, we will set the parent node to the current node:

```
...
child->mNodeNum = childNode;
child->mParentNode = shared_from_this();
mChildNodes.push_back(child);
...
```

Add the highlighted line in the preceding code to the code at the given position of the `addChilds()` method. Calling `shared_from_this()` creates a `std::shared_ptr` pointer from the current node and assigns the smart pointer to the `mParentNode` variable of the new child node instance.

To read out the stored parent node, we will add `getParentNode()` like this:

```
std::shared_ptr<GltfNode> GltfNode::getParentNode() {
  std::shared_ptr<GltfNode> pNode = mParentNode.lock();
  if (pNode) {
```

```
    return pNode;
  }
  return nullptr;
}
```

Calling the `lock()` function on the parent weak pointer is a required action to create `std::shared_ptr` from the weak pointer. If the `mParentNode` pointer is not set, (i.e., for the root node), or if the pointer is no longer valid because the node is already in the destruction phase, we will return `nullptr` to show that we cannot find the parent node. However, if we have a valid parent node, we will return the shared pointer to it.

For the update traversal of all child nodes, the `updateNodeAndChildMatrices()` method will be used:

```
void GltfNode::updateNodeAndChildMatrices() {
  calculateNodeMatrix();
  for (auto &node : mChildNodes) {
    if (node) {
      node->updateNodeAndChildMatrices();
    }
  }
}
```

We will simply call `calculateNodeMatrix()` to update the current node matrix, descending recursively to the child nodes until no more exist for the node.

The new `getLocalRotation()` method is simple:

```
glm::quat GltfNode::getLocalRotation() {
  return mBlendRotation;
}
```

Conversely, the `getGlobalRotation()` needs some explanation:

```
glm::quat GltfNode::getGlobalRotation() {
  glm::quat orientation;
  glm::vec3 scale;
  glm::vec3 translation;
  glm::vec3 skew;
  glm::vec4 perspective;
```

First, we must declare local variables for all components of the decomposed 4x4 transformation matrix. In such a transformation matrix, we have the rotation, scale, and translation stored but also values for a possible skew and perspective distortion. Even if we need only the rotation here, all the variables need to be declared for the function call.

By calling `glm::decompose()` on the `mNodeMatrix` node matrix, GLM extracts the parts of the transformation matrix and writes the values back to the remaining parameters:

```
  if (!glm::decompose(mNodeMatrix, scale, orientation,
      translation, skew, perspective)) {
    return glm::quat(1.0f, 0.0f, 0.0f, 0.0f);
  }
  return glm::inverse(orientation);
}
```

The Boolean return value of `glm::decompose()` signals whether the extraction was successful. In case of a failed matrix decomposing, we will return a non-rotating quaternion to gain a valid return value, and if the decomposing is successful, we will return the extracted `orientation` as a quaternion. I have chosen the variable name `orientation` here instead of the word `rotation`, because orientation is a better fit for a quaternion, even if the underlying operation is a rotation.

For the `getGlobalPosition()` method, the declaration part is identical, and only the returned value differs:

```
glm::vec3 GltfNode::getGlobalPosition() {
  ...
  if (!glm::decompose(mNodeMatrix, scale, orientation,
      translation, skew, perspective)) {
    return glm::vec3(0.0f, 0.0f, 0.0f);
  }
  return translation;
}
```

We will return the extracted `translation` instead of `orientation`, and a "null translation" if there is an error while decomposing the matrix.

The new `calculateNodeMatrix()` method is like the `getParentNode()` method:

```
void GltfNode::calculateNodeMatrix() {
  calculateLocalTRSMatrix();
  glm::mat4 parentNodeMatrix = glm::mat4(1.0f);
  std::shared_ptr<GltfNode> pNode = mParentNode.lock();
  if (pNode) {
    parentNodeMatrix = pNode->getNodeMatrix();
  }
  mNodeMatrix = parentNodeMatrix * mLocalTRSMatrix;
}
```

To simplify the node update process, we will recalculate the local TRS matrix before we attempt to update `mNodeMatrix`. The combined update simplifies the calls to the matrix update methods, as we cannot forget to update the local TRS matrix beforehand.

Then, we will define the identity matrix as the default parent node matrix. If the following locking of the parent node pointer fails, the identity matrix will be taken to update `nModeMatrix`, resulting in the values of `mLocalTRSMatrix`. If there is a successful retrieval of the parent node, we will read the node matrix of the parent and multiply the node matrix and the local TRS matrix normally.

We also need to update the `GltfModel` class to reflect the changes from the `GltfNode` class and collect the Inverse Kinematics nodes.

Updating the model class

As well as the removal of the `parentNodeMatrix` parameter from the declarations in the `GltfModel.h` file and the method definitions in the `GltfModel.cpp` file in the `model` folder, we must make some additions and changes.

First, we will clear the node data in the `getNodeData()` method in the `GltfModel.cpp` file for the translation, scale, and rotation, if no data is available in the `tinygltf` data element for the given node. Due to changes to the rotation data of a node during the Inverse Kinematic algorithms, we must reset the node if the original data contains no rotation.

Then, we will add a `public` method, called `setInverseKinematicsNode()`, to populate the node vector with all the nodes that will be affected by the Inverse Kinematics:

```
void GltfModel::setInverseKinematicsNodes(
    int effectorNodeNum, int ikChainRootNodeNum) {
```

At the start of the `setInverseKinematicsNode()` method, we will check whether the effector node or the chain root node is inside the skeleton:

```
  if (effectorNodeNum < 0 ||
      effectorNodeNum > (mNodeList.size() - 1)) ||
      ikChainRootNodeNum < 0 ||
      ikChainRootNodeNum > (mNodeList.size() - 1)) {
    return;
  }
```

Then, we will create a temporary vector of `GltfNode` smart pointers that should be included in the the Inverse Kinematics solving process:

```
  std::vector<std::shared_ptr<GltfNode>> ikNodes{};
```

The effector node will be the first element of the smart pointer vector:

```
    ikNodes.insert(ikNodes.begin(),
      mNodeList.at(effectorNodeNum));
```

In the following `while` loop, we will walk the skeleton tree backward to find the root node given by the `ikChainRootNodeNum` parameter:

```
    int currentNodeNum = effectorNodeNum;
    while (currentNodeNum != ikChainRootNodeNum) {
      std::shared_ptr<GltfNode> node = mNodeList.at(currentNodeNum);
      if (node) {
```

Next, we append each parent node we find in the path to the temporary `ikNodes` vector:

```
        std::shared_ptr<GltfNode> parentNode = node->getParentNode();
        if (parentNode) {
          currentNodeNum = parentNode->getNodeNum();
          ikNodes.push_back(parentNode);
```

If we find no valid parent, we will stop walking the skeleton tree because we reached the skeleton root node:

```
        } else {
          break;
        }
      }
    }
```

At the end of the `setInverseKinematicsNode()` method, we will hand over the node vector to the solver class:

```
    mIKSolver.setNodes(ikNodes);
  }
```

We will also add to the `public` helper methods, `setNumIKIterations()` and `solveIKByCCD()`, which call the underlying solver methods:

```
  void GltfModel::setNumIKIterations(int iterations) {
    mIKSolver.setNumIterations(iterations);
  }
  void GltfModel::solveIKByCCD(glm::vec3 target)
    mIKSolver.solveCCD(target);
    updateNodeMatrices(mIKSolver.getIkChainRootNode());
  }
```

The `solveIKByCCD()` method also updates the vertex skinning matrices after the Inverse Kinematics algorithm ends. We will only need to update the matrices, starting at the root node.

Finally, we must add these three `public` methods, `setInverseKinematicsNodes()`, `setNumIKIterations()`, and `solveIKByCCD ()`, to the `GtlfModel.h` header file, include the `IKSolver.h` header at the top of the file, and add a solver instance as the `private` member variable:

```
...
#include "IKSolver.h"
...
IKSolver mIKSolver{};
...
```

After the updates to the `GltfNode` and `GltfModel` classes, we can start the Inverse Kinematics `Solver` class. As the `Solver` class for Inverse Kinematics is tightly coupled to the `GltfModel` and `GltfNode` classes, the best place for the new class will be inside the `model` folder.

Outlining the new solver class

For the new `IKSolver` class, create the `IKSolver.h` file in the `model` folder, and start with the header guard and the included headers:

```
#pragma once
#include <vector>
#include <memory>
#include <glm/glm.hpp>
#include "GltfNode.h"
```

We will need the `vector` and the `memory` headers to store the smart pointers of the `GltfNode` instances of the skeleton, which will take part in the iterations of the Inverse Kinematics. Manipulating the nodes directly by using a reference to the smart pointers saves two assignments per node – we do not need to copy the node data to get the current position and rotation, and there is no need to write back the changed position and rotation after the solver algorithm finishes its work.

Now, we will start the `IKSolver` class itself and the `public` constructors:

```
class IKSolver {
  public:
    IKSolver();
    IKSolver(unsigned int iterations);
```

The first constructor creates an instance of the solver class with a reasonable number of iterations set, and the second constructor sets the number of iterations we want to have set as the initial value.

To get the references to the GltfNode smart pointers, the setNodes() method will be used:

```
void setNodes(std::vector<std::shared_ptr<GltfNode>>
  nodes);
```

For convenience, we will also add the getIkChainRootNode() method to access the root node of the skeleton chain directly:

```
std::shared_ptr<GltfNode> getIkChainRootNode();
```

After the solver algorithm has changed the skeleton nodes, we must update the joint matrices or dual quaternions to reflect the changes in the node orientation. As we only need to update the part of the skeleton that was changed by the solver, accessing the root node of the respective skeleton part becomes useful and saves some CPU cycles.

Adjusting the number of iterations for the Inverse Kinematics algorithm can be done by calling the setNumIterations() method:

```
void setNumIterations(unsigned int iterations);
```

Finally, the first solver method is added:

```
bool solveCCD(glm::vec3 target);
```

By calling solveCCD(), the CCD algorithm is used to adjust the configured skeleton nodes, trying to bring the effector node as close as possible to the point given as the target parameter.

We must also store the nodes taking part in the Inverse Kinematics solver process. This is because we need to access all nodes directly. An array of smart pointers called mNodes will be used as the first private member variable:

```
  private:
    std::vector<std::shared_ptr<GltfNode>> mNodes{};
```

The nodes will be saved with the effector node at position zero of the std::vector, and the root node of the skeleton chain will be the last element of the vector. Storing the effector first makes the implementation clearer, as the CCD algorithm starts with the rotation of the second node after the effector node (see *Figure 13.3*).

In the mIterations integer, the number of iterations of the algorithm is stored. The last member variable, mThreshold, is used to define the maximum distance of the effector from the target that will be used to set the condition "the effector has reached the target" to true:

```
    unsigned int mIterations = 0;
    float mThreshold = 0.00001f;
};
```

Now, we must implement the methods of the `IKSover` class. To do so, we will start with the new `IKSolver.cpp` file in the `model` folder.

Implementing the Inverse Kinematics solver class and the CCD solver

We will start again with the headers to include:

```
#include <glm/gtx/quaternion.hpp>
#include "IKSolver.h"
```

The GLM quaternion header is needed because CCD uses rotations to solve Inverse Kinematics, and the orientation in the `GltfNode` class is stored as a quaternion. Plus, we need the header for the `IKSolver` class here.

The implementations for the two constructors discussed in the *Outlining the new solver class* section and for the getter and the setter methods are simple; we will skip the listing here and continue directly with the CCD solver method.

The `solveCCD()` method will return a Boolean to signal whether the target has been reached by the effector or not. We will not use the returned value in this example; implementing a `true/false` check and a field to the user interface has been left as a practical session for you, which you can find in the *Practical sessions* section:

```
bool IKSolver::solveCCD(const glm::vec3 target) {
  if (!mNodes.size()) {
    return false;
  }
```

The first check in the `solveCCD()` method is whether the size of the stored `GltfNode` vector is greater than zero. If we initially forgot to add any nodes with the `setNodes()` method, we will return immediately, as there is nothing to do for the Inverse Kinematics solver.

The main part of the CCD solver starts with a `for` loop. We will do a maximum number of `mIterations` iterations of the CCD algorithm:

```
  for (unsigned int i = 0; i < mIterations; ++i) {
```

It is correct to phrase the number of loops as "a maximum number of iterations." The algorithm will terminate whether the length of the vector from the target position to the effector node position is less than `mThreshold` in size:

```
    glm::vec3 effector = mNodes.at(0)->getGlobalPosition();
    if (glm::length(target - effector) < mThreshold) {
      return true;
    }
```

Now, we will loop over the saved nodes, starting with the node *after* the effector:

```
for (size_t j = 1; j < mNodes.size(); ++j) {
```

If you refer back to *Figure 13.3* (**2**), you can see that the effector itself is skipped during the forward solving.

Now, we will get the smart pointer to the node at the position of the loop variable, `j`:

```
std::shared_ptr<GltfNode> node = mNodes.at(j);
if (!node) {
  continue;
}
```

We will check first whether we have a valid node in the vector at the position of the loop variable. Normally, all nodes should be valid, but the check helps to avoid the program crashing, caused by accessing an invalid node in the `mNodes` vector.

The next step is to read the global `position` of the current node as a 3-element vector and the global `rotation` as a quaternion:

```
glm::vec3 position = node->getGlobalPosition();
glm::quat rotation = node->getGlobalRotation();
```

Using the global position of the node, we will create two 3-element vectors called `toEffector` and `toTarget`:

```
glm::vec3 toEffector = glm::normalize(effector - position);
glm::vec3 toTarget = glm::normalize(target - position);
```

These two vectors contain the direction from the current node position to the effector, and the direction from the node position to the target. We will normalize the vectors right here because we only need the direction, not the length.

To calculate the rotation that is required to rotate the current node so that the `toEffector` vector equals the `toTarget` vector, GLM brings the `glm::rotation()` function:

```
glm::quat effectorToTarget = glm::rotation(toEffector,
  toTarget);
```

The GLM `rotation()` function returns the quaternion with the rotation that is needed to rotate the vector from the first parameter, `toEffector`, to the vector of the second parameter, `toTarget`. The result is exactly the rotation we need to make the effector touch the line between the target and the node position, as shown in *Figure 13.3* (**3**), *Figure 13.4* (**5**), and *Figure 13.4* (**7**).

However, the *global* rotation quaternion is not useful for us. We can only adjust the local rotation of the node. As the first step in rotating the node, we need to calculate the required *local* rotation of the node:

```
glm::quat localRotation = rotation * effectorToTarget *
  glm::conjugate(rotation);
```

To transform the `effectorToTarget` quaternion from a *global* rotation to a *local* rotation, we must reorient the quaternion first. This is done by appending the desired `effectorToTarget` rotation quaternion to the global `rotation` orientation of the node, and then undoing the global `rotation` again by rotating around the conjugate of the global `rotation`. The resulting `localRotation` quaternion contains the rotation of an imaginary unit quaternion around the local object axis, but with the same amount that the `effectorToTarget` quaternion has.

As the second step to rotate the node, we must read the local rotation from the node and calculate its new rotation:

```
      glm::quat currentRotation = node->getLocalRotation();
      node->blendRotation(currentRotation * localRotation,
        1.0f);
```

By multiplying the two quaternions, `currentRotation` and `localRotation`, we create a composed rotation. The result of the multiplication is the exact rotation of the node we need on a *global* level, aligning the effector with the virtual line between the target and the current node.

Here, we will use the `blendRotation()` method to adjust the rotation, as the local TRS matrix is built from the `mBlendRotation` variable in the `GltfNode` class.

After the rotation property of the node has been changed, we must update the local TRS matrix and the node matrix. Also, we must trigger node matrix recalculations from the current node "down" to the effector node of the skeleton chain, updating the orientation of the nodes. We will update the skeleton chain by calling the recursive `updateNodeAndChildMatrices()` method on the current node:

```
      node->updateNodeAndChildMatrices();
```

The resulting adjustment of the skeleton is shown in *Figure 13.4* (**5**) and (**7**).

At the end of each loop over the nodes, we will check again whether the effector node reached the target after the adjustment of the node matrices, and we will finish the Inverse Kinematics calculation if we are close enough:

```
      effector = mNodes.at(0)->getGlobalPosition();
      if (glm::length(target - effector) < mThreshold) {
        return true;
      }
    }
```

Finally, we will close the `for` loop of the iterations and end the `solveCCD()` method by returning `false`:

```
  }
  return false;
}
```

If we reach the end of the `solveCCD()` method, the algorithm was not able to bring the effector node closer than the value defined in `mThreshold` to the target. The most obvious reason for this is that the target is too far away, meaning that, even after rotation, all nodes pointing to the target are not enough to reach the target point.

Adding Inverse Kinematics to the renderer

To enable the Inverse Kinematics in the renderer, we have to add some variables to the `OGLRenderData.h` file in the `opengl` folder. First, we will create an `enum` class containing the `ccd` method, along with a setting named `off` to disable Inverse Kinematics solving:

```
enum class ikMode {
  off = 0,
  ccd
};
```

Then, the new Inverse Kinematics variables are added to the `OGLRenderData` struct:

```
  ikMode rdIkMode = ikMode::off;
  int rdIkIterations = 10;
  glm::vec3 rdIkTargetPos = glm::vec3(0.0f, 3.0f, 1.0f);
  int rdIkEffectorNode = 0;
  int rdIkRootNode = 0;
```

The new Inverse Kinematics variables are used globally, like previously defined variables; see, for instance, the animation variables in the *Adding new Control Variables for the Animations* section in *Chapter 10*. Hence, we can skip the detailed explanation here.

Another change to `OGLRenderData` is the renaming of the vector containing the skeleton names, as we will use them for more than the additive split node:

```
  std::vector<std::string> rdSkelNodeNames{};
```

In the `OGLRenderer.h` and `OGLRenderer.cpp` files in the `opengl` folder, we will reintroduce known code pieces:

- The coordinate arrows model and the separate mesh for it return
- We will add a new timer to take the Inverse Kinematics timings
- We must initialize the `OGLRenderData` values with reasonable defaults
- We must check the `OGLRenderData` Inverse Kinematics variables for changes and act accordingly – for example, we must re-upload the node vector if we change the effector or root node

The most important change in the renderer is the call to the `solveIKByCCD()` method in the `draw()` method of the `OGLRenderer.cpp` file. We must add the Inverse Kinematics calculation code *right after* the calculation of the animation and animation blending has finished:

```
if (mRenderData.rdPlayAnimation) {
...
} if (mRenderData.rdIkMode == ikMode::ccd) {
  mIKTimer.start();
  mGltfModel->solveIKByCCD(mRenderData.rdIkTargetPos);
  mRenderData.rdIKTime = mIKTimer.stop();
}
```

The `solveIKByCCD()` method hands over the target position to the CCD solver algorithm of the `IKSolver` instance in the `GltfModel` class, starting the solver and updating the model.

The reason for the order of operations is simple – the animation calls overwrite the node properties with values extracted from the animation channels. Moving the Inverse Kinematics above the animation calculation in the code would immediately undo all changes made by the Inverse Kinematics algorithm, resulting in an unchanged animation rendering.

Extending the user interface

For the user interface changes, the `UserInterface` class in the `UserInterface.h` and `UserInterface.cpp` files in the `opengl` folder needs to be extended.

Similar to the `GltfModel` changes, the extension consists of known code parts:

- We will add a new timer text field and plot for the Inverse Kinematics timings
- We will need a new collapsing header for the Inverse Kinematics settings
- The new settings contain radio buttons to select the algorithm, an integer slider for the number of iterations, a 3x float slider for the target position, and two combo boxes to select the effector and the root node

Adding these code parts is a matter of copying and pasting, and we will skip them here – the timer could be made similar to the FPS timer, using also an array of `float` values to collect the timing values. The collapsing header and the combo box code can be taken from the "glTF animation blending" portion of the `createFrame()` function in the `UserInterface` class code, introduced in the *Adding new control variables for the animations* section of *Chapter 9*. The integer slider from the "Field of view" control can be reused; we added the slider in the *Adding a slider to control the Field of View* section of *Chapter 5*. Finally, the 3x float slider was used last in the UI of *Chapter 7* to control the properties of the Cubic Hermite spline.

> **Note for the vulkan renderer**
>
> For the Vulkan example, the changes outside the renderer class are identical. For the renderer itself, the changes must be made in the `VkRenderData.h` file instead of `OGLRenderData.h`, and in the `VkRenderer.h` and `VkRenderer.cpp` files instead of `OGLRender.h` and `OGLRenderer.cpp`. The named files for the Vulkan renderer reside in the `vulkan` folder of the examples.

If you compile the example code and select CCD in the new **glTF Inverse Kinematic** part of the ImGui interface, you should see a result like *Figure 13.5*:

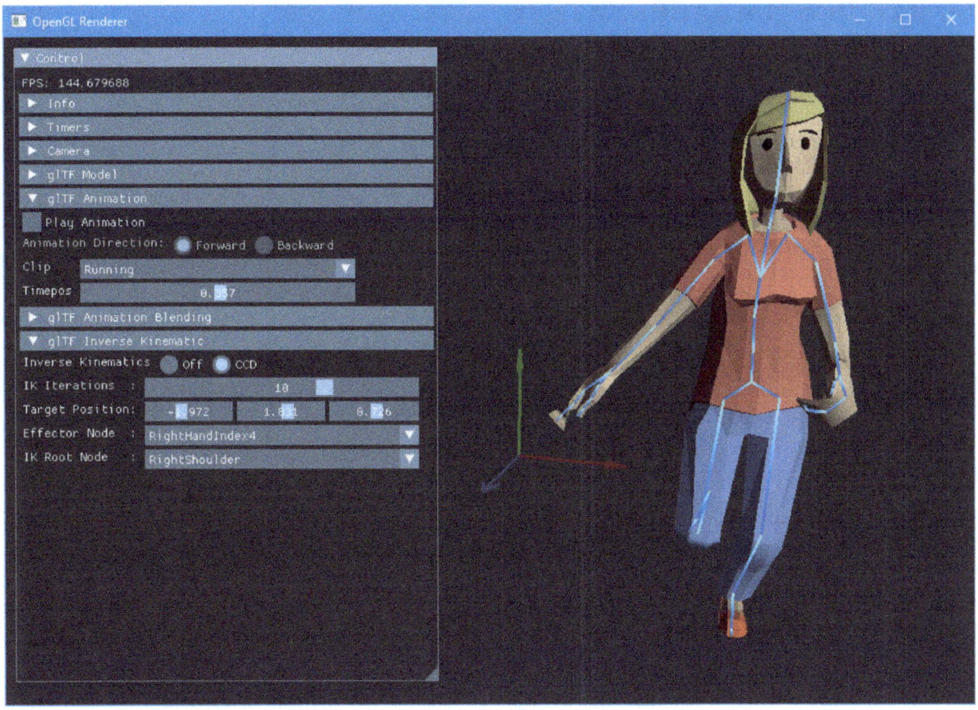

Figure 13.5: The hand of the glTF model tries to reach the target using CCD

You will see that the model tries to reach the target with the coordinate arrows. The target position itself can be moved in the *X*, *Y*, and *Z* directions, and the bones we chose will follow the target.

The main problem with CCD is the unintended twisting of the bones; this twisting can be seen especially during animations. The reason for this behavior is the continuous rotation of the bones to reach the target, and slight changes in the axis can lead to a rotation around a different quaternion axis.

A better algorithm is introduced next, the FABRIK solving algorithm.

Building a FABRIK solver

The second heuristic Inverse Kinematics solver to explore is **FABRIK**, the **Forward and Backward Reaching Inverse Kinematics** solver. FABRIK needs fewer iterations compared to CCD to find a satisfactory solution.

Similar to CCD, we will start with an overview of the FABRIK algorithm. After the basics have been explained, we will update the Inverse Kinematics `Solver` class, the user interface, and the renderer code to allow the selection of FABRIK as a second Inverse Kinematics solver.

Understanding the FABRIK basics

While CCD rotates the bones around the nodes to align the effector with the target, FABRIK moves and scales the bones to make the effector reach the target. Also, FABRIK moves along the chain of bones in two directions, forward and backward, hence its name.

Let us use the same simple robotics arm covered in the *Understanding the CCD Basics* section; the steps for a single iteration are shown in *Figures 13.6* to *13.9*. We can see the same initial position in the CCD example in *step 1* of the *Understanding the CCD basics* section. Three bones, the target, and the effector were drawn in that step, with the blue node attached to the ground and the outer red node used as the effector. Let us begin:

1. First, we will examine the *forward* solving part of FABRIK, as shown in *Figure 13.6* (**1**).

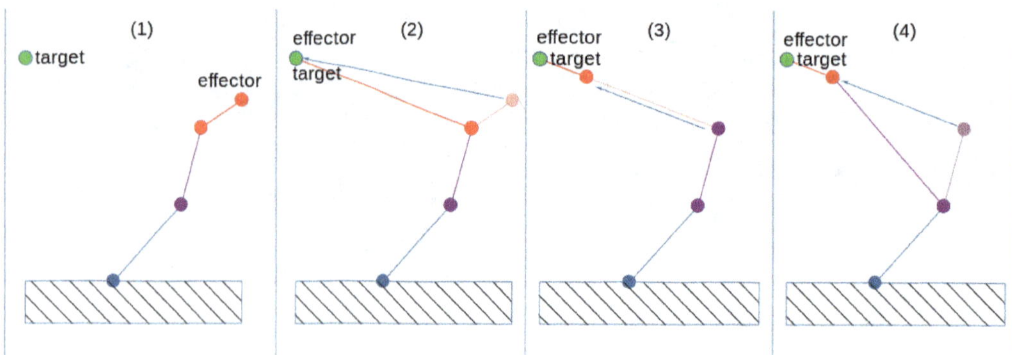

Figure 13.6: Solving Inverse Kinematics using FABRIK forward iteration – part 1

2. In *Figure 13.6* (**2**), we will *move* the effector to the position of the target. As you can see, moving the node stretches the red bone far beyond its original length.
3. As we must correct the length of the red bone, we will need to save the length of our bone before moving the effector. Also, we will scale the red bone back to the saved length after the effector has been moved, as shown in *Figure 13.6* (**3**). Scaling back the red bone to the previous length rips apart our robotics arm, as seen in *Figure 13.6* (**3**), but this is an intended behavior in FABRIK.

4. Then, we will move the outer node of the purple bone back to the end of the red bone, scaling it again to an arbitrary length. *Figure 13.6* (**4**) shows the result after the robotics arm has been reconnected.
5. The purple bone is scaled back to its previous length, as shown in *Figure 13.7* (**5**), moving the end node away from the blue bone.

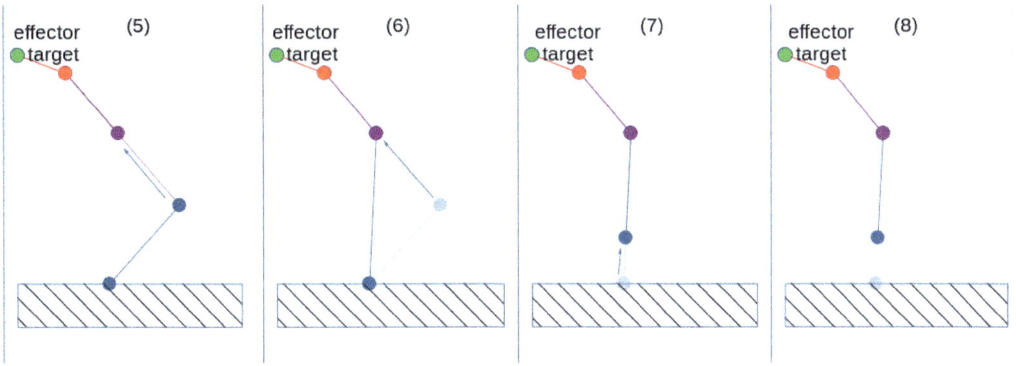

Figure 13.7: Solving Inverse Kinematics using FABRIK forward iteration – part 2

6. Finally, we will repeat *steps 4* and *5* of the purple bone movement, but also with the blue bone. We will reconnect the arm and scale the bone back to its original length, as shown in *Figure 13.7* (**6**) and *Figure 13.7* (**7**).

   Figure 13.7 (**8**) shows the result after the forward solving steps of the FABRIK algorithm.

   The robotic arm disconnected from the ground is not the result we want. To fix the arm, we will repeat the same steps, but this time backward on the same chain of bones.

   In the *backward* part of FABRIK, we will use the connection point of the arm as a target, and then the end of the blue bone becomes the effector.

7. As the first step in the backward operation, we will reconnect the arm to the ground, as shown in *Figure 13.8* (**9**).

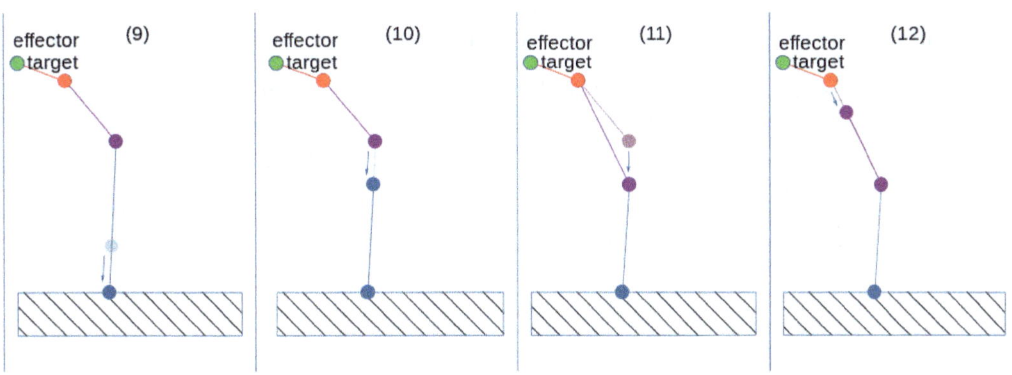

Figure 13.8: Solving Inverse Kinematics using FABRIK backward iteration – part 1

8. Then, we scale the blue bone back to its previous size and move the purple bone in the same way as we did initially in *steps 2* and *3*. In *Figure 13.8* (**10**), *Figure 13.8* (**11**), and *Figure 13.8* (**12**), the results of adjusting the blue and purple bones are shown.
9. Now, the lower node of the red bone will move, and the red bone is scaled back to its previous size, as shown in *Figure 13.9* (**13**) and *Figure 13.9* (**14**).

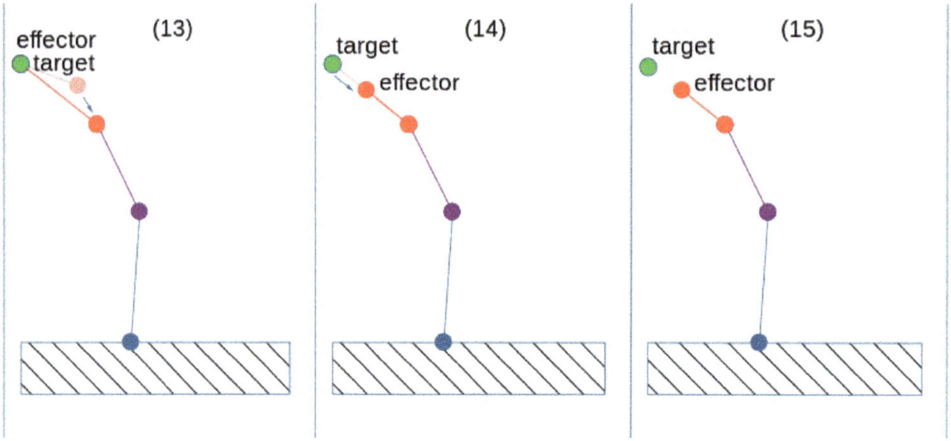

Figure 13.9: Solving Inverse Kinematics using FABRIK backward iteration part 2

Figure 13.9 (**14**) moves the effector away from the position of the target, but this is the intended behavior in FABRIK.

In *Figure 13.9* (**15**), a single FABRIK iteration has been done. If we compare the result with *Figure 13.4* (**7**) of the CCD solver, we can see that the effector has been moved much closer to the target in this single solver iteration.

For the next iterations of FABRIK, *steps 2* to *9* are repeated, until the effector reaches the target or we hit the maximum number of iterations.

After we have created all the parts for the solver class in the *Building a CCD Solver* section, the implementation of the FABRIK solver is completed with a couple of functions.

Here, we will again cover only the core functionality; the full source code for the Inverse Kinematics solver containing the CCD and the FABRIK algorithms is available in the `chapter13` folder, in the `02_opengl_fabrik` subfolder for the OpenGL renderer and the `04_vulkan_fabrik` subfolder for the Vulkan renderer.

Now, let us add the FABRIK solving algorithm to the `IKSolver` class.

Adding the methods for the FABRIK algorithm

First, we have to add new methods and member variables to the `IKSolver.h` file in the `model` folder. We will start with the `public` method, `solveFABRIK()`, which will be called to solve the Inverse Kinematics for the stored nodes:

```
bool solveFABRIK(glm::vec3 target);
```

The three-dimensional position given as the `target` parameter is the destination that we will try to reach with the effector node.

As the FABRIK algorithm consists of a forward and a backward step, we will add the two `private` methods, `solveFABRIKForward()` and `solveFABRIKBackward()`, to encapsulate the logic for the two separate parts of the algorithm. We can keep these two methods in the private part of the class; there is no need to call them from outside the class:

```
void solveFABRIKForward(glm::vec3 target);
void solveFABRIKBackward(glm::vec3 base);
```

While the forward solving method takes the three-dimensional location of the target that should be reached as the `target` parameter, the backward method will be given the three-dimensional `base` parameter with the location of the Inverse Kinematics root node.

Two specialties of the FABRIK algorithm require us to add more helper methods and member variables. As shown in *Figure 13.6* (**3**), we need the length of the bones to scale each one back to its original length after we moved the start point around. To achieve this, the `calculateBoneLengths()` method will be used, and the lengths of the nodes will be stored in the `mBoneLengths` vector:

```
void calculateBoneLengths();
std::vector<float> mBoneLengths{};
```

Also, we need to store the original global positions of the nodes to avoid destroying that information during the iterations. We will copy the global positions to a vector named `mFABRIKNodePositions`, and the `adjustFABRIKNodes()` method will be used to adjust the global position of the nodes after the algorithm is finished:

```
void adjustFABRIKNodes();
std::vector<glm::vec3> mFABRIKNodePositions{};
```

The next step to add the FABIRK algorithm is the implementation of the methods from the header file.

Implementing the FABRIK solving methods

We start with the first helper method, `calculateBoneLengths()`. Add the following code to the `IKSolver.cpp` file in the `model` folder:

```
void IKSolver::calculateBoneLengths() {
  mBoneLengths.resize(mNodes.size() - 1);
```

For the first operation, we will resize the `mBoneLengths` vector to store the bone lengths as the number of the saved nodes in `mNodes`, minus one. We can subtract one from the number of nodes, as every bone uses two nodes.

Then, we simply iterate on the saved nodes and store the differences between the starting and ending nodes in the `mBoneLengths` vector:

```
  for (int i = 0; i < mNodes.size() - 1; ++i) {
    std::shared_ptr<GltfNode> startNode = mNodes.at(i);
    std::shared_ptr<GltfNode> endNode = mNodes.at(i + 1);
    glm::vec3 startNodePos = startNode->getGlobalPosition();
    glm::vec3 endNodePos = endNode->getGlobalPosition();
    mBoneLengths.at(i) = glm::length(endNodePos - startNodePos);
  }
}
```

The initialization of the bone lengths is added at the end of the `setNodes()` method:

```
void IKSolver::setNodes(
    std::vector<std::shared_ptr<GltfNode>> nodes) {
    ...
    node->getNodeName().c_str());
    }
  }
  calculateBoneLengths();
  mFABRIKNodePositions.resize(mNodes.size());
}
```

Here, we will also resize the `mFABRIKNodePositions` vector, which will contain a copy of the original positions of the nodes.

Now, the implementation for the forward solving iteration step of FABRIK follows:

```
void IKSolver::solveFABRIKForward(glm::vec3 target) {
  mFABRIKNodePositions.at(0) = target;
  for (size_t i = 1; i < mFABRIKNodePositions.size(); ++i) {
    glm::vec3 boneDirection = glm::normalize(
      mFABRIKNodePositions.at(i) -
```

```
      mFABRIKNodePositions.at(i - 1));
    glm::vec3 offset = boneDirection * mBoneLengths.at(i - 1);
    mFABRIKNodePositions.at(i) = mFABRIKNodePositions.at(i - 1) +
      offset
  }
}
```

The `solveFABRIKForward()` method does the work shown in *Figure 13.6* (**3**), plus the other scaling steps. For every bone, we calculate its direction as a normalized three-dimensional `boneDirection` vector, scale it to its original length (named `offset`), and move the endpoint of the bone to the desired position in the correct direction and length from the start point.

Similarly, a backward iteration is done in the `solveFABRIKBackward()` method:

```
void IKSolver::solveFABRIKBackward(glm::vec3 base) {
  mFABRIKNodePositions.at( mFABRIKNodePositions.size() - 1) = base;
  for (int i = mFABRIKNodePositions.size() - 2; i>=0; --i) {
    glm::vec3 boneDirection = glm::normalize(
      mFABRIKNodePositions.at(i) -
      mFABRIKNodePositions.at(i + 1));
    glm::vec3 offset = boneDirection * mBoneLengths.at(i);
    mFABRIKNodePositions.at(i) = mFABRIKNodePositions.at(i + 1) +
      offset;
  }
}
```

This time, we walk the node positions backward, from the root node to the effector node, and adjust the start points of the bones back into the correct directions and lengths from the endpoints.

A bit more explanation is required for the adjustment of the nodes after the forward and backward steps are done. Most of the code for the `adjustFABRIKNodes()` method is similar to that for the CCD solving:

```
void IKSolver::adjustFABRIKNodes() {
  for (size_t i=mFABRIKNodePositions.size()-1; i>0; --i) {
    std::shared_ptr<GltfNode> node = mNodes.at(i);
    std::shared_ptr<GltfNode> nextNode = mNodes.at(i - 1);
    glm::vec3 position = node->getGlobalPosition();
    glm::quat rotation = node->getGlobalRotation();
    glm::vec3 nextPosition = nextNode->getGlobalPosition();
```

We will walk the node chain backward again, from the root node to the effector node. First, we will get the global position and rotation of the original nodes for the start and end node of every bone, plus the global position of the next node in the three-dimensional `nextPosition` vector.

Then, we will calculate the direction of the next original node from the current original node position, saving this direction in the `toNext` variable. We will also determine the direction of the next altered node in the copied vector. This is done relative to the current position of the altered node, and the result is saved in the `toDesired` variable. The altered node is located at the same position in the copied `mFABRIKNodePosition` vector as the original `mNodes` vector:

```
      glm::vec3 toNext = glm::normalize(nextPosition - position);
      glm::vec3 toDesired = glm::normalize(
        mFABRIKNodePositions.at(i - 1) - mFABRIKNodePositions.at(i));
```

Now, we have two vectors – one for the current orientation of the original bone, and one for the orientation of the same bone after the FABRIK solver has changed the copied positions of the nodes.

For every bone, we perform the same steps as the CCD solver. We calculate the global rotation and then the local rotation, which are required for the original bone to match the orientation of the copy, and adjust the current local rotation by concatenating the two quaternions:

```
      glm::quat nodeRotation = glm::rotation(toNext, toDesired);
      glm::quat worldRotation = rotation * nodeRotation *
        glm::conjugate(rotation);
      glm::quat currentRotation = node->getLocalRotation();
      node->blendRotation(currentRotation * localRotation,
        1.0f);
```

Finally, we will propagate the `node` property changes down the chain:

```
      node->updateNodeAndChildMatrices();
    }
  }
```

You might wonder why we adjust the bone by rotating the node instead of altering its translation.

The reason for this kind of adjustment is the vertex skinning. With a translation, the bone itself would be in the correct location after the Inverse Kinematics had been solved, but the matrices to calculate the weighted joint matrices or weighted dual quaternions in the vertex skinning process would have the old rotation values. As a result, the skin of the model would be badly distorted, as the matrices would not follow the bone direction correctly.

To finish the FABRIK algorithm, we must combine the methods.

Completing the FABRIK solver

The `solveFABRIK()` method starts with the same check as the `solveCCD()` method, and we will test whether we have any nodes in the `mNodes` vector:

```
bool IKSolver::solveFABRIK(glm::vec3 target) {
  if (!mNodes.size()) {
```

```
    return false;
  }
```

Then, we will copy the global node locations to the `mFABRIKNodePositions` vector:

```
  for (size_t i = 0; i < mNodes.size(); ++i) {
    std::shared_ptr<GltfNode> node = mNodes.at(i);
    mFABRIKNodePositions.at(i) = node->getGlobalPosition();
  }
```

Then, we will save the global location of the chain root node in the three-dimensional vector named `base`:

```
  glm::vec3 base =
    getIkChainRootNode()->getGlobalPosition();
```

We must store the original value too because we will alter the position of the chain root node during the forward solving steps.

Now, we will perform a `for` loop for a maximum number of `mIteration` times:

```
  for (unsigned int i = 0; i < mIterations; ++i) {
```

Again, it is possible that the real number of iterations done is smaller than the value of `mIterations` if the effector is close enough to the target. We will test for this condition right at the start of every iteration, calculating the distance between the effector node in the copied `mFABRIKNodePositions` vector and the target:

```
    glm::vec3 effector = mFABRIKNodePositions.at(0);
    if (glm::length(target - effector) < mThreshold) {
      adjustFABRIKNodes();
      return true;
    }
```

If the distance is smaller than the `mThreshold` value, we must adjust the original node positions by calling `adjustFABRIKNodes()` before we return from the method. The FABRIK algorithm works on the copy, and not changing the original nodes at the end would discard the calculations.

Then, the forward step toward the desired `target` position and the backward step towards the `base` position, which is the previously saved position of the chain root node, are executed for every iteration:

```
    solveFABRIKForward(target);
    solveFABRIKBackward(base);
  }
```

If the target is still too far away from the effector after all the FABRIK iterations have been applied, we still must adjust the original nodes with the copied values to make the result of the calculations available:

```
  adjustFABRIKNodes();
```

The last check is only for convenience. We will return `true` if the effector position is close to the target position after the last node adjustment, signaling that the algorithm was successful:

```
glm::vec3 effector = mNodes.at(0)->getGlobalPosition();
if (glm::length(target - effector) < mThreshold) {
  return true;
}
return false;
```

If the effector was unable to reach the target, we simply return `false`.

To activate the FABRIK algorithm as an alternative way to solve the application's Inverse Kinematics, we must adjust the renderer and user interface. Let us start with the renderer.

Updating the renderer

The first change must be made to the `ikMode` enum in the `OGLRenderData.h` file in the `opengl` folder. We will simply append the new `fabrik` mode to `enum`. Do not forget to also add a comma after `ccd`; otherwise, the compiling will fail.

Then, the selection of the solver algorithm needs to be added in the `draw()` method of the file `OGLRenderer.cpp` in the `opengl` folder:

```
if (mRenderData.rdIkMode != ikMode::off) {
  mIKTimer.start();
```

Instead of just checking explicitly for the CCD solving, we will test whether any of the two algorithms is selected, and whether the current Inverse Kinematics mode is not set to `off`.

Then, we will use `switch/case` to select the corresponding algorithm:

```
  switch (mRenderData.rdIkMode) {
    case ikMode::ccd:
      mGltfModel->solveIKByCCD(mRenderData.rdIkTargetPos);
      break;
    case ikMode::fabrik:
      mGltfModel->solveIKByFABRIK(mRenderData.rdIkTargetPos);
      break;
    default:
      break;
  }
```

At the end of `switch`, we stop the timer and update the timing value:

```
  mRenderData.rdIKTime = mIKTimer.stop();
}
```

In addition, we also must adjust the drawing of the coordinate arrows and the upload of the line mesh, by adding the new `fabrik` mode to the checks for the currently enabled Inverse Kinematics mode in the `rdIkMode` variable.

To be able to adjust the value of the `rdIkMode` variable in the `mRenderData struct`, we will also have to adjust the `UserInterface` class.

Allowing the selection of FABRIK in the user interface

Extending the user interface to allow us to select FABRIK next to CCD is done with only two changes to the `UserInterface.cpp` file in the `opengl` folder:

First, we must add a third radio button with FABRIK to the *glTF Inverse Kinematic* selection. Also, we will have to activate the subsection with the controls if `rdIkMode` is set to `fabrik`, in addition to `ccd`.

Compiling the example code and switching to FABRIK in the **glTF Inverse Kinematic** part of the ImGui interface will show a screen like the one shown in *Figure 13.10*:

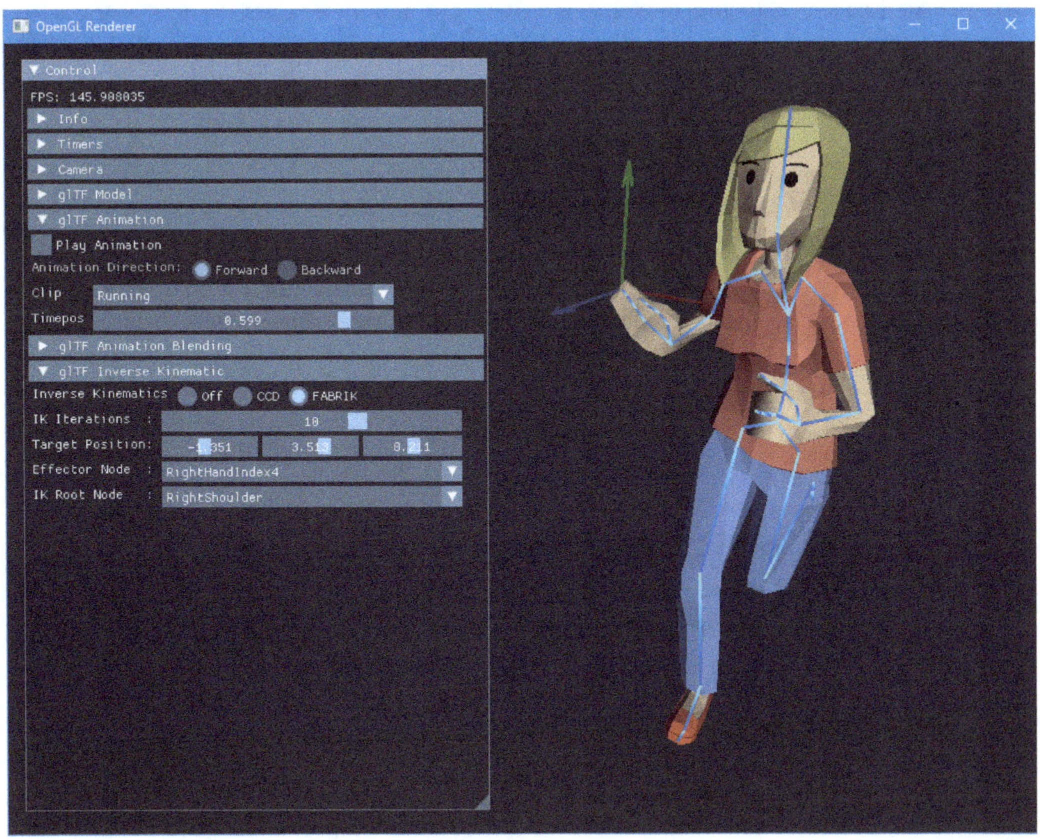

Figure 13.10: The hand of the glTF model reaching the target using FABRIK

Using the UI controls, you are again able to adjust the number of iterations used to solve the Inverse Kinematics via FABRIK. Also, like with the CCD solver, you can move the target around and control the start and end of the skeleton part that will be affected by the Inverse Kinematics.

Note that the hand reaches the target after fewer iterations than the CCD solver. Plus, the bones are not twisted as they were with CCD. The nodes are straight because the nodes were moved in FABRIK, instead of rotating at every step in the CCD algorithm.

Summary

In this chapter, we added Inverse Kinematics with the two algorithms, CCD and FABRIK. Both algorithms solve the problem of the so-called effector node reaching a target point in a heuristic manner, by rotating (CCD) or moving (FABRIK) the bones closer to the target.

After a general explanation of what Inverse Kinematics is about, we checked the basic function of the CCD algorithm.

Then, we created a solver class that implemented CCD. The new solver class required changes to the user interface to enable control of parameters, such as the number of iterations for the Inverse Kinematics algorithm, the position of the target, or the part of the skeleton that will be changed by the Inverse Kinematics solver.

Finally, we added the FABRIK algorithm to the solver class and extended the user interface, enabling us to switch the Inverse Kinematics solving between CCD and FABRIK.

In the following chapter, we will increase the number of glTF models on the screen. While we will render only a single model in this chapter, adding more models brings more life to the virtual world. Every model instance can be controlled individually, enabling us to see many animations simultaneously.

Practical sessions

You can try out these ideas to get a better understanding of Inverse Kinematics:

- Create a new text field in the `UserInterface` class to signal whether the Inverse Kinematics algorithm was successful. We previously created the two solving algorithms to return `true` if the target was reached, or `false` if reaching the target failed.
- **Advanced difficulty**: The two algorithms CCD and FABRIK can be extended by so-called constraints. This means you limit the amount of rotation for every node to mimic the behavior of a natural joint, such as the knee or the shoulder. Try to add some of those limits to the nodes, such as a minimum and a maximum angle for one or more of the rotational angles, and check how many iterations a constrained algorithm needs until the target reaches the effector, compared to the original algorithm.

- **Advanced difficulty**: Add the textured crate back to the screen, and implement a simple collision detection between the sides of the crate and the bones of the model. Then, change the node that would be inside the crate to be located at the intersection between the bone and the crate side, and activate Inverse Kinematics up to the shoulder or leg nodes. Ultimately, the model should, for example, be able to walk or run on a side of the crate, and the legs should be adjusted to always be visible instead of entering the crate.

Additional resources

- An introduction to `std::weak_ptr`: `https://en.cppreference.com/w/cpp/memory/weak_ptr`
- An introduction to the Jacobian matrix: `https://medium.com/unity3danimation/overview-of-jacobian-ik-a33939639ab2`
- A CCD original paper: `https://core.ac.uk/download/pdf/82473611.pdf`
- CCD with constraints: `https://diglib.eg.org/handle/10.2312/egt.20071063.173-243`
- A FABRIK original paper: `https://dl.acm.org/doi/10.1016/j.gmod.2011.05.003`
- FABRIK with constraints: `http://andreasaristidou.com/publications/papers/Extending_FABRIK_with_Model_C%CE%BFnstraints.pdf`
- The Möller–Trumbore algorithm for intersection checks: `http://www.lighthouse3d.com/tutorials/maths/ray-triangle-intersection/`

14
Creating Instanced Crowds

Welcome to *Chapter 14*! In the previous chapter, we explored the tech side of inverse kinematics. Using inverse kinematics, constrained movement of models can be made more natural-looking, such as climbing stairs or holding artifacts in their hands.

In this chapter, we will add more virtual people to our virtual world. We'll start with a brief overview of the right way to add multiple instances of the glTF model, as naive duplication raises a lot of problems.

Next, we'll split the model class into two parts, one for the shared part of the model data and the other one for the individual data of every instance on the screen. Moving the instance data to a separate class allows full control of every single model instance we draw on the screen.

Then, we'll extend the code to allow more than one model type and look at a GPU feature to let the graphics card do even more work while drawing instances. At the end of the chapter, we'll explore an alternative way to transfer instance data to the GPU and introduce **texture buffer obejcts** (**TBOs**).

In this chapter, we will cover the following topics:

- Splitting the model class into two parts
- Rendering instances of different models
- Using GPU instancing to reduce data transfers
- Textures are not just for pictures

Technical requirements

To follow along with this chapter, you will need the OpenGL and Vulkan renderer code from *Chapter 12*, plus the parent node changes in the `GltfNode` class in *Chapter 13*.

Splitting the model class into two parts

Right now, the code is made to show only a single glTF model. The options to show the model or the skeleton, the drawing settings, and the animation properties were created to support one and only one model on the screen. To render multiple models, we must adjust the application code.

In a naive solution, we would simply loop over a vector of glTF models and do all the preparation and drawing steps for every model. This way of drawing models works, but the loading and data extraction phases will take a lot of time and waste space in the main memory, as we need to add vertex data and animation clips to every single model.

To achieve proper instancing, we will split the model class into two separate classes. The original `GltfModel` class will keep the shared data for all instances, and a new `GltfInstance` class will maintain the variable per-instance data.

The full code for this section is available in the `chapter14` folder, in the `01_opengl_instances` subfolder for OpenGL and the `05_vulkan_instances` subfolder for Vulkan.

Before we start the split, we will get a quick overview of which kinds of variables could be kept in the model class, and what data needs to be moved to the new instance class.

Deciding which data to keep in the model class

The main responsibilities of the `GltfModel` class are to load the glTF file and the texture and to extract the various parts of the model data. All operations using the `tinygltf` loader should be kept in the `model` class so that the model instances do not need to know anything about the raw glTF model data.

These operations include the extraction of the vertex data and the animations as well as the joint and weight data or the inverse bind matrices. In addition, the low-level node operations to create the node tree and the node list will remain in the model class.

Collecting the data to move

On the other hand, all instances must maintain their own set of nodes, organized in a node tree. Different node properties are changed during the animations, and sharing this information between different instances is usually not what we want. Other instance properties, such as the animation replay speed or the blending mode, also need to be maintained on a per-instance basis.

Another property that needs to be set for every instance is the position in the virtual world and rotation around the *y* axis. Without a distinct world position, all model instances would spawn at the origin, and we would make only a *big ball of triangles*. Distributing the model instances across a small area will create a larger group of people standing, walking, or jumping around. The additional rotation is used to make the crowd of model instances appear more natural.

At the end of this section, all instances should be fully independent, but still individually configurable. To avoid adding dozens of getter and setter methods, we will use a new C-style struct called `ModelSettings` to store all the instance properties that can be controlled from the outside.

Adding a new ModelSettings struct to store the instance data

Add the following lines to the new `ModelSettings.h` file in the `model` folder:

```
#pragma once
struct ModelSettings {
  glm::vec2 msWorldPosition = glm::vec2(0.0f);
  glm::vec3 msWorldRotation = glm::vec3(0.0f);
```

As the instances should be at different locations in the virtual world, we must add a world location to the instance variables. We store only two dimensions in the `msWorldPosition` variable here: the *x* and *z* positions of the instance. The *y* position for the instance will be ignored here; an update of the variable to a three-dimensional vector could include the *y* position too.

Next, we'll add a three-dimensional `msWorldRotation` vector for the global rotation of the instance. We will use only the rotation about the *y* axis for now. A rotation around the *y* axis looks natural, while any rotation around the *x* and *z* axes tilts the model in a strange-looking fashion:

```
  bool msDrawModel = true;
  bool msDrawSkeleton = false;
  skinningMode msVertexSkinningMode = skinningMode::linear;
```

To enable the rendering of the model for any instance, the `msDrawModel` Boolean is used. The rendering of the optional model skeleton can be switched on and off by changing the `msDrawSkeleton` Boolean. We also want to be able to control the vertex skinning mode for every instance, so we need the `msVertexSkinningMode` variable to store the currently active type of vertex skinning.

The basic settings for the model animations follow:

```
  bool msPlayAnimation = true;
  replayDirection msAnimationPlayDirection = replayDirection::forward;
  int msAnimClip = 0;
  float msAnimSpeed = 1.0f;
  float msAnimTimePosition = 0.0f;
  float msAnimEndTime = 0.0f;
```

The variables in the preceding code have the same meaning as in the `OGLRenderData` struct.

We store the state of the animation replay per instance in the `msPlayAnimation` Boolean and the replay direction in the `msAnimationPlayDirection` enum. The current animation clip number is saved in the `msAnimClip` variable, and the replay speed will be controlled by the `msAnimSpeed` variable. The variable named `msAnimTimePosition` stores the time of the frame in the current animation clip to render if the animation is not played (`msPlayAnimation` is set to `false`). Finally, the end time of the animation clip is saved in the `msAnimEndTime` variable.

The settings for the different blending modes are also stored in the new struct:

```
blendMode msBlendingMode = blendMode::fadeinout;
float msAnimBlendFactor = 1.0f;
int msCrossBlendDestAnimClip = 0;
float msAnimCrossBlendFactor = 0.0f;
int msSkelSplitNode = 0;
```

First, we save the current blending mode (fade in/out, crossfading, and additive blending) in the `msBlendingMode` variable. If the fade in/out blending is selected, `msAnimBlendFactor` stores the blending factor between `0` and `1` for the current animation clip. For the cross-fading blending mode, we save the destination clip in `msCrossBlendDestAnimClip` and the blending factor between the two clips in the `msAnimCrossBlendFactor` variable. Finally, for the additive blending, the selected skeleton split node is saved in `msSkelSplitNode`:

```
  ikMode msIkMode = ikMode::off;
  int msIkIterations = 10;
  glm::vec3 msIkTargetPos = glm::vec3(0.0f, 3.0f, 1.0f);
  int msIkEffectorNode = 0;
  int msIkRootNode = 0;

glm::vec3 msIkTargetWorldPos = glm::vec3(0.0f, 0.0f,01.0f);
```

The variables for the inverse kinematics added in *Chapter 13* must be moved to the new `ModelSettings.h` header too. Plus, we added the new `msIkTargetWorldPos` variable to store the world coordinates of the inverse kinematics target, in addition to the position relative to the local model origin.

Two notable exceptions to the rule about storing only instance-related variables apply to the last two `msClipNames` and `msSkelNodeNames` vectors:

```
  std::vector<std::string> msClipNames{};
  std::vector<std::string> msSkelNodeNames{};
};
```

Storing the animation clip names in the `msClipNames` instance variable may seem a bit odd as the animations are on the model level not the instance level. However, we are sending the settings for the current instance to the user interface, and not the model data. So, saving the clip names in the instance simplifies the transfer to the user interface.

The strings for the `msSkelNodeNames` vector are used in the skeleton combo box and are generated from the skeleton nodes. As every instance has its own set of nodes, the data for the combo box will be available only in the instance class.

We could store the skeleton names in the model class, but this would result in additional complexity, either by creating a set of unused nodes in the model class or by ensuring only the first created instance writes the data to the model class. Both variants would bring no benefit compared to storing the strings in the instance.

After the new instance variables have been created in the ModelSettings struct, the old global counterparts from the OGLRenderData struct can be deleted.

Adjusting the OGLRenderData struct

Remove the following variables from the OGLRenderData struct in the OGLRenderData.h file in the opengl folder:

```
rdDrawGltfModel, rdDrawSkeleton, rdGPUDualQuatVertexSkinning,
rdPlayAnimation, rdClipNames, rdAnimClip, rdAnimClipSize,
rdAnimSpeed, rdAnimTimePosition,  rdAnimEndTime, rdModelNodeCount,
rdAnimationPlayDirection, rdAnimBlendFactor, rdBlendingMode,
rdCrossBlendDestAnimClip, rdAnimCrossBlendFactor, rdSkelSplitNode,
rdSkelNodeNames, rdIkMode, rdIkIterations, rdIkTargetPos,
rdIkEffectorNode, rdIkRootNode
```

All variables in the preceding code will be replaced by instance-level variables in the new ModelSetting struct.

To keep track of the overall number of instances and the currently selected instance, add the following two new variables at the end of the OGLRenderData struct:

```
  int rdNumberOfInstances = 0;
  int rdCurrentSelectedInstance = 0;
```

Now, we are ready to split the GltfModel class. First, we create the new GltfInstance class, and after that, we clean up and adjust the GltfModel class.

Cutting the model class into two pieces

We'll start by creating a new file called GltfInstance.h in the model folder. The full source code is available in the GitHub repository; we'll focus only on the important parts here.

The class begins with the public area and the constructor:

```
class GltfInstance {
  public:
    GltfInstance(std::shared_ptr<GltfModel> model,
      glm::vec2 worldPos, bool randomize = false);
```

The class constructor takes a shared pointer to the underlying model to access the model-level methods. As the second parameter, the *x* and *z* world coordinates for the instances must be set. The last parameter, `randomize`, can be set to fill the rotation of the model, the animation clip, and the animation speed with random values.

A substantial portion of the `public` methods can be taken directly from the `GltfModel` class into the new `GltfInstance` class:

```
void resetNodeData();
std::shared_ptr<OGLMesh> getSkeleton();
void setSkeletonSplitNode(int nodeNum);
int getJointMatrixSize();
int getJointDualQuatsSize();
std::vector<glm::mat4> getJointMatrices();
std::vector<glm::mat2x4> getJointDualQuats();
```

All methods in the preceding code will be reused in the new instance class, having the internal variables moved from the `OGLRenderData` struct to the new `ModelSettings` struct.

The animation part of the glTF model has been moved entirely from the `OGLRenderer` class to the `GltfInstance` class. We need only a generic method to let the instance update the internal animation states:

```
void updateAnimation();
```

Reading the current settings from the instance and saving any changes back to the instance can be achieved by the following two new methods:

```
void setInstanceSettings(ModelSettings settings);
ModelSettings getInstanceSettings();
```

We will load and save all individual settings at once, even if we change only a single setting.

To update the main properties, which may require more computational work (world position, world rotation, blending mode, and split node), a separate update method has been created. The content has been taken from the `draw()` method of the `OGLRenderer` class:

```
void checkForUpdates();
```

Calling `checkForUpdates()` after each setting save is not needed; the checks in this method need to run only once, at the end of the frame.

As the last two `public` methods, we add getters for the world position and rotation:

```
glm::vec2 getWorldPosition();
glm::quat getWorldRotation();
```

It is possible to extract both values from the `ModelSettings` struct. But having separate methods is handy for rendering coordinate arrows at the bottom of the model to show that the given model is currently selected.

The following `private` methods are also taken from the `GltfModel` class:

```
private:
  void playAnimation(int animNum,...);
  void playAnimation(int sourceAnimNum, int dest,...);
  void blendAnimationFrame(...);
  void crossBlendAnimationFrame(...);
  float getAnimationEndTime(int animNum);
```

The first batch of moved methods in the preceding code is responsible for the animations. We encapsulate the animation part in the instance class now. The second batch of moved methods in the following code is also known from the `GltfModel` class:

```
  void getSkeletonPerNode(...);
  void updateNodeMatrices(...);
  void updateJointMatrices(...);
  void updateJointDualQuats(...);
  void updateAdditiveMask(...);
  void setInverseKinematicsNodes(...);
  void setNumIKIterations(...);
```

For better separation of the update for the joint matrices and dual quaternions, the `updateJointMatricesAndQuats()` method from the `GltfModel` class has been split into two. And all methods have been adjusted to use the new `ModelSettings`-based variables. The opposite change was done for two inverse kinematics methods, `solveIKByCCD()` and `solveIKByFABRIK()`. Both methods were combined into the single `solveIK()` method of the `GltfInstance` class, selecting the correct solver by using the `msIkMode` member variable.

Most of the `private` data members in the following code are also known from the `GltfModel` class:

```
  std::shared_ptr<GltfNode> mRootNode = nullptr;
  std::vector<std::shared_ptr<GltfNode>> mNodeList{};
  std::vector<glm::mat4> mJointMatrices{};
  std::vector<glm::mat2x4> mJointDualQuats{};
  std::vector<bool> mAdditiveAnimationMask{};
  std::vector<bool> mInvertedAdditiveAnimationMask{};
  std::shared_ptr<OGLMesh> mSkeletonMesh = nullptr;
```

We also need a member variable for the parent glTF model we use:

```
  std::shared_ptr<GltfModel> mGltfModel = nullptr;
```

Some of the member variables are only for convenience:

```
    std::vector<std::shared_ptr<GltfAnimationClip>> mAnimClips{};
    std::vector<glm::mat4> mInverseBindMatrices{};
    std::vector<int> mNodeToJoint{};
```

By accessing the animation clips vector, translation from nodes to joints or inverse bind matrices from the model class is possible during the respective method calls. Using internal variables saves on the code that needs to be written and some method calls to the model class.

Similarly, the node count from the model class is saved locally for convenience:

```
    unsigned int mNodeCount = 0;
```

Finally, the header file ends with the variable for the instance-specific setting:

```
    ModelSettings mModelSettings{};
};
```

The implementation of most of the methods in the `GltfInstance.cpp` file in the `model` folder is like that of the original methods taken from the `GltfModel` class, so we will skip most of the walk-through here. You can find the complete source code in the example folders in the GitHub repository. We will explore only the constructor here, and even the `GltfInstance` constructor is partially identical to the original `GltfModel` constructor.

Implementing the logic in the new instance class

To create a new instance of a model, the custom constructor is used:

```
GltfInstance::GltfInstance(std::shared_ptr<GltfModel> model,
    glm::vec2 worldPos, bool randomize) {
  if (!model) {
    Logger::log(1, "%s error: invalid glTF model\n",
      __FUNCTION__);
    return;
  }
```

First, we check for a valid model. We need the nodes and the animation clip data from the `GltfModel` object, so it is useless to continue if no valid smart pointer to such an object has been given as a parameter. Next, we save the model pointer and update the global position of the new instance:

```
  mGltfModel = model;
  mModelSettings.msWorldPosition = worldPos;
```

Now, the convenience functions follow:

```
mNodeCount = mGltfModel->getNodeCount();
mInverseBindMatrices = mGltfModel->getInverseBindMatrices();
mNodeToJoint = mGltfModel->getNodeToJoint();
```

We grab the node count, the inverse bind matrices, and the node-to-joint mapping from the model itself.

Having the values available, we can resize some of the internal vectors:

```
mJointMatrices.resize(mInverseBindMatrices.size());
mJointDualQuats.resize(mInverseBindMatrices.size());
mAdditiveAnimationMask.resize(mNodeCount);
mInvertedAdditiveAnimationMask.resize(mNodeCount);
```

Here, the vectors for the joint matrices, the dual quaternions, and the masks for the additive animation blending are set to the correct size. Plus, we fill the additive animation mask and the inverted mask:

```
std::fill(mAdditiveAnimationMask.begin(),
  mAdditiveAnimationMask.end(), true);
mInvertedAdditiveAnimationMask = mAdditiveAnimationMask;
mInvertedAdditiveAnimationMask.flip();
```

Now, it is time to create the skeleton node tree and the node list:

```
GltfNodeData nodeData;
nodeData = mGltfModel->getGltfNodes();
mRootNode = nodeData.rootNode;
mRootNode->setWorldPosition(glm::vec3(mModelSettings.
  msWorldPosition.x, 0.0f, mModelSettings.msWorldPosition.y));
mRootNode->setWorldRotation(mModelSettings.msWorldRotation);
mNodeList = nodeData.nodeList;
updateNodeMatrices(mRootNode);
```

We let the `GltfModel` class create the node tree and node list for us, as this requires access to the `tinygltf` model. We also set the world position and rotation on the root node. All other nodes have only relative location and translation changes with respect to the root node, so we do an update of all nodes here, starting from the root node.

In the following code, the skeleton split node is set to the last node, and the vector containing the skeleton names is filled:

```
mModelSettings.msSkelSplitNode = mNodeCount - 1;
for (const auto &node : mNodeList) {
  if (node) {
    mModelSettings.msSkelSplitNodeNames.
      push_back(node->getNodeName());
```

```
    } else {
      mModelSettings.msSkelSplitNodeNames.push_back("(invalid)");
    }
  }
```

The same procedure is followed for the animations:

```
  mAnimClips = mGltfModel->getAnimClips();
  for (const auto &clip : mAnimClips) {
    mModelSettings.msClipNames.push_back(
      clip->getClipName());
  }
```

We grab all the animation clips from the `GltfModel` class and generate the vector for the animation clip names.

If the `randomize` parameter was set to `true`, we create random values for the animation clip played and the replay speed, plus the world rotation of the instance:

```
  unsigned int animClipSize = mAnimClips.size();
  if (randomize) {
    int animClip = std::rand() % animClipSize;
    float animClipSpeed = (std::rand() % 100) / 100.0f + 0.5f;
    float initRotation = std::rand() % 360 - 180;
    mModelSettings.msAnimClip = animClip;
    mModelSettings.msAnimSpeed = animClipSpeed;
    mModelSettings.msWorldRotation = glm::vec3(0.0f, initRotation,
      0.0f);
  }
```

Near the end, we run the `checkForUpdates()` method once to initialize the method-local variables containing the current state of the blending mode, the skeleton split, and the world position and rotation:

```
  checkForUpdates();
```

We also initialize the line mesh for the model skeleton and resize the vertices vector to be able to store two vertices for every bone of the skeleton:

```
  mSkeletonMesh = std::make_shared<OGLMesh>();
  mSkeletonMesh->vertices.resize(mNodeCount * 2);
```

Finally, the inverse kinematic solver class must be initialized with some default values. We use the nodes for the right arm here as default values to make the activation of the inverse kinematics solver easier:

```
  mModelSettings.msIkEffectorNode = 19;
  mModelSettings.msIkRootNode = 26;
```

```
setInverseKinematicsNodes(
   mModelSettings.msIkEffectorNode, mModelSettings.msIkRootNode);
setNumIKIterations(mModelSettings.msIkIterations);
```

As the last change, we add the following:

```
mModelSettings.msIkTargetWorldPos = getWorldRotation() *
  mModelSettings.msIkTargetPos +
  glm::vec3(worldPos.x, 0.0f, worldPos.y);
```

We have created new instances in the renderer. But we need adjustments not only to the renderer code itself but also to the shaders, both on the C++ side and in the GLSL code.

Enhancing the shader code

To be able to set the index of the current model skeleton joint inside the uniform buffer containing the joint matrices respective the dual quaternions, we must add a uniform variable inside the vertex shader and extend the `Shader` class with code to retrieve the location of this uniform variable.

Add these two `public` methods to the `Shader.h` file in the `opengl` folder:

```
    bool getUniformLocation(std::string uniformName);
    void setUniformValue(int value);
```

By calling the `getUniformLocation()` method with the textual string of the uniform variable, the location inside the shader will be stored. Using the second method, `setUniformValue()`, the uniform variable in the shader will be updated with `value` given as a parameter.

In the GLSL shader code, we must add the uniform variable to the vertex shader and use this variable inside some calculations. Just declaring the variable would not work, as the GLSL compiler will remove unused variables.

Add the new uniform variable to both vertex shader files, `gltf_gpu.vert` and `gltf_gpu_dquat.vert`, in the `shader` folder, right above the `main()` method:

```
uniform int aModelStride;
```

For the joint matrix shader, `gltf_gpu.vert`, adjust the calculation of the `skinMat` matrix in the `main()` method and extend the index by adding the uniform variable:

```
aJointWeight.x*jointMat[int(aJointNum.x) + aModelStride] +
aJointWeight.y*jointMat[int(aJointNum.y) + aModelStride] +
aJointWeight.z*jointMat[int(aJointNum.z) + aModelStride] +
aJointWeight.w*jointMat[int(aJointNum.w) + aModelStride];
```

Now, in the dual quaternion shader, `gltf_gpu_dquat.vert`, update the creation of the dual quaternions in the `getJointTransform()` method, also by adding the uniform variable to the index:

```
mat2x4 dq0 = jointDQs[joints.x + aModelStride];
mat2x4 dq1 = jointDQs[joints.y + aModelStride];
mat2x4 dq2 = jointDQs[joints.z + aModelStride];
mat2x4 dq3 = jointDQs[joints.w + aModelStride];
```

Before we complete instance rendering, we need to update the renderer class code. We will have to create the instances, keep the animations running, and enable updates to the instance settings.

Preparing the renderer class

To enable the renderer to manage the instances, we have to add some member variables to the `OGLRenderer` class. Adjust the `OGLRenderer.h` file in the `opengl` folder to include the following new `private` data members:

```
std::vector<std::shared_ptr<GltfInstance>>
  mGltfInstances{};
```

First, we add a vector of shared pointers to `GltfInstance` objects. This vector will contain all the instances we create. In addition to the data member definition, we need to include the `GltfInstance.h` header too.

Next, we add two vectors for the global joint matrix and dual quaternion data:

```
std::vector<glm::mat4> mModelJointMatrices{};
std::vector<glm::mat2x4> mModelJointDualQuats{};
```

The vectors will collect the joint matrices and dual quaternions for all instances, and eventually, both vectors will be uploaded into the GPU shader buffer.

Now, we re-introduce the three colored coordinate arrows, where the *x* axis is shown by the red arrow, the *y* axis by the green arrow, and the *z* axis by the blue arrow:

```
CoordArrowsModel mCoordArrowsModel{};
OGLMesh mCoordArrowsMesh{};
std::shared_ptr<OGLMesh> mLineMesh = nullptr;
unsigned int mSkeletonLineIndexCount = 0;
unsigned int mCoordArrowsLineIndexCount = 0;
```

Next to the model and the mesh, we add a line mesh to collect all the lines to draw. This includes the coordinate arrows and the skeleton lines, and we simply count the number of lines both types of lines may have in the rendering process.

For the coordinate arrows, the header file, `CoordArrowsModel.h`, must be included. We also need to get the `CoordArrowsModel.h` and `CoordArrowsModel.cpp` files from the `chapter07` | `model` folder.

The following three `private` data members should be *removed* as they are unused now:

```
std::shared_ptr<OGLMesh> mSkeletonMesh = nullptr;
unsigned int mSkeletonLineIndexCount = 0;
bool mModelUploadRequired = true;
```

Now, the implementation of the renderer must be changed. We will show only a broad overview here. You can check the full source code in the GitHub repository.

Changing the renderer to create and manage instances

First, the `init()` method of the `OGLRenderer` class in the `OGLRenderer.cpp` file in the `opengl` folder needs to be extended.

To achieve true random model locations, we set the random seed here:

```
std::srand(static_cast<int>(time(NULL)));
```

The preceding line initializes the internal pseudo-random number generator with the value of the current time as the seed, ensuring different random values at every start of the application.

If we omit the initialization of the pseudo-random number generator, the calls to the `std::rand()` function will return the same values in the same order, for every start of the application. Getting the same succession of values as the result of the location randomization would place each of the model instances at the same location in the virtual world on subsequent application invocations. You can comment out or remove the `std::srand()` call to see the effect of the pseudo-randomization of the instance locations.

After the shaders have been loaded, the location of the uniform variable must be set:

```
if (!mGltfGPUShader.getUniformLocation("aModelStride")) {
  return false;
}
```

We stop the initialization of an error that occurs as a missing uniform variable will break the rendering process.

The model instances are created by a simple `for` loop on a random world position, and with the other properties also randomized by using the `std::rand()` function:

```
int numTriangles = 0;
for (int i = 0; i < 200; ++i) {
  int xPos = std::rand() % 40 - 20;
```

```
    int zPos = std::rand() % 40 - 20;
    mGltfInstances.emplace_back(
      std::make_shared<GltfInstance>(mGltfModel,
      glm::vec2(static_cast<float>(xPos),
      static_cast<float>(zPos)), true));
   numTriangles += mGltfModel->getTriangleCount();
  }
  mRenderData.rdTriangleCount = numTriangles;
  mRenderData.rdNumberOfInstances = mGltfInstances.size();
```

We also count the number of triangles here to have the initial amount available in the user interface, and we also count the number of instances we created.

Calculating the combined size of the buffers for the joint matrices and dual quaternions can be achieved by multiplying the number of instances and the size of a single matrix (the same calculation is done for the dual quaternion sizes):

```
  size_t modelJointMatrixBufferSize =
    mRenderData.rdNumberOfInstances *
    mGltfInstances.at(0)->getJointMatrixSize() * sizeof(glm::mat4);
```

In the `draw()` method of the `OGLRenderer` class, we replace the entire animation part with a call to the `updateAnimation()` method of the instance, followed by solving the inverse kinematics (if enabled):

```
  for (auto &instance : mGltfInstances) {
    instance->updateAnimation();
    mIKTimer.start();
    instance->solveIK();
    mRenderData.rdIKTime += mIKTimer.stop();
  }
```

The instance itself handles all animation updates and the inverse kinematics by itself, corresponding to the settings we make at creation time and later in the user interface.

Next, we save the currently selected instance to a local variable:

```
  int selectedInstance = mRenderData.rdCurrentSelectedInstance;
```

Saving the value is required to avoid changes in the middle of the rendering process if another instance is selected in the user interface.

Before we fill the vectors – `mModelJointMatrices`, containing the changed joint matrices, and `mModelJointDualQuats` for the changed dual quaternions – we must clear both vectors:

```
mModelJointMatrices.clear();
mModelJointDualQuats.clear();
unsigned int matrixInstances = 0;
unsigned int dualQuatInstances = 0;
unsigned int numTriangles = 0;
```

Next, we initialize the counter to sum up the number of instances using the joint matrices and quaternions, plus a counter for the overall number of triangles shown.

Now, we loop across all instances:

```
for (const auto &instance : mGltfInstances) {
  ModelSettings settings = instance->getInstanceSettings();
  if (!settings.msDrawModel) {
    continue;
  }
```

As the first step, we get the settings from the model instance. If the rendering of the model itself is disabled, we skip the remaining part of the loop.

Depending on the vertex skinning mode, the corresponding vector is updated, and the counter for that skinning mode type is raised by one:

```
  if (settings.msVertexSkinningMode == skinningMode::dualQuat) {
    std::vector<glm::mat2x4> quats = instance->getJointDualQuats();
    mModelJointDualQuats.insert(
      mModelJointDualQuats.end(),
      quats.begin(), quats.end());
    ++dualQuatInstances;
  } else {
    … // same updates for the matrix skinning mode
  }
  numTriangles += mGltfModel->getTriangleCount();
}
```

We also count the number of triangles during the loop, and update the global counter:

```
mRenderData.rdTriangleCount = numTriangles;
```

Once the vectors are filled, we upload the data to the GPU:

```
mGltfShaderStorageBuffer.uploadSsboData(
  mModelJointMatrices, 1);
mGltfDualQuatSSBuffer.uploadSsboData(
  mModelJointDualQuats, 2);
```

Everything is now prepared for drawing. First, we get the size of a single joint matrix vector and initialize the position with zero:

```
unsigned int jointMatrixSize =
  mGltfInstances.at(0)->getJointMatrixSize();
unsigned int matrixPos = 0;
```

In the following `for` loop, we set the uniform variable to the current matrix position and issue a `draw()` call on the model. At the end of the loop, we advance the position in the buffer:

```
mGltfGPUShader.use();
for (int i = 0; i < matrixInstances; ++i) {
  mGltfGPUShader.setUniformValue(matrixPos);
  mGltfModel->draw();
  matrixPos += jointMatrixSize;
}
```

The loop in the preceding code draws all models using joint matrices; the same principle applies to the models configured to use dual quaternions.

At the end of the `draw()` call, we get the settings of the currently selected instance and use these settings to show the values in the user interface:

```
ModelSettings settings = mGltfInstances.at(selectedInstance)->
  getInstanceSettings();
mUserInterface.createFrame(mRenderData, settings);
mGltfInstances.at(selectedInstance)-> setInstanceSettings(settings);
mGltfInstances.at(selectedInstance)->checkForUpdates();
```

In case the settings were changed in the user interface, we save them again after the user interface has been created.

As the last step for instance rendering, we force an update for possible changes to the rendering mode or skeleton settings made in the user interface. In between the preceding steps, the skeleton lines are also collected, the coordinate arrows are placed, and all the lines are drawn.

To show the data for instances in the user interface and to allow changes to the instance settings, we need to make some additions and changes to the `UserInterface` class.

Displaying the instance data in the user interface

The control elements in the user interface remain identical to the previous, non-instanced version of the code. Only the `createFrame()` method must be extended by the model settings as the additional parameter:

```
void createFrame(OGLRenderData &renderData,
  ModelSettings &settings);
```

Inside the `createFrame()` method, the references to the (now removed) `OGLRenderData` variables must be changed to the new `ModelSettings` variables, taken from the new `settings` parameter. Now, the values for the ImGui widgets are read from the currently selected instance.

Changing from one instance to another is done by a new widget section called **glTF Instances**, as shown in *Figure 14.1*. Also, the world position and world rotation of the currently selected instance can be changed here:

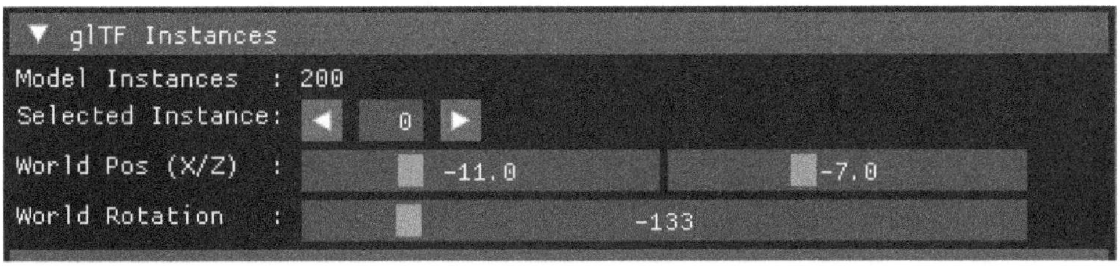

Figure 14.1: User interface changes for instance selection

The **Selected Instance** section uses arrow buttons to allow the easy selection of the next or the previous instance. The settings for the selected instance are read in by the renderer and sent to the user interface. A double-click into the instance number field jumps directly to the specific instance. For the world position and world rotation, sliders for `float` values are used.

What about Vulkan?

For the Vulkan renderer-based application code, all changes apply. Splitting the `GltfInstance` class from the `GltfModel` class is done in the same way, the `UserInterface` changes are the same, and also the adjustments inside the `VkRenderer` class are mostly identical.

Instead of a uniform variable for the matrix stride, we use a Vulkan push constant to adjust the position for the joint matrix/dual quaternion shader storage buffers. A push constant is perfect for this use case, as it does not need to be uploaded in a complex way. We can set this constant with a single Vulkan command, just like a uniform variable in an OpenGL shader. Push constants were explained in *Chapter 4*, in the *Using push constants in Vulkan* section.

If you compile and run the code now, you will get an embarrassing result. Even when you cut down the number of instances to something like 10 or 20, the matrix updates will take ages, resulting in *seconds per frame* instead of *frames per second*. We must tell the compilers to optimize the code, or else we'll be unable to continue in the chapter.

The need for application speed

In the default configuration, all compilers used for the book will generate a debug-ready binary. This means the binary will not be optimized. This is important to have a direct mapping of the source code and the instructions for the CPU. To get an optimized binary using GCC or Clang, add the following lines after the `project` definition in the `CMakeLists.txt` file in the project root:

```
if(CMAKE_CXX_COMPILER_ID MATCHES "GNU" OR
    CMAKE_CXX_COMPILER_ID MATCHES "Clang")
  set(CMAKE_CXX_FLAGS "-O3")
endif()
```

For Visual Studio, a new `Release` block must be added to the `CmakeSettings.json` file, also located in the project root:

```
    {
      "name": "x64-Release",
      "generator": "Visual Studio 17 2022 Win64",
      "configurationType": "RelWithDebInfo",
      "buildRoot": "${projectDir}\\out\\build\\${name}",
      "installRoot": "${projectDir}\\out\\install\\${name}",
      "cmakeCommandArgs": "",
      "buildCommandArgs": "",
      "ctestCommandArgs": "",
      "inheritEnvironments": [ "msvc_x64_x64" ],
      "variables": []
    }
```

Rebuilding the code using optimization and running the new executables eventually shows the desired result. Even low-end machines should be able to render about 200 model instances with a reasonable frame time, as shown in *Figure 14.2*. Whoa, what a crowded place we have created here:

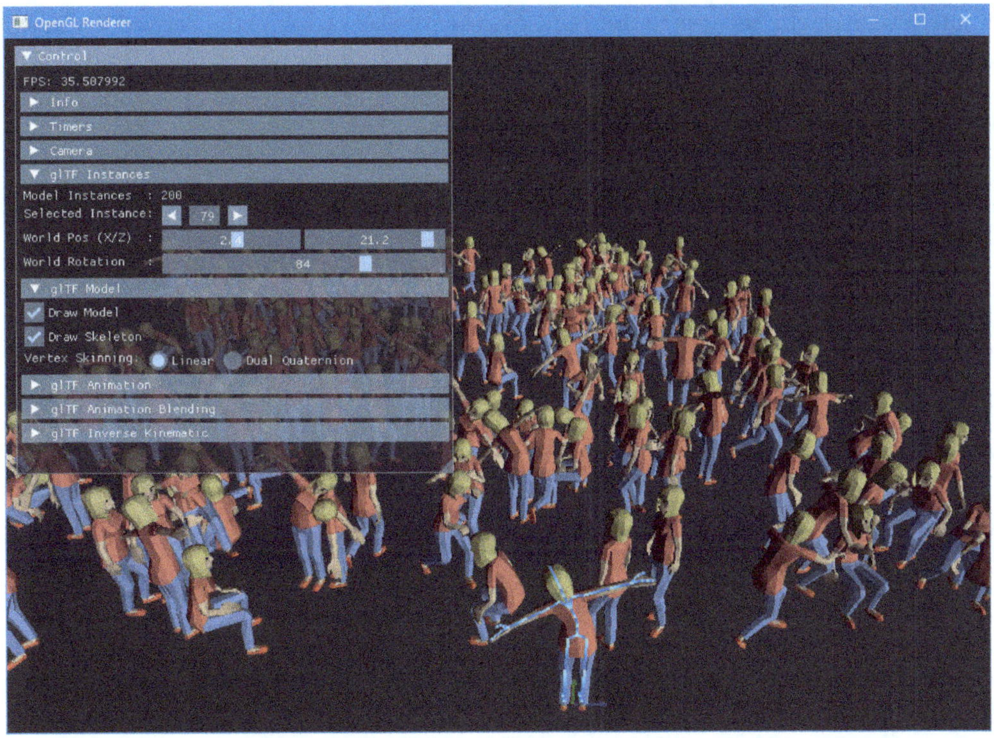

Figure 14.2: The OpenGL Renderer displaying 200 instances of the glTF model

You can select any of the instances on the screen using the new ImGui section and modify this instance in the same way as the single model before. The instance settings are remembered during the current program run, and every fresh start gives you another set of randomized virtual people on the screen.

Drawing multiple instances of the same model looks neat, but what about different models? In fact, loading more than one model and using different models as sources for instances is easy with the current code.

The full source code for this section can be found in the `chapter14` folder's `02_opengl_multiple_models` and `06_vulkan_multiple_models` subfolders.

Rendering instances of different models

First, we need a small extension of the `GltfInstance` class, a getter for the saved glTF model. The declaration in the `GltfInstance.h` file and the implementation in the `GltfInstance.cpp` file in the model folder are trivial, so we can skip a listing.

More interesting are the changes to the `OGLRenderer` class. Change the declaration of the `private` member variable storing the glTF model in the `OGLRenderer.h` file in the `opengl` folder to `std::vector`:

```
std::vector<std::shared_ptr<GltfModel>> mGltfModels{};
```

Also, add two new vectors to store the pointers to the instances using joint matrices or dual quaternions:

```
std::vector<std::shared_ptr<GltfInstance>>
  mGltfMatrixInstances{};
std::vector<std::shared_ptr<GltfInstance>>
  mGltfDQInstances{};
```

Due to the possible mixing of the model types within the instances, we need to adjust the calculation of the overall size of the SSBO:

```
size_t modelJointMatrixBufferSize = 0;
size_t modelJointDualQuatBufferSize = 0;
int jointMatrixSize = 0;
int jointQuatSize = 0;
for (const auto &instance : mGltfInstances) {
  jointMatrixSize += instance->getJointMatrixSize();
  modelJointMatrixBufferSize +=
    instance->getJointMatrixSize() * sizeof(glm::mat4);
  jointQuatSize += instance->getJointDualQuatsSize();
  modelJointDualQuatBufferSize +=
    instance->getJointDualQuatsSize()*sizeof(glm::mat2x4);
}
```

We simply loop over all the created instances and sum up the sizes of each instance.

The collection of the joint matrix and dual quaternion data into the `mModelJointMatrices` and `mModelJointDualQuat` vectors also needs a minor change:

```
mGltfMatrixInstances.clear();
mGltfDQInstances.clear();
for (const auto &instance : mGltfInstances) {
  ...
  if (settings.msVertexSkinningMode ==
      skinningMode::dualQuat) {
    std::vector<glm::mat2x4> quats =...
    mModelJointDualQuats.insert(...);
    mGltfDQInstances.emplace_back(instance);
  } else {
    ...
```

```
    }
    ...
  }
```

Instead of summing up the number of instances for every vertex skinning mode, we append the current instance to the new `mGltfMatrixInstances` and `mGltfDQInstances` vectors.

The rendering itself iterates over these new vectors and calls the drawing using the new model-getter method of the instance:

```
  mGltfGPUShader.use();
  for (const auto &instance : mGltfMatrixInstances) {
    mGltfGPUShader.setUniformValue(matrixPos);
    instance->getModel()->draw();
    matrixPos += instance->getJointMatrixSize()
  }
```

Adding the size of the current joint matrix or dual quaternions to the uniform variable assures that we step the exact right number of elements forward in the SSBO.

Compiling and running the optimized version of the code will result in a more diverse crowd, as shown in *Figure 14.3*:

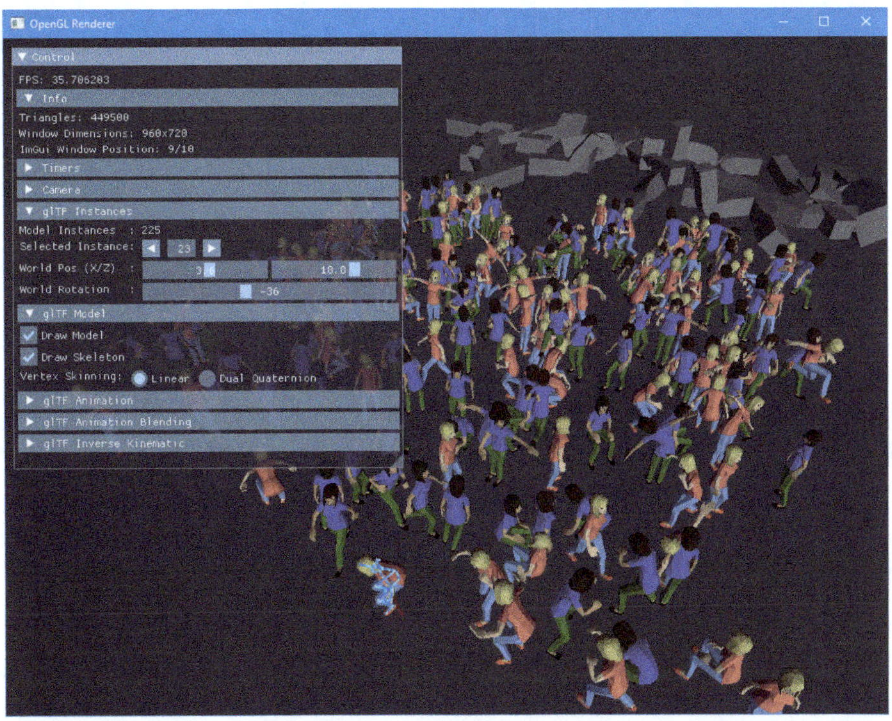

Figure 14.3: Rendering random instances of three different gLTF models

You can still navigate through all models and change the settings. The two woman models with different clothing are indeed different glTF models, sharing the same geometrical data. The dual quaternion test blocks from *Chapter 9* at the back of the crowd can be controlled in the same way as the other models. The user interface values for the animation clips are automatically adjusted depending on the chosen model.

Up to now, we had to make a `draw()` call for every instance we wanted to render to the screen. Modern graphics cards enable us to move some of the vertex-based work entirely to the GPU.

You will find the full source code for this section in the `chapter14` folder – for OpenGL, in the `03_opengl_instanced_drawing` subfolder, and for Vulkan in the `07_vulkan_instanced_drawing` subfolder.

> **Note on the code base for this section**
>
> In case you are wondering, the examples for this section are based on the first examples in the `01_opengl_instances` and `05_vulkan_instances` folders. Using instanced drawing with instances of multiple models adds a lot of extra complexity to the code. You may make these changes as part of the *Practical sessions* section.

Using GPU instancing to reduce data transfers

By using so-called instanced drawing, the graphics card duplicates the vertex data for the model instances by itself. All we must tell the GPU is the location of the vertex or index buffer data to use, and the number of instances to create.

The normal call telling OpenGL to start drawing looks like this:

```
void glDrawElements(drawMode, indexCount,
  componentType, indices);
```

For the drawing mode, we are using `GL_TRIANGLES` to draw triangles, defined by groups of three vertices. The index count is the number of entries in the index buffer. If some vertices are shared between triangles, the number of index entries may be lower than the overall number of vertices. Depending on the amount of index entries, the component type could be a byte, a short integer with 16 bits, or an integer with 32 bits. As we are using an index buffer to store the index elements, the last parameter is `nullptr`.

The call to tell OpenGL to create more than one instance of a set of index elements has an additional parameter, stating the number of instances to draw:

```
void glDrawElementsInstanced(drawMode, indexCount,
   componentType, indices, instanceCount);
```

Inside the shaders, the same vertices are taken for every model, but they can be altered by using shader-internal variables, such as the `gl_InstanceID` variable in OpenGL shaders and the `gl_InstanceIndex` variable in Vulkan shaders, to access specific positions in additional buffers. These internal variables are increased automatically, allowing us to create many model instances with a single call to the graphics library.

Drawing many models at once is beneficial for the code complexity and also leads to a large performance leap if we render many larger models.

Changing the model class to use instanced drawing

In the `GltfModel` class, we add a new method called `drawInstanced()`:

```
void GltfModel::drawInstanced(int instanceCount) {
  ...
  mTex.bind();
  glBindVertexArray(mVAO);
  glDrawElementsInstanced(drawMode, indexAccessor.count,
   indexAccessor.componentType, nullptr, instanceCount);
  glBindVertexArray(0);
  mTex.unbind();
}
```

The differences from the normal `draw()` method are the additional parameter, stating the number of instances to draw, and the `glDrawElementsInstanced()` call. The remaining part of the method is identical.

Firing the turbo boost in the renderer

To draw the models using the GPU instancing, the `draw()` call of the `OGLRenderer` class must be changed too.

We can *remove* the entire `for` loop over the `matrixInstances` or `dualQuaternion` integer values, including the helper variables:

```
  unsigned int jointMatrixSize =
    mGltfInstances.at(0)->getJointMatrixSize();
  unsigned int matrixPos = 0;
  mGltfGPUShader.use();
  for (int i = 0; i < matrixInstances; ++i) {
    mGltfGPUShader.setUniformValue(matrixPos);
    mGltfModel->draw();
    matrixPos += jointMatrixSize;
  }
```

Instead, instanced rendering is done with an overall count of three lines:

```
mGltfGPUShader.use();
mGltfGPUShader.setUniformValue(
  mGltfInstances.at(0)->getJointMatrixSize());
mGltfModel->drawInstanced(matrixInstances);
```

After activating the shader program, we upload the size of the joint matrices to the shader uniform variable. Remember: we draw identical models here, so there is no need for more than one value.

In the third line, we issue the instanced drawing command, instructing OpenGL to render the number of instances using the joint matrices from the single set of vertices in the active vertex buffer.

The two glTF vertex shaders also need to know that we will use instanced rendering. Instead of manually altering the position in the SSBO, we let the shader use the `gl_InstanceID` variable to advance to the correct position in the buffer.

For the `gltf_gpu.vert` shader in the `shader` folder, simply multiply the `aModelStride` uniform variable with the value of the `gl_InstanceID` variable when the `skinMat` matrix is calculated:

```
aJointWeight.x * jointMat[int(aJointNum.x) +
  gl_InstanceID * aModelStride] +
aJointWeight.y * jointMat[int(aJointNum.y) +
  gl_InstanceID * aModelStride] +
aJointWeight.z * jointMat[int(aJointNum.z) +
  gl_InstanceID * aModelStride] +
aJointWeight.w * jointMat[int(aJointNum.w) +
  gl_InstanceID * aModelStride];
```

For the `gltf_gpu_quat.vert` shader, do the same multiplication in the `getJointTransform()` function:

```
mat2x4 dq0 = jointDQs[joints.x + gl_InstanceID * aModelStride];
mat2x4 dq1 = jointDQs[joints.y + gl_InstanceID * aModelStride];
mat2x4 dq2 = jointDQs[joints.z + gl_InstanceID * aModelStride];
mat2x4 dq3 = jointDQs[joints.w + gl_InstanceID * aModelStride];
```

If you compile the code and run the optimized executable, you'll see no difference compared to the screenshot in *Figure 14.2*. Even the timer values should be in the same range. But, why?

The application is currently limited by the CPU, not the GPU. Calculating all the matrix updates takes a lot of time, and uploading the data to the GPU plus issuing the draw calls is done quickly. Optimizing the GPU transfers brings no visible benefits for us.

And it gets even worse: as we are unable to update the shader data between the calls, we cannot change simple elements such as the texture on the fly, without also storing that data in a buffer and advancing over the buffer using the `gl_InstanceID` variable.

Using GPU-based instancing is good for many models drawn on the screen. The differences between loop-based drawing with multiple draw calls and a single draw call will be visible when we get to the GPU analysis part in *Chapter 15*. For now, the main goal of this section is to explore some of the advanced capabilities of modern GPUs.

Another *good-to-know* section follows as the last section of this chapter. Now we will explore another method to upload structured data to the graphics card: texture buffers.

You can check the full source code for the section in the `chapter14` folder, in the `04_opengl_tbo` subfolder for OpenGL and the `08_vulkan_tbo` subfolder for Vulkan.

Textures are not just for pictures

In the previous chapters, we used two different methods to upload larger amounts of arbitrary data to the GPU: in *Chapter 4*, we added uniform buffers, and in *Chapter 9*, shader storage buffers were introduced. The push constants for Vulkan are not added to this list because of the limited size of only 128 bytes.

Uniform buffer objects, abbreviated to **UBOs**, were introduced in OpenGL 3.1. UBOs can contain data shared across all shaders, ideal for uploading central data such as matrices or light parameters. But alas, the minimum guaranteed size of uniform buffers is only 64 KB, a limit one could reach quickly on complex virtual scenes.

Also introduced in OpenGL 3.1 were **texture buffer objects**, or for short, **TBOs**. Technically, a TBO is closely related to a texture, but it is not backed by an image like a real texture. Instead, a separate buffer is bound to the texture unit, and every texel of that texture can be read by its position. The value is returned without any filtering or interpolation that a real texture image may have, making it perfect for the transport of data larger than the minimal 64 KB of a UBO to the GPU.

Today, TBOs are replaced by SSBOs, as they are bigger and easier to use. SSBOs are also writable by shaders, allowing computations to be made entirely on the GPU.

Let us start by adding the new buffer type to the code base.

YABT – Yet Another Buffer Type

For the texture buffer, we create a new `TextureBuffer` class in the `opengl` folder. This new class is a mix between the texture class and the buffer classes. The `public` methods in the `TextureBuffer.h` file are more like a buffer:

```
  public:
    void init(size_t bufferSize);
    void uploadTboData(std::vector<glm::mat4> bufferData,
      int bindingPoint);
    void bind();
    void cleanup();
```

On the other hand, the `private` member variables remind us more of a texture:

```
private:
  size_t mBufferSize = 0;
  GLuint mTexNum = 0;
  GLuint mTexture = 0;
  GLuint mTextureBuffer = 0;
```

The implementation of the `init()` method is also a wild mix between a texture and a buffer:

```
mBufferSize = bufferSize;
glGenBuffers(1, &mTextureBuffer);
glBindBuffer(GL_TEXTURE_BUFFER, mTextureBuffer);
glBufferData(GL_TEXTURE_BUFFER, bufferSize, NULL,
  GL_STATIC_DRAW);
```

After saving the buffer size, we create a buffer of type `GL_TEXTURE_BUFFER`, similar to a buffer of type `GL_UNIFORM_BUFFER` or `GL_SHADER_STORAGE_BUFFER`. But, in the next lines, we also create a texture:

```
glGenTextures(1, &mTexture);
glBindTexture(GL_TEXTURE_BUFFER, mTexture);
glTexBuffer(GL_TEXTURE_BUFFER, GL_RGBA32F, mTextureBuffer);
```

The most important line in the preceding code is the last one. The `glTexBuffer()` call attaches the texture buffer to the `mTexture` texture. Any data uploaded into the buffer defined by `mTextureBuffer` appears as a texture with four 32-bit float components, usable in the vertex shader.

When we check the `bind()` method of the `TextureBuffer` class, the similarities to a default OpenGL texture are also visible:

```
glActiveTexture(GL_TEXTURE0 + mTexNum);
glBindTexture(GL_TEXTURE_BUFFER, mTexture);
glActiveTexture(GL_TEXTURE0);
```

We must activate a texture unit first, and bind the active texture unit to the texture buffer value stored in the `mTexture` variable. After this binding operation, the buffer data is visible as a `samplerBuffer` (OpenGL) or `textureBuffer` object in the shader (Vulkan).

Updating the vertex shader one last time

For demonstration purposes, we will change only the joint matrix vertex shader, `gltf_gpu.vert`, in the `shader` folder to use the TBO for uploads. The dual quaternion shader, `gltf_gpu__dquat.vert`, will still get the data from an SSBO.

First, *remove* the SSBO binding from the shader:

```
layout (std430, binding = 1) readonly buffer JointMatrices {
  mat4 jointMat[];
};
```

Then, *add* a samplerBuffer uniform buffer type with the same name and binding:

```
layout (binding = 1) uniform samplerBuffer JointMatrices;
```

Above the main() function, add a new getMatrix() function to retrieve a 4x4 matrix from a specified offset inside the samplerBuffer buffer:

```
mat4 getMatrix(int offset) {
  return mat4(texelFetch(JointMatrices, offset),
    texelFetch(JointMatrices, offset + 1),
    texelFetch(JointMatrices, offset + 2),
    texelFetch(JointMatrices, offset + 3));
}
```

Finally, the calculation of the skinMat matrix in the main() function must be adjusted again:

```
    aJointWeight.x * getMatrix((int(aJointNum.x) +
      gl_InstanceID * aModelStride) * 4) +
    aJointWeight.y * getMatrix((int(aJointNum.y) +
      gl_InstanceID * aModelStride) * 4) +
    aJointWeight.z * getMatrix((int(aJointNum.z) +
      gl_InstanceID * aModelStride) * 4) +
    aJointWeight.w * getMatrix((int(aJointNum.w) +
      gl_InstanceID * aModelStride) * 4);
```

As the TBO contains float values instead of the mat4 values from the SSBO, we must multiply the offset by a factor of four to reach the same data as before.

For the renderer, the changes are minimal. The new TextureBuffer and the previously used ShaderStorageBuffer classes are compatible with the initialization and the data upload methods. We can simply change the type and the name of the joint matrix buffer and adjust the upload method name and we are ready to go.

The only important change is the binding of the texture buffer. This activation must happen prior to the drawInstanced() call of the glTF model:

```
  mGltfGPUShader.use();
  mGltfTextureBuffer.bind();
  mGltfGPUShader.setUniformValue(
    mGltfInstances.at(0)->getJointMatrixSize());
  mGltfModel->drawInstanced(matrixInstances);
```

Calling `bind()` activates configured texture unit number one on the GPU, and as we are using binding point number one for the buffer named `samplerBuffer` in the vertex shader, the matrix data is accessible for the shader.

If you compile the code and run the optimized executable, you will again see no difference. For our amounts of data, it simply makes no difference whether we upload the data via a TBO or SSBO to the GPU.

Having several different methods to transfer data to the GPU will help us in *Chapter 15*, where we look at optimizations on the CPU and GPU sides.

Summary

In this chapter, we upgraded our renderer from showing only a single model to rendering a larger crowd of models.

First, we split the `GltfModel` class into two parts, adding a new `GltfInstance` class for the instance-specific variables and methods. This split enabled us to enhance the renderer to draw many instances of the same model. Next, we upgraded the renderer to draw instances of different models on the screen.

Then, we used the code of the first example with the split of the model and the instance class as the basis and added GPU-side instancing to the code to offload the drawing of the instances to the graphics card. Lastly, we explored TBO as an alternative way to transfer data to the GPU.

In the next chapter, we look deeper *under the hood* of the created application. We had to add an optimization in this chapter, but there is much more to explore and check on the CPU and GPU sides to make the application even faster.

Practical sessions

You may try out the following exercises to get a deeper insight into rendering multiple instances of glTF models:

- Enable the dynamic addition of new instances. While the addition of a new instance to the `std::vector` array is easy, the buffer sizes require more attention. You need to check for a sufficient size and re-create or adjust the GPU buffers.
- Add more than one model per instance on the screen when using GPU-instanced rendering. You could calculate the joint matrices and dual quaternions normally but add multiple `GltfInstance` models with the same buffer data while altering the world position and rotation values. This addition would create a much larger crowd with the same amount of CPU load. Think of thousands or tens of thousands of models jumping on the screen. Due to the spacing between the models sharing the animation clip and animation replay speed, the crowd will still look random.

- Medium difficulty: Add both the non-instanced and instanced drawing methods plus the upload of the buffer data via an SSBO and TBO to the code, and make the different methods selectable via ImGui. The differences between the example sources in the `01_opengl_instances`, `03_opengl_instanced_drawing`, and `04_opengl_tbo` folders and their Vulkan counterparts in the `chapter14` folder are small. Adding extra radio buttons to toggle the instancing on and off, or to change between shader storage buffers and texture buffers, to upload the data to the GPU, should not be too hard. You will need more shaders, and for Vulkan, this also requires new pipelines. A direct comparison between different drawing modes is a good start for *Chapter 15*, where we dive deeper into optimization topics.
- Enhanced difficulty: Add the ability to draw different models with the instanced rendering code. This is complex, as all the matrix/dual quaternion data for every model type is best saved to a continuous memory area on the GPU. So, you would have to add separate buffers for every model or upload the data for the next model type after the instanced draw call for the current model is finished. As an alternative, you may try to add the different strides into another buffer and use the shader internal instance index as a pointer to get the correct stride for the specific instance.
- Enhanced difficulty: Add graphical selection. You do not have to work with projection and deprojection; there is a simpler way: Add a unique index number to every model at creation time, hand over the index to the shader, and draw the triangles for the model with the index as a color into a separate buffer. When the user clicks into the window, retrieve the color of the extra buffer from the GPU and do a reverse lookup to get the instance from the index. See the *Additional resources* section for an example of how to do such graphical selection.

Additional resources

- OpenGL instancing: `https://learnopengl.com/Advanced-OpenGL/Instancing`
- Vulkan instancing example: `http://xdpixel.com/vulkan-draw-call-instancing/`
- OpenGL TBO example: `https://gist.github.com/roxlu/5090067`
- Mouse picking with a shader storage buffer: `https://blog.gavs.space/post/003-vulkan-mouse-picking/`

15
Measuring Performance and Optimizing the Code

Welcome to *Chapter 15*! In the previous chapter, we extended the glTF application to render a large crowd of model instances at the same time on the screen.

In this chapter, we will search for performance problems by measuring the time the application needs for some function calls, such as the calculation of the joint matrices for the vertex skinning or the upload of the matrix data into the buffers of the graphics card. This measurement allows us to find so-called **hotspots**, which are parts of the code that are called many times during the program execution.

First, we discuss some basic dos and don'ts of code optimization. Then, we explore a couple of different methods to make the code – at least theoretically – faster. There is no guarantee that an optimization will have a positive effect on the speed of a program, as using the wrong data type or algorithm can even slow down the code. Therefore, we need to check our application code with a **profiling** tool to detect hotspots before and after we apply our optimizations.

Next, we use **RenderDoc** to analyze a frame the application sends to the graphics card. RenderDoc hooks itself into the call to the graphics API and records the data sent to the GPU. At the end of the chapter, we look at some more tips to measure and optimize code.

In this chapter, we will cover the following topics:

- Measure twice, cut once!
- Moving computations to different places
- Profiling the code to find hotspots
- Using RenderDoc to analyze a GPU frame
- Scale it up and do A/B tests

Technical requirements

For this chapter, you will need the OpenGL and Vulkan renderer code from *Chapter 14*.

Before we go into details about code optimization, let us discuss some "rules of thumb" regarding optimization in the software development process.

Measure twice, cut once!

The saying, "*Measure twice, cut once,*" is popular among carpenters. Cutting a wooden plank is irreversible, and if the resulting plank is too short due to inaccurate measurements, the carpenter must start over with a new plank.

Thanks to **Source Code Management** (**SCM**) software such as Git, code changes are not irreversible in the way that cutting wood is. But you will waste precious time if you start optimizing without a plan.

Always measure before you take actions

If you find a performance problem in your application, you may feel the urge to optimize it somehow. However, making code changes by following gut feelings is a bad idea, as you will most likely not end up optimizing the actual code responsible for the slow performance, instead just making assumptions about which part of the code may be slow.

So, before you dive into the code and try your best to make it faster, you should at least start measuring the times taken by different parts of the application. Adding timers and drawing plots with the values, as we did in *Chapter 5* and *Chapter 12*, will quickly help you to identify the broad locations of the parts of code negatively affecting the performance of your program. It makes sense to check the time-consuming sections of the code first, even if this is only to confirm that a blocking operation such as an OpenGL draw call is responsible for a large proportion of the time taken for execution.

For a more detailed view of the code, you should profile the application. A profiling tool checks every function of your application at runtime, measuring how often the function was called and how much time it took to complete. At the end of the profiling run, you get a textual or graphical representation of the results, allowing you to locate the hotspots where the application demands the most time to process. We will do a profiling run of the glTF model application in the *Profiling the code to find hotspots* section.

Three steps of code optimization

The following is a quote from Kent Beck, one of the three people who invented **Extreme Programming** (**XP**):

Make it work, make it right, make it fast.

Extreme programming follows a set of rules to minimize the formalities and concentrate on the process of writing code and automated tests. Nevertheless, the aforementioned quote can be applied to other types of software development processes, as it states three steps you should do in the right order, which are as follows:

1. As a first step, you could add some new functionality or change the code by simply adding or changing the code in place. There is little reason to think a lot about the runtime complexity, memory management, or clean class or code design at this moment. At this point, you only want to know whether the code (still) works as expected.
2. After the added or changed code has been found to solve your problem or fulfill the desired functionality, you should "do it right." This is the perfect time to refactor your changes with the right classes, ensure they have the correct access specifiers, the required sets of parameters and return types, and so on. But... do not start to optimize the code yet, as more changes may occur.
3. Optimizations come at step three, after your code changes or additions have been proven to deliver the correct results, including any edge cases, and form a stable part of the API your code exposes to other parts of the code or to the "outside world," where other programmers may include your code in their own programs.

Failing to wait for step three to begin optimizing will in the best case waste your time, and in the worst case, risk compromising the entire project timeline.

Avoid premature optimizations

Another important sentence to remember as a software developer is this quote by Donald E. Knuth:

Premature optimization is the root of all evil.

You could start optimizing your web application code to support tens of thousands of users right from the get-go, or tune your 3D model renderer to be able to show thousands of different models.

But you have other more pressing problems to solve first. You can *think* about scaling your application or supporting different file formats and 3D APIs during the initial phases of development. Sadly, however, most of the time you end up starting with a new application, a new set of functions, new APIs, and so on, so none of the optimized parts matter.

It is much more important to build the required functionality, make the code stable and robust, and add a suitable user interface to the application. Taking performance problems into account and working on optimizations usually comes *after* you get the application or new functions ready.

> **Note on compiler optimization flags**
>
> In *Chapter 14*, we added compiler optimization flags for GCC and Clang and a release version to Visual Studio, just to continue with the development, as the generated debug code was too slow to get a reasonable frame rate. This kind of adjustment does not count as premature optimization because we did not change any code.

Once we reach the point in the development process where we do need to optimize the application code, we have several methods available to avoid wasting CPU time. Let us have a quick examination of some of the methods you will find in different software products as kinds of optimization.

Moving computations to different places

Even with the current multi-core processors and several GHz of core frequencies, CPU power is still a scarce and precious resource. Every CPU cycle you waste by doing unnecessary calculations, using the wrong algorithms, or repeating operations is lost for the remaining parts of the program. Therefore, it is important to identify how to save CPU cycles while still doing the intended computations.

Recalculate only when necessary

There are essentially two opposite paths available to optimize code. You can try to optimize the code in a way that computes the results on every call with low overhead – or you can be lazy, cache the results, and recalculate new results only when some of the parameters have changed.

Both paths have their pros and cons. While continuously computed results will produce smooth and uniform calculation times in the functions, you do a lot of unnecessary operations if the input values never change. With the lazy solution, you recalculate new results only if any parameters change, but a lot of changes at once can result in performance hits.

It is up to you which path you choose, and your choice can vary between different functions. The best way to find out which is best is to try and measure.

Utilize compile time over runtime

You have already seen an example of precalculation in *Chapter 3*, with the SPIR-V shader format for the Vulkan renderer.

In an OpenGL renderer, you usually load and compile the shaders at runtime, during the initialization phase. This means you must do the same operations repeatedly. Plus, any errors in the shader code result in graphical errors or the complete abortion of the application.

For the Vulkan renderer, the entire shader compile process has been moved to compile time. The application can load the precompiled, error-checked byte code of the shader and use it directly. Logical errors may still distort the resulting images, but any syntactical errors will already have been caught during the shader compilation.

Another example of the effective utilization of compile time over runtime is format conversions of images, videos, or other assets that take place during the compilation process. The dependency checks of the build systems will trigger any conversions if the source material has changed, reducing the compile time required.

On the code side, using the `constexpr` qualifier (since C++ 11) allows you to execute functions at compile time if possible. The resulting dual-use functions could help move calculations to the compilation process. The new `consteval` qualifier in C++ 20 forces execution at compile time, and you can create complex code snippets that do their work during compilation.

Convert your data as soon as possible

There may be cases where you cannot convert data elements to a different format during compilation time. This happens mostly because you only have loader code for the original file format, and writing a load is too complex a task just for this project. Think of the glTF file format we explored in *Chapter 8*... you do not want to invent a similar format.

Instead, use a common loader for the file format, and convert the data in your application into the destination format. Either you interleave the vertex, normal, and texture data in your code, or put it into separate buffers – it is up to you. But you had better convert all files to be loaded to exactly the same format the GPU uses in the shaders, as further conversion during the upload will waste CPU time.

For small datasets, this suggestion can be ignored. Once you scale up, every conversion on the internal path from the loaded data to the final format uploaded to the GPU makes your application slow. The best way to upload the data to the graphics card is still a simple `std::memcpy` call, letting the processor move all data in a single run to a buffer used by the GPU. Extensive `for` loops converting the data "on the fly" to a GPU-compatible format will always make your code slower than a simple memory copy would.

Split the calculations into multiple threads

Even if you were to optimize all data conversions at compile time and runtime, and moved all calculations to return cached results, if any changes were to occur in the meantime, you could run out of CPU cycles on even a high-end processor.

The main reason for this is that your code will use only a single CPU core by default. Although C++ 17 started to add concurrency to some of the STL algorithms, your default code is still limited to a single core.

Utilizing multiple CPU cores by using **threads** is a common way to overcome this limitation. In theory, you just start a new thread and hand over the computations it must do. But, in practice, you must handle a lot of extra work, including managing dependencies between data elements, or so-called race conditions, where multiple threads update the same list, array, or plain value and overwrite the data in a non-deterministic order.

Multithreading is a complex topic, but once you master it, you will unleash the full power of your CPU. But alas… the path to understanding and using multiple threads in a program is paved with large rocks; many hidden traps are waiting for you, and you should expect dragons on your voyage. Using multiple threads is out of the scope of this book, but if you are interested in this topic, some links are included in the *Additional resources* section.

Use compute shaders on your graphics card

Another way to parallelize calculations is by letting the GPU do the work. OpenGL added the so-called **compute shaders** in version 4.3, and Vulkan has had support for compute shaders since its initial version 1.0.

This new shader type is not necessarily part of the image creation in the way the vertex and fragment shaders are. Instead, compute shaders do what the name suggests: they do pure computational work. And, due to the enormous number of shader units on current graphics cards, they can do their job in a massively parallel manner, especially operations containing vectors and matrices, which are made for compute shaders, as it is the primary job of the shader units to work blazingly fast with these data types.

Thanks to GLSL being like simple C code, creating a compute shader requires no magic or wizardry. As an additional advantage, the resulting data can be written to a shader storage buffer on the GPU, ready to use in another shader stage. You not only use computational power on the graphics card, but you also save the transfer of the data to the GPU.

On the shadow side of the GPU shaders lies the synchronization part. Running the computer shader before the graphics shaders will count toward the overall frame time, lowering your maximum FPS. As an alternative solution, you can run the compute shaders in parallel to the graphics shaders, or after the image creation has been finished. But this setup will delay the compute shader result by at least one frame. You also must test directly what works for your code and what does not.

Now we have reviewed some of the common solutions to optimize code, let's go for a practical profiling session in the next section.

Profiling the code to find hotspots

For code performance profiling, the executable is instrumented by a profiling tool, and every function call is counted, including the execution time. Depending on the OS and the compiler, different settings are required to enable proper application profiling.

We will now begin with a practical profiling session and search for hotspots in the code used in *Chapter 14*: `03_opengl_instanced_drawing`. The optimized code can be found in the folder for `chapter15` in the `01_opengl_optimize` subfolder.

Profiling code using Visual Studio

Visual Studio comes with an internal performance profiler. The profiler can be started in the **Debug** menu of Visual Studio, as shown in *Figure 15.1*:

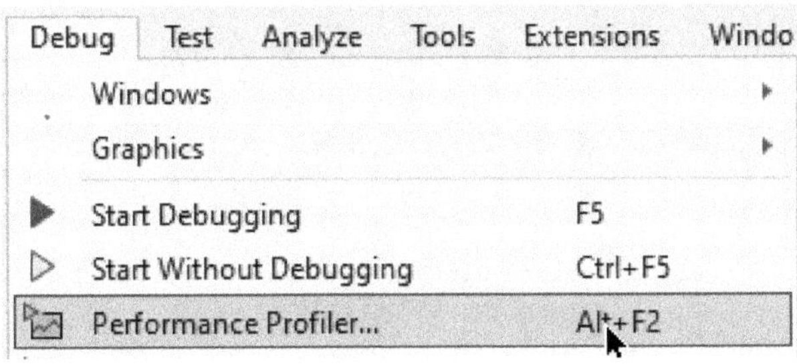

Figure 15.1: Starting the profiler from Visual Studio 2022

In the new Visual Studio tab, select **Executable** as the desired **Analysis Target**. Navigate to the `chapter14\03_opengl_instanced_drawing` folder and select the executable file in the following subfolder:

```
out\build\x64-Release\RelWithDebInfo\Main.exe
```

If the file is missing, you need to build a `Release` executable first.

Next, start the profiler and let the application run for a number of seconds. Close the application window to let Visual Studio collect the required information.

After the performance data is processed, the five top functions are shown. For non-optimized code, your display should be like *Figure 15.2*:

Top Insights

No insights found.

Top Functions

Function Name	Total CPU [unit, %]	Self CPU [unit, %]
glm::operator*<float,0>	7275 (40,95 %)	7241 (40,76 %)
glm::translate<float,0>	1291 (7,27 %)	1289 (7,26 %)
GltfNode::calculateLocalTRSMatrix	10308 (58,03 %)	1263 (7,11 %)
glm::mat4_cast<float,0>	938 (5,28 %)	935 (5,26 %)
GltfNode::calculateNodeMatrix	11755 (66,17 %)	785 (4,42 %)

Figure 15.2: Top functions in the non-optimized code

Two methods of the `GltfNode` class appear in the "top five." These two methods, `calculateLocalTRSMatrix()` and `calculateNodeMatrix()`, are the first candidates to check and optimize their code – they are the CPU hogs in the code.

Clicking the left mouse button on one of the methods, for example, `calculateLocalTRSMatrix()`, opens a new window, marking the hotspots in the source code using different shades of red. The darker the shade of red, the more time was spent on that given line of code. *Figure 15.3* shows the `calculateLocalTRSMatrix()` method of a performance profiling run:

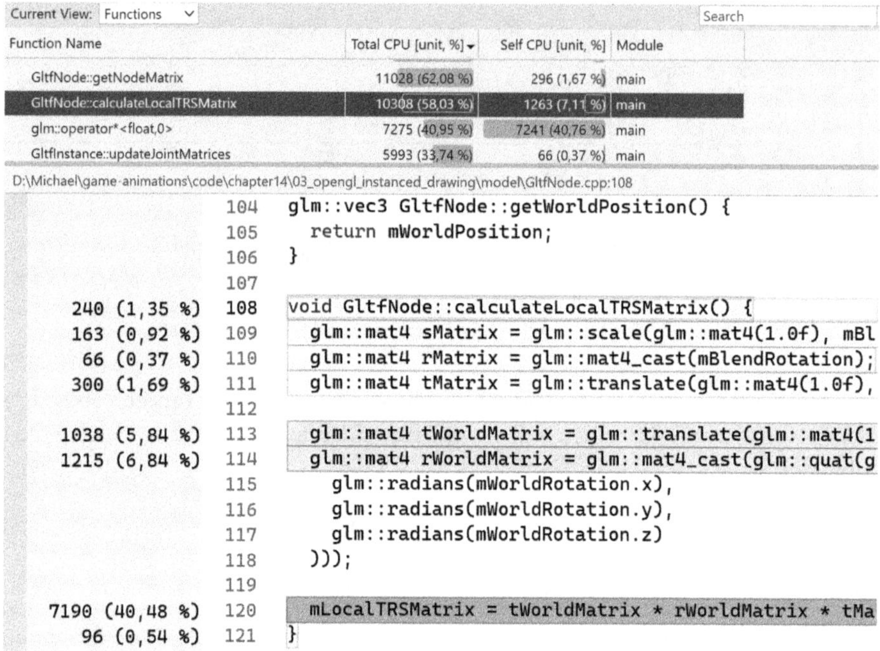

Figure 15.3: CPU usage of the operations in the calculateLocalTRSMatrix() method

As you can see in *Figure 15.3*, the multiplication of the five matrices containing local translation, the local rotation, the local scale, and the global translation and rotation took nearly 40% of the total time spent on the code.

Before we change the code of the `GltfNode` class, let us check how to activate the profiler for GCC and Clang.

Profiling code using GCC or Clang on Linux

For GCC and Clang on Linux, the Unix tool **gprof** will be used. The package manager on your distribution will have a recent version available to download if required.

To activate the profiling with gprof, add the `-pg` flag to the compiler flags. The best way to achieve this is to append the flag to the following line in the `CMakeLists.txt` file:

```
set(CMAKE_CXX_FLAGS "-O3 -pg")
```

Now, rebuild the project to activate the flag and start the executable to let the application collect the profiling data:

```
mkdir build
cd build
cmake .. && make -j5 && ./Main
```

After you close the application window, a file named `gmon.out` appears in the current folder. This file is where the collected performance data is saved.

The contents of the file can be viewed by running `gprof` with the executable file as a parameter. We pipe the output to the `less` tool to get scrollable text:

```
gprof ./Main | less
```

We see the two `GltfNode` methods, `calculateLocalTRSMatrix()` and `calculateNodeMatrix()`, are also in Linux , at the top of the list:

```
Flat profile:

Each sample counts as 0.01 seconds.
  %   cumulative   self              self     total
 time   seconds   seconds    calls  s/call   s/call  name
 52.30      2.73     2.73 27419790     0.00     0.00  GltfNode::calculateLocalTRSMatrix()
 24.14      3.99     1.26  3284526     0.00     0.00  GltfNode::calculateNodeMatrix()
  5.75      4.29     0.30  1305600     0.00     0.00  GltfAnimationChannel::getRotation(float)
  3.64      4.48     0.19  1305600     0.00     0.00  GltfAnimationChannel::getScaling(float)
  3.64      4.67     0.19  1305600     0.00     0.00  GltfAnimationChannel::getTranslation(flo>
  1.92      4.77     0.10    38400     0.00     0.00  GltfInstance::blendAnimationFrame(int, f>
  1.72      4.86     0.09  1621242     0.00     0.00  GltfInstance::updateJointMatrices(std::s>
  1.53      4.94     0.08    38601     0.00     0.00  GltfInstance::updateNodeMatrices(std::sh>
```

Figure 15.4: The result of the profiling using gprof on Linux

Even if the percentage numbers differ, we can clearly see that those two methods need our attention.

Profiling code using Eclipse

For Eclipse on Windows, we are using MSYS2 to provide the compiler and build tools. We will use the Unix tool gprof, which is already installed in MSYS2, so there is nothing we need to do.

Sadly, Eclipse has trouble profiling applications when the `cmake4eclipse` plugin is installed. We must switch to the manual way that was described in the *Profiling code using GCC or Clang on Linux* section.

First, edit the `CMakeList.txt` file and change the C++ flags line to the following:

```
set(CMAKE_CXX_FLAGS "-O3 -pg -no-pie")
```

The extra `-no-pie` flag is required for GCC on Windows as without the flag, the created `gmon.out` file will not be usable.

Now, run the `Main.exe` executable within Eclipse as **Local C++ Application** (or start it from Windows Explorer) and let it run for a number of seconds to collect the profiling information.

After you close the application window, open a CMD window, navigate to the `chapter14\03_opengl_instanced_drawing` folder, and run `gprof.exe`:

```
gprof _build\Release\Main.exe | less
```

The result looks different than the Linux executable built with GCC, but the topmost `GltfNode` entries are the same:

```
Flat profile:

Each sample counts as 0.01 seconds.
  %   cumulative   self              self     total
 time   seconds   seconds    calls  ns/call  ns/call  name
 38.33     13.30    13.30                             sincosf
 30.95     24.04    10.74 8902365062     1.21     1.21  GltfNode::calculateLocalTRSMatrix()
  6.14     26.17     2.13 64461897798     0.03     0.12  GltfNode::calculateNodeMatrix()
  4.90     27.87     1.70                             __sinl_internal
  3.43     29.06     1.19                             _mcount_private
  2.54     29.94     0.88                             __fentry__
  2.05     30.65     0.71 4310076896     0.16     0.16  GltfAnimationChannel::getScaling(float)
  2.02     31.35     0.70                             acosf
  1.96     32.03     0.68 4310076896     0.16     0.16  GltfAnimationChannel::getRotation(float)
  1.70     32.62     0.59 4310076896     0.14     0.14  GltfAnimationChannel::getTranslation(float)
```

Figure 15.5: GCC profiling under Windows

We have determined that the two matrix calculations of the `GltfNode` class should be examined and optimized. So, let us check what options we have.

Analyzing the code and planning the optimizations

In *Figure 15.3*, the matrix multiplication of the `calculateLocalTRSMatrix()` method is highlighted in dark red, a clear sign that we should start our optimization right there. The `calculateLocalTRSMatrix()` method itself is split into three distinct parts. First, the new matrices for the scaling, rotation, and transformation values are calculated. We create three local 4x4 matrices on every method call:

```
void GltfNode::calculateLocalTRSMatrix() {
  glm::mat4 sMatrix = glm::scale(glm::mat4(1.0f), mBlendScale);
  glm::mat4 rMatrix = glm::mat4_cast(mBlendRotation);
  glm::mat4 tMatrix = glm::translate(glm::mat4(1.0f),
    mBlendTranslation);
```

Next, the new global translation and rotation matrices are created and filled. Again, we are using local variables in every run:

```
  glm::mat4 tWorldMatrix = glm::translate(glm::mat4(1.0f),
    mWorldPosition);
  glm::mat4 rWorldMatrix = glm::mat4_cast(glm::quat(glm::vec3(
    glm::radians(mWorldRotation.x),
    glm::radians(mWorldRotation.y),
    glm::radians(mWorldRotation.z)
  )));
```

As the last step, a very expensive matrix multiplication of all local matrices is created:

```
    mLocalTRSMatrix = tWorldMatrix * rWorldMatrix * tMatrix * rMatrix *
      sMatrix;
  }
```

Do we really need to create and calculate all the matrices on every single call of the `calculateLocalTRSMatrix()` method? The simple answer: *no!*

So, let us split the optimization into four steps:

1. Create member variables to avoid the handling of the local matrices.
2. Combine the global translation/rotation matrix.
3. Recalculate the matrices only when the values have changed.
4. Recalculate the final `mLocalTRSMatrix` only if at least one other matrix was changed.

We will now discuss these four steps in detail in the next two subsections.

Promoting the local matrices to member variables

Per the steps listed in the *Analyzing the code and planning the optimizations* section, *step1* can be done straightforwardly. First, we create three new `private` members in the `GltfNode.h` file in the `model` folder:

```
    glm::mat4 mTranslationMatrix = glm::mat4(1.0f);
    glm::mat4 mRotationMatrix = glm::mat4(1.0f);
    glm::mat4 mScaleMatrix = glm::mat4(1.0f);
```

Then, for *step 2*, we create another triplet of new `private` members:

```
    glm::mat4 mWorldTranslationMatrix = glm::mat4(1.0f);
    glm::mat4 mWorldRotationMatrix = glm::mat4(1.0f);
    glm::mat4 mWorldTRMatrix = glm::mat4(1.0f);
```

We will see in the implementation why three matrices are required here instead of two. The first and second matrices, `mWorldTranslationMatrix` and `mWorldRotationMatrix`, store the global translation and global rotation of the model instance. The third matrix, `mWorldTRMatrix`, is used to precalculate the product of the `mWorldTranslationMatrix` and `mWorldRotationMatrix` matrices. Calculating the product in advance saves a matrix-matrix-multiplication when we need to update the local TRS matrix.

Additionally, we create a Boolean `private` member as a flag to signal any matrix changes for *step 4*:

```
    bool mLocalMatrixNeedsUpdate = true;
```

Step 3 is more work as we have to move the calculations to different methods. Let us take a look at what is needed to fulfill the third optimization step.

Moving the matrix calculations

In the `GltfNode.cpp` file, we adjust the three `set*()` and the three `blend*()` methods to calculate the matrices on every call of those methods. As an example, see the following changes in the `blendRotation()` method:

```
void GltfNode::blendRotation(glm::quat rotation, float blendFactor) {
  float factor = std::min(std::max(blendFactor, 0.0f), 1.0f);
  mBlendRotation = glm::slerp(mRotation, rotation, factor);
  mRotationMatrix = glm::mat4_cast(mBlendRotation);
  mLocalMatrixNeedsUpdate = true;
}
```

The new `mRotationMatrix` member is updated directly every time we set a new value. So, if we do only a rotation, the translation and scaling matrices are not touched. At the end of the `blendRotation()` method, we also set the `mLocalMatrixNeedsUpdate` flag to true, signaling that one of the TRS matrices was changed.

For the `setWorldPosition()` method, we calculate two matrices on every call:

```
void GltfNode::setWorldPosition(glm::vec3 worldPos) {
  mWorldPosition = worldPos;
  mWorldTranslationMatrix = glm::translate(glm::mat4(1.0f),
    mWorldPosition);
  mWorldTRMatrix = mWorldTranslationMatrix * mWorldRotationMatrix;
  mLocalMatrixNeedsUpdate = true;
  updateNodeAndChildMatrices();
}
```

In the new `mWorldTranslationMatrix` variable, the new world translation is saved. We also update `mWorldTRMatrix` with the product of the world translation and the world rotation matrix. The combined `mWorldTRMatrix` matrix is created as a member variable in *step 2* of the *Promoting the local matrices to member variables* section. We also set the notification flag for matrix changes here.

Similar changes are done for the `setWorldRotation()` method:

```
void GltfNode::setWorldRotation(glm::vec3 worldRot) {
  mWorldRotation = worldRot;
  mWorldRotationMatrix = glm::mat4_cast(glm::quat(glm::vec3(
    glm::radians(mWorldRotation.x),
    glm::radians(mWorldRotation.y),
    glm::radians(mWorldRotation.z)
```

```
    )));
    mWorldTRMatrix = mWorldTranslationMatrix * mWorldRotationMatrix;
    mLocalMatrixNeedsUpdate = true;
    updateNodeAndChildMatrices();
}
```

The calculation of the new world rotation matrix `mWorldRotationMatrix` is moved into the method, and we also update the combined `mWorldTRMatrix` matrix and flag the required local TRS matrix update.

A bigger change has to be made for the `calculateLocalTRSMatrix()` method. After all the matrix calculations were moved, we must check whether any of the matrices we multiply were changed:

```
void GltfNode::calculateLocalTRSMatrix() {
    if (mLocalMatrixNeedsUpdate) {
        mLocalTRSMatrix = mWorldTRMatrix * mTranslationMatrix *
            mRotationMatrix * mScaleMatrix;
        mLocalMatrixNeedsUpdate = false;
    }
}
```

If the check is true, we update the `mLocalTRSMatrix` matrix and reset the flag. This check makes sure we only multiply the four matrices if at least one of them was changed, and without matrix changes for the node, `calculateLocalTRSMatrix()` does nothing. Plus, the combined world transformation matrix removes one matrix multiplication. The code should run a lot faster now.

Fixing the getNodeMatrix() method

The second slow method of the `GltfNode` class is `getNodeMatrix()`, and we can immediately see why the method does more work than required:

```
glm::mat4 GltfNode::getNodeMatrix() {
    calculateNodeMatrix();
    return mNodeMatrix;
}
```

Every time we get the node matrix, we recalculate the node matrix first. And the first line of the `calculateNodeMatrix()` method looks like this:

```
void GltfNode::calculateNodeMatrix() {
    calculateLocalTRSMatrix();
    ...
}
```

On every node matrix retrieval, we also recalculate the local TRS matrix. No wonder the calculateLocalTRSMatrix() method was the most-called one.

The fix in this case is simple, we just *remove* the calculateNodeMatrix() call:

```
glm::mat4 GltfNode::getNodeMatrix() {
  return mNodeMatrix;
}
```

If the glTF model viewer behaved strangely after this change, we could add the call to the node matrix calculation to run before the getNodeMatrix() call. But running the updated code shows the same result as before, meaning no further changes are necessary.

Re-profiling the application

Now that we have changed the GltfNode class, we should check whether our optimizations improve the performance. Recompile the code and restart the profiler. As shown in *Figure 15.6*, we used the profiling tool from Visual Studio 2022:

Top Insights

No insights found.

Top Functions

Function Name	Total CPU [unit, %]	Self CPU [unit, %]
glm::operator*<float,0>	1812 (10,72 %)	1805 (10,68 %)
GltfAnimationChannel::getRotation	1578 (9,33 %)	1209 (7,15 %)
GltfNode::blendRotation	1603 (9,48 %)	994 (5,88 %)
GltfAnimationChannel::getTranslation	966 (5,71 %)	950 (5,62 %)
GltfAnimationChannel::getScaling	911 (5,39 %)	884 (5,23 %)

Figure 15.6: Top 5 functions after implementing the optimizations

The two slow GltfNode methods, calculateLocalTRSMatrix() and calculateNodeMatrix(), are no longer in the top 5, and the new slowest functions have a significantly lower **Total CPU** value. Now, the slowest method is the GLM matrix multiplication, denoted as glm::operator*<float,0>, used many times in the code. The next runners-up in the list of slow methods are getRotation(), getTranslation(), and getScaling() from the GltfAnimationChannel class. The property retrieval methods for the animations are called for every node in every frame, so we also use them a lot. Finally, the last of the new "top 5 slow methods" is blendRotation() from the GltfNode class. Rotation blending uses SLERP interpolation and involves quite expensive calculations.

Searching for the `calculateLocalTRSMatrix()` method confirms the success of our work, as shown in *Figure 15.7*:

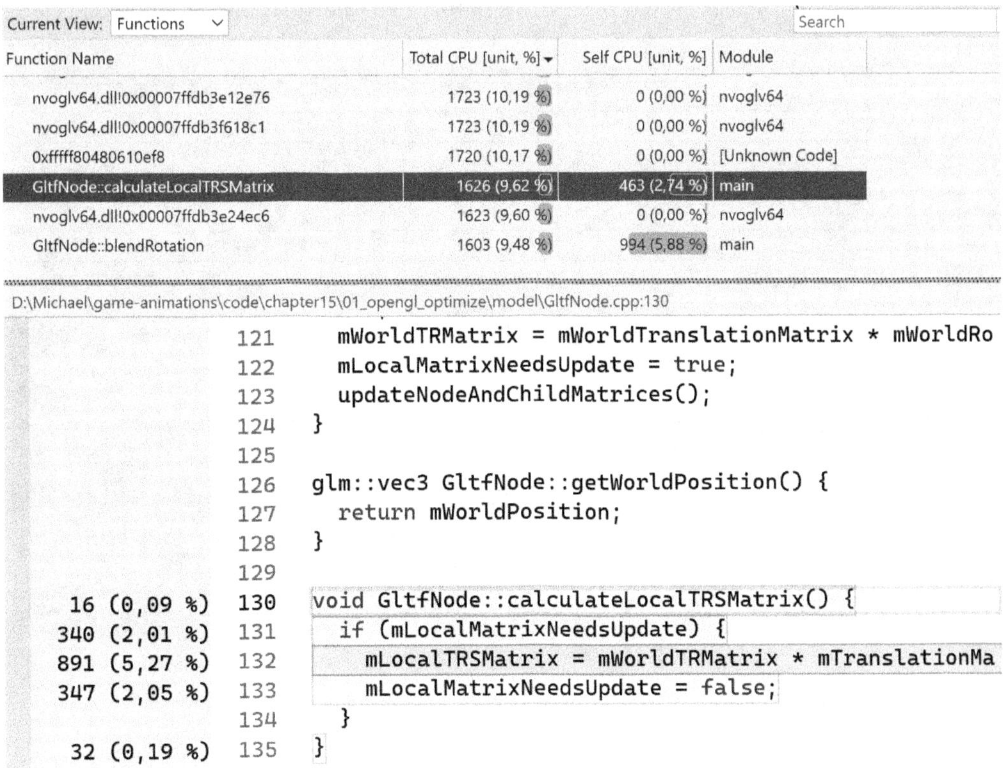

Figure 15.7: The calculateLocalTRSMatrix() method after the optimization

The CPU usage of the matrix multiplication line has been cut down to ~12% of the value we saw in *Figure 15.3* in the *Profiling code using Visual Studio* section. The calculation of the local TRS matrix uses only about 5% of the CPU time now, instead of nearly 40% prior to this optimization.

And this was only the first round of optimizing the application. As the next step, we could search for solutions to lower the CPU usage of the now-slowest functions, apply the proposed changes, and profile the code again.

Once we get to the point where no direct optimizations are possible, as discussed in this section, we should change our technique and try out other solutions, such as multithreading or compute shaders, to reduce the calculation time even more.

Nonetheless, the results of the optimization are already visible. In *Figure 15.8*, a picture with 1,000 model instances is shown, running at ~25 FPS. The matrix update time has been cut down to roughly ~20% of the values from *Chapter 14*, where we had a similar FPS value for only 200 instances:

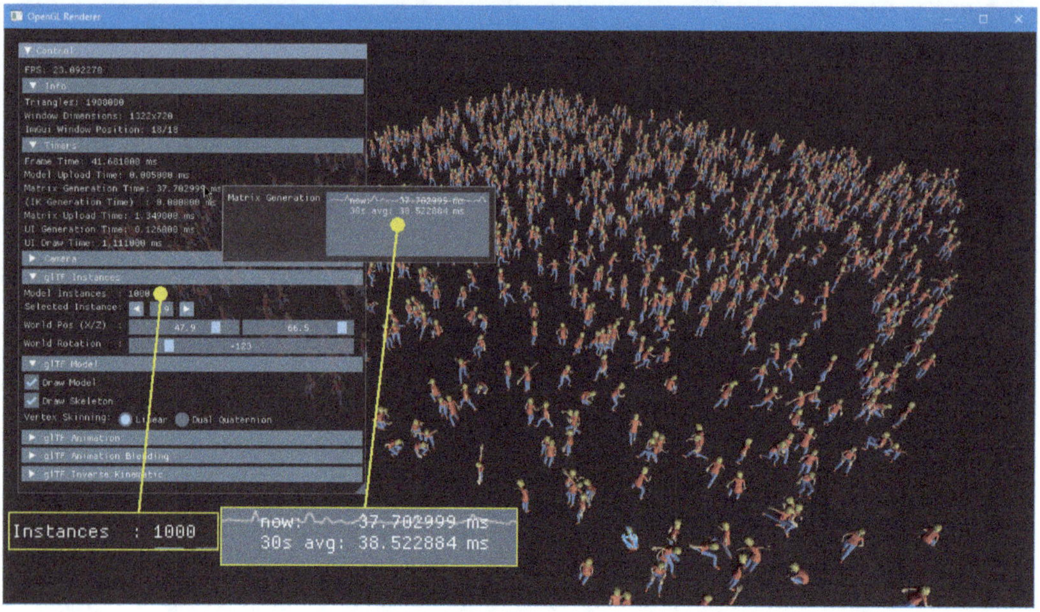

Figure 15.8: The application performance boost after the first optimizations

Another possible bottleneck when displaying many model instances is the upload of the data to the graphics card, plus the kind of draw call for the triangle rendering process. Choosing the wrong solution here will also result in performance drops when too much data must be uploaded in every frame or, for instance, every model is drawn with a separate drawing call. Investigating the GPU activity can be tricky as we normally cannot see what is happening after we send the data to the graphics card driver. Luckily, the free tool RenderDoc allows us to get detailed insights into what the GPU is doing during the creation of the image for a single 3D frame. Let us take a look at RenderDoc now.

Using RenderDoc to analyze a GPU frame

RenderDoc is a free tool to capture and analyze the frames our application draws. The program supports OpenGL and Vulkan, and also Direct 3D on Windows and OpenGL ES on mobile devices.

In *Figure 15.9*, a single frame of the `04_opengl_tbo` example of *Chapter 14* has been captured:

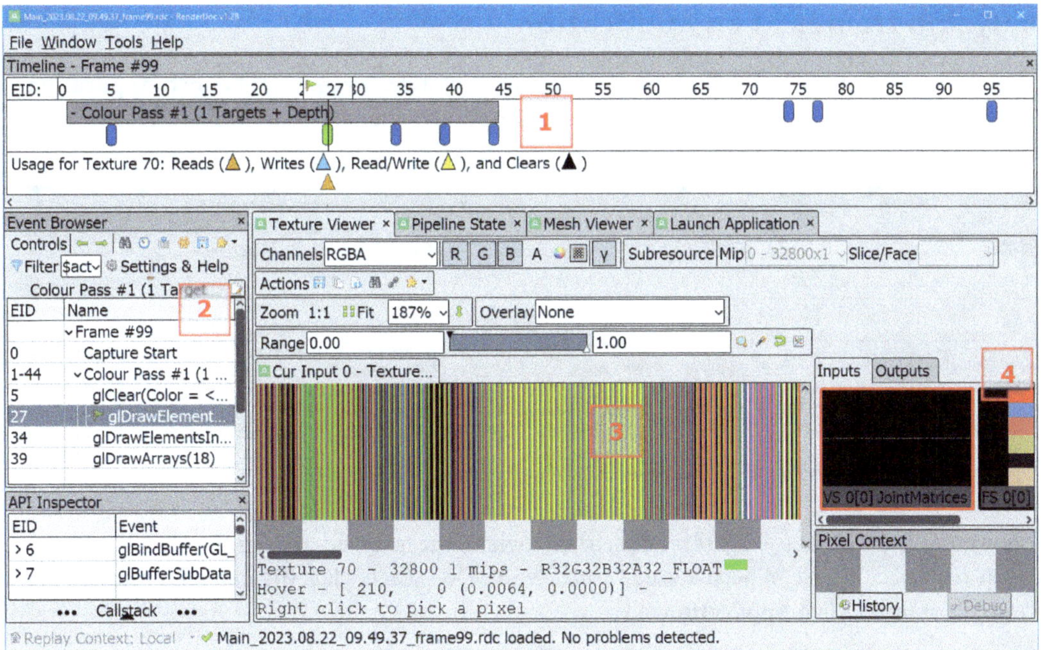

Figure 15.9: RenderDoc analyzing an OpenGL version of the model viewer

In *Figure 15.9*, at the top of the RenderDoc window labeled with number **1**, the overall timing of the frame is shown. On the left side, at number **2**, the recorded OpenGL calls are presented. Selecting one block or command advances the frame and the timing bar in the window with the number **1** to the frame state at that specific time.

The colored bars at number **3** are the joint matrices that were uploaded to the texture buffer. We use a texture buffer to upload the matrix data to the GPU, and the uploaded data is visible as a one-dimensional texture in RenderDoc. On the lower-right side, at number **4**, the content of the `Woman.png` texture in the `textures` folder is shown, as this file was loaded as the color texture for the glTF model.

In the next subsections, we explore how to download and install RenderDoc, and we analyze the GPU usage of the four examples in this chapter. Afterward, we compare the generated RenderDoc charts of the different versions of the program.

Downloading and installing RenderDoc

To download RenderDoc, head to the official website: `https://renderdoc.org`

Download the appropriate version for your operating system. For Windows, an installer is available, while the Linux version comes as a `.tar` archive and needs to be unpacked locally.

Start the program, and you are ready to go ahead with the analysis of an OpenGL application.

Analyzing frames of an application

Launching an application in RenderDoc is a bit counterintuitive. If you select **Launch Application** from the **File** menu, you are moved to the **Launch Application** tab in the user interface, as shown in *Figure 15.10*:

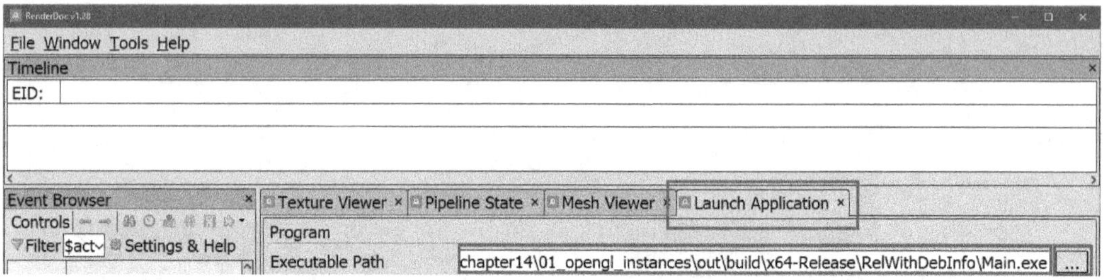

Figure 15.10: The executable path to launch in RenderDoc

As shown in *Figure 15.10*, use the three dots to the right of the text field to open the file selector and navigate to the executable to be analyzed inside RenderDoc. Then, click the **Launch** button at the lower right of the **Launch Application** tab.

RenderDoc will start your application as normal and draw an overlay on top of the rendered graphics containing some status information:

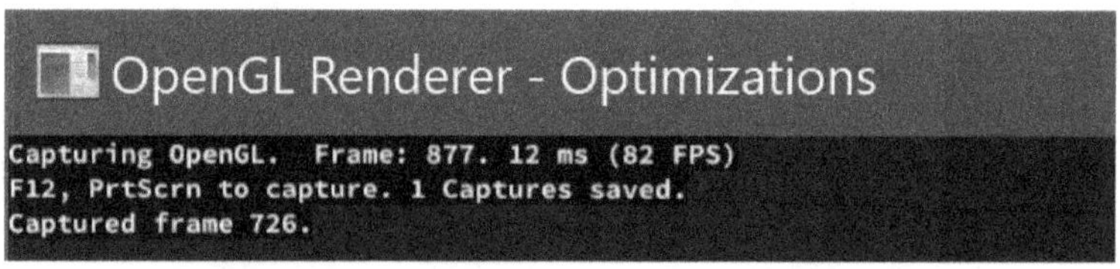

Figure 15.11: Status information overlay generated by RenderDoc

Pressing the *F12* or *PrintScreen* keys will capture the currently rendered frame. You can capture multiple frames of the application and analyze all of them. If you capture only a single frame, this frame will be selected automatically as the target for the analysis.

Comparing the results of different versions of our application

To explore the differences in the GPU usage of our application, we will investigate the timings of some of the code examples from *Chapter 14*.

We start with the `01_opengl_instances` example, where we issued a `draw()` call to the model class for every instance. *Figure 15.12* shows the timings of the first-instance version of the application:

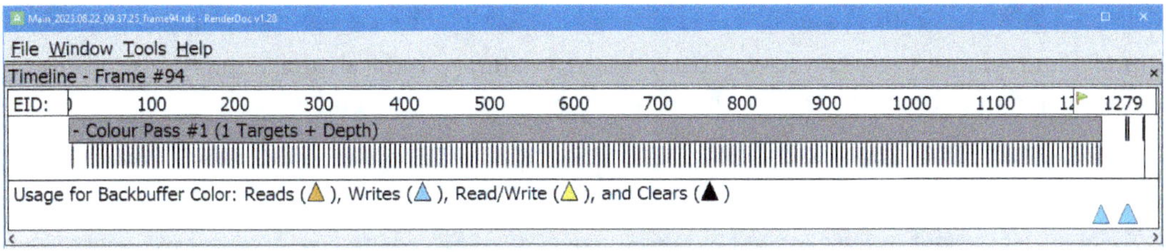

Figure 15.12: A frame from the 01_opengl_instances example

Every single small vertical line in the screenshot is one call to `glDrawElements()`. Issuing the drawing call over and over results in many small events, as the event ID (**EID**) counter shows in *Figure 15.12*.

Now, let us compare the timings from the simple instancing version with a screenshot from the `03_opengl_instanced_drawing` example. In *Figure 15.13*, a frame from the version using the `glDrawElementsInstanced()` drawing command has been captured:

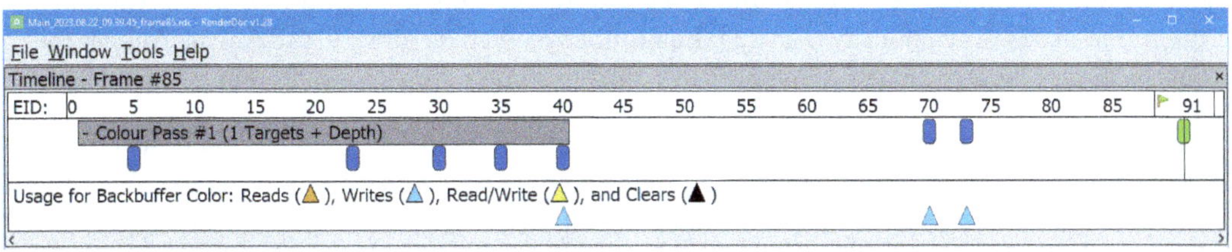

Figure 15.13: A frame from the 03_opengl_instanced_drawing example

Instead of around 1,300 OpenGL events for a single frame, the GPU-instanced drawing needs fewer than a hundred events for the same result to be drawn on the screen. A lot of work is done by the graphics card itself, and fewer commands needed to be sent.

Using RenderDoc, we are also able to compare the outcome of different buffer usages. In the `04_opengl_tbo` example, we changed the code for the joint matrices from a shader storage buffer to a texture buffer. *Figure 15.14* shows the result from the fourth example:

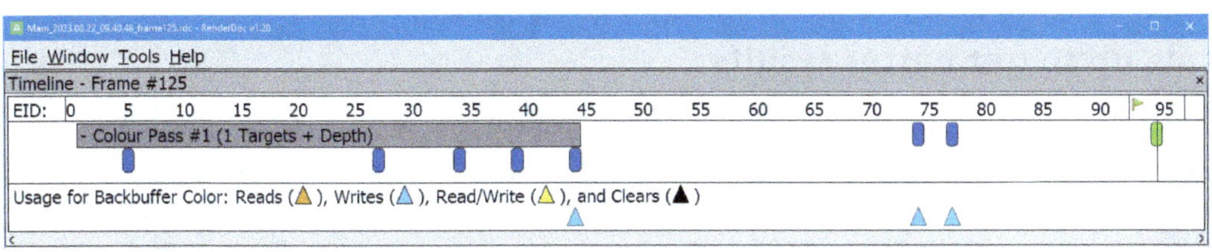

Figure 15.14: A frame from the 04_opengl_tbo example

The differences between the graphs in *Figure 15.13* and *Figure 15.14* are small. The example using the texture buffer had four events more, compared to the version with the shader storage buffer. These extra commands are the setup steps for the texture to be used as a data buffer.

Now, let us take the number of events from the OpenGL code in *Figure 15.13* and compare it to a frame from the Vulkan renderer:

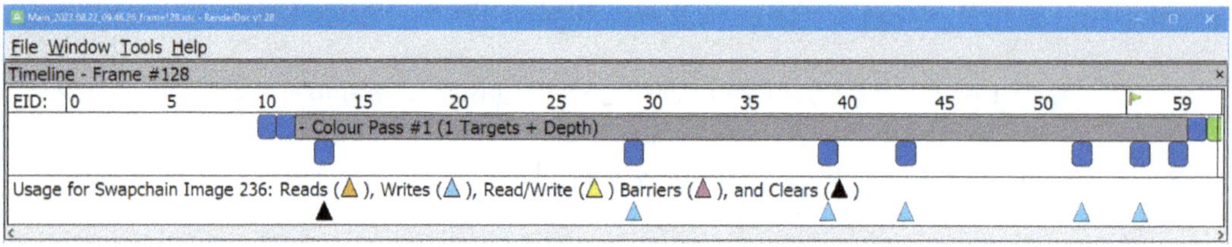

Figure 15.15: A frame from one of the Vulkan examples

At the frame start shown in *Figure 15.15*, we can see quite a large setup delay without events. The rendering process itself takes a similar number of events (around 45) just like the OpenGL rendering, but the frame needs only about two-thirds the number of events from start to finish. You get the controls back a lot faster from the graphics driver, enabling you to push more frames to the GPU.

RenderDoc is a versatile tool for GPU analysis and gives you tons of insights into the rendering process and the textures, buffers, and commands sent to the graphics card. For more information about the features of RenderDoc, check the link to the documentation in the *Additional resources* section.

Now we have completed the basic performance analysis of the CPU and GPU parts of the application, two tips for further optimizations follow in the last section of this chapter.

Scale it up and do A/B tests

At this point, the optimization journey has just begun. After the first rounds of digging into possible performance issues for the processor and the graphics card, you need to re-iterate the status of the application. Two pieces of advice will help you to tickle even more frames per second out of your application.

Scale up to get better results

If we profile the first version of your shiny new glTF model viewer application from *Chapter 8*, where we are loading and rendering only the single model, the results may lead to the wrong conclusions. The differences between the calls are too small to allow us to discern the cause for any slowdowns, and many generic calls to STL or GLM functions are shown, as you can see in *Figure 15.16*:

```
Flat profile:

Each sample counts as 0.01 seconds.
  %   cumulative   self              self     total
 time   seconds   seconds    calls  ms/call  ms/call  name
  5.19      0.04     0.04  2868572     0.00     0.00  nlohmann::detail::lexer<nlohmann::basic_json<std::map, std::vector, std::__cxx11
  5.19      0.08     0.04     2314     0.02     0.02  ImGui::UpdateKeyboardInputs()
  2.60      0.10     0.02  2897199     0.00     0.00  char& std::vector<char, std::allocator<char> >::emplace_back<char>(char&&)
  2.60      0.12     0.02  2897199     0.00     0.00  std::vector<char, std::allocator<char> >::back()
  2.60      0.14     0.02   893796     0.00     0.00  ImVec2::ImVec2(float, float)
  2.60      0.16     0.02   561509     0.00     0.00  stbi__zhuffman_decode(stbi__zbuf*, stbi__zhuffman*)
  2.60      0.18     0.02   164294     0.00     0.00  glm::vec<4, float, (glm::qualifier)0>::operator[](int)
  2.60      0.20     0.02    18512     0.00     0.00  ImFont::RenderText(ImDrawList*, float, ImVec2 const&, unsigned int, ImVec4 const
  2.60      0.22     0.02    18512     0.00     0.00  ImFont::CalcTextSizeA(float, float, float, char const*, char const*, char const*
  2.60      0.24     0.02     9256     0.00     0.00  SetCurrentWindow(ImGuiWindow*)
  2.60      0.26     0.02     4628     0.00     0.03  ImGui::Begin(char const*, bool*, int)
  2.60      0.28     0.02     4628     0.00     0.01  ImGui::UpdateWindowManualResize(ImGuiWindow*, ImVec2 const&, int*, int, unsigned
  2.60      0.30     0.02        1    20.00    20.00  tinygltf::base64_decode(std::__cxx11::basic_string<char, std::char_traits<char>,
```

Figure 15.16: Profiling the code from Chapter 8, example 01_opengl_gltf_load

If you start optimizing on the basis of these results, you will waste your time working on completely the wrong parts of your code.

Instead of profiling the minimal version, scale your application up to do as much work as possible, both on the CPU and GPU sides. This means you should draw as many triangles as you can, create lots of objects, instantiate many models, and animate them.

The more work your CPU must do inside the classes and methods you created, the better your chances are of finding the real hotspots in the code. In *Figure 15.4*, you saw the profiling of a later version of the application, and the functions we had to optimize could easily be found in the output.

Make one change at a time and profile again

The second piece of advice comes from the realm of web software development. In large applications, or during UI changes, so-called **A/B tests** are used. This means delivering the current version of the software to some users (this is the "A" version of the application), while others get the slightly changed "B" version, which usually contains only minor updates. If the number of users and the randomization are broad enough, conclusions can be drawn about which of the two versions gives better results, without the changes ("A") or with the changes ("B").

A similar approach should be used during optimization. Instead of changing a whole bunch of parameters, do only one change at a time. Then, profile and test the new application, and compare the collected profiling data. For better results, do several runs, throw away the data from the startup phase, and calculate a weighted average across all application runs. You may even have to record all the results in spreadsheets and create graphs for different versions of your application.

Advancing in small steps may look like it takes more time, but in the long run, you get fine-grained results of which changes make your application faster, and which changes caused new performance issues. These results will be helpful once you start the next round of optimizations after fixing the worst parts of the code and scaling up again.

Summary

In this chapter, we explored performance measurements and optimization of the code we created throughout all the chapters of this book.

First, we looked at the basic dos and don'ts of optimization. You should do any optimizations as late as possible and avoid premature optimization at all costs, as it will slow down the development and eventually delay your product. Also, we talked about some basic ideas on how to make code run faster.

Next, we checked our code examples from *Chapter 14* for hotspots and bottlenecks on both the CPU and GPU sides. By using a profiling tool, we detected the code parts where the processor spent more time than necessary. RenderDoc helped us to analyze the frames that are sent from the application to the graphics card, and to compare the effects of different variants of the rendering code sent to the GPU.

Finally, two pieces of advice for the optimization process were given. Scaling up the application helps you to find the real bottlenecks, and working in small steps helps you avoid introducing new hotspots in the code. With these last lines of *Chapter 15*, my job as your "tour guide" into the world of game character animations ends. I hope you enjoyed reading the book, and I also hope you gained a lot of new knowledge during the long journey from a file residing on your computer to the large crowd of animated models walking and jumping across your screen.

Since opening the very first pages of *Chapter 1*, you have learned how to create an application window and how to read the data from the mouse and the keyboard to roam within a virtual world. You also learned how to load and animate a glTF model, how to draw multiple models at the same time, and how you can use inverse kinematics to make even more realistic animations. Plus, you were given hints on how to measure the application performance and find the right spots that need optimization.

So... what to do next? Well, that's completely up to you!

You could extend the code to load and animate different glTF models. The current application code has been created to work only with the simple models included in the examples. Follow the link given in the *Additional resources* section to the official example models of the Khronos Group to browse and download different kinds of glTF models. Then try to update the code to support more formats.

Or, you could include the `Assimp` asset importer library to load other types of 3D models, such as those from Blender, 3ds Max, or from games such as the Quake and Half-Life series, and then render and animate those models. `Assimp` supports more than 50 file formats, and you may find the one 3D model that you always wanted to see on the screen, rendered by an application you created. Check the *Additional resources* section for the link to the asset importer library.

Lastly, by using the Inverse Kinematics solvers from *Chapter 13* and a simple collision detection algorithm, you could even make the model run across a virtual landscape, climb some stairs, or open and close virtual doors. Your toolbox to create such a virtual world is now brimming with potential, and you can use the application we created in this book as a starting point to continue your journey into the virtual worlds of computer games.

Stay curious and experiment with the code.

Practical sessions

You can try out these ideas to get deeper insights into the process of code optimization:

- Search for more hotspots using a profiler and try to reduce the calculation time for every instance even more.

  The optimized code from *Chapter 15* needs about 0.02 milliseconds for the creation of the joint matrices or dual quaternions of every model on a recent CPU. For 1,000 models drawn using the GPU instancing, the matrix data update takes about 20 milliseconds per frame. Maybe you will find more places where a couple of CPU cycles can be saved.

- *Advanced difficulty*: Use multithreading for the update of the matrix data.

  You could try to update more than one model at once by parallelizing the joint matrix update process. This may be done by a simple worker or consumer/producer model, where you add the update tasks to a list or vector and let the threads take the topmost entry to work on the matrices. But beware, synchronization between threads can be difficult, and the startup of threads is also not free.

- *Advanced difficulty*: Offload the computation to a compute shader.

  As an alternative solution to parallelize the joint matrix updates of the model, you could try out a compute shader. You would need to upload the animation data to the GPU and calculate the joint matrices in a shader. The results can be written into a shader storage buffer that will be handed directly to the vertex buffer of the graphics shader.

Additional resources

For further reading, please check these links:

- Linux profiling: `http://euccas.github.io/blog/20170827/cpu-profiling-tools-on-linux.html`
- Windows profiling: `https://learn.microsoft.com/en-us/visualstudio/profiling/cpu-usage?view=vs-2022`
- Multithreading in C++: `https://db.in.tum.de/teaching/ss21/c++praktikum/slides/lecture-10.2.pdf`
- Mastering multithreading: `https://www.packtpub.com/product/mastering-c-multithreading/9781787121706`
- Concurrency with Modern C++: `https://www.grimm-jaud.de/index.php/concurrency-with-modern-c`
- OpenGL compute shaders: `https://antongerdelan.net/opengl/compute.html`

- Vulkan compute shaders: `https://saschawillems.de/vulkantutorial/en/Compute_Shader.html`
- RenderDoc documentation: `https://renderdoc.org/docs/index.html`
- C++ constexpr and consteval: `https://lemire.me/blog/2023/03/27/c20-consteval-and-constexpr-functions/`
- glTF Sample Models: `https://github.com/KhronosGroup/glTF-Sample-Models`
- Asset Importer (Assimp): `https://github.com/assimp/assimp`

Index

A

B

C

D

E

F

G

H

I

K

O

P

Q

R

S

W

Y

Z

Other Books You May Enjoy

If you enjoyed this book, you may be interested in these other books by Packt:

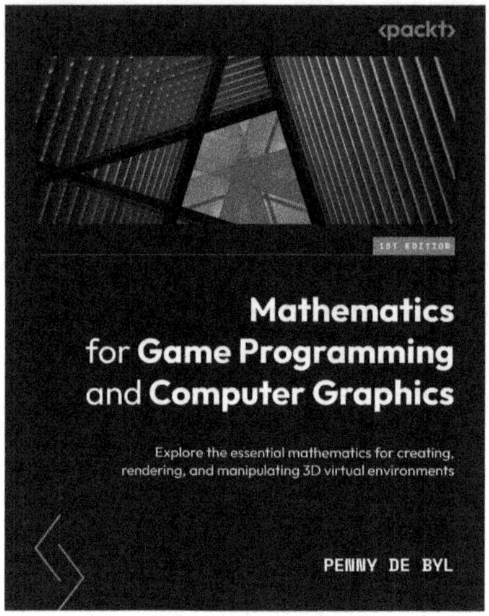

Mathematics for Game Programming and Computer Graphics

Penny de Byl

ISBN: 978-1-80107-733-0

- Get up and running with Python, Pycharm, Pygame, and PyOpenGL
- Experiment with different graphics API drawing commands
- Review basic trigonometry and how it's important in 3D environments
- Apply vectors and matrices to move, orient, and scale 3D objects
- Render 3D objects with textures, colors, shading, and lighting
- Work with vertex shaders for faster GPU-based rendering

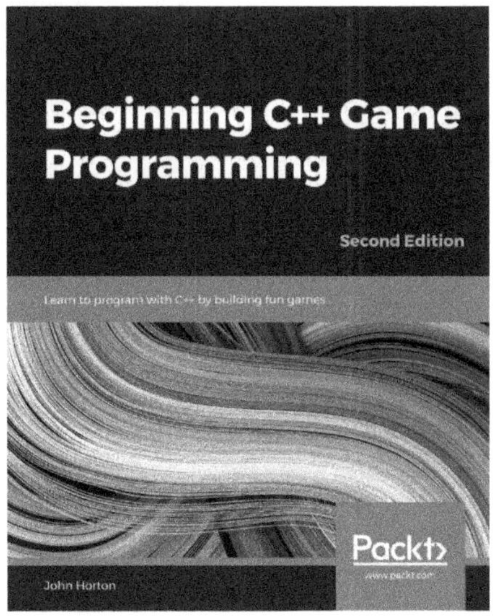

Beginning C++ Game Programming

John Horton

ISBN: 978-1-83864-857-2

- Set up your game development project in Visual Studio 2019 and explore C++ libraries such as SFML
- Explore C++ OOP by building a Pong game
- Understand core game concepts such as game animation, game physics, collision detection, scorekeeping, and game sound
- Use classes, inheritance, and references to spawn and control thousands of enemies and shoot rapid-fire machine guns
- Add advanced features to your game using pointers, references, and the STL
- Scale and reuse your game code by learning modern game programming design patterns

Packt is searching for authors like you

If you're interested in becoming an author for Packt, please visit `authors.packtpub.com` and apply today. We have worked with thousands of developers and tech professionals, just like you, to help them share their insight with the global tech community. You can make a general application, apply for a specific hot topic that we are recruiting an author for, or submit your own idea.

Hi!

We're Michael Dunsky and Gabor Szauer, the authors of C++ Game Animation Programming, Second Edition. We really hope you enjoyed reading this book and found it useful for increasing your productivity and efficiency in C++ Game Animation Programming.

It would really help us (and other potential readers!) if you could leave a review on Amazon sharing your thoughts on C++ Game Animation Programming, Second Edition here.

Go to the link below or scan the QR code to leave your review:

`https://packt.link/r/1803246529`

Your review will help us to understand what's worked well in this book, and what could be improved upon for future editions, so it really is appreciated.

Best Wishes,

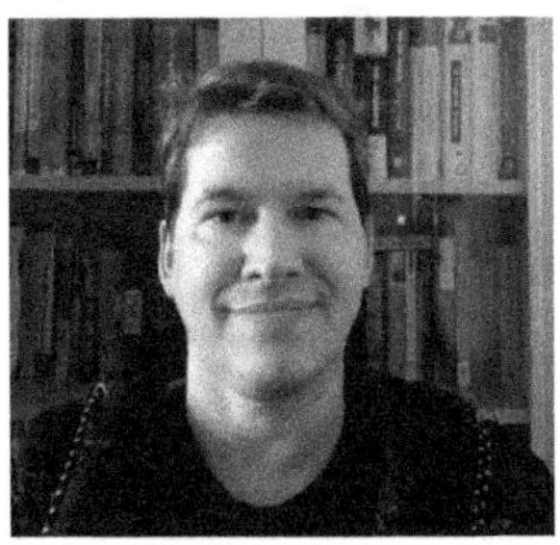

Michael Dunsky

Download a free PDF copy of this book

Thanks for purchasing this book!

Do you like to read on the go but are unable to carry your print books everywhere?

Is your eBook purchase not compatible with the device of your choice?

Don't worry, now with every Packt book you get a DRM-free PDF version of that book at no cost.

Read anywhere, any place, on any device. Search, copy, and paste code from your favorite technical books directly into your application.

The perks don't stop there, you can get exclusive access to discounts, newsletters, and great free content in your inbox daily

Follow these simple steps to get the benefits:

1. Scan the QR code or visit the link below

`https://packt.link/free-ebook/9781803246529`

2. Submit your proof of purchase
3. That's it! We'll send your free PDF and other benefits to your email directly

www.ingramcontent.com/pod-product-compliance
Lightning Source LLC
LaVergne TN
LVHW060017210926
848481LV00013B/3728